The *Perfect Guide to the Sciences of the Qur'ān*

Volume I

Muḥammad b. Hamad Al-Thani Center for
Muslim Contribution to Civilization

The Perfect Guide to the Sciences of the Qur'ān

Volume I

Al-Itqān fī ʿUlūm al-Qur'ān

Imām Jalāl-al-Dīn al-Suyūṭī

Translated by Professor Ḥamid Algar,
Dr. Michael Schub and Mr Ayman Abdel Ḥaleem

Reviewed by Professor Osman S. A. Ismaʿīl A. al-Bīlī

Garnet
PUBLISHING

The Perfect Guide to the Sciences of the Qur'ān
Al-Itqān fī ʿUlūm al-Qur'ān
Volume I

Published by
Garnet Publishing Limited
8 Southern Court
South Street
Reading
RG1 4QS
UK

First Edition

ISBN-13: 978-1-85964-242-9

British Library Cataloguing-in-Publication Data
A catalogue record for this book is available from the British Library

Typeset by Samantha Barden
Jacket design by Garnet Publishing

Printed and bound in Lebanon by International Press:
interpress@int-press.com

Contents

Foreword	vii
About this Series	ix
Muḥammad bin Hamad Al-Thani Center for Muslim Contribution to Civilization: Founding Board of Trustees	xi
Muḥammad bin Hamad Al-Thani Center for Muslim Contribution to Civilization: Advisory Committee	xii
Introduction	xiii
Author's Introduction	xix
Chapter one	1
Chapter two	25
Chapter three	31
Chapter four	35
Chapter five	37
Chapter six	39
Chapter seven	41
Chapter eight	49
Chapter nine	55
Chapter ten	71
Chapter eleven	75
Chapter twelve	77
Chapter thirteen	81
Chapter fourteen	83
Chapter fifteen	87
Chapter sixteen	91
Chapter seventeen	117
Chapter eighteen	137
Chapter nineteen	155
Chapter twenty	169
Chapter twenty-one	177
Chapter twenty-two to twenty-seven	181
Chapter twenty-eight	201
Chapter twenty-nine	221
Chapter thirty	225
Chapter thirty-one	233
Chapter thirty-two	241
Chapter thirty-three	247
Chapter thirty-four	251
Chapter thirty-five	263
Index	295

In the Name of God, the Beneficent, the Merciful

Foreword

THE interrelationship and interaction of human cultures and civilizations has made the contributions of each the common heritage of men in all ages and all places. Early Muslim scholars were able to communicate with their Western counterparts through contacts made during the Crusades; at Muslim universities and centres of learning in Muslim Spain (al-Andalus, or Andalusia) and Sicily to which many European students went for education; and at the universities and centres of learning in Europe itself (such as Salerno, Padua, Montpellier, Paris and Oxford), where Islamic works were taught in Latin translations. Among the Muslim scholars well-known in the centres of learning throughout the world were al-Rāzī (Rhazes), Ibn Sīnā (Avicenna), Ibn Rushd (Averroës), al-Khwārizmī and Ibn Khaldūn. Muslim scholars such as these and others produced original works in many fields. Many of them possessed encyclopaedic knowledge and distinguished themselves in many disparate fields of knowledge.

The Center for Muslim Contribution to Civilization was established in order to acquaint non-Muslims with the contributions Islam has made to human civilization as a whole. The Great Books of Islamic Civilization Project attempts to cover the first 800 years of Islam, or what may be called Islam's Classical Period. This project aims at making available in English and other European languages a wide selection of works representative of Islamic civilization in all its diversity. It is made up of translations of original Arabic works that were produced in the formative centuries of Islam, and is meant to serve the needs of a potentially large readership. Not only the specialist and scholar, but also the non-specialist with an interest in Islam and its cultural heritage will be able to benefit from the series. Together, the works should serve as a rich source for the study of the early periods of Islamic thought.

In selecting the books for the series, the Center took into account all major areas of Islamic intellectual pursuit that could be represented. Thus the series includes works not only on better-known subjects such as law, theology, jurisprudence, history and politics, but also on subjects such as literature, medicine, astronomy, optics and geography. The specific criteria used to select individual books were these: that a book should give a faithful and comprehensive account of its field; and that it should be an authoritative source. Readers thus have at their disposal virtually a whole library of informative and enlightening works.

Each book in the series has been translated by a qualified scholar and reviewed by another expert. While the style of one translation will naturally differ from another – as do the styles of the authors – the translators have endeavoured, to the extent it is possible, to make the works accessible to the common reader. As a rule, the use of footnotes has been kept to a minimum, though a more extensive use of them was necessitated in some cases.

This series is presented in the hope that it will contribute to a greater understanding in the West of the cultural and intellectual heritage of Islam and will therefore provide an important means towards greater understanding of today's world.

May God Help Us!

Muḥammad bin Hamad al-Thani
Chairman of the Founding Board of Trustees

About this Series

This series of Arabic works, made available in English translation, represents an outstanding selection of important Islamic studies in a variety of fields of knowledge. The works selected for inclusion in this series meet specific criteria. They are recognized by Muslim scholars as being early and important in their fields as works whose importance is broadly recognized by international scholars, and as having had a genuinely significant impact on the development of human culture.

Readers will therefore see that this series includes a variety of works in the purely Islamic sciences, such as Qurʾān, *ḥadīth*, theology, prophetic traditions (*sunna*), and jurisprudence (*fiqh*). Also represented will be books by Muslim scholars and scientists on belles lettres, sufism, psychology, medicine, astronomy, geography, physics, chemistry, horticulture and other fields.

The work of translating these texts has been entrusted to a group of professors in the Islamic and Western worlds who are recognized authorities in their fields. It has been deemed appropriate, in order to ensure accuracy and fluency, that two persons, one with Arabic as their mother tongue and another with English as their mother tongue, should participate together in the translation and revision of each text.

This series is distinguished from other similar intercultural projects by its distinctive objectives and methodology. These works will fill a genuine gap in the library of human thought. They will prove extremely useful to all those with an interest in Islamic culture, its interaction with Western thought, and its impact on culture throughout the world. They will, it is hoped, fulfil an important role in enhancing world understanding at a time when there is such evident and urgent need for the development of peaceful coexistence.

This series is published by the Center for Muslim Contribution to Civilization (CMCC), now a member of the Faculty of Islamic Studies of Qatar Foundation, Doha, Qatar. The Center was established in 1983 under the patronage of H.E. Sheikh Muḥammad bin Hamad al-Thani, the former Minister of Education of Qatar, who also chaired the Board of Trustees. The Board comprised a group of prominent scholars. These included His Eminence Sheikh al-Azhar, Arab Republic of Egypt, and Dr Yousef al-Qaradhawi, Director of the Sira and Sunna Research Center. At its inception the Center was directed by the late Dr Muḥammad Ibrahim Kazim, former Rector of Qatar University, who established its initial objectives.

Until 1997, the Center was directed by the late Dr Kamal Naji, the Foreign Cultural Relations Advisor of the Ministry of Education of Qatar. He was assisted by a Board comprising a number of academicians of Qatar University, in addition to a consultative committee chaired by the late Dr Ezzeddin Ibrahim, former Rector of the University of the United Arab Emirates. A further committee acting on behalf of the Center comprises prominent university professors who act under the chairmanship of Dr Raji Rammuny, Professor of Arabic at the University of Michigan. This committee is charged with making known, in Europe, in America, in Asia and elsewhere the books selected for translation, and in selecting and enlisting properly qualified university professors, orientalists and students of Islamic studies to undertake the work of translation and revision, as well as overseeing the publication process. In 1997, Professor Professor Osman Sid Aḥmad Ismaʿīl al-Bīlī took over as General Supervisor of the Centre.

In January 2009, the CMCC joined Qatar Foundation as part of the Faculty of Islamic Studies. In May 2010 Her Highness Sheikha Moza bint Naser Al-Misnad, the Chairperson of Qatar Foundation named the Center as Muḥammad bin Hamad Al-Thani Center for Muslim Contribution to Civilization. Currently Professor Osman Sid Aḥmad Ismaʿīl al-Bīlī is the Director of the Center.

MUḤAMMAD BIN HAMAD AL-THANI CENTER FOR MUSLIM CONTRIBUTION TO CIVILIZATION

FOUNDING BOARD OF TRUSTEES

H.E. Sheikh Muḥammad bin Hamad al-Thani
Chairman

MEMBERS

1. H.E. Sheikh al-Azhar, Cairo, Arab Republic of Egypt.
2. Director-General of the Islamic Educational, Scientific and Cultural Organization (ISESCO).
3. Director-General of the Arab League Educational, Cultural and Scientific Organization (ALECSO).
4. H.E. the Minister of Education, State of Qatar.
5. H.E. the Minister of Education, Kuwait.
6. H.E. the Minister of Education, Oman.
7. H.E. the Secretary-General of the Muslim World Association, Saudi Arabia.
8. H.E. Dr Ezzeddin Ibrahim, Cultural Advisor to H.H. the President of the U.A.E.
9. Professor Yousef al-Qaradhawi, Director, Sira and Sunna Research Centre, University of Qatar.
10. Chairman, Arab Historians' Union.
11. Professor Cesar Adib Majul, Professor at the American Universities.

Following are the names of the late prominent Muslim figures who (may Allāh have mercy upon them) passed away after they had taken vital roles in the preliminary discussions of the Center's goals, work plan and activities. They are:

1. Dr Kamal Naji, former General Supervisor, Center for Muslim Contribution to Civilization, Qatar (7 October 1997).
2. Sheikh Jad al-Haq Ali Jad al-Haq, Sheikh al-Azhar, Cairo, Arab Republic of Egypt.
3. Dr Muḥammad Ibrahim Kazim, former Rector, University of Qatar.
4. Sheikh ʿAbdullah bin Ibrahim al-Ansari, former Chairman, Department for the Revival of Islamic Cultural Heritage, State of Qatar.
5. Muḥammad al-Fasi, former Honorary Chairman, Islamic University Rabat, Kingdom of Morocco.
6. Dr Abul-Wafa al-Taftazani, former Deputy Rector, University of Cairo, Arab Republic of Egypt.
7. Senator Mamimatal Tamano, former member of the Philippino Congress and Muslim leader in the Philippines.

7\. Dr Ezzeddin Ibrahim (March 2010).

MUḤAMMAD BIN HAMAD AL-THANI CENTER FOR MUSLIM CONTRIBUTION TO CIVILIZATION

Advisory Committee

1. H.E. Sheikh Muḥammad bin Hamad al-Thani, Honorary Chairman of the Advisory Committee
2. Professor Osman Sid Aḥmad Ismaʿīl al-Bīlī, Professor of Middle Eastern and Islamic History at QFIS and Director of the Center.
3. Professor Hatem al-Karnashawi, Dean QFIS.
4. Professor Muḥammad Khalifa al-Ḥasan, Director, Al-Qaradawi Center for Islamic Moderation and Renewal.
5. Professor Ibrahim Saleh al-Nuaimi, former Rector, University of Qatar, Chairman of Doha International Center for Interfaith Dialogue.
6. Professor Husam al-Khateeb, Professor of Arabic Language.

Center's Advisor

Professor Raji Mahmoud Rammuny
Director of the Center's Translation Committee in the U.S.A.
Professor of Arabic Studies, Department of Near Eastern Studies,
University of Michigan, U.S.A.

INTRODUCTION

Age and time of al-Suyūṭī 849–911/1445–1505

Contrary to what is commonly believed, the Abbāsid Caliphate did not end with the fall of Baghdad and the murder of the then incumbent caliph al-Mustanṣir (640–656/1242–58), in the year 656/1258. Nor did the interregnum and the appointment of a new Abbāsid caliph take long. Within one year, the vacuum was filled. Al-Mustanṣir 659/1261, a member of the same dynasty and the same family, was paid homage to as the Mamluks in Cairo declared him caliph in the year 659–660/1261. His attempt to re-capture Baghdad from the Mongols failed. He lost his life on the battlefield. A successor was immediately proclaimed. This was Caliph al-Hakim I – 660–701/1261–1302. Thus, the Abbāsid Caliphate of Cairo began in 659/1261.

What is important in this respect is that the era of isolation of the caliphs had set in since the days of Samarra, almost immediately after the end of the reign of the eighth Abbāsid Caliph al-Muʾtasim 218–227/833–842. The caliphs, isolated in their new capital Samarra, became regional governors in Iraq. As caliphs, they gave legitimacy to the generals and regional governors who often played major roles in the appointment, the deposition and sometimes the murder of caliphs. The caliphs were the ones who sanctioned the legitimacy of their vassals or deputies as regional governors. It was those governors, especially those of Syria and Egypt, the Ayyubids and the Mamluks, who held power in their provinces and dominance in the region and over the caliphs in Baghdad before its fall to the Mongols in 656/1258 and after.

In two years after the fall of Baghdad, the Mamluks continued the struggle against the Mongols in the name of the Abbāsid caliphs and Caliphate. Sultan al-Muzaffar Sayf al-Dīn Qutz 657–658/1259–60 defeated the Mongols in Ayn Jalut in 1258/1260. His successor, Sultan Baybars (al-Zahir Rukn al-Dīn) 659–676/1260–1277, consolidated that victory. The threat of the Mongols continued for decades after that. However, the Abbāsid Caliphate was saved and the line of Abbāsid caliphs continued. Under the Mamluks, the Abbāsid caliphs were tolerated guests and hostages of the sultans.

It was the Ayyubids who earlier wrested Egypt from the Fatimids and returned the rich and powerful province to the Abbāsids' Sunni fold. With the unity of Syria and Egypt under the Ayyubids and the Mamluks 564–922/1169–1517, the Abbāsid Caliphate could successfully face its enemies in the East (the Mongols) and the West (the Crusaders) until the Ottoman

Sultan Selim the Grim took both provinces, Syria and Egypt, in 922–923/1516 and 1517. On his return to Istanbul, he took with him the then incumbent Abbāsid Caliph al-Mutawakil III. Not very much is known about the fate of the deported caliph or any other Abbāsid caliph ever since.

However it is important to note that the Ottomans saw as a sign of their legitimacy the blessings given to them by the Abbāsid caliph at the rise of their ghazi emirate under ʿUthmān (Osman I b. Ertoghril) 680/1281 and ever since until Sultan Selim took what seems to be the last Abbāsid caliph from Cairo to Istanbul. It is equally important to note that the Ottomans, true to the nature of their rule, took "sultan" as their official title. "Sultan" means power, or the one who holds power. "Caliph" means successor in the line of the Patriarchal Caliphs who succeeded Prophet Muḥammad (peace and blessings be upon him) as heads of the Muslim State. Ottoman sultans recognized Abbāsid caliphs as long as those existed.

At the time of al-Suyūṭī (ninth–tenth A.H./15–16 A.D.), Egypt was the capital province of the Abbāsids under Mamluk rule. Cairo was the capital city of the Abbāsid world, if not all the Muslim world – or maybe of the civilized world at the time. The New World had just been discovered. At that time, one could contour a web of Muslim cities spreading from Portugal and Spain to Bukhara and Samarqand, and from Cairo to Timbuktu and Kano, which al-Suyūṭī had chance to visit. Sharing one common faith, Islam, one common divine book, the Qurʾān, they also mostly shared one common alphabet, the Arabic alphabet, as well as one language, the Arabic language. Arab numerals were also known to most literate people of those places. There was also the Shariʿa, the common law for all Muslims, applied and respected throughout the Muslim world. Centres for reading, writing, rhetoric and reckoning, beacons of knowledge and culture, these cities had wealth, power and pomp.

Cairo was perhaps the most outstanding in that glorious web of cities at that time. Ibn Khaldun, the famous Arab Muslim savant 732–808/1332–1408, in spite of all he saw of cities in Spain and North Africa, was so overwhelmed by the city's character and splendour that he described it as "the capital of the world". That was not because of the Sphinx and the Pyramids, but because of the grandeur, cultural and civic qualities of the place. Here is what he wrote about Cairo on his first visit to it in the year 784/1382.

> "I stayed in Alexandria for a month preparing to go to pilgrimage. However, it was destined that I did not do it that year. I then proceeded to Cairo on the first day of Dhu al-Qaida 784/1382. In Cairo, I saw the capital of the world, the garden of the universe, the congregation of nations, the home of countless number of people, the city of Islam and the abode of monarchy. Palaces and mansions lie open unto the fields and to the sky. Schools and Sufi centres flourish in abundance. The stars and planets are lit by the "wisdom and knowledge" of the scholars. The Nile resembles the river of Paradise and the

rush of heavenly waters, providing sweet balmy drink and producing plenty of crops and fruits. I passed through the alleys and back ways of the city. They were congested with the passers-by. The markets were full of merchandise.

We continued to talk about this great city, the expanse of its built area and the opportunities it offered. Comments of our pilgrim and merchant friends differed. I asked our friend Abū ʿAbd Alla al-Maqri, the leading scholar of Fez and all the Maghreb, on his return from pilgrimage "How is this Cairo?" He answered, "He who did not see Cairo can not know the greatness of Islam." I put the same question to our friend Abū al-ʿAbbās b. Idris, the leading scholar of Bujaya. He said, "As if the dwellers of the place descended from the clouds", pointing to their great numbers and the security they were in. I asked our friend Abū Qāsim al-Burji, the scribe and army judge – Qadi al-Aʾskar – of Fez on his return from a mission to the rulers of Egypt in the year 756/1355 about Cairo. He said, "In brief I say. When one imagines something and sees it, one finds the real less than the imagined, as imagination is wider than reality, except for Cairo. It is much more than one imagines it to be."

When I entered Cairo, I stayed for some days. Students flocked to me seeking knowledge although (humbly) I professed that I had little of that. However, they would not excuse me. So I stayed to teach at the mosque of al-Azhar.

It was in that Cairo, home of al-Azhar Mosque University, the leading centre of Islamic learning, capital of the civilized world, abode of Abbāsid caliphs and Mamluk sultans, that al-Suyūṭī was born. The year of his birth was 849/1445, four decades after the death of Ibn Khaldun 808/1406. The reign was that of Caliph al-Mustakfi II 845–855/1441–1451. The rule was that of Sultan al-Zahir Sayf al-Dīn Jaqmaq 842–857/1438–1453. It was in that year 857/1453 that the Ottoman Sultan Muḥammad II al-Fatih (the conqueror) captured Constantinople, thereby setting the stage for what came to be the Ottoman Empire, which lasted until the year 1342/1924. Al-Suyūṭī died in the year 911/1505, only eleven years before the Ottomans took both Syria and Egypt. That ended Mamluk hegemony in both provinces. The deportation of the last Abbāsid caliph from Cairo to Istanbul virtually spelt the end of the Abbāsid Caliphate.

However, neither the fall of Baghdad nor the demise of the Abbāsid caliphs spelt the end of the flourishing or progress of the Islamic Civilization and its contributions to the world. Al-Suyūṭī's Cairo as described by Ibn Khaldun was gradually surpassed by Istanbul or Islambul. Islambul, the city of Islam, capital of the Ottomans to which a lot of the knowledge, the learning, the culture, the crafts, the merchandise, the learned men, the scholars, the students and fortune hunters from all over the Islamic world flocked, became the real centre of the Muslim world.

The Ottomans turned Egypt into a pashalik, a province ruled by an Ottoman pasha. There were no more Mamluk sultans or shadow Abbāsid caliphs. Yet the Mamluks' military caste continued to control Egypt until Muḥammad ʿAlī Pasha made an end to their existence in the famous massacre of the citadel in

Cairo in the year 1226/1811. All the time Egypt remained powerful and rich. Cairo was becoming more cosmopolitan. Al-Azhar Mosque University continued to be the foremost centre of Sunni Islam, a position it holds to the present day.

The assumed cultural decline is now refuted by the massive evidence of the names of savants, the great works, and the rise of urban centres, the spread of knowledge and learning, and the growth in the paper industry that was to be used in the printing machines in Europe. Europe was then a veritable student of Avicenna, Averroës, Ibn Tufayl, al-Zohr, al-Khowarazmi, Leo Africanus and others.

In the field of Qurʾānic sciences, the works of al-Suyūṭī came at a time when both Abbāsid caliphs and Mamluk sultans were to be overthrown. Nevertheless, the works in their originality, quality and sheer size show that knowledge has a logic of its own. It is limitless. It is the fruit of labour, search and divine guidance, where when there is a will there is always a way. In Cairo, there was a lot that sharpened the wills and many who lighted the way.

Imām Jalal al-Dīn ʿAbd-al-Raḥmān b. Abū Bakr b. Muḥammad al-Suyūṭī 849–911/1445–1505 was born, lived and died in Cairo. The ascription "al-Suyūṭī" is a reference to Asyut, a town in Upper Egypt from which his family hailed. Born into a family of devout Muslims, losing his father in his early years the young orphan had the best education of his time. In his famous work "Husn al-Muhadara", he says: "My birth was in the evening of Saturday, the night before Sunday, the first of Rajab of the year 849/1445. During the life of my father, I was taken as a baby to be blessed by Shaykh Abū Muḥammad al-Majdhoub, one of the great men of God who lived near al-Ḥusayn tomb. I grew up an orphan."

The young orphan al-Suyūṭī lived to fulfil that blessing. He learned the Qurʾān by heart before he was eight years old. When he was sixteen he had already learned such of Jurisprudence, Obligations, Language, Grammar and Traditions that he was accredited to teach the Arabic language. Known as the "son of books" for the numerous books he studied and referred to in his works, he could equally be called "the father of books" because of the many books he produced. Ibn Iyās said that al-Suyūṭī had 600 books to his name. The German scholar Carl Brockelmann counted 415 from books to manuscripts. Al-Suyūṭī himself said that he was bestowed with the blessing to study extensively seven major sciences. These he enumerated as Tafsīr, Commentary on the Qurʾān; *Ḥadīth*, Traditions of Prophet Muḥammad (peace and blessings be upon him); Fiqh, Jurisprudence; Nahw, Grammar; al-Maʾani, connotations; al-Badi, figures of speech; and al-Bayan, eloquence. Of the seven sciences, he said that none of his masters reached what he reached in them except for the science of Fiqh, Jurisprudence. In that he said his master Shaykh Alam al-Dīn al-Balqini had more of knowledge and insight.

Jalal al-Dīn al-Suyūṭī was not the first in his family to have the title of Imām. In fact, his father, ʿAbd-al-Raḥmān b. Abū Bakr, had the same title before him – albeit that the father did not attain the influence and the fame the son was destined to have. The title "Imām" is usually given to the most outstanding

Muslim scholars. It implies great knowledge and leadership in theology, jurisprudence, Traditions, Arabic language, grammar and literature as well as all the allied Islamic and secular sciences that were the making of a greatly enlightened age of Islamic civilization. One has to see the number of such sciences drawn from Muslim, Arabic, Greek, Persian, Indian, Biblical and other sources applied by al-Suyūṭī and others in dealing with different aspects of the Qurʾān to appreciate what makes an "Imām". It equally shows how great Muslim scholars and scholarships were.

Imām Jalal al-Dīn al-Suyūṭī read a lot, wrote a lot, taught a lot, and fought many literary battles against his critics and adversaries. He also travelled quite a lot. He went to Hijaz for pilgrimage where he visited the two holy cities of Mecca and Medina. He visited Syria. He travelled to Morocco. He made a visit to the ruler of Kano in Bilad al-Takrur, present-day Nigeria, where he delivered sermons and gave dispensations, which echoed in Muslim cities of Nigeria as part of the heritage of Sokoto State 1783–1903.

Most of al-Suyūṭī's works were on the Qurʾān. However, being the all-round scholar he was, his works also covered almost all the fields of the sciences of the Qurʾān, the Tradition, Jurisprudence, Arabic, History and Literature. They had such superb qualities that he earned the respect and sometimes the envy of his generation and the generations that followed.

In the last two decades of his life, he led a life of seclusion in his home in al-Rawda on the Nile bank in Cairo. It was a life of prayer, meditation and writing. Most of his great works belong to this period.

It is generally agreed that "Kitab al-Itqān fī ʿUlūm al-Qurʾān", here presented as the "Perfect Guide to the Sciences of the Qurʾān", is not only the most important of Imām al-Suyūṭī's many works but also it is one of the most comprehensive and authoritative in the field of Qurʾānic studies to which many before and after him contributed. Exhaustive in its sources, in its subjects, thoughtfully and lucidly written, the work is also well arranged.

The work gained fame and found its way to many circles near and far in the Islamic world of the author's time. It came in many manuscripts referring to an original dictated by the author himself. The book was first published in the years 1271, 1278, 1279, 1306, 1317 and 1318 A.H., in two parts in one volume, but the translation presented here is from a publication of four parts in two volumes edited by Muḥammad Abū al-Faḍl Ibrāhīm, published in Cairo in the year 1387/1967. Reference to earlier editions was also made.

Dr Ḥamid Alger translated Chapters 1–14. Dr Michael Chop translated Chapters 15–32 and the last part of Chapter 35. Ayman ʿAbd al-Halim translated Chapter 32 up to the first part of Chapter 35. Thanks to their perseverance, we now have this publication: Part 1 Volume 1 of the Itqān. I hope the other three parts will follow in good time.

In his preface Imām Jalal al-Dīn al-Suyūṭī left nothing unsaid about the motivation and the manner in which he devoutly pursued his subject to ultimately crown his lifelong desire to write a magnum opus on the Qurʾān. It was for him to be the be-all and end-all of all works on the subject. The contents of all parts of the work are set before the reader in that preface. His undoubtedly great accomplishment could be true to his time and indeed later times but only in the subjects he dealt with. Those were the concerns of the classical approach to the sciences of the Qurʾān. Now the concern is the relevance of the Qurʾān as a source of divine revelation to all the sciences and all problems of man in a daily changing modern age.

In chapter 41 verses 41–42, the Qurʾān is described as: "It is a divine writ. No falsehood can ever attain to it, neither from before or from behind; being bestowed from on high, by One who is truly wise, ever to be praised."

Some reliable sources state that the Qurʾān is the most read, most recited and most learned-by-heart book in the world. Its relevance to the billion and more adherents of Islam who hold no doubt about its divine origin demands continuous and careful attention to the book. Al-Suyūṭī's work in its classical concerns sets the base for such studies.

* * *

Early at the dawn of Friday 19, Jumada the first, in the year 911/1505 Imām Jalal al-Dīn al-Suyūṭī, may God bless his soul, passed away. He was buried in Hawsh Qusun outside the gate of al-Garafa cemetery in Cairo. His great legacy lives on.

Osman S.A. Ismaʿīl al-Bīlī (reviewer)

Author's Introduction

In the name of God, the Merciful, the Compassionate
Peace and blessing upon our master Muḥammad and his family and Companions

Thus says the learned and erudite shaykh and imām, the sage and ocean of learning, the perspicacious instigator of truth and its subtleties, he whose word is a proof, the hafiz and the mujtahid, the shaykh of Islam and the Muslims, the heir to the knowledge of the Master of God's Messengers, the glory of religion and one peerless among the mujtahids, Abū al-Faḍl ʿAbd al-Raḥmān, Abū Bakr al-Suyūṭī al-Shāfiʿī, son of our master the late Shaykh Kamal al-Dīn:

Praise be to God, Who sent the Book down to His slave as an admonition to the possessors of intelligence; placed in it wondrous forms of knowledge and wisdom; and made it the most glorious of books in value, the most abundant in knowledge, the most pleasing in arrangement, and the most eloquent in address – "an Arabic Qurʾān", without any crookedness, uncreated, and beyond all doubt and hesitation. I bear witness that there is no god but God alone. He has no partner, and He is the Lord of all lords; all faces are humbled before His eternity and all necks are bowed before His splendour. I bear witness, too, that our master Muḥammad is His slave and messenger, raised up from the noblest of peoples and the most honourable of clans and sent to the best of communities with the best of books. May God grant him, his family and his noble Companions peace and blessings, perpetually until the Day of Return!

Knowledge is a turbulent ocean the floor of which cannot be reached and a lofty mountain the summit of which cannot be scaled or approached.

Whoever wishes to exhaust it will be unable and whoever desires to measure it fully will fail. For did the Almighty not say, addressing His creation: "You have been given but a slight part of knowledge" (v. 85, al-Isrāʾ). Our book the Qurʾān is the wellspring and source of all knowledge; it is the orbit in which the sun of knowledge rises and sets. In it God Almighty has placed the knowledge of all things, and expounded all forms of guidance and misguidance. Thus the practitioners of every art seek aid from the Qurʾān and rely upon it. The *faqīh* (religious scholar) derives from it the ordinances of the law, drawing from it the distinctions between permissible and forbidden. The grammarian builds up from it his rules of vocalization and refers to it in order to distinguish incorrect speech from correct. The rhetorician is guided by it to the understanding of proper arrangement and by means of it he traverses the paths of eloquence in the ordering of speech.

The Qurʾān contains, moreover, stories and narrations that will admonish the people of insight and counsels and similitudes that will rein in the thoughtful and reflective, in addition to other types of knowledge that cannot be computed except by the One Who knows their full extent.

Add to this an eloquence in wording and style that bewilders the intellect and enraptures the heart, an inimitability of arrangement possible only for the One Who knows all hidden things.

When a student I was surprised to see that the ancient scholars had not composed a book on the sciences of the Qurʾān as they had for the science of *ḥadīth*. But then, I heard our shaykh, the supreme master and the pupil of the eye of all who beheld him, the essence of existence, the supreme scholar of the age, the pride of the epoch, Abū Abdillah Muhyi a-Din al-Kāfījī – may God prolong his life and cover him with His protective shade! – say:

> "I have compiled a unprecedented book on the sciences of the Qurʾān."

I copied the book from him. It is slight in girth and consists essentially of two chapters: the first, on the meanings of the words tafsīr, taʾwīl, Qurʾān, *sūrah* and ayah, and the second on the conditions necessary for expressing an opinion on the Qurʾān. To these is appended a conclusion on the behavioural norms incumbent on the scholar and the student. This book did not quench my thirst nor guide me on the path to my goal.

Then our shaykh, the supreme shaykh of Islam, the chief judge and the foremost among men, bearer of the standard of the Shāfiʿī school Alam ad-Dīn al-Bilqīnī – may God Almighty have mercy upon him! – guided me to a book on the subject written by his brother, the Chief Judge Jalal ad-Dīn entitled Mawaqiʿ al-ʿUlūm min Mawāqiʿal-Nujūm. I saw it to be a fine book, an elegant composition, well arranged and well written, with rich and varied contents. In the exordium to his book, Jalāl al-Dīn writes: "Imām Shāfiʿī delivered a well-known address to one of the Abbāsid caliphs in which he enumerated some of the forms of knowledge touching on the Qurʾān. To quote it here will aid us in attaining our goal. A number of people have written on the sciences of *ḥadīth*, in both ancient and modern times, but their works discuss the sanad (chain of transmitters) of the Qurʾān, not its text, or those who specialize in it and establish its sanad; whereas the sciences of the Qurʾān include many other matters and thus require a complete exposition.

"In this work I intend to set out the knowledge I have attained of the various kinds of elevated science the Qurʾān contains. They can be summarized as follows.

1 The places, times and occasions of revelation, consisting of the following twelve categories: Meccan, Medinan, verses revealed while the Messenger

– upon whom be peace and blessings – was journeying, verses revealed while he was in his place of residence, verses revealed at night, verses revealed during the day, verses revealed in summer, verses revealed in winter, verses revealed to the Messenger – upon whom be peace – in his sleep, the occasions of revelation, the first verses to be revealed, and the last verses to be revealed.

2 The sanad, consisting of the following six categories: the universally accepted, the unique, the exceptional, the variant readings established by the Prophet – upon whom be peace and blessings – the narrators, the memorizers.

3 Recitation (adā), consisting of six categories: the pause, the beginning, modifying the 'ā', the lengthening vowels, the lightening of the hamza, and elision.

4 Lexicology, consisting of seven categories: the unusual, the Arabicized, the metaphorical, words of multiple meaning, the synonym, the metaphor, the simile.

5 Topics concerning legal ordinances, consisting of fourteen categories: the ordinance originally universal in scope and retaining its universality; the ordinance once universally applicable but now specific; the ordinance apparently general in its applicability but of specific applicability; the ordinance whereby the Qur'ān makes specific the sunnah; the ordinance whereby the sunnah makes specific the Qur'ān; the summary; the explicatory; the interpreted; the comprehensible; the absolute; the delimited; the abrogating; the abrogated; the ordinance that is enacted for a specific period; and the ordinance that a specific person is called on to observe.

6 Topics concerning words, consisting of five categories: joining; separation; conciseness; prolixity; brevity. The total number of categories contained under these six headings is fifty. There are other topics not included among them, such as names, patronymics, titles and ambiguous words. Once these are added to the list presented above, we have a complete enumeration of the sciences pertaining to the study of the Qur'ān."

This is what Qadī Jalāl al-Dīn enumerates in the introduction to his book. He then goes on to discuss each topic in an extremely brief manner that calls for much significant elaboration, supplementation and addition. I therefore composed a book called al-Taḥbīr fī ʿUlūm al-Tafsīr, in which I incorporated the topics discussed by al-Bilqīnī and added to them an equal number of further topics and useful discussions that my talent permitted me to include. I said the following in my introduction to that book:

"Although the sciences are numerous and their cultivation has spread out across the horizons, they have as their common goal an ocean the bed of which cannot be fathomed and a lofty mountain the peak of which is unattainable. Hence these are opened to every scholar doors of knowledge to which previous scholars had no means of access. Among certain matters earlier scholars neglected to write on until it became adorned in recent times in the finest of garb was the science of tafsīr, which resembled the science of *ḥadīth* terminology in that no one had written on it, in times ancient or modern, until there came the shaykh al-Islām, the support of mankind, the supreme scholar of the age, the chief among judges, Jalāl al-Dīn al-Bilqīnī, may God Almighty have mercy upon him, and wrote on the subject his book, Mawāqiʿ al-ʿUlūm min Mawāqiʿ al-Nujām. He refined and clarified the whole subject and divided and arranged its subject matter in unprecedented fashion.

His book contained fifty odd chapters, arranged in six parts, and he discussed each section in a firm and clear style. But as al-Imām Abū al-Saʾadat Ibn al-Athīr said in the introduction to his Nihāya: 'Whoever embarks on a matter where none has preceded him or undertakes a task in which none has gone before him, the result is something slight that increases something small that grows.' It therefore occurred to me to include sections Bilqīnī had omitted and to add important matters he had not adequately treated.

Thus I formed the resolve to compile a book concerning this science; in it, I will gather together all the miscellaneous aspects of the subject, and include various useful information, as if I were stringing rare pearls together. Thus I may hope to be the second among two in the creation of this science and unique in the joining together of the scattered, the only one in this field or one of the two, making the two sciences of tafsīr and *ḥadīth*, stand tall together in the perfection of arrangement and line.

When its bud blossomed and exuded perfume, when the full moon of its perfection rose and shone forth, and when its herald called the reader to prosperity, I called it al-Taḥbīr fī ʿUlūm al-Tafsīr (An Elegant Composition on the Sciences of Qurʾānic Exposition).

This is the list of its contents:

Introduction	
Chapter one	Verses revealed in Mecca
Chapter two	Verses revealed in Medina
Chapter three	Verses revealed while the Prophet was in residence
Chapter four	Verses revealed while the Prophet was travelling
Chapter five	Verses revealed during the day
Chapter six	Verses revealed during the night

Chapter seven	Verses revealed during the summer
Chapter eight	Verses revealed during the winter
Chapter nine	Verses revealed while the Prophet was in bed
Chapter ten	Verses revealed while the Prophet was asleep
Chapter eleven	The occasions of revelation
Chapter twelve	The first verses to be revealed
Chapter thirteen	The last verses to be revealed
Chapter fourteen	Verses the time of the revelation of which is known
Chapter fifteen	Verses that were not revealed to any of the preceding prophets
Chapter sixteen	Verses that were revealed to the preceding prophets
Chapter seventeen	Verses that were revealed more than once
Chapter eighteen	Verses that were revealed in parts
Chapter nineteen	Verses that were revealed as a whole
Chapter twenty	The manner of revelation

All these chapters are concerned with the process of revelation:

Chapter twenty-one	Variant readings related by numerous authorities
Chapter twenty-two	Variant readings related by few authorities
Chapter twenty-three	Anomalous traditions
Chapter twenty-four	Variant readings sanctioned by the Prophet
Chapter twenty-five	Narrators
Chapter twenty-six	Memorizers
Chapter twenty-seven	The means of preservation
Chapter twenty-eight	Degrees of transmission (see section 21) inter-connected.

This is related to the narrators:

Chapter twenty-nine	Variant readings related by narrators of uniform quality

All these chapters are concerned with the sanad (transmission):

Chapter thirty	The beginning
Chapter thirty-one	The pause
Chapter thirty-two	Modifying the 'ā'

Chapter thirty-three	Lengthening of vowels
Chapter thirty-four	The lightening of the hamza
Chapter thirty-five	Elision
Chapter thirty-six	Lowering of the voice
Chapter thirty-seven	Inversion
Chapter thirty-eight	The articulation of sounds

All these chapters are concerned with recitation (adāʾ):

Chapter thirty-nine	Unusual words
Chapter forty	Vocalization
Chapter forty-one	Metaphors
Chapter forty-two	Words with multiple meaning
Chapter forty-three	Synonyms
Chapter forty-four	Verses of clear and obvious meaning (*al-muhkam*)
Chapter forty-five	Verses of allegorical meaning (*al-mutashābih*)
Chapter forty-six	Verses difficult to interpret (*al-mushkil*)
Chapter forty-seven	Verses summary in meaning (*al-mujmil*)
Chapter forty-eight	Verses expository in meaning (*al-mubayyin*)
Chapter forty-nine	Metaphors (*al-istiāra*)
Chapter fifty	Similes (*al-tashbih*)
Chapter fifty-one	Allusions (*al-kināya*)
Chapter fifty-two	Indirect statements (*al-taʾrīd*)
Chapter fifty-three	Verses general in their scope at the time of revelation and retaining their general validity
Chapter fifty-four	Verses specific in their reference (*al-makhsūs*)
Chapter fifty-five	Verses general in nature but specific in their intent
Chapter fifty-six	Matters concerning which the Qurʾān has made specific the intent of the Sunnah
Chapter fifty-seven	Matters concerning which the Sunnah has made specific the intent of the Qurʾān
Chapter fifty-eight	The interpreted
Chapter fifty-nine	The clearly understood
Chapter sixty	The absolute
Chapter sixty-one	The restricted
Chapter sixty-two	The abrogating
Chapter sixty-three	The abrogated
Chapter sixty-four	Verses that served as a basis for action by a single individual and were then abrogated
Chapter sixty-five	Verses containing a command that was obligatory for a single individual

Chapter sixty-six	Concision
Chapter sixty-seven	Prolixity
Chapter sixty-eight	Symmetry
Chapter sixty-nine	Making similar
Chapter seventy	Separation
Chapter seventy-one	Connection
Chapter seventy-two	Abbreviation
Chapter seventy-three	Overlapping
Chapter seventy-four	The mentioning of the cause
Chapter seventy-five	Juxtaposing the mention of two contrasting things
Chapter seventy-six	The mention of two or more corresponding things
Chapter seventy-seven	The mention of two or more things belonging to the same genus
Chapter seventy-eight	Ambiguity
Chapter seventy-nine	The use of a word with several meanings intending more than one of them
Chapter eighty	The mention of things first through summary in a single word and then in detailed enumeration
Chapter eighty-one	Enallage
Chapter eighty-two	Terminations of verses and endings
Chapter eighty-three	The best verses of the Qurʾān
Chapter eighty-four	The preferred verses of the Qurʾān
Chapter eighty-five	The verses of the Qurʾān to which they are preferred
Chapter eighty-six	The simple, non-compound words of the Qurʾān
Chapter eighty-seven	Parables
Chapter eighty-eight	The code of behaviour to be observed by the reciter of the Qurʾān
Chapter eighty-nine	Code of behaviour to be observed by one who is learning the recitation of the Qurʾān
Chapter ninety	The arts of the interpreter of the Qurʾān
Chapter ninety-one	Those whose interpretations are to be accepted and those whose interpretations are to be rejected
Chapter ninety-two	Unusual interpretations
Chapter ninety-three	Knowledge of the interpreters
Chapter ninety-four	The writing down of the Qurʾān
Chapter ninety-five	The naming of the *sūrahs*
Chapter ninety-six	The arrangement of the verses and *sūrahs*
Chapter ninety-seven	Names (*al-asmāʾ*)

Chapter ninety-eight	Patronymics
Chapter ninety-nine	Titles
Chapter one hundred	Ambiguous matters
Chapter one hundred and one	The names of those concerning whom verses were revealed
Chapter one hundred and two	History (Dating)

This ends the enumeration of the chapters I made in the prologue to the Taḥbīr. Praise be to God, the book was completed in the year (8)72 and it was written out by an accomplished scholar who counts as one of my masters."

Then it occurred to me to write an extensive book, a precise compendium, following the path of comprehensiveness and travelling on the road of exhaustiveness. All the while I imagined that I stood alone in that undertaking and that none had preceded me on those paths. But then, while I was letting my thoughts range back and forth and advancing with one foot and retreating with the other, I learned that al-Shaykh al-Imām Badr al-Dīn Muḥammad b. Abdillah al-Zarkashī, a late scholar belonging to our Shāfiʿī school, had compiled a rich book on the same subject, entitling it al-Burhān fī ʿUlūm al-Qurʾān.

So I acquired a copy to acquaint myself with its contents and I found the author writing in his prologue:

> "Since the sciences of the Qurʾān are beyond enumeration and its meanings are inexhaustible, it is incumbent upon us (only) to concern ourselves with what lies within our reach. I have therefore composed a book including what my predecessors have overlooked and containing the various categories of the sciences of the Qurʾān, by analogy with the books that have been written on the sciences of Prophetic tradition. I sought the blessing of God – may He be exalted and praised – in writing a book on the subject that should include what has already been said concerning the different aspects, points and topics of the Qurʾān. I filled my work with fine meanings and elegant, wise sayings, of a nature to overwhelm men's hearts with astonishment in order that it might serve them as a key to the gates of the Qurʾān and a guide to it; assist the interpreter in uncovering its truths; and make him aware of some of its mysteries and subtleties.
>
> I entitled it al-Burhān fī ʿUlūm al-Qurʾān (The Proof of the Sciences of the Qurʾān), and these are its contents:

Chapter one	Occasions of revelation
Chapter two	The mutual congruity of verses
Chapter three	Terminations of verses
Chapter four	Words with multiple meanings and near-synonyms

Chapter five	Verses of allegorical meaning
Chapter six	Ambiguous matters
Chapter seven	The mysteries contained in certain opening verses
Chapter eight	The conclusions of *sūrahs*
Chapter nine	Meccan and Medinan verses
Chapter ten	The first verses to be revealed
Chapter eleven	The dialects (lughah) in which the Qurʾān was revealed
Chapter twelve	The manner of its revelation
Chapter thirteen	How it was collected and preserved by the Companions
Chapter fourteen	The division of the Qurʾān
Chapter fifteen	The names of the Qurʾān
Chapter sixteen	Words in the Qurʾān not belonging to the dialect of the Hejaz
Chapter seventeen	Non-Arabic words contained in the Qurʾān
Chapter eighteen	Unusual words in the Qurʾān
Chapter nineteen	Declension
Chapter twenty	Ordinances
Chapter twenty-one	Whether a simple word (*lafz*) or a compound (*tarkīb*) is better and more eloquent
Chapter twenty-two	The variation of words through augmentation or diminution
Chapter twenty-three	Dialectics
Chapter twenty-four	Pauses
Chapter twenty-five	Orthography
Chapter twenty-six	Virtues and properties of the Qurʾān
Chapter twenty-seven	Properties of the Qurʾān
Chapter twenty-eight	Is one part of the Qurʾān better than another?
Chapter twenty-nine	The arts of the recitation of the Qurʾān
Chapter thirty	Is it permissible to use verses of the Qurʾān in compositions, letters and sermons?
Chapter thirty-one	The parables contained in the Qurʾān
Chapter thirty-two	The ordinances contained in the Qurʾān
Chapter thirty-three	The disputations contained in the Qurʾān
Chapter thirty-four	Abrogating and abrogated verses
Chapter thirty-five	Verses that give rise to disagreement (that give the appearance of contradiction)
Chapter thirty-six	How to distinguish clear, unambiguous verses from the allegorical
Chapter thirty-seven	Allegorical verses concerning the divine attributes
Chapter thirty-eight	The miraculous nature (inimitability) of the Qurʾān
Chapter thirty-nine	The unanimously accepted obligatory nature of unanimously accepted Qurʾān

Chapter forty	The reinforcement of the Qur᾿ān by the Sunnah
Chapter forty-one	The interpretation of the Qur᾿ān
Chapter forty-two	The different forms of address contained in the Qur᾿ān
Chapter forty-three	The real and the allegorical
Chapter forty-four	Allusions and indirect references
Chapter forty-five	Different types of meaning of the Divine Word
Chapter forty-six	The styles of the Qur᾿ān, to the degree that they are accessible
Chapter forty-seven	Particles

Know that if a man wished to study exhaustively a single one among these topics and devoted to it his whole life, he would be unable to do it justice. We have therefore restricted ourselves to the main principles of each topic together with an indication of some of the details, for learning is long and life is short. How might the tongue of deficiency expound all these matters?"

Thus concludes the prologue to the book of al-Zarkashī.

I rejoiced to make the acquaintance of this book and I praised God greatly, being strengthened in my resolve to carry out my intention. I made firm my determination to compose the work I had in mind, and I therefore set down this book of exalted rank and manifest proof, full of benefit and firm of meaning. I arranged its subject matter in a way more suitable than that of the Burhān, combining certain topics with each other and separating those that deserved to remain distinct as well as adding to the useful and unique matters contained in the Burhān, its general principles and the miscellaneous information, topics that will delight the ear of the reader.

I have entitled the book al-Itqān fī ᶜUlūm al-Qur᾿ān. God Almighty willing, you will note in each of its chapters matters each of which calls for a separate book, and your thirst will be slaked at its limpid springs for all eternity. I have made this book an introduction to the great commentary on the Qur᾿ān on which I have embarked and which I have called Majma al-Bahrayn wa Matla al-Badrayn. This commentary is to combine the narration of traditions and the examination of meaning. I seek success, guidance, assistance and solicitude from God; certainly He is near and answers all prayers. God alone grants success; upon Him is my reliance and unto Him I repent.

These are the contents of the book:

Chaper one	Meccan and Medinan verses
Chapter two	Verses revealed while the Prophet was in residence and verses revealed while he was travelling

Chapter three	Verses revealed in the daytime and verses revealed at night-time
Chapter four	Verses revealed in the summer and verses revealed in the winter
Chapter five	Verses revealed while the Prophet was in bed or sleeping
Chapter six	Verses revealed on the earth and verses revealed in the heavens
Chapter seven	The first parts of the Qurʾān to be revealed
Chapter eight	The last parts of the Qurʾān to be revealed
Chapter nine	Occasions of revelation
Chapter ten	Verses revealed in conformity with the sayings of certain of the Companions
Chapter eleven	Verses that revealed more than once
Chapter twelve	Verses which anticipated the promulgation of an ordinance and verses which were anticipated by the promulgation of an ordinance
Chapter thirteen	*Sūrahs* that were revealed in successive segments and *sūrahs* that were revealed as a whole
Chapter fourteen	Parts of the Qurʾān that were revealed accompanied by angels and parts that were revealed unaccompanied
Chapter fifteen	Verses revealed to the preceding prophets and verses revealed only to the Prophet and to none other before him
Chapter sixteen	The manner of revelation
Chapter seventeen	The names of the Qurʾān and the names of its *sūrahs*
Chapter eighteen	The collection and arrangement of the Qurʾān
Chapter nineteen	The number of the *sūrahs*, verses, words and letters of the Qurʾān
Chapter twenty	The memorizers and narrators of the Qurʾān
Chapter twenty-one	The exalted or lowly status of narrators
Chapter twenty-two	Variant readings related by numerous authorities
Chapter twenty-three	Well-known variant readings
Chapter twenty-four	Variant readings related by few authorities
Chapter twenty-five	Anomalous variant readings
Chapter twenty-six	Invented variant readings
Chapter twenty-seven	Variant readings resulting from the insertion of extraneous matter
Chapter twenty-eight	Termination and beginning

Chapter twenty-nine	Sentences that are verbally linked to each other but semantically separate
Chapter thirty	Deflection and the vowelling with *a*
Chapter thirty-one	Elision, retention of separate phonetic value, suppression and inversion
Chapter thirty-two	Lengthening and shortening
Chapter thirty-three	Lightening of the *hamza*
Chapter thirty-four	The means of learning (*tahammul*) the Qurʾān
Chapter thirty-five	The arts of reciting the Qurʾān
Chapter thirty-six	Unusual words in the Qurʾān
Chapter thirty-seven	Words in the Qurʾān not belonging to the dialect of the Hejaz
Chapter thirty-eight	Non-Arabic words in the Qurʾān
Chapter thirty-nine	Words with multiple meanings and near-synonyms
Chapter forty	The meanings of the particles which the interpreter must know
Chapter forty-one	The vocalization of the Qurʾān
Chapter forty-two	Important rules of which the interpreter must be aware
Chapter forty-three	Verses of firm and obvious meaning and verses of allegorical meaning
Chapter forty-four	The earlier and later parts of the Qurʾān
Chapter forty-five	General and specific verses of the Qurʾān
Chapter forty-six	Summary verses and verses that expound in detail
Chapter forty-seven	Abrogating and abrogated verses
Chapter forty-eight	Difficult verses of the Qurʾān and verses suggestive of contradiction
Chapter forty-nine	Absolute and restricted verses
Chapter fifty	The recited form of the Qurʾān and its semantic content
Chapter fifty-one	Different forms of address found in the Qurʾān
Chapter fifty-two	The real and the allegorical
Chapter fifty-three	Similes and metaphors of the Qurʾān
Chapter fifty-four	Allusions and indirect references in the Qurʾān
Chapter fifty-five	Restriction and specification
Chapter fifty-six	Conciseness and prolixity
Chapter fifty-seven	Narration and composition
Chapter fifty-eight	Original forms of expression (*al-badāʾi*) in the Qurʾān
Chapter fifty-nine	Terminations of verses

Chapter sixty	Beginnings of *sūrahs*
Chapter sixty-one	Endings of *sūrahs*
Chapter sixty-two	Mutual congruity of verses and *sūrahs*
Chapter sixty-three	Verses similar to each other
Chapter sixty-four	The miraculous nature (inimitability) of the Qurʾān
Chapter sixty-five	Sciences that can be deduced from the Qurʾān
Chapter sixty-six	Parables of the Qurʾān
Chapter sixty-seven	Oaths in the Qurʾān
Chapter sixty-eight	Arguments in the Qurʾān
Chapter sixty-nine	Names, patronymics and epithets in the Qurʾān
Chapter seventy	Ambiguous matters in the Qurʾān
Chapter seventy-one	The names of persons concerning whom verses were revealed
Chapter seventy-two	The virtues of the Qurʾān
Chapter seventy-three	The excellent and most excellent parts of the Qurʾān
Chapter seventy-four	The simple, non-compound words of the Qurʾān
Chapter seventy-five	The properties and special characteristics of the Qurʾān
Chapter seventy-six	Orthography of the Qurʾān and the customs connected with writing it
Chapter seventy-seven	The exegesis and interpretation of the Qurʾān, and the nobility and the necessity thereof
Chapter seventy-eight	The conditions and customs to be observed by the interpreter of the Qurʾān
Chapter seventy-nine	Unusual interpretations
Chapter eighty	Classes and categories of interpreters

Numerous matters have been condensed within each of these eighty chapters; were each of them to be treated separately, the book would have more than three hundred chapters. Most of the topics treated in each chapter have been made the subject of separate works, the majority of which have come to my notice.

Among the books that belong to the same category as the present work (although, in reality, they do not resemble it and are not even close to it, apart from being extremely few in number) are: Funūn al-Afnān fī ʿUlūm al-Qurʾān by Ibn al-Jauzī; Jamāl al-Qurrāʾ by al-Shaykh Alam al-Dīnal-Sakhāwī; al-Murshid al-Wajīz fī Ulūm tataallaq bi l-Qurʾān al-Azīz by Abū Shamah; and al-Burhān fī Mushkilāt al-Qurʾān by Abū al-Maālī Azīz b. Abd al-Mālik, known as Shaydhalah. In comparison with the present work, all of them are like a grain of sand compared to a sand desert or a minute drop next to a surging ocean.

These are the books I have consulted in preparing the present work and the contents of which I have summarized for inclusion in it:

Books of tradition: the Qurʾānic commentaries of Ibn Jarīr, Ibn Abī Ḥātim, Ibn Mardawayh, Abū al-Shaykh, Ibn Habbān, al-Firyabi, Abd al-Razzāq, Ibn al-Mundhir, Saʿīd b. Manṣūr (his collection being a part of his Sunan), and al-Ḥākim (his collection being a part of his Mustadrak); the commentary on the Qurʾān of al-Hāfiz Imād al-Dīn b. Kathīr; Fadāʾil al-Qurʾān by Abū ʿUbayd; Fadāʾil al-Qurʾān by Ibn al-Darīs; Fadāʾil al-Qurʾān by Ibn Abī Shaybah; al-Masāhif by Ibn Ashtah, al-Masāhif by Ibn Abī Dawūd; al-Radd alā man khālafa Mishaf Uthmān by Ibn Abī Bakr al-Anbārī; Akhlāq Hamalat al-Qurʾān by al-Ājarī; al-Tibyān fī Ādāb Hamalat al-Qurʾān by al-Nawawī; Sharh al-Bukhārī by Ibn Hajar; and other collections of traditions and narrations too numerous to be mentioned.

Books concerning variant readings of the Qurʾān and its pronunciation: Jamāl al-Qurrāʾ by al-Sakhāwī; al-Nashr wa l-Taqrīb by Ibn al-Jazarī; al-Kāmil by al-Hudhalī; al-Irshād fī l-Qiraʾāt al-Ashr by al-Wāsitī; al-Shawwādh by Ibn Ghalbūn; books entitled al-Waqf wa l-Ibtidāʾ by Ibn al-Anbārī, al-Sajāwandī, al-Naḥḥās, al-Dānī, al-Umānī and Ibn al-Nakzāwī; and Qurrat al-Ayn fī l-Fath wa l-Imālah bayn al-Lafzayn by Ibn al-Qāsih.

Books concerning words, unusual words, the sciences of the Arabic language, and vocalization: Mufradāt al-Qurʾān by al-Rāghib; Gharīb al-Qurʾān by Ibn Qutaybah; the work of the same title by al-Azīzī; al-Wujūh wa l-Nazāʾir by al-Nīsābūrī; a work of the same title by ʿAbd al-Samad; al-Wāhid wa l-Jam fī l-Qurʾān by Abū l-Ḥasan al-Akhfash al-Ausat; al-Zāhir by Ibn al-Anbārī; Sharh al-Tashīl wa l-Irtishāf by Abū Ḥayyān; al-Mughnī by Ibn Hishām; al-Jany al-Dānī fī Hurūf al-Maānī by Ibn Umm Qāsim; works entitled Irāb al-Qurʾān by Abū l-Baqāʾ, al-Samīn and al-Safāqsī, and Muntakhab al-Dīn; al-Muhtasib fī Taujīh al-Shawwadh by Ibn Jinni; al-Khasāʾis, al-Khātiriyāt and Dhū l-Qadd by the same author; al-Amālī by Ibn al-Hājib; al-Muʿarrab by Ibn al-Jawālīqī; Mushkil al-Qurʾān by Ibn Qutaybah; al-Lughāt allatī nazala bihā l-Qurʾān by Abū l-Qāsim Ibn Sallam; al-Gaharaib wa l-Ajaib by al-Kirmānī, Qawaid fī al-Tafsīr by Ibn Taimiya.

Books concerning ordinances of the Qurʾān and matters related to them: works entitled Ahkām al-Qurʾān by Ismail al-Qadi, Bakr b. al-Alāʾ, Abū Bakr al-Rāzī, al-Kayā al-Hirāsī, Ibn al-Furs, and Ibn Khuwayz Mindād; works entitled al-Nāsikh wa l-Mansūkh by Ibn al-Hassār, al-Saʿīdī, Abū Jaʿfar al-Naḥḥās, Ibn al-Arabī, Abū Dawūd al-Sijistānī, Abū ʿUbayd al-Qāsim b. Raslān, and Abū Manṣūr ʿAbd al-Qāhir b. Tāhir al-Tamīmī; al-Imām fī Adillat al-Ahkām by al-Shaykh Izz al-Dīn b. Abd al-Salam.

Books concerning the miraculous nature of the Qurʾān and the various branches of rhetoric: works entitled Ijāz al-Qurʾān by al-Khattābī, al-Rummānī, Ibn Abī Sarrāqah, al-Qādī Abū Bakr al-Bāqillānī, Abd al-Qāhir al-Jurjānī, al-Imām Fakhr al-Dīn; works entitled al-Burhān by Ibn Abī l-Asba and al-Zamlakānī; the abbreviated version of the latter, entitled al-Majīd; Majāz al-Qurʾān by Ibn ʿAbd al-Salam; al-Ījāz fī l-Majāz by Ibn al-Qayyim; Nihāyat al-Ta'mīl fī Asrār al-Tanzīl by al-Zamlakānī; al-Tibyān fī l-Bayān and al-Manhaj al-Mufīd fī Ahkām al-Taukīd, also by al-Zamlakānī; Badā'i al-Qurʾān, al-Tahbīr, al-Khawātir al-Sawānih fī Asrār al-Fawātih, all by Ibn Abī l-Asba; Asrār al-Tanzīl by al-Sharaf al-Bārizī; al-Aqsa al-Qarīb by al-Tanukhī; Minhāj al-Bulaghāʾ by Hāzim; al-Umdah by Ibn Rashīq; al-Sināatayn by al-Askarī; al-Misbāh by Badr al-Dīn b. Mālik; al-Tibyān by al-Tayibī; al-Kināyāt by al-Jurjānī; al-Ighrīd fī l-Farq bayn al-Kināyah wa l-Tarīd by al-Shaykh Taqī l-Dīn al-Subkī; al-Iqtinās fī l-Farq bayn al-Hasr wa l-Ikhtisās by the same author; Ārūs al-Afrāh by his son, Bahāʾ al-Dīn; Raud al-Afhām fī Aqsām al-Istifhām by al-Shaykh Shams al-Dīn b. al-Sāʾigh; Nashr al-Abīr fī Iqāmat al-Zāhir Maqām al-Damīr, al-Muqaddimah fī Sirr al-Alfāz al-Muqaddamah, and Ahkām al-Raʾy fī Ahkām al-Āyy all by the same author; Munāsabat Tartīb al-Suwar by Abū Jaʿfar b. al-Zubayr; Fawāsil al-Āyāt by al-Tūfī; al-Mathal al-Sā'ir by Ibn al-Athīr; al-Falak al-Daʾir alā al-Mathal al-Sāʾir by Ibn Abī l-Hadīd; Kanz al-Barāah by Ibn al-Athīr; and Sharh Badi Qudāmah by al-Muwaffaq ʿAbd al-Latīf.

Books concerning other subjects: al-Burhān fī Mutashābih al-Qurʾān by al-Kirmānī; Durrat al-Tanzīl wa Ghurrat al-Ta'wīl fī l-Mutashābih by Abū ʿAbdillah al-Rāzī; Kashf al-Maānī fī Mutashābih al-Mathānī by al-Qādī Badr al-Dīn b. Jamāah; Amthāl al-Qurʾān by al-Māwardī; Aqsām al-Qurʾān by Ibn al-Qayyim; Jawāhir al-Qurʾān by al-Ghazālī; al-Tarīf wa l-Ilām fī mā waqaa fī l-Qurʾān min al-Asma' wa l-Alām by al-Suhaylī; the supplement to this work by Ibn Asākir; al-Tibyān fī Mubhamāt al-Qurʾān by al-Qādī Badr al-Dīn b. Jamāah; Asmaʾ man nazala fīhim al-Qurʾān by Ismail al-Darīr; Dhāt al-Rushd fī Adad al-Āyy and its commentary by al-Mausilī; Sharh Āyāt al-Sifāt by Ibn al-Labbān; and al-Durr al-Nazīm fī Manāfi al-Qurʾān al-Azīm by al-Yāfiī.

Books concerning orthography: al-Muqni by al-Dāni; Sharh al-Rāʾiya by al-Sakhāwī; another work of the same title by Ibn Jabbārah.

Books comprehensive in nature: Badāʾi al-Fawāʾid by Ibn al-Qayyim; al-Fawāʾid by al-Shaykh Izz al-Dīn b. Abd al-Salam; al-Ghurar wa l-Durar by al-Sharīf al-Murtāda; al-Tadhkīr by al-Badr b. al-Sāhib; Jāmi al-Funūn by Ibn Shabīb al-Hanbalī; al-Nafīs by Ibn al-Jauzī; and al-Bustān by Abū l-Layth al-Samarqandī.

Commentaries on the Qurʾān other than those compiled by traditionalists: al-Kashshāf by al-Zamakhsharī; glosses on al-Kashshāf by al-Taiyibī; the tafsīr of al-Imām Fakhr al-Dīn al-Rāzī; the tafsīrs of al-Isbahānī, al-Hūfī, Abū Ḥayyān, Ibn Aṭiyyah, al-Qushayrī, al-Mursī, Ibn al-Jauzī, Ibn Aqīl, Ibn Razīn, al-Wāhidī, al-Kawāshī, al-Māwardī, Salīm al-Razī, Imām al-Haramayn al-Juwaynī, Ibn Burjān, Ibn Burayzah and Ibn al-Munīr; the Amālī of al-Rāfiī concerning al-Fātiḥah; the introduction to the tafsīr of Ibn al-Naqīb; al-Gharāʾib wa l-Ajāʾib by al-Kirmānī; Qawāid al-Tafsīr by Ibn Taymiyah.

Now let us begin on our undertaking, with the aid of the Sovereign King to whom all worship is due.

Chapter one

MECCAN AND MEDINAN VERSES

Among those who have written separate works on this topic are al-Makkī and al-Izz ad-Dīrīnī. One of the benefits of knowing which verses were revealed in Mecca and which in Medina is learning which verse was revealed later and is thereby an abrogating or a specifying verse, according to those who believe that a specifying verse always comes later.

Abū l-Qāsim al-Ḥasan b. Muḥammad b. Ḥabīb al-Nīsābūrī says in his book al-Tanbīh alā Faḍl Ulūm al-Qur'ān:

Among the most noble of the Qur'ānic sciences is that which enables us to learn the occasions of revelation of the verses; the ordering of the verses that were revealed in Mecca and those that were revealed in Medina; those that were revealed in Mecca but whose ordinance relates to Medina; those that were revealed in Medina but whose ordinance relates to Mecca; those that were revealed in Mecca and refer to the people of Medina; those that were revealed in Medina and refer to the people of Mecca; those that were revealed in Medina and resemble those revealed in Mecca; those that were revealed in Mecca and resemble those revealed in Medina; those that were revealed in al-Juhfah, Jerusalem, Ṭā'if, and al-Hudaybiyah; those revealed at night-time and those revealed during the day; those that were revealed accompanied by angels and those that were not; the Medinan verses contained in the Meccan *sūrahs* and the Meccan verses contained in the Medinan *sūrahs*; those transferred from Mecca to Medina and those transferred from Medina to Mecca; those transferred from Medina to Abyssinia; those that are summary and those that are detailed; and those that are varyingly said to be either Meccan or Medinan. If one is ignorant of these twenty-five categories and is unable to distinguish them from each other, it is not permissible for him to speak concerning God's book.

In my book, I shall give abundant information concerning each category, devoting separate chapters to some of them and combining others together.

Ibn al-ʿArabī says in his book al-Nāsikh wa l-Mansūkh:

According to our general knowledge of the Qur'ān, some of its verses were revealed in Mecca and others in Medina; some were revealed while the Prophet – peace and blessings be upon him – was travelling and others while he was in a place of residence; some verses were revealed at night and others during the day; some were revealed in the heavens, some were revealed on earth, some were revealed between the heavens and the earth, and some were revealed beneath the earth, in the cave.

Ibn Naqīb supplies the following information on the subject in the introduction to his tafsīr:

The *sūrahs* of the Qurʾān can be divided into four categories: Meccan; Medinan; partially Meccan and partially Medinan; neither Meccan nor Medinan. The scholars have put forward three views concerning the Meccan and Medinan *sūrahs*. The best known view is that a *sūrah* counts as Meccan if it was revealed before the Hijra and Medinan if it was revealed after the Hijra, irrespective of whether it was actually revealed in Mecca or Medina, in the Year of the Conquest, the Year of the Farewell Pilgrimage, or in the course of travel.

Uthmān b. Saʿīd al-Rāzī on the authority of Yahyā b. Salam said that the verses revealed to the Prophet – peace and blessings be upon him – as he travelled from Mecca to Medina count as Meccan, and those revealed after the migration to Medina, in the course of travel, count as Medinan. This is a precious narration from which we can deduce that verses revealed in the course of the Hijra count as Meccan.

The second view is that whatever was revealed at Mecca, even if after the Hijra, counts as Meccan, and whatever was revealed at Medina counts as Medinan. This view gives rise to an intermediate category: whatever was revealed in the course of a journey cannot be regarded as either Meccan or Medinan.

According to the Sunan al-Kabīr of al-Ṭabarānī, al-Walīd b. Muslim, on the authority of Ufayr b. Midān, on the authority of Salīm b. Āmir, on the authority of Abū Umāmah, relates that the Messenger of God – peace and blessings be upon him – said: "The Qurʾān was revealed in three places: Mecca, Medina and Syria." According to Walīd b. Muslim what is meant by Syria is Jerusalem, but Imād al-Dīn b. Kathīr is of the opinion that it is preferable to interpret Syria as referring to Tabūk.

In addition to this, I wish to remark that verses revealed in the environs of Mecca – Minā, Arafāt and al-Hudaybiyah – are to be included among the Meccan, and verses revealed in the environs of Medina – Badr, Uḥud and Sala – are to be included among the Medinan.

The third view is that verses addressed to the Meccans are to be regarded as Meccan, and verses addressed to the Medinans are to be regarded as Medinan. The words of Ibn Masūd, quoted below, are to be interpreted in this sense.

Al-Qāḍī Abū Bakr says in his book al-Intisar: "In distinguishing the Meccan and Medinan verses from each other we must refer to whatever the Companions and the Followers remember on this subject. No pronouncements on this subject have been recorded from the Prophet – peace and blessings be upon him – since he was not commanded to concern himself with it and God did not make it an obligatory concern for the community as a whole. In the case of some verses, it may be a duty for the scholars to know the history of abrogating and abrogated verses, but this can be had without an explicit statement from the Prophet – peace and blessings be upon him."

Al-Bukhārī relates Ibn Masūd to have said: "I swear by the God other than Whom there is no god that I know concerning whom each verse of the Qurʾān was revealed and where it was revealed."

According to Ayyūb, someone once asked ʿIkrimah about a certain verse of the Qurʾān. He pointed to Mount Salah and said: "It was revealed on the slopes of that mountain." This narration is mentioned by Abū Nuaym, in his Hilyat al-Awliyāʾ.

There are traditions both from Ibn ʿAbbās and from others concerning whether a given verse is Meccan or Medinan. I will cite those of their traditions I have encountered, and then discuss the verses which are in dispute.

Ibn Saʿd says in his Ṭabaqāt: "I was informed by al-Wāqidī, who heard it from Qudāmah b. Mūsā, who had it in turn from Abū Salma al-Haḍramī, that Ibn ʿAbbās said: 'I asked Ubayy b. Kaʿb which *sūrahs* of the Qurʾān had been revealed in Medina. He replied that twenty-seven *sūrahs* had been revealed there, and all the others in Mecca.'"

Abū Jaʿfar al-Naḥḥās says in his book *al-Nāsikh wa l-Mansūkh*: "I heard from Yamūt b. Muzarra, who had it from Abū Ḥātim Sahl b. Muḥammad al-Sijistānī, who had it from Abū ʿUbaydah Mamar b. al-Muthannā, who had it from Yūnus b. Habīb, that Abū ʿAmr b. al-Alāʾ had said: 'I asked Mujāhid about distinguishing the Meccan from the Medinan verses. He replied that he had asked Ibn ʿAbbās about the same subject, and that Ibn ʿAbbās had answered that Sūrat *al-Anʿam* had been revealed in Mecca as a single unit so that it counts as Meccan, with the exception of three verses which were revealed in Medina, beginning: "Say, 'Come, and I will recite to you . . .'" (v. 151). The preceding *sūrahs*, he said, were Medinan. *al-Aʿraf*, *Yūnus*, *Hūd*, *Yūsuf*, *Raʿd*, *Ibrāhīm*, *al-Ḥijr*, *al-Naḥl* (with the exception of the last three verses which were revealed between Mecca and Medina while the Prophet – peace and blessings be upon him – was returning from Uḥud) were all Meccan. Likewise *Banī Israʾīl*, *al-Kahf*, *Maryam*, *Tāhā*, *al-Anbiyāʾ*, and *al-Ḥajj* (with the exception of verses 19–21 which were revealed in Medina). Also Meccan were *al-Muʾminūn*, *al-Furqān*, *al-Shuʿarā* (with the exception of the last five verses which were revealed in Medina), al-*Naml*, *al-Qasas*, *al-ʿAnkabūt*, *al-Rūm* (with the exception of verses 27–29 which were revealed in Medina), *al-Sajdah* (with the exception of verses 32–34 which were revealed in Medina), *Sabaʾ*, *Fāṭir*, *Yasin*, *al-Ṣāffāt*, *Ṣād*, *al-Zumar* (with the exception of verses 39–41 which were revealed in Medina concerning Waḥshī, the killer of Ḥamzah), verses 53 *al-Zumar* to the end of the verses, the seven *sūrahs* beginning with *Hā-Mīm* (*Ghāfir*, *Fussilat*, *al-Shūrā*, *al-Zukhruf*, *al-Dukhān*, *al-Jāthiyah*, *al-Aḥqāf*), *Qāf*, *al-Dhāriyāt*, *al-Ṭūr*, *al-Najm*, *al-Qamar*, *al-Raḥmān*, *al-Wāqiah*, *al-Ṣaff*, *al-Taghābun* (with the exception of some verses at the end which were revealed in Medina), *al-Mulk*, *Nūn*, *al-Hāqqa*, *al-Maʿārij*, *al-Jinn*, *al-Muzammil* (with the exception of verses 73–74), and from *al-Muddaththir* to the end of the Qurʾān (with the exception of *al-Zalzāla*, *al-Naṣr*, *al-Ikhlās*, *al-Falaq* and *al-Nās*, which were revealed at Medina) – all these *sūrahs* are Meccan. The following *sūrahs* were revealed in Medina: *al-Anfāl*, *al-Barāʾa*, *al-Nūr*, *al-Aḥzāb*, *Muḥammad*, *al-Fatḥ*, *al-Ḥujurāt*, and all the *sūrahs* from *al-Ḥadīd* to *al-Taḥrīm*.'"

Ibn Saʿd has narrated this tradition in its complete form. Its chain of transmission is excellent, all the narrators being trustworthy men and well-known scholars of Arabic.

Al-Bayhaqī relates in his *Dalāʾil al-Nubuwwah* the following narration: "I was informed by Abū ʿAbd-Allāh al-Hāfiz, on the authority of a chain of transmission going back through Abū Muḥammad b. Ziyād al-Adl, Muḥammad b. Ishāq, Yaqūb b. Ibrāhīm al-Dauraqī, Aḥmad b. Naṣr b. Mālik al-Khuzzaʾī, ʿAlī b. al-Ḥusayn Wāqid, and Wāqid, back to Yāzīd al-Nahwī, that ʿIkrimah and Ḥusayn b. Abī l-Ḥasan said: 'God revealed these *sūrahs* in Mecca: *al-ʿAlaq*, *al-Nūr*, *al-Muzammil*, *al-Muddaththir*, *Tabbat*, *al-Takwīr*, *al-Alā*, *al-Layl*, *al-Fajr*, *al-Ḍuḥā*, *al-Inshirāh*, *al-Aʾsr*, *al-Ādiyāt*, *al-Kauthar*, *al-Māūn*, *al-Kāfirūn*, *al-Fīl*, *al-Falaq*, *al-Nās*, *al-Ikhlāṣ*, *al-Najm*, *Abasa*, *al-Qadr*, *al-Shams*, *al-Burūj*, *al-Tīn*, *Quraysh*, *al-Qāriʿah*, *al-Qiyāmah*, *al-Humazah*, *al-Mursalāt*, *al-Balad*, *Qāf*, *al-Ṭāriq*, *al-Qamar*, *Ṣād*, *al-Jinn*, *Yāsīn*, *al-Furqān*, *al-Malāʾikah*, *Ṭāhā*, *al-Wāqiʿah*, *al-Shuarāʾ*, *al-Naml*, *al-Qasas*, *al-Isrāʾ*, *Hūd*, *Yūsuf*, *al-Hijr*, *al-Anām*, *al-Sāffāt*, *Luqmān*, *Sabaʾ*, *al-Zumar*, *al-Muʾmin*, *al-Ḍuḥā*, *Fuṣṣilat*, *al-Shūrā*, *al-Zukhruf*, *al-Jāthiyah*, *al-Aḥqāf*, *al-Dhāriyāt*, *al-Ghāshiyah*, *al-Kahf*, *al-Naḥl*, *Nūḥ*, *Ibrāhīm*, *al-Anbiyāʾ*, *al-Muʾminūn*, *al-Sajdah*, *al-Tūr*, *al-Mulk*, *al-Hāqqah*, *al-Maārij*, *al-Nabaʾ*, *al-Nāziʿāt*, *al-Inshiqāq*, *al-Fāṭir*, *Rūm*, and *al-ʿAnkabūt*. The *sūrahs* revealed in Medina are the following: *al-Muṭaffifūn*, *al-Baqara*, *Āl ʿImrān*, *al-Anfāl*, *al-Aḥzāb*, *al-Maʾidah*, *al-Mumtaḥinah*, *al-Nisāʾ*, *al-Zalzāla*, *al-Ḥadīd*, *Muḥammad*, *al-Raʿd*, *al-Raḥmān*, *al-Ṭalāq*, *al-Bayyinah*, *al-Hashr*, *al-Naṣr*, *al-Nūr*, *al-Ḥajj*, *al-Munāfiqūn*, *al-Mujādilah*, *al-Ḥujurāt*, *al-Taḥrīm*, *al-Ṣaff*, *al-Jumuʿah*, *al-Taghābun*, *al-Fatḥ* and *al-Taubah*.' "

Al-Bayhaqī remarks: "The *sūrahs al-Fātiḥah*, *al-Arāf* and *Maryam*, which were revealed in Mecca, are not included in this narration."

Al-Bayhaqī adds to this list the ninth *sūrah* by which he means *Yūnus*, and remarks that the *sūrahs al-Fātiḥah*, *al-Aʿrāf* and *Maryam*, which were revealed in Mecca, are not mentioned in this narration.

He also cites this narration: "Alī b. Aḥmad informed us, on the authority of a chain of transmission going back through Aḥmad b. ʿUbayd al-Ṣaffār, Muḥammad b. al-Faḍl, Ismāʿīl b. ʿAbdillah b. Zurāra al-Raqqī, Abd al-ʿAzīz b. ʿAbd-al-Raḥmān al-Qurashī and Khasīf to Mujāhid, that Ibn ʿAbbās said: 'The first part of the Qurʾān revealed by God to His Prophet – peace and blessings be upon him – was "recite in the name of Your Lord . . ." (*al-Alaq*).' "

Al-Bayhaqī then explains the meaning of this tradition from Ibn ʿAbbās and goes on to add the *sūrahs* not included in his first narration concerning the *sūrahs* revealed in Mecca. He says that the *Tafsīr* of Muqātil and others supports the tradition – sound (in its text) although having gaps in its chain of transmission – of Ibn ʿAbbās.

Ibn al-Durays says in his *Faḍāʾil al-Qurʾān*: "Muḥammad b. ʿAbd Allāh informed us, on the authority of a chain of transmission going through ʿAmr b. Hārūn and ʿUthmān b. Atāʾ al-Khūrāsānī to ʿAtāʾ al-Khūrāsānī, that Ibn ʿAbbās had said: 'When the beginning of a *sūrah* was revealed in Mecca, it was written down in Mecca, and then God would add to it whatever He wished. The first *sūrah* of the Qur'ān to be revealed was *al-Alaq*. Then the other *sūrahs* were revealed in the following order: *al-Muzammil*, *al-Muddaththir*, *Tabbat*, *al-Takwīr*, *al-Aʿlā*, *al-Layl*, *al-Fajr*, *al-Ḍuhā*, *al-Inshirāḥ*, *al-ʿAṣr*, *al-Ādiyāt*, *al-Kauthar*, *al-Takāthur*, *Māʿūn*, *al-Kāfirūn*, *al-Falaq*, *al-Nās*, *al-Ikhlāṣ*, *al-Najm*, *Abasa*, *al-Qadr*, *al-Shams*, *al-Burūj*, *al-Tīn*, *Quraysh*, *al-Qāriha*, *al-Qiyāmah*, *al-Humaza*, *al-Mursalāt*, *Qāf*, *al-Balad*, *al-Tāriq*, *al-Qamar*, *Sād*, *al-Arāf*, *Yāsīn*, *al-Furqān*, *al-Malā'ikah*, *Maryam*, *Ṭāhā*, *al-Wāqiʿah*, *al-Shuarā'*, *al-Naml*, *al-Qiṣaṣ*, *al-Isrā'*, *Yūnus*, *Hūd*, *Yūsuf*, *al-Ḥijr*, *al-Anʿām*, *al-Ṣāffāt*, *Luqmān*, *Saba'*, *al-Zumar*, *al-Mu'min*, *Fuṣṣilat*, *al-Shūrā*, *al-Zukhruf*, *al-Dukhān*, *al-Jāthiyah*, *al-Aḥqāf*, *al-Dhāriyāt*, *al-Ghāshiyah*, *al-Kahf*, *al-Naḥl*, *Nūḥ*, *Ibrāhīm*, *al-Anbiyā'*, *al-Mu'minūn*, *al-Sajdah*, *al-Ṭūr*, *al-Mulk*, *al-Ḥāqqa*, *al-Maʿārij*, *al-Naba'*, *al-Infiṭār*, *al-Inshiqāq*, *Rūm*, *al-ʿAnkabūt* and *al-Muṭaffifūn*. Then these *sūrahs* were revealed in Medina in the following order: *al-Baqara*, *al-Anfāl*, *Āl ʿImrān*, *al-Ahzāb*, *al-Mumtahinah*, *al-Nisā'*, *al-Zalzāla*, *al-Hadīd*, *al-Qitāl*, *al-Ra'd*, *al-Raḥmān*, *al-Dahr*, *al-Ṭalāq*, *al-Bayinah*, *al-Ḥashr*, *al-Naṣr*, *al-Nūr*, *al-Ḥajj*, *al-Munāfiqūn*, *al-Mujādilah*, *al-Ḥujurāt*, *al-Taḥrīm*, *al-Jumuah*, *al-Taghābun*, *al-Ṣaff*, *al-Fatḥ*, *al-Mā'idah* and *al-Taubah*.

Abū ʿUbayd says in his *Faḍā'il al-Qur'ān*: "I was told by ʿAbdullah b. Ṣālih who had it from Muāwiyah b. Ṣālih that ʿAlī b. Abī Talḥah had said: 'There were revealed in Medina *al-Baqara*, *Āl ʿImrān*, *al-Nisā'*, *al-Mā'idah*, *al-Anfāl*, *al-Taubah*, *al-Ḥajj*, *al-Nūr*, *al-Aḥzāb*, *Muḥammad*, *al-Fatḥ*, *al-Ḥadīd*, *al-Mujādilah*, *al-Ḥashr*, *al-Mumtaḥinah*, *al-Ṣaff*, *al-Taghābun*, *al-Ṭalāq*, *al-Taḥrīm*, *al-Fajr*, *al-Layl*, *al-Qadr*, *al-Bayyinah*, *al-Zalzāla*, and *al-Naṣr*. All other *sūrahs* were revealed in Mecca.' " ' "

Abū Bakr b. al-Anbārī relates the following: "I was told by Ismāʿīl b. Isḥāq al-Qāḍī, who had it from Hajjāj b. Minhāl, who was told by ʿAbd al-Razzāq b. Hammām, that Qatāda said: '*al-Baqara*, *Āl ʿImrān*, *al-Nisā'*, *al-Mā'idah*, *al-Taubah*, *al-Raʿd*, *al-Naḥl*, *al-Ḥajj*, *al-Nūr*, *al-Aḥzāb*, *Muḥammad*, *al-Fatḥ*, *al-Hujurāt*, *al-Hadīd*, *al-Raḥmān*, *al-Mujādilah*, *al-Hashr*, *al-Mumtahinah*, *al-Ṣaff*, *al-Jumuʿah*, *al-Munāfiqūn*, *al-Taghābun*, *al-Ṭalāq*, the first nine verses of *al-Taḥrīm*, *al-Zalzāla*, and *al-Naṣr* were revealed in Medina and all other *sūrahs* were revealed in Mecca.' "

Abū l-Ḥasan b. al-Ḥassār says in his book *al-Nāsikh wa l-Mansūkh* that twenty *sūrahs* were revealed by general agreement in Medina, that twelve others are also said to have been revealed there, although there is disagreement on the subject, and that all other *sūrahs* are agreed to have been revealed in Mecca. He then expounded the matter in the following verses:

O you who inquire earnestly concerning the Book of God –
  The order in which the recited *sūrahs* were revealed
How the Chosen One of Mudar delivered those verses,

May peace and blessings be upon him!
Which of its verses preceded the Hijra and which followed,
Which were received while journeying and which in residence.
This, so the *mujtahid* might learn cases of abrogation and specification,
Aided in his judgement by knowing the date of revelation.
Traditions contradict each other concerning the Mother of the Book,
But *al-Ḥijr* gives lessons to the thoughtful.
The Mother of the Qur᾽ān was revealed in the Mother of Cities;
There was no trace of the five prayers before *al-Ḥamd*.
After the Hijra of the Best of Mankind were revealed
Twenty *sūrahs* of the Qur᾽ān, then ten more.
First came four of the seven long *sūrahs*,
And the fifth was *al-Anfāl*, full of lessons.
Al-Taubah comes sixth in our counting,
Followed by the celebrated *al-Nūr* and *al-Ahzāb*.
Then the *sūrah* named for God's Prophet, a firm one;
Then *al-Fatḥ* and the glorious *al-Hujurāt*.
Next comes *al-Ḥadīd*, followed by *al-Mujādilah*;
Then *al-Ḥashr* and God's testing of man.
Then a *sūrah* in which God disgraces the hypocrites *al-Munafiqun*
And the *sūrah* of the assembly al-Jumu᾽a in which God is mentioned.

Then *sūrahs* with the ordinances concerning divorce (*al-Talāq*) and prohibition (*al-Tahrīm*).

Next *al-Naṣr* and *al-Fatḥ*, with its allusion to the appointed time of the Prophet.

On all these the narrators are fully agreed,
But reports differ concerning the rest.
When was *al-Raʿd* revealed? Men disagree,
Although most say it is like *al-Qamar*.
Like it, too, is *al-Raḥmān*, the proof being
The mention of the jinn it contains.
Well-known is the *sūrah* of the disciples,
And then *al-Taghābun* and *al-Taṭfīf* with its warnings.

The Night of Power *al-Qadr* is exclusively for our community;

Then comes *lam yakun*, followed by *al-Zalzālah*, to take note.

"Say: 'He is God'" is in description of our Creator;
Then come the two Repellers, which repel disaster, if that be God's will.
These are the *sūrahs*, on which the narrators disagree,
And sometimes, too, certain verses of the *sūrahs* are excluded.

All other *sūrahs* were revealed in Mecca;
Do not be distressed if some disagree.
Not every dissenting opinion is of value,
Only the opinion that rests on reflection.

Section

Sūrahs concerning which there is difference of opinion

Al-Fātiḥah Most scholars accept that this *sūrah* is Meccan. As will be seen in the second chapter, it is even said that it was the first *sūrah* to be revealed.

As proof of this, *al-Ḥijr* 72 ("Indeed We gave you seven oft-repeated verses") is cited. According to al-Bukhārī, the Prophet – peace and blessings be upon him – interpreted this as referring to *al-Fātiḥah*.

Al-Ḥijr It is Meccan by general agreement. The fact that God makes mention in it of the favour He has shown the Prophet – peace and blessings be upon him – with *al-Fātiḥah* shows that it was revealed later than *al-Fātiḥah*, for it is unlikely that He would make mention of a favour that had not already been granted. There is in addition no disputing that prayer was made obligatory in Mecca, and there is no record that prayer was ever performed in Islam without *al-Fātiḥah*. This has been related by Ibn Aṭiyyah and others.

Al-Wāḥidī and al-Thalabī relate from ʿAlāʾ b. al-Musayyab, who heard it from Faḍl b. ʿAmr, that ʿAlī b. Abī Ṭālib said: "*Al-Fātiḥah* which is one of the treasures of the Throne, was revealed in Mecca."

Mujāhid's affirmation that *al-Fātiḥah* was revealed in Medina is well known. His narration on this subject is contained in the *Tafsīr* of al-Firyābī and recorded by Abū ʿUbayd in *Faḍāʾil al-Qurʾān* with a sound chain of transmission. Ḥusayn b. al-Faḍl regards Mujāhid's view as erroneous because most of the scholars disagree with it. Ibn Aṭiyyah has recorded opinions to the same effect from al-Zuhrī, Atāʾ, Sawādah b. Ziyād and ʿAbdullah b. ʿUbayd b. ʿUmayr.

Al-Ṭabarānī reports in his *Awsat* a narration of Abū Hurayrah on the subject, with the following excellent chain of transmission: ʿUbayd b. Ghanām, Abū Bakr b. Abī Shaybah, Abū l-Ahwas, Manṣūr, Mujāhid, Abū Hurayrah. Abū Hurayrah is reported as saying: "When *al-Fātiḥah* was revealed, Satan threw himself to the ground. *Al-Fātiḥah* was revealed in Medina." There is a possibility that the second sentence was grafted on from the statement of Mujāhid.

According to some people, this *sūrah* was revealed twice – once in Mecca and once in Medina – in order to emphasize its value and honour. There is even a fourth opinion, to the effect that half the *sūrah* was revealed in Mecca and half in Medina. This is reported by Abū l-Layth al-Samarqandī.

Al-Nisā᾽ Pointing out that verse 58, with its reference to the keys of the Kaba, was revealed in Mecca by general agreement, al-Naḥḥās maintains that the whole of the *sūrah* is Meccan. However, his reasoning is faulty, because if one or more verses of a *sūrah* which is for the most part Medinan were revealed in Mecca, this does not suffice to make the whole *sūrah* Meccan. There is, moreover, the preferred view that all *sūrahs* revealed after the Hijra are to be counted as Medinan. In addition, if one investigates the occasion for the revelation of the verses in this *sūrah* he will be still further inclined to reject the view of al-Naḥḥās. Arguing against his view is a tradition from Ā᾽ishah reported by al-Bukhārī. She is reported to have said: "*Al-Baqara* and *al-Nisā᾽* were revealed when I was in his presence." It is unanimously agreed that Ā᾽ishah entered the house of the Prophet – peace and blessings be upon him – as his wife after the Hijra.

It is also said that *al-Nisā᾽* was revealed at the time of the Hijra.

Yūnus The generally accepted view is that this *sūrah* is Meccan. There are two traditions from Ibn ʿAbbās on this subject. In one of them, cited above, this *sūrah* is said to be Meccan. This is reported by Ibn Mardawayh on the authority of al-Awfī, by Ibn Jurayj on the authority of Atā᾽, and by Khasīf on the authority of Mujāhid, who had it from Ibn al-Zubayr. In the other – reported on the authority of Uthmān b. Atā᾽ who heard it from Atā᾽ – Ibn ʿAbbās pronounced this *sūrah* to be Medinan.

The tradition of Ibn ʿAbbās narrated by Ibn Abī Ḥātim on the authority of al-Dahhāk supports the generally accepted view. According to this tradition Ibn ʿAbbās says: "When God sent Muḥammad as a messenger, the Arabs – or some among them – rejected him, saying God is too exalted to choose a messenger for Himself from among men. God thereupon revealed the second verse of sūrat *Yūnus*: 'Is it a matter of wonderment to men that We have sent Our revelation to a man from among them . . .?' "

Al-Raʿd According to previously cited traditions of Ibn ʿAbbās and ʿAlī b. Abī Talḥa narrated on the authority of Mujāhid, this *sūrah* is Meccan, although other traditions maintain that it is Medinan. Ibn Mardawayh reports Ibn ʿAbbās to have expressed the latter view on the authority of al-Awfī and on the authority of Ibn Jurayj who had it from ʿUthmān b. Atā᾽. Abū l-Shaykh reports Qatāda to have held the same view, while also attributing the view that the *sūrah* is Meccan to Ibn ʿAbbās on the authority of Saʿīd b. Jubayr.

Saʿīd b. Manṣūr relates the following in his *Sunan*: "Abū Awānah informed us that Abū Bishr told him of having asked Saʿīd b. Jubayr whether or not God intended by 'the one having knowledge of the Book' in verse 43 of *al-Rad* ʿAbdullah b. Salam. He answered: 'How could that be, given that this is a Meccan *sūrah*?' "

On the other hand, the tradition of Anas narrated by al-Ṭabarānī and others supports the view that this is a Medinan *sūrah*. Anas says that verses eight to thirteen of the *sūrah* were revealed in connection with the episode of Arbad b. Qays and Āmir b. Ṭufayl coming to Medina to see the Messenger of God.

The difference of opinion can be solved by concluding that the *sūrah* is Meccan with the exception of certain verses.

Al-Ḥajj According to the previously cited tradition of Ibn ʿAbbās, related on the authority of Mujāhid, this *sūrah* is Meccan, with the exception of the verses that he excluded. According to other traditions, it is Medinan. Ibn Mardawayh reports, on the authority of al-Awfī and on that of Ibn Jurayj, that Ibn ʿAbbās regarded the *sūrah* as Medinan. ʿUthmān reports a similar tradition on the authority of Atāʾ, as well as a tradition of Ibn al-Zubayr to the same effect, related on the authority of Mujāhid.

Ibn al-Faras reports in his *Aḥkām al-Qurʾān* that the *sūrah* has been said to be Meccan with the exception of all verses after the nineteenth, or with the exception of ten verses. He also reports the view that it is Medinan, with the exception of verses 52–55, this being the opinion of Qatāda and others, as well as the view of al-Dahhāk and others that it is Medinan in its entirety. Finally, he mentions the common view that it is a mixed *sūrah* containing both Meccan and Medinan verses. This view is supported by the fact that many of its verses are related to have been revealed in Medina, as we have set forth in our book *Asbāb al-Nuzūl*.

Al-Furqān According to Ibn al-Faras, the common view is that this *sūrah* is Meccan, but al-Dahhāk regards it as Medinan.

Yāsīn According to an opinion cited by Abū Sulaymān al-Dimishqī and described by him as uncommon this *sūrah* is Medinan.

Sād Al-Jaʾbarī records an opinion to the effect that this *sūrah* is Medinan, contrary to the consensus that it is Meccan.

Muḥammad Al-Nasafī cites an unusual opinion to the effect that this *sūrah* is Meccan.

Al-Ḥujurāt According to a rare opinion, this *sūrah* is Meccan.

Al-Raḥmān The majority view is that this *sūrah* is Meccan, and this is correct. This is indicated by the tradition related by al-Tirmidhī and al-Ḥākim on the authority of Jābir: "After reciting *al-Raḥmān* from beginning to end, the Messenger of God – peace and blessings be upon him – said to his Companions: 'Why are you thus silent? When I recited this *sūrah* to the jinn, they responded better than you. Whenever I recited the verse, "which, then, of the blessings of your Lord do you deny?" they replied, "O Lord, we deny none of your blessings, and you alone do we praise."'" Al-Ḥākim remarks that this tradition is fully authentic, according to the criteria set by al-Bukhārī and Muslim. This encounter with the jinn took place in Mecca.

A still clearer proof that *al-Raḥmān* is a Meccan *sūrah* is provided by the tradition of Asmā', the daughter of Abū Bakr, recorded in the *Musnad* of Aḥmad b. Hanbal with a strong chain of transmission. Asmā' said: "I heard the Messenger of God – peace and blessings be upon him – while he was praying towards the Black Stone, reciting the verse, 'Which, then, of the blessings of your Lord do you deny?' before 'expound openly what you are commanded . . .' (*al-Hijr*, 94) had been revealed." This tradition demonstrates that *al-Raḥmān* was revealed before *al-Hijr*.

Al-Ḥadīd According to Ibn al-Faras, the majority opinion is that this *sūrah* is Medinan. Others regard it as Meccan. There is no disputing that it contains Medinan verses, but its opening verses appear to be Meccan.

I am of the same opinion as Ibn al-Faras, given the tradition concerning ʿUmar by al-Bazzāz in his *Musnad* and others: "ʿUmar once entered his sister's house before he had embraced Islam and saw a page containing the opening verses of *al-Ḥadīd*. He read them, and this was the cause for his accepting Islam."

Al-Ḥākim and others relate Ibn Masūd to have said: "Not more than four years passed between ʿUmar's acceptance of Islam and the revelation of a verse in which God reprimands the believers: '. . . that they not be like those who were given revelation before them' (*al-Ḥadīd*, 16)."

Al-Ṣaff According to the generally adopted opinion, this *sūrah* is Medinan. Ibn al-Faras attributes this opinion to the majority of scholars and himself regards it as preferable. One indication of its correctness is a tradition from ʿAbdullah b. Salam reported by al-Ḥākim and others. He said: "A group of us Companions of the Messenger of God were sitting engaged in conversation, and we said that if we knew what deed was most beloved of God we would certainly do it. Thereupon God Almighty revealed the first two verses of *al-Ṣaff* – 'Whatever is in the heavens and the earth glorifies God; He is the Powerful, the Wise. O you who believe! Why do you say what you do not do?' – followed by the rest of the *sūrah*. The Messenger of God – peace and blessings be upon him – then recited the entire *sūrah* to us."

Al-Jumuʿah The correct view is that this is Medinan on account of this tradition from Abū Hurayrah reported by al-Bukhārī: "We were sitting with the Prophet – peace and blessings be upon him – when God revealed the verse '. . . and others who have not already joined them' (*al-Jumuʿah* 3). I asked the Messenger of

God who these others might be." It is well known that Abū Hurayrah embraced Islam some time after the Hijra. Moreover, verse 6 of this *sūrah* – "Say: 'O Jews'" – is an address to the Jews who were living in Medina. The last verse of this *sūrah* was revealed concerning those who rushed away while the *khutbah* was still in progress because a trading caravan had arrived; this is confirmed by authentic traditions. It is thus proven that the entire *sūrah* is Medinan.

Al-Taghābun It has been said both to be Medinan and to be Meccan with the exception of its last verse.

Al-Mulk There is an uncommon view that this *sūrah* is Medinan.

Al-Insān Although it is said that the entire *sūrah* is Medinan, it is also said to be Meccan with the exception of verse 24 (". . . and do not obey any sinful ingrate from among them").

Al-Muṭaffifūn Ibn al-Faras relates a number of views concerning this *sūrah*. One is that it was revealed in Mecca, given its mention of legends, and another is that it was revealed in Medina, because the Medinans were the most dishonest people in weighing and measuring. A third view is that it was revealed in Mecca with the exception of the verses concerning fraudulent dealing. There are also people who say the *sūrah* was revealed between Mecca and Medina.

In addition, I wish to point out that al-Nasāʾī and others have narrated the following tradition from Ibn ʿAbbās, with a sound chain of transmission: "When the Prophet – peace and blessings be upon him – arrived in Medina, its people were extremely dishonest in weighing and measuring. God therefore revealed 'Woe upon those who deal fraudulently' (*al-Muṭaffifūn*, 1), and they began to weigh and measure correctly."

Al-Alā According to majority opinion, this *sūrah* is Meccan, but Ibn al-Faras records an opinion that it is Medinan, given the mention it contains of Īd prayer and the zakāt paid on Īd al-Fitr.

I wish to point out, however, that this view is refuted by a tradition of al-Barāʾ b. ʿĀzib reported by al-Bukhārī: "The first of the Companions of the Prophet – peace and blessings upon him – to come to us were Musab b. ʿUmayr and Ibn Umm Maktūm; they began teaching us the recitation of the Qurʾān. Then came ʿAmmār, Bilāl and Sad, followed by ʿUmar b. al-Khaṭṭāb, accompanied by twenty people. Then the Prophet – peace and blessings be upon him – himself arrived, and I had never seen the Medinans rejoice as they did then. As soon as he arrived, I recited *al-ʿAlā*."

Al-Fajr According to Ibn al-Faras, there are two views concerning this *sūrah*, but the opinion of Abū Ḥayyān and the majority of scholars is that it is Meccan.

Al-Balad Ibn al-Faras says that there are two views concerning this *sūrah* also, but that "by this city" (*al-Balad*, 1–2) refutes the view that it is Medinan.

Al-Layl The common view is that this *sūrah* is Meccan, but it is also said to be Medinan on account of the episode of the palm tree, as we have demonstrated, citing the relevant traditions, in our *Asbāb al-Nuzūl*. A third opinion holds that this *sūrah* contains both Meccan and Medinan verses.

Al-Qadr There are two views concerning this *sūrah* but the majority view is that it is Meccan. The evidence cited in favour of its being Medinan is a tradition reported from Ḥasan b. ʿAlī by al-Tirmidhi and al-Ḥākim to the effect that the Prophet – peace and blessings be upon him – foresaw that the Banu Umayyah would mount the minbar, and this made him unhappy. Thereupon al-Kawthar and al-Qadr were revealed. Al-Mazzī classifies this tradition as unknown.

Al-Bayinah Ibn al-Faras states that this *sūrah* is Meccan according to the prevalent view. However, the opposite is indicated by this tradition of Abū Hayya al-Badrī reported by Aḥmad b. Hanbal: "The Messenger of God – peace and blessings be upon him – said that when this *sūrah* was revealed to him, Gabriel ordered him to recite it to Ubayy." Relying on this tradition, Ibn Kathīr states categorically that this *sūrah* is Medinan.

Al-Zalzāla There are also two views concerning this *sūrah*. The evidence for its being Medinan is this tradition of Abū Saʿīd al-Khudrī reported by Ibn Abī Ḥātim: "When the verse, 'Whosoever does an atom's worth of good shall see it' (*al-Zalzāla*, 7), was revealed, I told the Messenger of God – peace and blessings be upon him, 'Indeed I can see the good deeds I have performed.' " Now Abū Saʿīd was definitely in Medina, having come there after the Battle of Uḥud.

Al-Ādiyāt There are also two views on this *sūrah*; the evidence for its being Medinan is this tradition of Ibn ʿAbbās reported by al-Ḥākim and others: "The Messenger of God sent forth a group of horsemen, and although a month passed, no news was heard of them. Thereupon *al-Ādiyāt* was revealed."

Al-Takāthur The prevalent view is that this *sūrah* is Meccan, but according to a tradition of Ibn Buraydah reported by Ibn Abī Ḥātim and others it is Medinan; this is the view I prefer. Ibn Buraydah says: "This *sūrah* was revealed concerning two tribes Ansār that were vying with each other."

According to a tradition of Qatāda, this *sūrah* was revealed concerning the Jews.

Bukhārī reports Ubayy b. Kaʿb to have said: "Until *sūrat al-Takāthur* was revealed, we thought that the *ḥadīth* 'if there were a valley of gold beneath man . . .' was part of the Qurʾān."

According to a tradition recorded by al-Tirmidhī, ʿAlī said: "Until the verse concerning torment in the grave was revealed, we were in doubt on this subject." Because of the *ḥadīth* recorded by Bukhārī concerning the Jewish woman, we know that the torment in the grave began to be mentioned only in Medina.

Al-Maʿūn According to Ibn al-Faras, there are two views concerning this *sūrah*.

Al-Kauthar The truth of the matter is that this *sūrah* is Medinan. In his commentary on Muslim, al-Nawawī prefers this view, basing himself on a tradition of Anas b. Mālik reported by Muslim. Anas said: "The Messenger of God, peace and blessings be upon him, fell asleep for a time while we were at his side. Then he awoke, he smiled and raised his head, saying, 'This *sūrah* was revealed to me a short time ago.' He then pronounced the *basmala* and recited the whole of *sūrat al-Takāthur*."

Al-Ikhlāṣ There are two views on this *sūrah*, arising from two contradictory versions of the occasion for its revelation. Some scholars claim that it was revealed more than once, thus reconciling the two versions.

As I explain in my *Asbāb al-Nuzūl*, it appears to me preferable to regard this *sūrah* as Medinan.

Al-Muʿawidhdhatān According to the preferred view, both *sūrahs* are Medinan, because, as al-Bayhaqī mentions in his *Dalāʾil al-Nubuwwah*, they were revealed with reference to Labīd b. al-Aʿsam's efforts to work magic on the Messenger of God, peace and blessings upon him.

Section

Sūrahs some of the verses of which were revealed in Mecca and others of which were revealed in Medina

According to *Dalāʾil al-Nubuwwah* of al-Bayhaqī, the verses making up certain Meccan *sūrahs* were completed in Medina and then added to them.

Ibn al-Haṣṣār similarly says: "Some verses are excepted from the general characterization of the *sūrahs* in which they occur as either Meccan or Medinan. Then making these exceptions, some people rely on their own judgement, to the exclusion of any tradition."

Section

Verses excepted from the Meccan and Medinan

Ibn Hajar says in his commentary on al-Bukhārī: "Certain leading scholars have given care to identifying the Medinan verses that are contained in Meccan *sūrahs*. The converse of this also obtains: part of a *sūrah* may have been revealed in Mecca, but the revelation of the *sūrah* as a whole was postponed to Medina. However, I have rarely observed this kind of revelation."

It will be fitting if I now set forth in detail the information I have collected concerning these two types of exception, emphasizing the first of them and indicating the evidence for the exceptions, in accordance with the view of al-Hassār. For the sake of brevity, I will not cite the evidence verbatim, referring the reader instead to my book on the occasions of revelation, where it is set out in full.

Al-Fātiḥah As we said above, half of the *sūrah* was revealed in Medina, apparently the second half, although there is no clear proof for this.

Al-Baqara Verses 109 and 122 have been excepted.

Al-Anʿām Ibn al-Haṣṣār says: "Nine verses are said to have been excepted from this *sūrah*, but there is no tradition authenticating this view, and the whole *sūrah* is reported, moreover, to have been revealed at once." Let me state, however, that this view is indeed correct, because according to a narration reported from Ibn ʿAbbās, verses 151–153 are to be excepted. Furthermore, verse 91 ("They did not estimate God justly") was revealed concerning Mālik b. al-Sayf, according to a tradition recorded by Ibn Abī Ḥātim, and verses 21–22 were revealed concerning Musaylamah. It is also said that these verses are excepted: verse 20 ("Those to whom We gave the Book and who know it as they know their own sons") and verse 114 ("and those to whom We gave the Book know that it [the Qurʾān] is sent down by your Lord". Al-Kalbī is reported by Abū al-Shaykh to have said: "With the exception of two verses revealed in Medina concerning a Jew who said that God reveals nothing to man, the whole of *sūrat al-Anʿām* is Meccan." Al-Firyabī heard from Sufyān that Layth had told him that Bishr had informed him that with the exception of verses 151–152 ("Say: come that I may recite to you . . .") the whole of *sūrat al-Anʿām* was revealed in Mecca.

Al-Aʿrāf Qatāda is reported by Abū al-Shaykh b. Ḥayyān to have said: "With the exception of verse 163 ('Ask them concerning the city on the seashore'), the whole of the *sūrah* is Meccan." Others say that the verses following 163, as far as 173 ("When your Lord took from the sons of Ādam . . .") are Medinan, and the rest are Meccan.

Al-Anfāl Verse 30 ("When those who disbelieve were plotting against you . . .") has been excepted from this *sūrah*, Muqātil saying that it was revealed in Mecca.

As we have mentioned in our book on the occasions of revelation, this view is refuted by the authentic tradition of Ibn ʿAbbās to the effect that precisely this verse was revealed in Medina. Some also regard verse 64 ("O Prophet, sufficient for you is God . . .") as Meccan, a view regarded by Ibn al-ʿArabī and others as correct. Let me point out that its correctness is confirmed by a tradition of Ibn ʿAbbās, related by al-Bazzāz, to the effect that this verse was revealed when ʿUmar accepted Islam.

Al-Taubah Ibn al-Faras says that this *sūrah* is Medinan, with the exception of verses 128 and 129. ("A messenger has come to you from among yourselves . . ."). I regard this view as unlikely. How can these two verses be Meccan, given the fact that they are said to be among the last verses of the Qurʾān to be revealed? Some also except from this *sūrah* verse 113 ("it is not fitting for the Prophet . . ."), which was revealed with respect to the Prophet's saying to Abū Ṭālib: "I will seek forgiveness for you as long as I am not forbidden to do so."

Yūnus According to Ibn al-Faras and the *Jamāl al-Qurrāʾ* of al-Sakhāwī, the verses of this *sūrah* are Meccan, with the exception of verses 94 and 95 (beginning with "If you are in doubt concerning what We have revealed unto you") and verse 40 ("and among them are those who believe in it . . ."), which is said to have been revealed concerning the Jews. It is also said that the first forty verses of the *sūrah* are Meccan and the remaining verses Medinan.

Hūd This *sūrah* is Meccan, with the exception of verses 12 ("Perhaps you may abandon . . ."), 17 ("Is he who possesses a clear proof from his Lord . . .?") and verse 114 ("Establish the prayer at the beginning and end of the day"). It is indeed established by sound traditions, transmitted by different chains, that the last of these was revealed in Medina concerning Abū l-Yusr.

Yūsuf According to Abū Ḥayyān, the first three verses of the *sūrah* are Medinan, and the rest are Meccan. This view is so aberrant as to be unworthy of consideration.

Al-Raʿd According to a statement of Qatāda recorded by Abū l-Shaykh, this *sūrah* is Medinan with the exception of verse 31 ("Disaster continually afflicts those who disbelieve on account of what they have wrought"). If we accept the opposing view that the *sūrah* is Meccan, verses 8 ("God knows . . .") to 13 (". . . extremely powerful") must be excepted as Medinan, as mentioned before. Ibn Mardawayh cites this saying of Jundab: "ʿAbdullah b. Salam came to the mosque and laying hold of the rings on each panel of its door said, 'O people, I ask you in the name of God, do you know that I am the one concerning whom "the one who has knowledge of the book" (verse 43) was revealed?' They replied, 'O God, yes!'"

Ibrāhim According to a statement of Qatāda recorded by Abū l-Shaykh, this *sūrah* is Meccan, with the exception of verses 28 and 29 ("Do you not see those who have met God's blessing with ingratitude? . . . How evil a place of repose!")

Al-Ḥijr Some people say that this *sūrah* is Meccan with the exception of verse 87 ("Indeed We have given you seven oft-repeated verses"). Let me add that verse 24 ("Indeed we were aware of those who preceded you") ought also to be excepted, given the traditions reported by al-Tirmidhī and others concerning the occasion for its revelation, which was the formation of rows in prayer.

Al-Naḥl As mentioned above, Ibn ʿAbbās regards this *sūrah* as Meccan, with the exception of its last verse. Evidence in support of this will be mentioned in the chapter concerning verses revealed while the Prophet – peace and blessings be upon him – was travelling. According to a tradition of al-Shabī reported by Abū l-Shaykh, the whole *sūrah* was revealed in Mecca with the exception of verses 126–128, beginning "If you are to punish . . ." According to a tradition of Qatāda, also reported by Abū l-Shaykh, verses 41 ("Those who migrate after suffering injustice . . .") to the end are Medinan, and the verses preceding it are Meccan. In the chapter on the first verses of the Qurʾān to be revealed we will cite a tradition from Jābir b. Zayd to the effect that the first forty verses of this *sūrah* were revealed in Mecca, and the rest in Medina. This is refuted by a tradition of ʿUthman b. Abī I-ʿĀs reported by Aḥmad b. Ḥanbal; concerning the revelation of verse 90 ("God commands justice and beneficence . . ."). We will deal with this subject again in the chapter on the arrangement of the *sūrahs*.

Al-Isrāʾ According to a tradition of Ibn Masʿūd reported by al-Bukhārī, this *sūrah* is Meccan with the exception of verse 85 ("They will ask you concerning the spirit"), which was revealed in answer to the question of the Jews concerning the spirit. In accordance with the traditions we cite in our book on the occasions of revelations, the following verses are also Medinan: 73 ("They were about to cast you into temptation . . .") to 81 (". . . certainly falsehood was destined to vanish"); 88 ("Say: if they [mankind and jinn] come together . . ."); 60 ("We made the vision We showed you a trial for men . . ."); and 107 ("those to whom knowledge has been given").

Al-Kahf This *sūrah* is Meccan with the exception of the first eight verses: verse 28 ("Be patient in your soul . . ."); and verses 30 ("Those who believe . . .") to the end.

Maryam This *sūrah* is Meccan, with the exception of verse 58 (the Verse of Prostration) and verse 71 ("There is none among you but will pass over the fire").

Ṭāhā This *sūrah* is Meccan, with the exception of verse 130 ("endure patiently what they say"). In my opinion, another verse should also be excepted, bearing in mind what Abū Rāfi is recorded by al-Bazzāz and Abū Yalā to have said: "Some guests came to visit the Prophet – peace and blessings be upon him – and he sent me to a Jew to buy some flour on credit, the payment to fall due at the beginning of Rajab. The Jew refused to agree unless I gave him a pledge, and I returned to the Prophet – peace and blessings be upon him – and told him what the Jew had said. Thereupon he said: 'By God, I have been recognized as trustworthy in the heavens and on earth.' I had not left his presence when this verse was revealed: 'Do not strain your eyes in longing for the things we have given for enjoyment to parties of them . . .' (verse 131)." This verse must, then, also be regarded as Medinan.

Al-Anbiyāʾ This *sūrah* is entirely Meccan with the exception of verse 44 ("Do they not see that we gradually reduce the land from its outlying borders?").

Al-Ḥajj The Medinan verses of this predominantly Meccan *sūrah* have been discussed above.

Al-Muʾminūn Verses 64 ("Finally we seize the affluent among them with chastisement") to 77 (". . . they will be plunged in despair") are Medinan; the remaining verses are Meccan.

Al-Furqān This *sūrah* is Meccan, with the exception of verses 68 ("Those who do not call on any god together with God . . .") to 70 (". . . God is forgiving, merciful").

Al-Shuʿarāʾ As mentioned above, Ibn ʿAbbās describes this *sūrah* as Meccan, with the exception of verses 224 ("and the poets – it is those straying in evil who follow them") to the end. According to what has been reported by Ibn al-Faras, some people also include verse 197 ("Is it not for them a sign that the scholars of the Children of Israel know it . . .?") among the non-Meccan verses.

Al-Qiṣaṣ Verses 52 ("Those to whom we gave the Book . . .") to 55 ("We seek not the ignorant") are Medinan, the rest of the *sūrah* being Meccan. According to a tradition of Ibn ʿAbbās related by al-Ṭabarānī, these verses – together with the last verses of *sūrat al-Ḥadīd* – were revealed concerning the troops of the Negus who came to Medina and participated in the Battle of Uhud. Verse 85

("The One Who ordained the Qurʾān for you") is also Medinan, for reasons that will be cited below.

Al-ʿAnkabūt As related by Ibn Jarīr al-Ṭabarī, when discussing the occasion for the revelation of the verses, this *sūrah* is Meccan, with the exception of the first three verses. It can be added that according to traditions reported by Ibn Abī Ḥātam verse 60 ("How many creatures there are . . .") should also be excepted.

Luqmān Ibn ʿAbbās says that verses 27–29 ("If all the trees on earth were pens . . .") are Medinan.

Al-Sajdah As mentioned above, Ibn ʿAbbās says that verses 18 ("Is the believer at all like the sinner . . .?") to 20 are Medinan. Some would also add verse 16 ("Their sides avoid their beds . . ."). This is supported by a tradition from Bilāl al-Ḥabashī, reported by al-Bazzāz: "While we were sitting in the mosque, some of the Companions prayed continuously from the time of the sunset prayer to the time of the night prayer. The verse (in question) was then revealed."

Sabaʾ This *sūrah* was revealed in Mecca, with the exception of verse 6 ("Those who have received knowledge see that the revelation sent down to you from your Lord is the truth"). Farwah b. Nusayk al-Muradī is said by al-Tirmidhī to have come to the Prophet – peace and blessings be upon him – saying, "O Messenger of God, shall I not fight against those of my people who turn their backs to the enemy?" In the same tradition, the words occur, "and there was revealed concerning Sabaʾ what was revealed". Thereupon a man asked, "O Messenger of God, what is Sabaʾ?"

Ibn al-Hassār remarks: "This shows that the episode in question occurred in Medina, because Farwah's migration to Medina took place after the tribe of Thāqif accepted Islam in the ninth year of the Hijra." He adds that the word *unzila* ("was revealed") occurring in the tradition probably refers to what was revealed before his migration.

Yāsīn Verse 12 ("We it is who restore life to the dead . . .") has been regarded as an exception to this otherwise Meccan *sūrah*, because of a tradition from Abū Saʿīd, related by al-Tirmidhī and al-Ḥākim: "The Banu Salamah were living in a distant area of Medina. They wished to move closer to the mosque, whereupon this verse was revealed. The Prophet – peace and blessings be upon him – told them that every step they took (from home to come to the mosque) would be recorded (and rewarded), and they therefore abandoned the idea of moving."

Some people say that verse 47 ("When they are told, 'spend from the sustenance God has given you' . . ."), said to have been revealed concerning the Hypocrites, was also revealed in Medina.

Al-Zumar According to a tradition of Ibn ʿAbbās, this *sūrah* is Meccan, with the exception of verses 53 ("Tell them (on My behalf), 'O My servants . . .'") to 55. According to another tradition of Ibn ʿAbbās, related by al-Ṭabarānī with a different chain of transmission, verse 53 was revealed concerning Wahshī, the killer of Ḥamza. As is stated in al-Sakhāwi's *Jamāl al-Qurrā*ʾ, some people add to the non-Meccan verses of this *sūrah* verse 10 ("Tell them (on My behalf), 'O My servants who believe, fear your Lord . . .'"). Ibn al-Jazarī says that some people would also add verse 23 ("God revealed the best of speech").

Ghāfir Verses 35 ("Those who dispute . . .") to 58 (". . . they do not know") were revealed in Medina. As I have explained in my book on the occasions of revelation, these verses were revealed concerning the Jews when they began discussing the Dajjāl, as Ibn Abī Ḥātim records Abū l-Āliyah and others to have said.

Shūrā This *sūrah* is Meccan, with the exception of verses 24 ("Or do they say, 'he has invented a lie against God'?") to 27 (". . . He is well aware of His servants, all-seeing"). With respect to the occasion for the revelation of these three verses, let me say, relying on traditions related by al-Ṭabarānī and al-Ḥākim, that they were revealed concerning the Ansār.

Verse 27 (beginning "Were God to enlarge the provision for His servants . . .") is also said to have been revealed concerning the Companions of the Bench.

According to a tradition related by Ibn al-Faras, verses 39 ("Those who when wrong is inflicted on them . . .") to 41 (". . . there is no cause to blame them") are also Medinan.

Al-Zukhruf This *sūrah* is Meccan, with the exception of verse 45 ("Ask those of Our messengers whom We sent before you . . ."). It is said that this verse was revealed either in Medina or in the heavens.

Al-Jāthiyah Qatāda is reported by the author of *Jamāl al-Qurrā*ʾ to have regarded verse 14 ("Tell those who believe to forgive . . .") as Medinan; the rest of the *sūrah* is Meccan.

Al-Aḥqāf Verse 10 of this Meccan *sūrah* ("Say, 'Do you see?'") is Medinan. According to a tradition from ʿAuf b. Mālik al-Ashjaʿī, related by al-Ṭabarānī with a sound chain of transmission, this verse was revealed in Medina with reference to the acceptance of Islam by ʿAbdullah b. Salam. The same tradition has been recorded with different chains of transmission.

However, according to a tradition of Masrūq reported by Ibn Abī Ḥātim, this verse was revealed in Mecca, although ʿAbdullah b. Salam's acceptance of Islam took place in Medina; this verse referred, then, to the enmity he then felt towards Muḥammad, peace and blessings be upon him.

According to a tradition related from al-Shabī, the verse does not concern ʿAbd Allah b. Salam and was revealed in Mecca.

According to the Jamāl al-Qurrā᾿, verses 15 ("We have enjoined on man kindness to his parents . . .") to 18, as well as verse 35 ("Therefore patiently persevere . . ."), were revealed in Medina.

Qāf With the exception of verse 38 ("Indeed We have created the heavens and the earth . . .") this *sūrah* was revealed in Mecca. According to traditions related by al-Ḥākim and others, this verse was revealed concerning the Jews.

Al-Najm This *sūrah* is Meccan with the exception of verses 32 ("Those who avoid great sins . . .") to 51 (". . . nor did He give them a perpetual lease of life"). The nine verses beginning with verse 33 ("Have you seen the one who turns back . . .?") have also been regarded as Medinan.

Al-Qamar This *sūrah* is Meccan, and the view that verse 45 ("Soon will their multitude be put to flight . . .") is Medinan is to be rejected, for reasons to be discussed in Chapter twelve. The last two verses of the *sūrah* are also said to be Medinan.

Al-Raḥmān According to *Jamāl al-Qurrā᾿*, verse 29 ("Every creature in the heavens and on earth seeks its need of Him . . .") of this Meccan *sūrah* is Medinan.

Al-Wāqiah According to traditions related by Muslim concerning the occasion for their revelation, verses 39 and 40 ("A goodly number from those of early times and a goodly number from those of later times") and verses 75 ("I swear by the setting of the stars . . .") to 82 ("Have you made it your livelihood that you should declare it false?") are Medinan; the rest of the *sūrah* is Meccan.

Al-Ḥadīd The whole *sūrah* is said to be Meccan with the exception of the last verse.

Al-Mujādilah According to Ibn al-Faras and others, this *sūrah* is Medinan, with the exception of verse 7 (". . . if three people converse in secret, the fourth among them is He . . .").

Al-Taghābun According to traditions reported by al-Tirmidhī and al-Ḥākim concerning the occasion of its revelation, this *sūrah* is Medinan, with the exception of its last verse.

Al-Taḥrīm It has already been mentioned that according to Qatāda the first nine verses of this *sūrah* are Medinan and the rest is Meccan.

Al-Mulk In his commentary on the Qur'ān, on the authority of Dahhāk, Jubayr relates Ibn ʿAbbās to have said that the whole of *sūrat al-Mulk* was revealed concerning the people of Mecca, with the exception of three verses.

Nūn According to al-Sakhāwi's *Jamāl al-Qurrā'*, verses 17 ("We have tried them . . .") to 33 (". . . If they but knew") and 48 ("So wait with patience for the command of your Lord . . .") to 50 (". . . from among the righteous") are Medinan in this otherwise Meccan *sūrah*.

Al-Muzammil According to al-Isbahānī, verses 10 ("Be patient in the face of what they say . . .") and 11 are Medinan in this otherwise Meccan *sūrah*. According to Ibn al-Faras, the last verse of the *sūrah* is also Medinan, but this is refuted by a tradition of Ā'ishah, reported by al-Ḥākim, to the effect that it was revealed one year after the revelation of the beginning of the *sūrah*. This was at a time soon after Islam had first appeared, when night vigils were obligatory and the five prayers had not yet been made obligatory in their stead.

Al-Insān With the exception of verse 24 ("So wait with patience for the command of your Lord . . .") this *sūrah* is Medinan.

Al-Mursalāt According to Ibn al-Faras and others, this *sūrah* is Meccan with the exception of verse 48 ("When they are told to bow down . . .").

Al-Muṭaffifūn This *sūrah* is said to be Meccan with the exception of the first six verses.

Al-Balad This *sūrah* is said to be Medinan apart from the first four verses.

Al-Layl This *sūrah* is said to be Meccan with the exception of its beginning.

Al-Māʿūn The first three verses were revealed in Mecca and the rest in Medina.

Section

Respective characteristics of the Meccan and Medinan verses

According to al-Ḥākim in *al-Mustadrak*, al-Bayhaqī in *Dalā'il al-Nubuwwah*, and al-Bazzāz in his *Musnad* (all of them citing a tradition that goes back from Amash through Ibrāhīm and Alqamah to ʿAbdullah b. Masūd), verses that open with the formula of address "O believers" were revealed in Medina and *sūrahs* that open with the formula of address "O people" were revealed in Mecca. The same tradition is cited by Abū ʿUbayd in his *Faḍāʾil al-Qurʾān* but with a defective chain of transmission that goes back only as far as Alqamah.

According to a tradition of Maymūn b. Mihrān, verses beginning either "O people" or "O sons of Ādam" are Meccan, and those beginning "O you who believe" are Medinan.

Ibn Aṭiyyah, Ibn al-Faras and others confirm that verses beginning "O you who believe" are indeed Medinan, but they point out that the formula "O people" can sometimes be found in Medinan as well as Meccan verses.

Ibn al-Ḥaṣṣār says: "Those who concern themselves with distinguishing abrogating and abrogated verses rely upon this tradition (that of ʿAbdullah b. Masʿūd) despite its weakness. However, there is unanimous agreement that *sūrat al-Nisāʾ* is Medinan, although it begins with the address 'O people', and that *sūrat al-Ḥajj* is Meccan, although it contains the verse 'O you who believe! Bow down and prostrate yourselves . . .'" (verse 77).

Other scholars have said that although the distinction is generally valid, it calls for some examination. For although *sūrat al-Baqara* is Medinan, verse 21 contains the address "O people" ("O people, worship your Lord Who created you and those before you"), as does verse 168 ("O people, eat of the lawful and good things the earth contains"). Similarly, although *sūrat al-Nisāʾ* is Medinan, it begins with the address "O people".

Makkī says: "Although this view is often correct, it does not form a general rule, for many Meccan *sūrahs* contain the address, 'O you who believe.'"

Someone else says: "The preferable view is that if those intended by the formula of address are the Meccans, then the verses in which it occurs are Meccan, and if those intended by it are the Medinans, then the verses are Medinan."

Al-Qāḍī said: "If the view (that verses addressed to 'people' are Meccan and verses addressed to 'you who believe' are Medinan) is based on sound tradition, it is to be accepted. But if it is based only on the fact that the believers in Medina were more numerous than those in Mecca, it must be regarded as weak. For not only is it possible for the believers to be addressed with respect to their attributes, names and genders, it is also possible for those who are not believers to be commanded to engage in worship. After all, the believers are commanded to continue with their worship and augment it." This has been recorded by al-Imām Fakhr al-Dīn in his commentary on the Qurʾān.

In the *Dalāʾil* of al-Bayhaqī, Yūnus b. Bakir is reported to have heard from Hishām b. ʿUrwah – who transmitted it from his father – that whatever part of the Qurʾān contains the mention of past peoples and nations was revealed in Mecca, and whatever part contains mention of obligatory and recommended actions was revealed in Medina.

Al-Jabarī says: "There are two ways of judging whether a *sūrah* is Meccan or Medinan: the hearing (of a sound tradition) and comparison (according to certain criteria). The first informs us that a given verse was revealed in either Mecca or Medina. As for the criteria involved in the second, any *sūrah* that contains as its sole form of address 'O people', that contains the particle *kallā* (indeed not), that begins with disconnected letters (with the exception of *sūrat al-Baqara* and *sūrat Āl ʿImrān*) or that contains the story of Ādam and Iblīs (again with the exception of *sūrat al-Baqara*) – such a *sūrah* is Meccan. Likewise, all *sūrahs* containing mention of past prophets and peoples are also Meccan. By contrast, all *sūrahs* containing the mention of duties and punishments are Medinan."

Makkī regards all *sūrahs* containing mention of the Hypocrites as Medinan; some people consider *sūrat al-Ankabūt* an exception to this rule.

Al-Hudhalī says in his *Kāmil* that all *sūrahs* containing a mention of prostration are Meccan.

Al-Dīrīnī has the following verse:

Kallā was never revealed in Yathrib, and know, too,
Nowhere in the first half of the Qurʾān does it occur.

The reason for this is that the second half of the Qurʾān was revealed in Mecca. Since most of the people of that city were arrogant oppressors, the word *kallā* was used repeatedly to threaten and intimidate and condemn them. There was no need to use this word in those verses in the second half of the Qurʾān, revealed in Medina, that refer to the Jews, given their lowliness and weakness. This is mentioned by al-Ammānī.

Addendum

Al-Ṭabarānī reports Ibn Masūd to have said: "*Al-Mufassal* was revealed in Mecca. We recited it for several years, because no other verses were revealed."

Note

We have now set forth the following aspects of the topic from among those which Ibn Ḥabīb mentioned: Meccan and Medinan *sūrahs*; *sūrahs* the Meccan or Medinan identity of which is disputed; the order in which the *sūrahs* were revealed; the Medinan verses contained in the Meccan *sūrahs* and the Meccan verses contained in the Medinan *sūrahs*.

There remain now to be mentioned certain other aspects of this topic, together with examples illustrating them.

Verses revealed in Mecca but counted as Medinan

An example is verse 13 of *sūrat al-Ḥujurāt* ("O people, We have created you from a single male and female . . ."), which was revealed in Mecca after the conquest but is regarded as Medinan because its revelation came after the Hijra.

Other examples of this category are verse 3 of *sūrat al-Māʾidah* ("This day I have completed for you your religion") and verse 58 of *sūrat al-Nisāʾ* ("God commands you to return trusts to their owners . . ."). Further examples could also be mentioned.

Conversely, *sūrat al-Mumtaḥinah* was revealed in Medina but it counts as Meccan because it addresses the people of Mecca. Verse 41 of *sūrat al-Nahl* ("and those who migrate . . .") was also revealed in Medina, but addressed to the Meccans. The same holds true of the beginning of *sūrat al-Taubah*; it was revealed in Medina but addressed to the polytheists among the people of Mecca.

Verses resembling Medinan verses but contained in Meccan *sūrahs*

An example of this category is verse 31 of *sūrat al-Najm* ("Those who avoid major sins, abominations, falling only into small faults . . ."). Abominations (*al-fawāhish*) are all those sins the fixed commission of which entails fixed punishment (*hadd*); major sins (*al-kabāʾir*) are all those sins the commission of which results in hellfire; and small faults (*al-lamam*) are those sins that fall between the two other categories. Now although this verse was revealed in Mecca, there were no fixed punishments or anything resembling them.

Verses resembling Meccan verses but contained in Medinan *sūrahs*

An example of this category is provided by the first verse of *sūrat al-ʿĀdiyāt* ("By the steeds that run with panting breath") and verse 32 of *sūrat al-Anfāl* ("When they say, 'O God, if this be a truth coming from You . . .' ").

***Sūrahs* transferred from Mecca to Medina**

Examples are *sūrat Yūsuf* and *sūrat al-Ikhlāṣ*. As can be seen from a tradition from al-Bukhārī quoted above, *sūrat al-Aʿlā* can also be added to these.

***Sūrahs* transferred from Medina to Mecca**

Examples are verse 27 of *sūrat al-Baqara* ("They will ask you concerning the Sacred Month and fighting therein"), verse 275 of the same *sūrah* ("Those who devour usury . . ."), the opening verses of *sūrat al-Taubah* ("A proclamation from God and His Messenger . . .") and verse 97 of *sūrat al-Nisāʾ* ("When the angels take the souls of those who die in sin against their own souls . . .").

Verse 64 of *sūrat Āl ʿImrān* ("Say, 'O People of the Book, agree on a word shared equally by us and by you . . .' "), together with the following verses, counts as a verse transferred to Abyssinia. However, it counts as a verse transferred to the Byzantines, according to an authentic tradition, and it is more appropriate to cite *sūrat Maryam* as a group of verses transferred to Abyssinia, because – according to the *Musnad* of Aḥmad b. Ḥanbal – Jaʿfar b. Abī Ṭālib recited this *sūrah* to the Negus.

As for verses revealed in al-Juḥfah, Ṭāʾif, Jerusalem and al-Ḥudaybiyah, these will be discussed in the next chapter. Verses revealed in Minā, ʿArafāt, Asfān, Tabūk, Badr, Uḥud, Ḥirāʾ and Ḥamrāʾ al-Asad will be discussed in conjunction with them.

Chapter two

VERSES REVEALED WHILE THE PROPHET – PEACE AND BLESSINGS BE UPON HIM – WAS IN RESIDENCE AND VERSES REVEALED WHILE HE WAS TRAVELLING

The verses revealed while he was in residence are numerous. As for those revealed while he was travelling, I have researched and confirmed the examples which follow.

Verse 125 of *sūrat al-Baqara* ("Take the station of Ibrāhīm as a place for prayer . . .") was revealed in Mecca during the Farewell Pilgrimage. Ibn Abī Ḥātim and Ibn Mardawayh record Jābir to have said: "While the Prophet – peace and blessings be upon him – was circumambulating the Kaʿba, ʿUmar asked him, 'Is this the station of our ancestor, Ibrāhīm the Friend of God?' The Prophet replied that it was, and ʿUmar then asked, 'Would it not be suitable for us to make it a place for prayer?' The verse (in question) was then revealed."

Ibn Mardawayh also reports the following concerning ʿUmar b. l-Khattāb, on the authority of ʿAmr b. Maymūn: "He passed by the station of Ibrāhīm and said, 'O Messenger of God, shall we not stand in the station of Ibrāhīm, the Friend of our Lord?' The Prophet replied that indeed they should, whereupon ʿUmar said, 'Shall we then not take it as a place for prayer?' Not long passed before the verse (in question) was revealed."

Ibn al-Haṣṣār says: "This verse was revealed on the occasion either of the compensatory *ʿumrah*, the conquest of Mecca, or the Farewell Pilgrimage."

Verse 189 of *sūrat al-Baqara* ("It is no virtue to enter houses from the back . . .") was also revealed while the Prophet – peace and blessings be upon him – was travelling. According to a tradition of al-Zuhrī recorded by Ibn Jarīr, it was revealed during the *ʿumrah* that followed the conclusion of the Treaty of al-Hudaybiyah. According to al-Suddī, it was revealed during the Farewell Pilgrimage.

Verse 196 of *sūrat al-Baqara* ("and complete the hajj and the *ʿumrah* for God . . .") was also revealed while the Prophet – peace and blessings be upon him – was travelling. According to a tradition of Ṣafwān b. Umayyah reported by Ibn Abī Ḥātim, a man wearing a cloak and perfumed with saffron came to the Prophet – peace and blessings be upon him – and asked him, "What are your commands with respect to the *ʿumrah*?" Then this verse was revealed, and the Prophet said, "Where is the man who is inquiring concerning the *ʿumrah*? Take off your garments and wash."

Another portion of verse 196 ("If any among you is ill, or has an ailment in his scalp . . .") was also revealed at al-Ḥudaybiyah, as is reported by Aḥmad

b. Ḥanbal from Kaʿb b. ʿUjrah, concerning whom it was revealed and by al-Wāhidī from Ibn ʿAbbās.

Verse 285 of *sūrat al-Baqara* ("The Messenger believes") is said to have been revealed on the day of the conquest of Mecca, but I have not been able to find any proof of this.

Verse 281 of *sūrat al-Baqara* ("Fear the day on which you will be brought back to God . . .") was revealed at Minā during the year of the Farewell Pilgrimage, according to traditions recorded by al-Bayhaqī in his *Dalāʾil.*

Verse 172 of *sūrat Āl ʿImrān* ("Those who follow the call of God and His Messenger . . .") was also revealed during a journey. According to a tradition of Ibn ʿAbbās related by al-Ṭabarānī with sound chain of transmission, this verse was revealed at Hamrāʾ al-Asad.

Verse 43 of *sūrat al-Nisāʾ*, which concerns dry ablution, was revealed during one of the journeys of the Prophet – peace and blessings be upon him – according to a tradition of Asla b. Shurayk recorded by Ibn Mardawayh.

Verse 58 of *sūrat al-Nisāʾ* ("God commands you to return trusts to their owners . . .") was revealed on the day of the conquest of Mecca inside the Kaʿba, according to a tradition of Ibn Jurayj reported by Sunayd in his commentary on the Qurʾān, as well as a tradition of Ibn ʿAbbās reported by Ibn Mardawayh.

Verse 102 of *sūrat al-Nisāʾ* ("When you are among them and establish prayer for them") was revealed at Asfān, between the midday and the afternoon prayers, according to a tradition of Abū Ayyāsh al-Zarqī reported by Aḥmad b. Ḥanbal.

Verse 176 of *sūrat al-Nisāʾ* ("They ask you for a judgement. Say, 'God will provide you with a judgement concerning those who die with no heirs . . .' ") was revealed to the Prophet – peace and blessings be upon him – in the course of a journey, according to a tradition of Hudhayfah reported by al-Bazzāz and others.

The first part of *sūrat al-Māʾidah* was revealed at Minā, according to a tradition of Asmāʾ bt. Yāzīd reported by al-Bayhaqī in *Shuʿab al-Imān*. In his *Dalāʾil*, he reports a tradition from Umm ʿAmr to the effect that her uncle said that it was revealed during a journey.

Abū ʿUbayd reports a tradition from Muḥammad b. Kaʿb to the effect that *sūrat al-Māʾidah* was revealed during the Farewell Pilgrimage between Mecca and Medina.

Verse 3 of *sūrat al-Māʾidah* ("This day I have completed for you your religion . . .") was revealed in the evening of the Day of ʿArafah during the Farewell Pilgrimage, a Friday, according to a sound tradition of ʿUmar, related with many chains of transmission. But according to a tradition of Abū Saʿīd al-Khudrī related by Ibn Mardawayh, it was revealed on the Day of Ghādir Khumm. The same is stated in a tradition of Abū Hurayrah, where it is said that the day in question was the eighteenth day of Dhū l-Hijjah, the day of his return from the Farewell Pilgrimage. Neither of the two traditions is correct.

Verse 6 of *sūrat al-Māʾidah* concerning dry ablution was revealed at al-Baydāʾ while the Muslims were entering Medina, according to a tradition of Āʾishah related in the *Ṣaḥīḥ* of al-Bukhārī. In another version of the same tradition, the names of both al-Baydāʾ and Dhāt al-Jaysh are to be found. Ibn ʿAbd al-Barr says in *al-Tamhīd* that this verse may have been revealed concerning the *ghazwah* against the Banu Mustaliq, and he expounds the same view more emphatically in *al-Istidhkār*. He was preceded in this view by Ibn Sad and Ibn Habbān.

The *ghazwah* against the Banu Mustaliq is the same as the *ghazwah* of al-Marīsīʿ. This has been regarded as unlikely by a certain scholar of recent times, because – he says – al-Marīsīʿ is a locality of Mecca, situated between Qadīd and the coast, whereas the episode referred to in the verse took place in the region of Khaybar, given the mention by Āʾishah of al-Baydāʾ or Dhāt al-Jaysh, both of which are situated between Medina and Khaybar, as has been established by al-Nawawī.

However, Ibn al-Tīn is convinced that al-Baydāʾ is the same as al-Ḥalīfah. Abū ʿUbayd al-Bakrī says that al-Baydāʾ is the name given to the heights near al-Halīfah, in the direction of Mecca, and he says, too, that Dhāt al-Jaysh is one *barīd* [a distance of about twelve miles] from Medina.

Verse 11 of *sūrat al-Māʾidah* ("O you who believe, remember God's bounty towards you when a people intended . . .") was also revealed during a journey. Qatāda is reported by Ibn Jarīr to have said that it was revealed to the Messenger of God – peace and blessings be upon him – when he was at Batn al-Nakhl, during the seventh *ghazwah*; the Banu Thalabah and the Banu Muhārib wished to kill him, but God alerted him to their intentions.

Similar is verse 67 of *sūrat al-Māʾidah* ("God protects you from people . . ."). According to a tradition from Abū Hurayrah recorded in the *Ṣaḥīḥ* of Ibn Habbān, it was revealed during a journey. According to a tradition of Jābir related by Ibn Abī Ḥātim and Ibn Mardawayh, it was revealed at Dhāt al-Raqī near Batn al-Nakhl during the *ghazwah* against the Banu Anmār.

According to a tradition of Saʿd b. Abī Waqqās reported by Aḥmad b. Hanbal, the beginning of *sūrat al-Anfāl* was revealed at Badr, following on the battle that took place there. Verse 9 of this *sūrah* ("When you seek aid from your Lord . . .") was also revealed at Badr, according to a tradition of ʿUmar reported by al-Tirmidhī.

According to a tradition of Thaubān reported by Aḥmad b. Hanbal, verse 35 of *sūrat al-Taubah* ("Those who hoard gold and silver . . .") was revealed during one of the journeys of the Prophet, peace and blessings be upon him.

Similarly, verse 42 of this *sūrah* ("If it were a worldly benefit . . .") and the verses following on it were revealed during the expedition to Tabūk, according to a tradition of Ibn ʿAbbās recorded by Ibn Jarīr.

Verse 65 of *sūrat al-Taubah* ("If you ask them they will certainly say, 'We were only talking loosely and playing' . . .") was also revealed during the expedition to Tabūk, according to a tradition of Ibn ʿUmar recorded by Ibn Abī Ḥātim.

According to a tradition of Ibn ʿAbbās recorded by al-Ṭabarānī and Ibn Mardawayh, verse 113 of *sūrat al-Taubah* ("It is not fitting for the Prophet and those who believe . . .") was revealed when the Prophet – peace and blessings be upon him – set out to perform the umrah and descended the slopes of Asfān to visit the tomb of his mother and sought permission to ask forgiveness for her.

According to a tradition of Abū Hurayrah recorded by al-Bayhaqī in his *Dalāʾil* and al-Bazzāz, the last verse of *sūrat al-Nahl* was revealed at Uḥud when the Prophet – peace and blessings be upon him – was standing over the martyred body of Hamzah. According to a tradition of Ubayy b. Kaʿb reported by al-Tirmidhī and al-Ḥākim, this verse was revealed on the day of the conquest of Mecca.

According to a tradition of ʿAbd-al-Raḥmān b. Ghanam, recorded by al-Bayhaqī in the *Dalāʾil* and by Abū l-Shaykh on the authority of Shahr b. Hūshab, verse 76 of *sūrat al-Isrāʾ* ("Their purpose was to scare you off the land . . .") was revealed at Tabūk.

According to a tradition of Imrān b. Ḥusayn related by al-Tirmidhī and al-Ḥākim, the opening verses of *sūrat al-Hajj* – from "O mankind! Fear your Lord, for the convulsion of the hour will be a terrible thing . . ." to ". . . dreadful will be the wrath of God" (verse 2) – were revealed during a journey. According to a tradition of Ibn ʿAbbās, reported by Ibn Mardawayh on the authority of al-Kalbī who had it from Abū Sālih, these verses were revealed while the Prophet – peace and blessings be upon him – was journeying to do battle with the Banu l-Musṭaliq.

According to al-Qādī Jalāl al-Dīn al-Bulqaynī, verse 19 of *sūrat al-Ḥajj* ("These two enemies . . .") may have been revealed during the Battle of Badr when the two sides were clashing, thus giving rise to the dual expression *hādhāni*.

According to a tradition of Ibn ʿAbbās recorded by al-Tirmidhī, verse 39 of *sūrat al-Ḥajj* ("It is permitted to those who are fought against . . .") was revealed when the Prophet – peace and blessings be upon him – was compelled to leave Mecca. He recounts that Abū Bakr said: "They have expelled their prophet and they will certainly be destroyed." The verse in question was thereupon revealed. Ibn al-Hassār says that basing themselves on this tradition some people have reached the conclusion that this verse was revealed during the Hijra itself.

According to Ibn Habīb, verse 45 of *sūrat al-Furqān* was revealed in Tāʾif, but I have not encountered any proof in support of his view.

According to a tradition of al-Dahhāk recorded by Ibn Abī Ḥātim, verse 85 of *sūrat al-Qisas* ("He Who ordained the Qurʾān for you . . .") was revealed in al-Juhfah during the Hijra.

The opening verses of *sūrat al-Rūm* were revealed during a journey. According to a tradition of Abū Saʿīd al-Khudrī reported by al-Tirmidhī, the Byzantines defeated the Persians on the same day as the Battle of Badr, and the believers were surprised to hear of it; the first four verses of the *sūrah* were thereupon revealed. Al-Tirmidhī remarks, in connection with this tradition, that the word *gh-l-b-t* in the second verse must be read *ghalabat* (that is, in the active, not the passive form) to conform to the meaning of the tradition.

According to Ibn Ḥabīb, verse 45 of *sūrat al-Zukhruf* ("Ask those messengers whom He sent before you") was revealed in Jerusalem on the night of the *Isrāʾ*.

According to al-Sakhāwī in his *Jamāl al-Qurrāʾ*, verse 13 of *sūrat Muḥammad* ("and how many cities there are, more powerful than your city which has driven you out . . .") was revealed when the Prophet – peace and blessings be upon him – set out on the Hijra and looking back on Mecca wept. Thereupon the verse in question was revealed.

According to a tradition of Miswar b. Makhramah and Marwān b. Ḥakam recorded by al-Hakim and others, the whole of *sūrat al-Fath*, from beginning to end, was revealed between Mecca and Medina, with reference to what happened at al-Ḥudaybiyah. In addition, al-Hakim reports in his *Mustadrak* a tradition from Majma b. Jāriyah to the effect that the first verses of the *sūrah* were revealed at a place called Kurā al-Ghamīm.

According to a tradition of Ibn Abī Mulaykah recorded by al-Wāhidī, verse 13 of *sūrat al-Ḥujurāt* ("O mankind, certainly We have created you from a single male and a single female . . .") was revealed on the day of the conquest of Mecca when Bilāl mounted the Kaʿba to call the *adhān* and someone said, "Look at this black slave climbing on top of the Kaʿba to call the *adhān*."

According to a tradition related by Ibn al-Faras, verse 45 of *sūrat al-Qamar* ("that group will soon be dispersed . . .") was revealed during the Battle of Badr. As will be seen in Chapter twelve, this is to be rejected. However, I have seen a tradition of Ibn ʿAbbās that supports it.

Verses 13 ("A goodly number from early generations . . .") and 81 ("Is it this Word that you belittle?") of *sūrat al-Wāqiah* are said to have been revealed during the journey of the Prophet – peace and blessings be upon him – to Medina. However, I have not encountered any evidence in support of this view.

Verse 82 ("Have you made it your livelihood to declare it false?") is also said to have been revealed during a journey. Ibn Abī Ḥātim relates a tradition of Abū Ḥirzah, with a chain of transmission that passes from Mujāhid through Yaqūb, to the effect that this verse was revealed during the expedition to Tabūk concerning one of the Ansār. When the Prophet – peace and blessings be upon him – and those accompanying him came to the place known as al-Hijr, he forbade them to take water from there. They then set out and came to another stopping place, and they complained to him that their supplies of water were exhausted. So he prayed, and God sent a cloud and caused it to rain on their heads so that their thirst became quenched. One of the Hypocrites said, "We owe this rain to the rain-star", whereupon this verse was revealed.

According to a tradition of al-Zuhrī recorded by Ibn Jarīr, verse 10 of *sūrat al-Mumtaḥinah* ("O you who believe, when the believing women come to you in migration . . .") was revealed on the lower slopes of al-Hudaybiyah.

According to a tradition of Zayd b. Arqam reported by al-Tirmidhī, the entirety of *sūrat al-Mujahidin* was revealed at night during the expedition to Tabūk. According to a tradition of Sufyān reported by al-Tirmidhī, it was revealed during the *ghazwah* against the Banu l-Musṭaliq, which is also the firm opinion of Ibn Ishāq and others.

Ibn Masᶜūd says, in a tradition reported by both al-Bukhārī and Muslim, that *sūrat al-Mursalāt* was revealed while he and other Companions were with the Prophet – peace and blessings be upon him – in a cave at Mina.

According to traditions narrated by al-Nasafī and others, *sūrat al-Muṭaffifīn* was revealed during the Hijra before the Prophet – peace and blessings be upon him – entered Medina, either in whole or in part.

The opening verses of *sūrat al-Alaq* were revealed in the cave of Hira, as is recorded by al-Bukhārī and Muslim.

According to a tradition of Saᶜīd b. Jubayr recorded by Ibn Jarīr, *sūrat al-Kauthar* was revealed on the day of the Treaty of al-Hudaybiyah, but this is not certain.

According to a tradition of Ibn ᶜUmar reported by al-Bazzāz and al-Bayhaqī in his *Dala᾿il*, *sūrat al-Naṣr* was revealed to the Prophet – peace and blessings be upon him – during the days of *tashrīq*. He knew that the time to bid farewell had come, so he called for his camel, named al-Quswā᾿, and had a saddle placed on it. He then stood on the back of the camel and delivered his sermon. (In the remaining part of the tradition, Ibn ᶜUmar quotes the well-known Sermon of Farewell.)

Chapter three

VERSES REVEALED IN THE DAYTIME AND VERSES REVEALED AT NIGHT-TIME

There are abundant examples of verses revealed in the daytime, and Ibn Ḥabīb says indeed that most of the Qurʾān was revealed in the daytime.

As for those revealed at night-time, I have researched and confirmed the examples which follow.

According to a tradition of Ibn ʿUmar, recorded by al-Bukhārī and Muslim, verse 144 of *sūrat al-Baqara*, which deals with the change of the *qiblah*, was revealed at night-time. Ibn ʿUmar says: "While people were performing the dawn prayer at the mosque of Qubāʾ someone came and told them, 'The Prophet – peace and blessings be upon him – has received revelation tonight, and a change in the *qiblah* has been ordained.'"

According to a tradition of Anas recorded by Muslim, the Prophet – peace and blessings be upon him – was praying in the direction of Jerusalem when the verse "We see you turning your face to the heavens . . ." was revealed. Someone from the Banu Salamah then passed by the Muslims as they were engaged in the bowing of the second rakah of prayer and called out to them that the *qiblah* had been changed.

However, according to a tradition of al-Barrāʾ reported by al-Bukhārī and Muslim, the Prophet – peace and blessings be upon him – prayed in the direction of Jerusalem for sixteen or seventeen months, and it was his desire that his *qiblah* should be the Kaʿba. The first prayer he performed in the direction of the Kaʿba was the afternoon prayer. A number of people prayed it together with him, and one of them left and passed by the people in the mosque when they were bowing. He told them, "I call God to witness that I have just prayed with the Prophet – peace and blessings be upon him – in the direction of the Kaʿba," and they immediately turned to face in the direction of the Kaʿba.

This tradition suggests that the verse was revealed in the daytime, between the midday and afternoon prayers. However, according to al-Qādī Jalal al-Dīn, it is preferable to deduce that the verse was revealed at night-time because the people in the mosque at Qubāʾ were engaged in the morning prayer when they heard the news, and Qubāʾ is close to Medina; it is, moreover, unlikely that the Messenger of God – peace and blessings be upon him – should have postponed communicating the matter to them from the afternoon to the morning of the next day.

Ibn Ḥajar regards it as more likely that the verse should have been revealed in the daytime, the explanation of the tradition of Ibn ʿUmar being that the news reached those within Medina – that is, the Banū Ḥārithah – in the afternoon and reached those outside Medina – that is, the Banu ʿAmr b. ʿAuf, the people of Qubāʾ - the morning of the following day. As for his saying that the verse was revealed at night, the expression can be taken in an extended sense to include part of the preceding day.

Let me state that a tradition of Abū Saʿīd b. al-Mualla, recorded by al-Nisāʾī, supports this explanation. Abū Saʿīd says: "One day we passed by the Messenger of God – peace and blessings be upon him – while he was seated on the *minbar*. I said to myself, 'Maybe something has happened,' so I sat down, and the Messenger of God – peace and blessings be upon him – recited this verse: 'We see you turning your face to the heavens . . .' When he had completed it, he descended from the *minbar* and prayed the midday prayer."

The closing verses of *Āl ʿImrān* were also revealed at night-time. Ibn Habbān (in his *Ṣaḥīḥ*), Ibn Mundhir, Ibn Mardawayh and Ibn Abī l-Dunyā in his *Kitāb al-Tafakkur*, all relate that Āʾishah said: "Bilāl came to the Prophet – peace and blessings be upon him – to make the morning *adhān*, and he found him weeping. He said, "O Messenger of God, what causes you to weep?" He responded, "Why should I not weep? Tonight the verse, 'Truly in the creation of the heavens and the earth and the alternation of night and day there are signs for the possessors of intelligence' (verse 190, *sūrat Āl ʿImrān*) was revealed to me." Then he added: "Woe upon those who do not recite this verse and reflect on it."

Verse 67 of *sūrat al-Māʾidah* ("God protects you from men . . .") was also revealed at night-time. Al-Tirmidhī and al-Ḥākim record Āʾishah as saying that the Prophet – peace and blessings be upon him – used to have a guard until this verse was revealed. Then he put his head out of his dwelling and called out, "Disperse, o men! God has promised to protect me."

Al-Ṭabarānī reports Ismah b. Mālik al-Khutamī to have said: "We used to guard the Messenger of God – peace and blessings be upon him – at night until this verse was revealed. Then the practice of guarding him was abandoned."

Sūrat al-Anām was revealed in its entirety at night-time. Al-Ṭabarānī and Abū ʿUbayd, in his *Faḍāʾil*, record Ibn ʿAbbās as saying: "*Sūrat al-Anām* was revealed at night in Mecca, as a single unit, to the accompaniment of seventy thousand angels proclaiming aloud the glory of God."

Verse 118 of *sūrat al-Taubah* ("He turned in mercy to the three who were left behind . . .") was revealed at night-time, for al-Bukhārī and Muslim record Kaʿb as having said: "God revealed that our repentance had been accepted during the last third of the night."

Sūrat Maryam was also revealed at night-time. Al-Ṭabarānī reports Abū Maryam al-Ghassānī to have said: "I came to the Messenger of God – peace and blessings be upon him – and when I informed him that a girl had been born to me that night he said, 'Tonight *sūrat Maryam* has been revealed to me, so call her Maryam.' "

The opening verses of *sūrat al-Ḥajj* were revealed at night-time. This is mentioned by Ibn Habīb and by Muḥammad b. Barakāt al-Saʿdī in his book *al-Nāsikh wa l-Mansūkh*, and stated categorically by al-Sakhāwī in his *Jamal al-Qurrāʾ*. The evidence is a tradition of Imrān b. Ḥusayn reported by Ibn Mardawayh to the effect that it was revealed when the Prophet – peace and blessings be upon him – was on one of his journeys and some of the Companions had fallen asleep and others had scattered. So he raised his voice to proclaim to them the newly revealed verse.

The verse of *sūrat al-Ahzāb* that permits women to go out was also revealed at night-time. Al-Qādī Jalāl al-Dīn regards it as likely that the verse in question is "O Prophet, tell your wives and daughters . . ." (verse 59). According to a tradition of Āʾishah recorded by al-Bukhārī, Saudah left the house for a certain purpose after veiling had been made obligatory. She was a full-bodied woman, recognizable to everyone who knew her. ʿUmar saw her on this occasion and said: "O Saudah, I swear by God that you are recognizable to us; think well in what state you leave the house." Āʾishah relates that Saudah then returned to the house of the Messenger – peace and blessings be upon him. He was eating his evening meal and holding a bone in his hand. She said: "O Messenger of God, I went out for certain purposes and ʿUmar told me such-and-such." Then God revealed to him, while he was still holding the bone in his hand, the verse in question, and he said to Saudah, "You and the other wives have permission to go out to take care of your needs." Al-Qādī Jalal al-Dīn says that this verse must have been revealed at night because the wives would go out only at night to take care of their needs, as is apparent from the tradition of Āʾishah concerning the lie (*al-ifk*) recorded by al-Bukhārī.

According to Ibn Habīb, verse 45 of *sūrat al-Zukhruf* ("Ask the messengers whom We have sent before you . . .") was revealed on the night of the *Isrāʾ*.

The beginning of *sūrat al-Fath* was revealed at night. According to a tradition of ʿUmar recorded by al-Bukhārī, the Prophet – peace and blessings be upon him – said: "Tonight a *sūrah* has been revealed to me that is more beloved of me than anything over which the sun has ever risen." He then recited "Certainly we have granted you a manifest victory . . .".

According to a tradition of Zayd b. Arqam recorded by al-Tirmidhī, *sūrat al-Munāfiqūn* was revealed at night.

According to a tradition of Ibn Masūd, recorded by al-Sakhāwī in his *Jamal al-Qurrāʾ*, *sūrat al-Mursalāt* was revealed at Hiraʾ on the night of the jinn (*laylat al-jinn*). This is an obscure tradition, in my opinion.

I have seen in the *Ṣaḥīḥ* of al-Ismaʿīlī a tradition – derived by him from al-Bukhārī – to the effect that this *sūrah* was revealed on the Night of ʿArafah in the cave of Mina. The same tradition is indeed to be found in both al-Bukhārī and Muslim, but without mention of the Night of ʿArafah. What is meant by the Night of ʿArafah is the night of the ninth of Dhu l-Hijjah, because the Prophet – peace and blessings be upon him – spent that night at Mina.

The *Muʾawidhdhatān* were also revealed at night-time. Ibn Ashtah says in his *Kitāb al-Masāhif*: "I was told by Muḥammad b. Yaʾqub, who heard it from Abū Dāwūd, who heard it from Uthmān b. Abī Shaybah, who heard it from Jarīr, who heard it from Bayyān, who heard it from Qays, who heard it from ʿUqbah b. Āmir al-Juhanī, that the Messenger of God – peace and blessings be upon him – said: 'Verses the like of which have never been seen were revealed to me tonight: "Say, 'I take refuge in the Lord of the dawn . . .'" and "Say 'I take refuge in the Lord of mankind . . .'."'"

Part

Another category relevant to the concern of this chapter consists of verses revealed at dawn, between night and day. The verse dealing with dry ablution ("O you who believe! when you rise up for prayer . . ."; verse 6, *sūrat al-Māʾidah*) is one such verse. Al-Bukhārī records Āʾishah to have said: "It became morning, and he sought water, but none was to be found. Then verse 6 ('O you who believe . . .') was revealed."

Another verse belonging to this category is verse 128 of *sūrat Āl ʿImrān* ("No part of that affair belongs to you . . ."). According to a tradition recorded in al-Bukhārī, it was revealed when the Prophet – peace and blessings be upon him – was performing the last *rakah* of his dawn prayer and wished to curse Abū Sufyān and his associates in the *qunūt*.

Note

In conclusion, let us mention the tradition of Jābir, related with a defective chain of transmission by al-Ḥākim in his *Tārīkh* that the Prophet – peace and blessings upon him – said, "The most truthful of dreams are the dreams that come during the day, because God has distinguished me through the receipt of revelation during the day." If I be asked how I deal with this tradition, I reply that it is an unknown tradition that cannot be cited as proof.

Chapter four

VERSES REVEALED IN THE SUMMER AND VERSES REVEALED IN THE WINTER

Al-Wāḥidī says: "God has revealed two verses concerning dying without heirs, one of them in winter, towards the beginning of *sūrat al-Nisa'* (verse 12) and the other in summer, which is the last verse of the *sūrah* (verse 176)."

ʿUmar is recorded in the *Ṣaḥīḥ* of Muslim to have said: "There is no subject on which I queried the Messenger of God – peace and blessings be upon him – as much as I did on the state of those who die without heirs, and there is no subject on which he answered me more firmly, to the point of thrusting his fingers against my chest and saying, 'O ʿUmar, is not the verse at the end of *sūrat al-Nisā'*, the verse revealed in summer, enough for you?' "

Al-Ḥākim relates in *al-Mustadrak* that Abū Hurayrah said: "Someone asked the Messenger of God what was meant by *al-kalālah* (dying without heirs). He replied, 'Have you not heard the verse that was revealed in summer – they will ask you for a judgement; say, God will give you a ruling concerning those who die without heirs?' " As mentioned above, this verse was revealed during the Farewell Pilgrimage.

The first verse of *sūrat al-Mā'idah*; the third verse of the same *sūrah* ("This day I have completed for you your religion . . ."); verse 281 of *sūrat al-Baqara* ("Fear that day when you will all be returned to God"); the next verse in *sūrat al-Baqara*, which deals with debts; and the whole of *sūrat al-Naṣr* – all these were revealed during the summer.

The verses that were revealed during the expedition to Tabūk, which came at the height of the hot season, also count among the verses revealed during the summer. In his *Dala'il*, al-Bayhaqī reports on the authority of Ibn Isḥāq that Āṣim b. ʿUmar b. Qatāda and ʿAbdullah b. Abī Bakr b. Ḥazm said that the Messenger of God – peace and blessings be upon him – would never depart on an expedition without pretending that his destination was a place other than where he was heading. The expedition to Tabūk was an exception; he said, "O people, I am heading to the Byzantines," thus informing the Muslims of his intentions. This was at a time of hardship, extreme heat and scarcity in the land. One day while the Messenger of God – peace and blessings be upon him – was busy making his preparations, he said to al-Jadd b. Qays, "Do you like the women of the Banu l-Asfar (that is, the Byzantines)?" He replied, "O Messenger, my people know that no one loves women more than I do. I fear that if I see the women of the Banu l-Asfar, they will tempt me, so permit me to stay behind." Thereupon verse 49 of *sūrat al-Taubah* was revealed: "There are among them those who say, 'Permit me to stay behind and draw me not into temptation' . . ."

Similarly, when one of the Hypocrites said, "Do not go out to war in this heat," verse 81 of *sūrat al-Taubah* was revealed ("Say, 'The fire of hell is much hotter . . .' ").

As for verses revealed in the winter, verses 11 ("Those who bring false report . . .") to 26 (". . . and generous provision") of *sūrat al-Nūr* belong to this category, according to a tradition of Āʾishah reported by al-Bukhārī.

The verses in *sūrat* al-Aḥzāb concerning the Battle of the Moat were also revealed during the cold season. According to a tradition of Hudhayfah, on the night of the Battle of the Confederates, everyone had moved away from the Prophet – peace and blessings be upon him – with the exception of twelve people. The Prophet then came to Hudhayfah and said to him, "Arise and go to the camp of the Confederates." He replied, "By the One Who sent you in truth, in this cold it is only my shame before you that compels me to rise." Thereupon verse 9 of *sūrat al-Ahzāb* ("O you who believe, remember the favour of God bestowed on you when hosts came down upon you . . ."). This tradition of Ḥudhayfah is recorded by al-Bayhaqī in his *Dalāʾil.*

Chapter five

VERSES REVEALED WHILE THE PROPHET – PEACE AND BLESSINGS BE UPON HIM – WAS IN BED OR SLEEPING

Examples of verses revealed while the Prophet – peace and blessings be upon him – was in bed are verse 67 of *sūrat al-Māʾidah* ("God will protect you against men . . .") and verse 118 ("He turned in mercy to the three who were left behind . . .") of *sūrat al-Taubah*. According to al-Bukhārī, this latter verse was revealed when one-third was left of the night and the Prophet – peace and blessings be upon him – was with Umm Salamah. However, it is difficult to reconcile this tradition with the saying of the Prophet – peace and blessings be upon him – to the effect that he never received revelation while he was in the bed of any of his wives except Āʾishah. Al-Qādī Jalal al-Dīn suggests that he made this statement before the revelation that came to him while he was in the bed of Umm Salamah.

I can claim to have found a better way of solving the problem. Abū Yala records in his *Musnad* a tradition of Āʾishah in which she says that she was given nine things (that set her apart from the other wives). In the course of this tradition she says, "Whenever revelation came to him while he was with his wives, they would leave him. However, sometimes revelation would come to him while I was lying beneath the blanket with him." This resolves the apparent contradiction between the two traditions cited above.

As for verses revealed while the Prophet – peace and blessings be upon him – was asleep, an example is *sūrat al-Kauthar*. Muslim records Anas as saying: "Once the Messenger of God – peace and blessings be upon him – closed his eyes for a time while we were with him. Then he raised his head with a smile on his face. We asked him what had caused him to smile, and he replied, 'A *sūrah* has just been revealed to me.' He then recited the entirety of *sūrat al-Kauthar*."

Al-Imām al-Rāfiʿī says in his *Amālī*: "Some scholars have understood from this tradition that the *sūrah* was revealed to him in a state of sleep, and they have said that a part of revelation came to him while he was asleep, because the dreams of the prophets are in themselves revelation. This is indeed true, but it would be closer to the truth to say that the entirety of the Qurʾān was revealed to the Prophet – peace and blessings be upon him – while he was in a waking state. We may say that *sūrat al-Kauthar* came to his mind while he was asleep but that it had already been revealed to him in a waking state. Alternatively, it may be said that the spring of al-Kauthar was displayed to him in his dream, the spring that is mentioned in the *sūrah*, and that he recited and interpreted the *sūrah* to them after waking." Al-Rāfiʿī adds: "According to certain traditions, 'The Prophet fainted' and this expression may be taken to refer to the state that overcame him when he received revelation, a state known as *burḥāʾ l-waḥy*."

Let me say that al-Rāfiʿī's statement is eminently sensible; I was already inclined to the same view before I encountered his statement. The second of the two explanations he offers is more correct than the first, because the saying of the Prophet, "has just been revealed to me", shows in fact that the *sūrah* had not been revealed some time earlier. We can conclude rather that the closing of the eyes (*al-ighfāʾ*) was not that which takes place during sleep but that which took place during the state that overcame him during revelation. Scholars have recorded that the Prophet – peace and blessings be upon him – was made unconscious of the world at such times.

Chapter six

VERSES REVEALED ON THE EARTH AND VERSES REVEALED IN THE HEAVENS

As was seen from a statement of Ibn al-ʿArabī quoted above, part of the Qurʾān was revealed in the heavens, part on the earth, part between the heavens and the earth, and part beneath the earth in a cave.

Ibn al-ʿArabī says the following: "We were informed by Abū Bakr al-Fihrī, who had it from al-Tamimi, who had it from Hibatullah the exegete, that the entirety of the Qurʾān was revealed either in Mecca or in Medina with the exception of six verses, which were revealed neither in the heavens nor on the earth. They are verses 164 ('All things have from Us a fixed station . . .') to 166 of *sūrat al-Ṣāffāt*, verse 45 of *sūrat al-Zukhruf* ('Ask those of Our messengers whom We have sent before . . .'), and the last two verses of *sūrat al-Baqara*, which were revealed on the night of the Mirāj."

Ibn al-Arabī then adds: "What Hibatullah meant may have been that these verses were revealed in a space between heaven and earth." He goes on to say: "As for the part of the Qurʾān that was revealed in a cave beneath the earth, this is *sūrat al-Mursalāt*, in accordance with the tradition of Ibn Masūd reported by al-Bukhārī."

As for the first four of the six verses mentioned by Ibn al-Arabī, I am not aware of any proof for his assertion. However, it is possible to adduce as evidence for the last two verses of *sūrat al-Baqara* this tradition of Ibn Masūd recorded by Muslim: "When the Messenger of God – peace and blessings upon him – was transported by night, he reached the lote-tree of the limit . . .". The tradition includes this statement: "And the Messenger of God – peace and blessings be upon him – was given three things: the five prayers; the concluding verses of *sūrat al-Baqara*; and forgiveness of major sins (*al-muqḥimāt*) for all in his community who do not assign partners to God."

According to *al-Kāmil* of al-Hudhalī, the concluding verses of *sūrat al-Baqara* were revealed at "the distance of two bowstrings" (*qāba qausayn*).

Chapter seven

THE FIRST PARTS OF THE QUR'ĀN TO BE REVEALED

There are several differing views concerning which part of the Qur'ān was the first to be revealed.

The first view – and the correct one – is that it was the opening verses of *sūrat al-ʿAlaq*: "Recite, in the name of your Lord Who created . . .". Ā'ishah is recorded by al-Bukhārī, Muslim and others to have said: "Revelation first came to the Messenger of God – peace and blessings upon him – in the form of veracious dreams during his sleep, and his dreams were always as clear as the dawn. Then solitude became beloved of him and he would often retire to Hirā' spending certain nights there in worship. He would take provision with him for these retreats and then return to Khadījah – may God be pleased with her – who would renew his provisions. Thus matters continued until the truth came to him when he was in the cave on Ḥirā'. The angel came to him there and said, 'Recite!' The Messenger of God – peace and blessings be upon him – told me that he replied to the angel, 'I cannot recite.'

"He further told me: 'Then the angel seized me and pressed me until I could no longer endure it. Then he released me and again said, "Recite!" and I responded again, "I cannot recite." Again he pressed until I could no longer endure it, and then he released me, again with the command, "Recite!" I responded as before, and he pressed me a third time until I could no longer endure it. Then he released me and said, "Recite in the name of your Lord Who created, created man out of a clot (*a'laq* – a thing that hangs on) of congealed blood. Recite! and your Lord is most bountiful, He Who taught by means of the Pen, taught man what he knew not"' (verses 1 to 5, *sūrat al-Alaq*).

"Then the Messenger of God – peace and blessings be upon him – repeated these verses, and his whole body was shaking."

Al-Ḥākim in his *Mustadrak* and al-Bayhaqī in his *Dalā'il* also report this tradition of Ā'ishah, qualifying it as sound: "The first *sūrah* of the Qur'ān to be revealed was 'Recite, in the name of your Lord . . .'."

Al-Ṭabarānī reports in *al-Kabīr*, with a sound chain of transmission, the following tradition of Abū l-Rajā' al-Utārīdī: "Abū Mūsā had us sit in a circle and recited to us certain portions of the Qur'ān. He was wearing two white garments. When he recited *sūrat al-ʿAlaq*, he said it was the first *sūrah* to be revealed to Muḥammad, peace and blessings be upon him."

In his *Sunan*, Saʿīd b. Manṣūr reports from Sufyān who had it from ʿAmr b. Dinar, who had it from ʿUbayd b. ʿUmayr, that Gabriel came to the Prophet – peace and blessings be upon him – and said, "Recite!" He replied, "What should I recite? I swear by God that I cannot recite." Then Gabriel said, "Recite, in the name of your Lord Who created." The Prophet himself used to say that this was the first part of the Qurʾān to be revealed.

Abū ʿUbayd reports the following in his *Faḍāʾil*: "We heard from ʿAbd al-Raḥmān, who had it from Sufyān, who had it from Ibn Abī Najīh, who had it from Mujāhid, that the first parts of the Qurʾān to be revealed were 'Recite, in the name of your Lord Who created' and *sūrat al-Qalam*."

In his *Kitāb al-Maṣāhif*, Ibn Ashtah records this tradition of Ubayy b. ʿUmayr: "Gabriel came to the Prophet – peace and blessings be upon him – with a piece of cloth and said, 'Recite!' The Prophet replied, 'I cannot recite,' and then Gabriel said, 'Recite, in the name of your Lord Who created.' People are of the opinion that this was the first *sūrah* to be revealed from the heavens."

Ibn Ashtah also records this tradition of al-Zuhrī: "The Prophet – peace and blessings be upon him – was at Hirāʾ when an angel came with a piece of brocade on which was written, 'Recite, in the name of your Lord Who created, created man out of a clot of congealed blood (*ʿalaq* – a thing that hangs on). Recite and your Lord is most bountiful, He Who taught by means of the pen, taught man what he knew not.' "

The second view is that *sūrat al-Muddaththir* was the first part of the Qurʾān to be revealed. Al-Bukhārī and Muslim record this saying of Abū Salamah b. ʿAbd-al-Raḥmān: "I asked Jābir b. Abdillah which part of the Qurʾān was the first to be revealed. He replied, 'Al-Muddaththir.' I said, 'Not *sūrat al-ʿAlaq*?' He responded, 'Let me tell you what the Messenger of God – peace and blessings be upon him – told us.

" 'He told us: "I was staying at Hirāʾ engaged in worship, and when my stay was complete I descended into the valley. I looked in front of me and behind me, to my right and to my left, and then I looked up to the heavens and saw him – that is, Gabriel. A trembling took hold of me, and I came to Khadījah. She ordered me to be wrapped, and God thereupon revealed, O one enveloped arise and warn (verses 1 and 2, *sūrat al-Muddaththir*)." ' "

It is possible to interpret this tradition in the following ways.

1 The question related to the first *sūrah* of the Qurʾān to be revealed as a whole, and Jābir in his reply declared that *sūrat al-Muddaththir* was revealed before the completion of the revelation of *sūrat al-Alaq*, because initially only the opening part of that *sūrah* was revealed. This is confirmed by another tradition of Jābir, transmitted by Abū Salamah, recorded by al-Bukhārī and Muslim: "I heard the Messenger of God – peace and blessings be upon him – speaking of the period in which revelation was interrupted. He said: 'Once when I was walking I heard a sound in the heavens. I raised my head and saw seated on a throne between the heavens and the earth the same angel that had come to me at Hirāʾ. I returned home and told them, "Cover me, cover me." So they wrapped me up, and thereupon God revealed *sūrat al-Muddaththir*.' "

The occurrence in this tradition of the words "the same angel that had come to me at Ḥirāʾ" proves that this episode occurred later than that at Ḥirāʾ during which "Recite, in the name of your Lord Who created" was revealed.

2 What Jābir meant by "first to be revealed" may have been "first to be revealed after the period in which revelation was interrupted", not the first to be revealed in an absolute sense.

3 Again, what he meant may have been "the first to be revealed with the command to warn men". The matter has been expressed as follows by some people: the first part of the Qurʾān to be revealed with respect to prophethood was the first five verses of *sūrat al-ʿAlaq*, and the first part of the Qurʾān to be revealed with respect to messengerhood was *sūrat al-Muddaththir*.

4 Alternatively, what he meant may have been "the first to be revealed on account of a pre-existent cause", that is, the Prophet's enveloping himself as a result of his fear. As for "Recite, in the name of your Lord Who created . . .," this was a beginning not preceded by any cause. This view is mentioned by Ibn Hajar.

5 Jābir said what he did as a result of his own judgement, not by way of narrating a tradition. The tradition narrated by Āʾishah has precedence over his judgement. This possibility is mentioned by al-Kirmānī.

The first and last of these various possible interpretations are the soundest.

The third view is that *sūrat al-Fātiḥah* was the first part of the Qurʾān to be revealed.

The Kashshāf says: "Ibn ʿAbbās and Mujāhid were of the view that the first part of the Qurʾān to be revealed was the first five verses of *sūrat al-ʿAlaq*, but the majority of commentators are of the view that the first *sūrah* to be revealed was *sūrat al-Fātiḥah*."

Ibn Hajar says that most eminent scholars follow the first opinion, and the view attributed to the majority is espoused, in fact, by only a very small number when compared to the adherents of the first view. The proof of this is the tradition narrated by al-Bayhaqī in his *Dalāʾil* and al-Wāhidī with a chain of transmission going back from Yūnus b. Bakīr through Yūnus b. ʿAmr to ʿAmr and then to Abū Maysarah ʿAmr b. Shurahbīl:

"The Messenger of God said to Khadījah: 'Whenever I am in retreat and alone, I hear a voice calling me and I am afraid, by God, that it might be something unpleasant.' She said: 'God forbid, God would not inflict any harm on you. By God, you return trusts to their owners, observe the claims on you of your kinsfolk, and speak the truth.' When Abū Bakr entered the house, Khadījah repeated to him what the Prophet – peace and blessings be upon him – had told her, and she told him, 'Go with Muḥammad to Waraqah.' So the two of them departed, and they told Waraqah what had happened. The Prophet – peace and blessings be upon him – said, 'Whenever I am in retreat and alone, I hear a voice calling, "O Muḥammad, o Muḥammad!" Then I flee running towards the horizon.' Waraqah then said, 'If the angel comes to you again, do not flee as you did before. Remain to hear what he says, and then come and inform me.' When next the Prophet – peace and blessings upon him – was alone in retreat, the angel called out to him, 'O Muḥammad, say "In the Name of God the Compassionate, the Merciful," ' and he recited the whole of *sūrat al-Fātiḥah*."

This tradition has an unbroken chain of transmission, and all its links are trustworthy.

Al-Bayhaqī says: "If this tradition has been correctly preserved, it is probable that it relates to the revelation of *sūrat al-Fātiḥah* after the revelation of 'Recite, in the name of your Lord, Who created' and after the revelation of *sūrat al-Muddaththir*."

The fourth view is that "In the Name of God, the Compassionate, the Merciful" was the first part of the Qurʾān to be revealed. This is related by Ibn al-Naqīb in the introduction to his commentary on the Qurʾān as a "redundant statement". Al-Wāhidī quotes ʿIkrimah and al-Ḥasan (with the appropriate chain of transmission) as saying: "The first part of the Qurʾān to be revealed was 'In the Name of God, the Compassionate, the Merciful', and the first *sūrah* of the Qurʾān to be revealed was 'Recite, in the name of your Lord Who created.' "

Ibn Jarīr and others record this tradition of Ibn ʿAbbās, transmitted by al-Ḍahhāk: "The first thing that Gabriel revealed to the Prophet – peace and blessings be upon him – consisted in his telling him: 'O Muḥammad, seek refuge in God from Satan and then say, In the Name of God, the Compassionate, the Merciful.' "

In my opinion, "In the Name of God, the Compassionate, the Merciful" cannot be counted as a separate unit of revelation, for the revelation of any *sūrah* necessitates the revelation, together with it, of the *basmalah*. It is, in that sense, definitely the first verse to be revealed.

There is another tradition from Āʾishah concerning the first part of the Qurʾān to be revealed; it is recorded by both al-Bukhārī and Muslim. She said: "The first part of the Qurʾān to be revealed was one of the short *sūrahs* (*al-mufassal*) containing the mention of paradise and hellfire. Later, when people began to embrace Islam, verses concerning the permitted and the forbidden were revealed."

This tradition might appear to be problematic in that "Recite, in the name of your Lord Who created" – the first part of the Qurʾān to be revealed – contains no mention of paradise or hellfire. However, the problem can be solved, in my opinion, if one assumes a *min* before the *awwal* in the tradition of Āʾishah, so that the meaning becomes, "one of the first parts of the Qurʾān to be revealed . . .". The short *sūrah* in question might then be *al-Muddaththir*, which was indeed the first set of verses to be revealed after the interruption of revelation and which contains, at its end, a mention of paradise and hellfire. It is possible, moreover, that the ending of *sūrat al-Muddaththir* was revealed before the remainder of *sūrat al-ʿAlaq*.

Part

Al-Wāḥidī reports al-Ḥusayn b. Wāqid to have said: "I heard ʿAlī b. al-Ḥusayn say: 'The first *sūrah* to be revealed in Mecca was *sūrat al-ʿAlaq* and the last was *sūrat al-Muʾminūn.*' It is also said that the last *sūrah* to be revealed in Mecca was *al-Ankabūt*. The first *sūrah* to be revealed in Medina was *al-Muṭaffifīn*, and the last *sūrah* to be revealed, *al-Taubah*. The first *sūrah* to be publicly proclaimed by the Messenger of God – peace and blessings be upon him – in Mecca was *al-Najm*."

In his commentary on al-Bukhārī, Ibn Ḥajar says the following: "By general agreement, the first *sūrah* to be revealed in Medina was *al-Baqara*." However, the view of al-Ḥusayn b. Alī makes the assertion "by general agreement" questionable.

Al-Wāqidī is quoted in the Qurʾān commentary of al-Nasafī as saying that the first *sūrah* to be revealed in Medina was *al-Qadr*.

Abū Bakr b. al-Hārith b. Abyad says, in his well-known *juzʾ*, "We were told by Abū l-ʿAbbās ʿUbaydullah b. Muḥammad b. Ayun al-Baghdādī, who had it from Hassān b. Ibrāhīm al-Kirmānī, who had it from Umayyah al-Azdī, who had it from Jābir b. Zayd, that the first part of the Qurʾān to be revealed in Mecca was 'Recite, in the name of your Lord Who created . . .'. The *sūrahs* were then revealed in the following order: *al-Qalam*, *al-Muzammil*, *al-Muddaththir*, *al-Fātiḥah*, *al-Lahab*, *al-Takwīr*, *al-Aʿlā*, *al-Layl*, *al-Fajr*, *al-Ḍuḥā*, *al-Inshirāḥ*, *al-Aṣr*, *al-Ādiyāt*, *al-Kauthar*, *al-Takāthur*, *al-Māʿūn*, *al-Kāfirūn*, *al-Fīl*, *al-Falaq*, *al-Nās*, *al-Ikhlāṣ*, *al-Najm*, *ʿAbasa*, *al-Qadr*, *al-Shams*, *al-Burūj*, *al-Tīn*, *Quraysh*, *al-Qāriʿah*, *al-Qiyāmah*, *al-Humazah*, *al-Mursalāt*, *Qāf*, *al-Balad*, *al-Ṭāriq*, *al-Qamar*, *Ṣād*, *al-Aʿrāf*, *al-Jinn*, *Yāsīn*, *al-Furqān*, *Malāʾikah*, *Maryam*, *Ṭāhā*, *al-Wāqiʿah*, *al-Shuʿarāʾ*, *al-Naml*, *al-Qiṣaṣ*, *al-Isrāʾ*, *Yūnus*, *Hūd*, *Yūsuf*, *al-Ḥijr*, *al-Anām*, *al-Ṣāffāt*, *Luqmān*, *Sabaʾ*, *al-Zumar*, *al-Muʾmin*, *Fuṣṣilat*, *al-Zukhruf*, *al-Dukhān*, *al-Jāthiyah*, *al-Aḥqāf*, *al-Dhāriyāt*, *al-Ghāshiyah*, *al-Kahf*, *al-Shūrā*, *al-Sajdah*, *al-Anbiyāʾ*, the first forty verses of *al-Naḥl* (the rest being revealed in Medina), *Nūḥ*, *al-Ṭūr*, *al-Muʾminūn*, *al-Mulk*, *al-Ḥāqqah*, *al-Maʿārij*, *al-Nabaʾ*, *al-Nāziʿāt*, *Fāṭir*, *al-Inshiqāq*, *al-Rūm*, *al-ʿAnkabūt* and *al-Muṭaffifīn*.

"The Medinan *sūrahs* were revealed in the following order: *al-Baqara*, *Āl ʿImrān*, *al-Anfāl*, *al-Aḥzāb*, *al-Māʾidah*, *al-Mumtaḥinah*, *al-Naṣr*, *al-Nūr*, *al-Ḥajj*, *al-Munāfiqūn*, *al-Mujādilah*, *al-Ḥujurāt*, *al-Taḥrīm*, *al-Jumuʿah*, *al-Taghābun*, *al-Ṣaff*, *al-Fatḥ* and *al-Taubah*, which is the last *sūrah* of the Qurʾān to be revealed."

I wish to remark that this ordering of the *sūrahs* is unusual and that it requires examination; Jābir b. Zayd was, after all, one of the scholars of the Followers who had a special knowledge of the Qurʾān, and al-Burhān al-Jabarī has relied on this tradition in his *qaṣīdah* entitled *Taqrīb al-Maʾmūl fī Tartīb al-Nuzūl*:

Eighty-six in number are the Meccan *sūrahs*, exalted,
  Versified here are their names, in order of revelation, for the reader:

al-ʿAlaq, *al-Qalam*, *al-Muzammil*, *al-Muddaththir*,
al-Fātiḥah, *al-Lahab*, *al-Takwīr* and then *al-Alā*, the lofty.
al-Layl, *al-Fajr*, *al-Ḍuhā*, *al-Inshirāḥ*, *al-Aṣr*,
al-Ādiyāt, *al-Kauthar*, followed by *al-Takāthur*.
al-Māūn, *al-Kāfirūn*, *al-Fīl* and *al-Falaq*,
al-Nās, *al-Ikhlāṣ*, *al-Najm*, then *Abas* appears.
al-Qadr, *al-Shams*, *al-Burūj* and *al-Tīn*,
Quraysh, *al-Qāriʿah*, then comes *al-Qiyāmah*.
al-Humazah, *al-Mursalāt* and then *Qāf* with
al-Balad, and next *al-Tāriq* and *al-Qamar*.
Ṣād, *al-Aʿrāf* and *al-Jinn*; then *Yāsīn*,
al-Furqān and *Fāṭir*, the exalted.
Maryam and *Ṭāhā*, *al-Wāqiʿah* and *al-Shuarāʾ*,
al-Naml, *al-Qaṣaṣ*, *al-Isrāʾ*, followed by *Yūnus* and *Hūd*.
Yūsuf, *al-Ḥijr*, *al-Anām*, and *al-Ṣāffāt*, with its mention of sacrifice,
Then *Luqmān*, *Sabaʾ* and *al-Zumar* – these follow on.
al-Ghāfir, *Fuṣṣilat* and *al-Zukhruf*,
al-Dukhān, *al-Jāthiyah*, *al-Aʾḥqāf* – recite them in order.
al-Dhāriyāt, *al-Ghāshiyah* and *al-Kahf*,
al-Shūrā, *al-Sajdah*, *al-Anbiyāʾ* and *al-Naḥl*.
Nūḥ, *al-Ṭūr* and *al-Muʾminūn*,
al-Mulk which makes men aware
al-Nāziʿāt, *al-Infiṭār* and *Inshiqāq*,
Then *al-Rūm*, *al-ʿAnkabūt*, *al-Mutaffifīn*, last of the Meccan *sūrahs*.
Then in Medina came twenty-eight *sūrahs* –
al-Baqara the lengthy, *Āl ʿImrān* and *al-Anfāl*.
Next *al-Aḥzāb*, *al-Māʾidah*, *al-Mumtaḥinah*, *al-Nisaʾ*,
al-Zalzalah and *al-Ḥadīd*, *sūrahs* demanding reflection.
Muḥammad, *al-Raʾd*, *al-Raḥmān*, *al-Insān*,
al-Ṭalāq, *al-Bayyinah* and *al-Hashr*,
al-Naṣr, *al-Nūr*, *al-Ḥajj* and *al-Munāfiqūn*,
al-Mujādilah and *al-Ḥujurāt*.
al-Taḥrīm, *al-Jumuah* and *al-Taghābun*,
al-Ṣaff, *al-Fath*, and *al-Taubah*, last *sūrah* of all.

As for the verses revealed on a journey,

"This day I have completed for you" (verse 3, *al-Māʾidah*) revealed at ʿArafah,

And "When you arise for prayer . . ." (verse 6, *Māʾidah*) which counts as Abyssinian,

And "Ask those whom We sent . . ." (verse 45, *al-Zukhruf*), revealed in Syria.

"The One who ordained for you" (verse 85, *al-Qaṣaṣ*), was revealed in al-Juhfah.

And at al-Ḥudaybiyah its meaning became clear.

The first verses to be revealed concerning certain subjects

The first verse to be revealed concerning fighting

Al-Ḥākim relates in his *Mustadrak* that Ibn ʿAbbās said: "The first verse to be revealed concerning fighting was 'It is permitted to those who have been attacked to fight, because they have been wronged . . .' "(verse 39, *al-Ḥajj*)

According to a tradition of Abū l-Āliyah reported by Ibn Jarīr, the first verse concerning fighting to be revealed in Medina was verse 190 of *sūrat al-Baqara*: "Fight for God's sake against those who fight you . . .".

According to the *Iklīl* of al-Ḥākim, the first verse to be revealed concerning fighting was verse 111 of *sūrat al-Taubah*: "God has bought from the believers their souls and their belongings in exchange for Paradise."

Al-Dahhāk is reported by Ibn Jarīr to have said that the first verse to be revealed concerning killing was verse 33 of *sūrat al-Isrāʾ*: "Whoever is killed wrongfully . . .".

The first verse to be revealed concerning wine

In his *Musnad*, al-Ṭayālisī records Ibn ʿUmar to have said: "Three verses were revealed concerning wine, the first of them being verse 219 of *sūrat al-Baqara*: 'They ask you concerning wine and gambling . . .'. It was said then that wine had been prohibited, so they asked the Prophet – peace and blessings be upon him – 'O Messenger of God, let us benefit from wine.' He gave them no reply. Then verse 43 of *sūrat al-Nisaʾ* was revealed: 'Do not approach prayer while intoxicated.' Again it was said, 'Wine has been prohibited,' so they said, 'We will not drink close to the times of prayer.' Again he remained silent. Then verse 90 of *sūrat al-Māʾidah* was revealed: 'O you who believe, wine and gambling . . . are an abomination.' Then the Messenger of God – peace and blessings be upon him – said: 'Wine has been forbidden.' "

The first verse to be revealed in Mecca concerning foods was verse 145 of *sūrat al-Anām*: "I find not in that which has been revealed to me any meat forbidden except . . .". This was followed by verse 114 of *sūrat al-Nahl*: "So eat of that which God has provided you, licit and pure . . .". The first verses to be revealed on the subject in Medina were verse 173 of *sūrat al-Baqara*: "Carrion has been forbidden for you . . ." followed by verse 3 of *sūrat al-Māʾidah*: "Carrion has been forbidden to you." This has been reported by Ibn al-Hassār.

Al-Bukhārī reports Ibn Masūd to have said that the first *sūrah* to be revealed containing a verse of prostration was *sūrat al-Najm*.

Al-Firyābī records a tradition of Mujāhid – transmitted to him by way of Warqāʾ and Ibn Abī Najīḥ – to the effect that the first verse of *sūrat al-Taubah* to be revealed was verse 25: "God has granted you victory in many a place." However, al-Firyābī reports another tradition – that of Abū l-Ḍuhā, transmitted to him by Isrāʾīl, who had it from Saʿīd, who had it from Masrūq – which states that the first verse of the *sūrah* to be revealed was verse 41: "Go forth in battle, heavily or lightly armed . . .". Then the opening verses of the *sūrah* were revealed, and finally its closing verses.

In his *Kitāb al-Masāhif*, Ibn Ashtah similarly relates Abū Mālik to have said: "The first verse of *sūrat al-Taubah* to be revealed was verse 41. Several years later, the first forty verses were revealed."

On the authority of Dawūd, Ibn Ashtah also relates ʿĀmir to have said that verse 41 was the first verse of *sūrat al-Taubah* to be revealed and that it was revealed during the expedition to Tabūk; when the Prophet – peace and blessings be upon him – returned from Tabūk, the remainder of the *sūrah* was revealed, with the exception of the first thirty-eight verses.

Ibn Ashtah relates a tradition of Saʿīd b. Jubayr – with a chain of transmission going back through Sufyān and others to Ḥabīb b. Abī ʿAmrah – to the effect that the first verse of *sūrat Āl ʿImrān* to be revealed was verse 138 ("This is a declaration to mankind, guidance and a warning to the Godfearing . . ."), and that the remainder of the *sūrah* was revealed on the day of the Battle of Uhud.

Chapter eight

THE LAST PARTS OF THE QURʾĀN TO BE REVEALED

There is difference of opinion on this subject. Al-Bukhārī and Muslim record al-Barāʾ b. ʿĀzib to have said that the last verse to be revealed was verse 176 of *sūrat al-Nisaʾ* ("They ask you for a ruling; say 'God will provide you with a ruling concerning those who die without heirs . . .'") and that the last *sūrah* to be revealed was *sūrat al-Taubah*.

Al-Bukhārī reports Ibn ʿAbbās to have said that the verse concerning usury was the last to be revealed, and al-Bayhaqī reports a similar tradition from ʿUmar. The verse intended is verse 278 of *sūrat al-Baqara*: "O you who believe! Fear God, and abandon what remains of your demand for usury . . .". Both Aḥmad b. Ḥanbal and Ibn Mājah report ʿUmar to have regarded this as the last verse to be revealed. Similarly, Ibn Mardawayh reports Abū Saʿīd al-Khudrī to have heard ʿUmar saying, in the course of a sermon, that the last part of the Qurʾān to be revealed was the verse on usury.

Al-Nisāʾī, on the authority of ʿIkrimah, reports Ibn ʿAbbās to have said: "The last part of the Qurʾān to be revealed was verse 281 of *sūrat al-Baqara* ('Fear the day on which you will be returned . . .')." Ibn Mardawayh reports a similar tradition, also from Ibn ʿAbbās, and transmitted by Saʿīd b. Jubayr, with a slightly different wording ("The last verse" instead of "the last part"). It is also recorded by Ibn Jarīr with a chain of transmission going back through al-Aufī to al-Dahhāk.

In his commentary on the Qurʾān, al-Firyābī says: "I was told by Sufyān, who had it from al-Kalbī, who had it from Abū Sālih, that Ibn ʿAbbās said: 'The last verse of the Qurʾān to be revealed was verse 281 of *sūrat al-Baqara*, and eighty-one days elapsed between the revelation of this verse and the death of the Prophet, peace and blessings be upon him.'"

Ibn Abī Ḥātim reports Saʿīd b. Jubayr to have said that the last verse of the Qurʾān to be revealed was verse 281 of *sūrat al-Baqara*, but that the Prophet – peace and blessings upon him – lived thereafter for only nine nights, dying on the night of Monday, two nights after the beginning of Rabī al-Awwal.

Ibn Jarīr records a similar tradition from Ibn Jurayj, and Ibn Abī Ḥātim records a tradition from Abū Saʿīd, on the authority of Aṭiyyah, that verse 281 of *sūrat al-Baqara* was the last to be revealed.

In his *Faḍāʾil*, Abū ʿUbayd records Ibn Shihāb to have said that the last part of the Qurʾān to be sent down from the divine throne were the verses on usury (verse 278, *al-Baqara*) and debts (verse 282, *al-Baqara*). Similarly, a tradition of Saʿīd b. al-Musayyab reported by Ibn Jarīr on the authority of Ibn Shihāb states that the last verse to descend from the Throne was the verse on debts; this is a tradition with an uninterrupted and sound chain of transmission.

In my opinion, there is no contradiction among these various traditions concerning the verse on usury (verse 281 of *sūrat al-Baqara*) and the verse on debts, because it appears that they were all revealed at the same time, in the order in which they now appear in the Qurʾān, and because they all relate to a single episode. Each of the traditions just quoted is therefore correct in asserting that one or other of the verses in question was the last verse to be revealed.

The saying of al-Barāʾ that verse 176 of *sūrat al-Nisāʾ* was the last to be revealed must be taken in the sense of its being the last verse to be revealed containing a ruling.

In his commentary on al-Bukhārī, Ibn Ḥajar says that the way to reconcile the traditions concerning the verse on usury and the verse "Fear the day on which you will be returned . . ." is to regard the latter as the conclusion to the verses revealed concerning usury and as standing in apposition to them. Such a view can in turn be reconciled with that of al-Barāʾ that the two verses were revealed together, so that both can be said to have been the last to be revealed in relation to all other verses of the Qurʾān. It is also possible that verse 176 of *sūrat al-Nisāʾ* is the last verse to have been revealed concerning legacies, thus setting it apart from the verses in *al-Baqara*, although the opposite of this is also possible. However, it is preferable to regard verse 281 of *sūrat al-Baqara* as the last verse to be revealed because of the reference it makes to death, a topic congruent with the ending of revelation.

In his *Mustadrak*, al-Ḥākim relates Ubayy b. Kaʿb to have said that the last part of the Qurʾān to be revealed was the concluding two verses of *sūrat al-Taubah* ("A messenger has come to you from among yourselves . . .").

ʿAbd-Allah b. Aḥmad (in his *Zawāʾid al-Musnad*) and Ibn Mardawayh report on the authority of Ubayy b. Kaʿb that when during the caliphate of Abū Bakr the Qurʾān was being gathered and men were writing it down they reached the verse ". . . they turn away; God has turned their hearts aside, for they are a people that understand not" (verse 127, *al-Taubah*) and they imagined it to be the last verse of the Qurʾān to be revealed. But Ubayy b. Kaʿb told them: "The Messenger of God – peace and blessings be upon him – taught me two verses later than it, 'A messenger has come to you from among yourselves . . .' and '. . . He is the Lord of the Supreme Throne' (verses 128–129, *al-Taubah*). These form the last part of the Qurʾān to be revealed." Ubayy b. Kaʿb then continued: "God completed the Qurʾān with that whereby He had begun it – 'God, there is no god but Him' – by revealing the verse 'We sent no messenger before you without revealing to him that there is no god but I, so worship me'" (verse 25, *al-Anbiyāʾ*). Ibn Mardawayh also relates Ubayy to have said that the last verses of the Qurʾān to be revealed by God were the two beginning with "A messenger has come to you from among yourselves . . ." (verses 128–129, *sūrat al-Taubah*). The same tradition has been reported by Ibn al-Anbārī with a slightly different wording ("the verses closest in time to the heavens").

In his commentary on the Qur'ān, Abū 'l-Shaykh records this tradition of Ibn 'Abbās, on the authority of 'Alī b. Zayd who had it from Yūsuf al-Makkī: "The last verse of the Qur'ān to be revealed was 'A messenger has come to you from among yourselves . . .'."

However, Ibn 'Abbās is reported by Muslim to have said that the last part of the Qur'ān to be revealed was *sūrat al-Naṣr*.

Al-Tirmidhī and al-Ḥākim report Ā'ishah to have said: "The last *sūrah* to be revealed was *sūrat al-Mā'idah*; regard as licit whatever you see proclaimed in it as licit."

Again al-Tirmidhī and al-Ḥākim report 'Abdullah b. 'Amr as saying: "The last *sūrahs* of the Qur'ān to be revealed were *sūrat al-Mā'idah* and the *sūrah* of victory (that is, *sūrat al-Naṣr*)."

A well-known tradition of 'Uthmān states that *al-Taubah* was one of the last *sūrahs* of the Qur'ān to be revealed.

Al-Bayhaqī remarks that the only way to reconcile these traditions – always supposing them to be sound – is to regard everyone as having answered the question in accordance with his own knowledge. Al-Qāḍī Abū Bakr says in his *Intiṣar*: "None of these traditions go back to the Prophet himself, peace and blessings be upon him; everyone spoke in accordance with his own judgement and firm conviction. It is also possible that everyone reported the last verses they happened to hear from the Prophet himself – peace and blessings be upon him – on the day of his death or shortly before his illness, while others heard the Prophet recite other verses somewhat later. It is furthermore possible that the last verse to be recited by the Prophet – peace and blessings be upon him – was revealed together with other verses, and that he gave orders for it to be written down after those other verses, thus giving rise to the impression that the verse coming last in the arrangement of verses was also the last to be revealed."

An unusual tradition on the subject is that of Muāwiyah b. Sufyān reported by Ibn Jarīr: he recited verse 110 of *sūrat al-Kahf* ("Whoever wishes for the meeting with his Lord . . .") and said, "This is the last verse of the Qur'ān to have been revealed." Ibn Kathīr comments that this statement is problematic and that Muāwiyah may have meant that no verse was revealed after it, abrogating it or modifying its force, so that it counts as a fixed and firm verse.

I wish to remark that al-Bukhārī and others report a similar tradition from Ibn 'Abbās: "Whoever deliberately kills a believer shall have hellfire as his punishment . . .' (verse 93, *al-Nisā'*) was the last verse of the Qur'ān to be revealed; no verse was revealed in abrogation of it." Aḥmad b. Hanbal and al-Nisā'ī also record Ibn 'Abbās to have said that this was the last verse to be revealed, with no verse coming in abrogation of it.

Ibn Mardawayh, on the authority of Mujāhid, records Umm Salamah to have said: "The last verse of the Qur'ān to be revealed was 'Their Lord has accepted their prayer, saying, I will not permit the deed of any among you to be lost, male or female . . .'" (verse 195, *Āl ʿImrān*).

This is connected with another tradition of Umm Salamah, in which she is reported to have said: "O Messenger of God, I see that God mentions men and does not mention women." Thereupon verse 32 of *sūrat al-Nisāʾ* ("Do not desire that whereby God has preferred some of you over others . . .") was revealed followed by verse 35 of *sūrat al-Aḥzāb* ("Muslim men and Muslim women . . .") and verse 195 of *sūrat Āl ʿImrān* (". . . I will not permit the deed of any among you to be lost, male or female . . .") This verse is therefore either the last of the three verses in question to be revealed, or the last verse to be revealed after revelation had previously made exclusive mention of men.

Ibn Jarīr records Anas to have said: "The Messenger of God – peace and blessings be upon him – said: 'Whoever departs this world in a state of sincere devotion to God, worshipping Him without partner, performing regular prayer and paying the *zakāt*, departs this world having earned the satisfaction of God.' The confirmation of this is to be found in the Book of God where He says, in the last part of His revelation; 'If they repent, perform regular prayer and pay the *zakāt . . .*'" (verse 5, *sūrat al-Taubah)*.

It is my opinion that what Anas meant by "the last part of His revelation" was "the last *sūrah* to be revealed".

Imām al-Haramayn says in his *Burhān*: "'Say, I do not find in what has been revealed to me a prohibition . . .' (verse 145, *sūrat al-Anām*) was one of the last verses to be revealed." Ibn al-Ḥaṣṣār objects to this view, pointing out that this *sūrah* is universally agreed to be Meccan; that there is no evidence that the verse in question was revealed later than the rest of the *sūrah*; and that the verse was indeed revealed in dispute and argument with the polytheists, who were, of course, in Mecca, not in Medina.

Given all of the foregoing, verse 3 of *sūrat al-Māʾidah* ("This day I have completed for you your religion . . .") appears problematical. It was revealed at ʿArafah during the Farewell Pilgrimage. Its apparent meaning is that all ordinances and obligations previously revealed are now seen to be complete. This view is clearly expressed by some scholars including al-Suddī who says: "After this verse, no regulations concerning the permitted and the prohibited were revealed." However, there are traditions attesting to the fact that verses concerning usury, debts and the estates of those who die without heirs were revealed later than this verse.

Ibn Jarīr says the following in solution of this problem: "It is best to interpret the verse as meaning that God completed the religion of the Muslims by providing them with absolute control of Mecca and expelling the polytheists from the city, thus enabling the Muslims to perform the hajj without the presence of the polytheists among them."

In support of this interpretation, he cites a tradition of Ibn ʿAbbās, transmitted by Ibn Abī Ṭalḥah: "The polytheists and the Muslims would make the hajj together. When *sūrat al-Taubah* was revealed the polytheists were banned from the Kaʿba, and the Muslims performed the hajj alone. This represents the completion of the blessing mentioned in verse 3 of *sūrat Māʾidah*: '. . . and I have completed My blessing upon you.'"

Chapter nine

THE OCCASIONS OF REVELATION

A number of scholars have written independent works on the subject, the most ancient of them being Alī b. al-Midyānī, a teacher of al-Bukhārī. The most celebrated of the books they have written is that of al-Wāhidī, despite its deficiencies. Al-Jabarī abridged it by deleting the chains of transmission for the traditions it contains and adding nothing new of his own. Shaykh al-Islām Abū l-Faḍl b. Hajar wrote a book on the subject, but it never progressed beyond draft form because of his death, and I have been unable to find a complete copy of it. I, too, have written a book on the subject, comprehensive yet brief and unrivalled; I entitled it *Lubab al-Nuqul fī Asbab al-Nuzul*.

Al-Jaʿbarī says: "The revelation contained in the Qurʾān is of two types: a type that came without reference to any cause or occasion; and a type that came with reference to a given event or question."

There are several matters that arise in connection with the second type.

The first is that some people claim this branch of knowledge to be useless since it is virtually equivalent to history. This view is erroneous, because the subject is useful in a number of ways. It helps us, for example, to discover the wise purposes that led to the promulgation of certain ordinances and – in the view of those who regard the occasion of revelation as a factor of specificity – to make the force of ordinances specific to a given set of circumstances. Furthermore, the wording of a verse may sometimes be general, but there is some indication that the meaning intended is specific. If the occasion of revelation is known, a specificity not always evident from the verbal form of the verse will be discovered. To include the occasion of revelation in one's understanding of the verbal form is imperative, and to exclude it on the basis of independent judgement is forbidden; on this, consensus obtains, as al-Qāḍī Abū Bakr relates in *al-Taqrīb*. No attention should be paid to the deviant view which holds such exclusion to be permissible.

Furthermore, to know the occasion for the revelation of a verse helps us in understanding its meaning and in solving any problematical aspects. Al-Wāhidī remarks that it is impossible to interpret a verse without being aware of the episode to which it refers and the circumstances under which it was revealed. Ibn Daqīq al-Id says similarly that knowledge of the occasions of revelation is an effective way for understanding the meanings of the Qurʾān. Ibn Taymiyah is also of the opinion that knowing the occasion for the revelation of a verse is helpful in gaining an understanding of its meaning, for to know the cause of a thing permits one to know the effect to which it gives rise.

Marwān b. al-Ḥakam was experiencing difficulty in understanding verse 188 of *sūrat Āl ʿImrān*: "Think not that those who rejoice in what they have done and love to be praised for what they have not done – think not that they can escape the penalty, for they shall indeed have a grievous penalty." He said: "If it means that everyone who rejoices in what he has done and loves to be praised for what he has not done will be punished, then certainly we will all be punished!" Then Ibn ʿAbbās explained to him that the verse had been revealed concerning the People of the Book: the Prophet – peace and blessings be upon him – had asked them for information on a certain subject, but they withheld what they knew and presented him instead with misleading information, pretending that it was a suitable answer to his question. They expected to be praised for what they had done! This is reported by al-Bukhārī and Muslim.

ʿUthmān b. Maẓʿūn and ʿAmr b. Madī Karab are said to have believed that wine was permissible, citing as their evidence verse 93 of *sūrat al-Māʾidah*: "On those who believe and do good deeds there is no blame for what they ate . . .". If they had known the occasion, for the revelation of this verse, they would not have spoken thus. When wine was prohibited, some people asked what would become of those who had been killed fighting in God's path but had been in the habit of drinking wine – a substance now condemned as filth. The verse was thereupon revealed in answer to their question, as is recorded by *Aḥmad* b. Hanbal, al-Nisāʾī and others.

Another example is provided by verse 4 of *sūrat al-Ṭalāq*: "If you are in doubt concerning the waiting period of your women who have entered menopause, know that it is three months." The conditional clause contained in this verse has presented some of the leading jurisprudents with problems. Thus scholars of the Zāhirī School have said that there is no waiting period for a woman in menopause if she is free of all doubt. However, the matter is clarified by the occasion for the revelation of the verse. When the verse was revealed in *sūrat al-Baqara* concerning the waiting periods of women (verse 228), some people said that the waiting periods of young girls and old women still remained to be fixed. Verse 4 of *sūrat al-Ṭalāq* was therefore revealed to clarify the matter, as is reported by al-Ḥakim on the authority of Ubayy. The verse thus addressed the problem of those women whose waiting period had not been fixed; it answered the doubts of those who wondered whether or not such women had to observe a waiting period, and if so, whether it was the same as that of the women mentioned in verse 228 of *sūrat al-Baqara*. The meaning of "if you are in doubt" thus comes to be "if the status of such women is a problem to you and you do not know how to reckon their waiting period, then this is the ruling".

A further example is provided by verse 115 of *sūrat al-Baqara*: "Wheresoever you turn, there is the face of God . . .". Following the literal sense of the wording, we might say that one is not obliged to turn towards the *qiblah* when praying, whether one is on a journey or not, which would contradict the consensus of the community. Once we know the occasion for the revelation of this verse, we come to realize that it refers either to a supererogatory prayer performed during a journey, or to the case of a person who based on the determination of another imagines the *qiblah* to lie in a certain direction and then realizes that he was wrong. Both these possibilities are reflected in traditions relevant to the verse in question.

Yet another example is provided by verse 158 of *sūrat al-Baqara*: "Ṣafā and Marwā are among the signs of God . . .". The apparent meaning of the verse does not make running between the two places obligatory, for which reason some people have indeed claimed that it is not obligatory. ʿUrwah understood the verse in this sense, but Āʾishah refuted his view by recalling the occasion for its revelation. The Companions thought they were sinning by running between the two places, since the same custom had been practised during the Jāhiliyyah; the verse was therefore revealed to correct their opinion.

Another benefit of knowing the occasion for the revelation of a verse is that it prevents us from placing an erroneously restrictive meaning on a verse. Al-Shāfiʾī says concerning the meaning of verse 145 of *sūrat al-Anām* ("Say, 'I find not in that which has been revealed to me any prohibition' . . ."): "When the unbelievers forbade what God had made permissible and permitted what God had forbidden, in sharp and obstinate enmity, this verse was revealed in utter contradiction of them. It was as if God said: 'There is nothing permissible except what you count as forbidden, and nothing forbidden except what you count as permissible.' This is comparable to someone telling you not to eat any sweets today, and your replying that you will eat nothing else. The purpose then is to express opposition to the unbelievers, not to negate or affirm anything. We may again paraphrase the divine intention as follows: 'There is nothing forbidden except what you have made permissible – carrion, blood, pig meat and animals sacrificed to other than God.' This does not mean that everything else is permitted, for here the emphasis is on establishing a prohibition, not on establishing what is permitted."

Imām al-Haramayn says: "This is an excellent statement on the part of al-Shāfiʾī. If he had not shown the way by making it, I would not have considered it permissible to oppose the view of Mālik that the foods forbidden are restricted to those mentioned in this verse."

A further benefit of knowing the occasion for the revelation of a verse is that it permits us to know the person concerning whom it was revealed and to resolve ambiguities. Thus Marwān used to say that verse 17 of *sūrat al-Ahqāf* ("There is one who says to his parents, 'Woe upon you . . .' ") referred to ʿAbd-al-Raḥmān b. Abī Bakr, but then Āʾishah refuted this by explaining to him the occasion for the revelation of the verse.

The second matter that arises in connection with verses revealed with reference to a given event or occasion is whether the general sense yielded by the wording of a verse or the specific one implied by the occasion of revelation should be given primacy. The scholars of *usūl* hold differing views on this question, but in my opinion it is the first of the alternatives that is preferable. Verses have been revealed with reference to specific occasions, but by general agreement the force of the verses in question goes beyond the original occasion. Examples are the verse on the type of repudiation of a wife known as *zihār* (verse 4 of *sūrat al-Ahzāb*) which was revealed concerning Salamah b. Ṣakhr; the verse on *liʿān*, the invocation of curses on oneself if one makes a false accusation against one's wife (verse 6 of *sūrat al-Nūr*), which was revealed concerning Hilāl b. Umayyah; and the verse specifying punishment for slanderous accusations against a woman (verse 23, *sūrat al-Nūr*), which was revealed concerning the accusers of Āʾishah. The provisions contained in these verses transcend in their applicability the original occasions of revelation.

Those who do not give primacy to the general sense yielded by the wording of a verse say that the verses we have cited are exempt from the rule they propose by virtue of a particular reason, other than the wording of the verse itself; in just the same way, the force of other verses is specific to the occasion of revelation because of particular reasons that apply in each case.

Al-Zamakhsharī says, concerning *sūrat al-Humazah*, "It is possible that the occasion for revelation should in this case be specific, but the threat that this *sūrah* contains is general in scope, encompassing whoever engages in the abominable act of scandal mongering, by way of implicit allusion."

I wish to point out that one of the proofs for the correctness of assigning primacy to the general sense of a verse is the fact that the Companions and others on several occasions deduced general rulings from verses that had specific occasions of revelation; this practice was widespread among them.

Ibn Jarīr reports, on the authority of Muḥammad b. Abī Maʾshar, that Abū Maʾshar Najīḥ heard Saʿīd al-Maqbarī talking to Muḥammad b. Kaʿb al-Quraẓī. He told him: "In one of God's books there is mention made of servants of God whose tongues are sweeter than honey but whose hearts are more bitter than al-sabr (a plant with very bitter-tasting juice); they wear garments softer to the touch than sheep's wool and they attract worldly gain by means of religion." Muḥammad b. Kaʿb replied: "There is a similar statement in the Book of God: 'There are those whose speech about the life of this world may dazzle you, and he calls God to witness about what is in his heart; yet he is the most contentious of enemies' (verse 204, *al-Baqara*)." Saʿīd asked: "Do you know concerning whom it was revealed?" Muḥammad b. Kaʿb answered: "Yes; it was revealed concerning a certain man, but then it became general in force."

It may be objected that Ibn ʿAbbās did not regard God's saying, "Think not that those who rejoice in what they have done and love to be praised for what they have not done – think not that they can escape the penalty, for they shall have indeed a grievous penalty" (verse 188, *sūrat Āl ʿImrān*), as general in its force, restricting it instead to those among the People of the Book concerning whom it was revealed.

To this my answer is that he was certainly aware that the wording of the verse is inclusive of more than the occasion for its revelation. However, he wished to make clear that a particular case was intended in this verse. Parallel to this is the interpretation by the Prophet – peace and blessings be upon him – of "wrongdoing" in verse 82 of *sūrat al-Anʿām* (". . . they did not cloak their faith in wrongdoing . . .") to carry the meaning it has in verse 13 of *sūrat Luqmān*: "Certainly *shirk* is great wrongdoing." This refuted the view of the Companions that all kinds of wrongdoing – not only *shirk* – were intended in the verse.

Moreover, another tradition of Ibn ʿAbbās indicates that in his view primacy should be given to the general meaning implied by the wording: he expresses this view in connection with the verse on theft. Ibn Abī Ḥātim says that ʿAlī b. al-Ḥusayn relates from Muḥammad b. Abī Ḥammād, who had it from Abū Thumaylah b. Abd al-Muʾmin, that Najdat al-Ḥanafī said: "I asked Ibn ʿAbbās whether the verse, 'Cut off the hands of the thief, male or female' (verse 38, *al-Māʾidah*) was general or specific in force. He replied that it was general."

Ibn Taymiyah said: "It is often said in this connection that a verse was revealed concerning such-and-such an incident, especially when it concerns a person. Thus it is said that the verse about *liān* was revealed concerning the wife of Thābit b. Qays and that the verse about dying without heirs was revealed concerning Jābir b. Abd-Allah. Likewise verse 49 of *sūrat al-Māʾidah* ('Judge among them . . .') concerns the Banu Qurayzah and the Banu Naḍir. Then there are verses which are said to have been revealed about a group of the polytheists in Mecca, a party of Jews or Christians, or some of the believers. But those who mention these facts do not mean that the rulings contained in the verses apply only to those groups; no Muslim – indeed, no intelligent person – would maintain such a thing.

"It must be noted that although there is disagreement on whether or not the general wording that is used with respect to a specific occasion of revelation is restricted in its applicability to that particular occasion, no one has ever said that the general provisions of the Qurʾān and the Sunnah are specific to a certain person. All that can be said is that they are specific to the category to which that person belongs, and that their general applicability does not derive from the wording as such. A verse for which there was a particular occasion of revelation, if it contains a command or a prohibition, is applicable both to the person first intended and to all those who are comparable to him. Similarly, if it contains praise or blame, it embraces both that person and all who share in his qualities."

Note

You will have understood from the foregoing that the discussion has been based on the assumption of a verse being general in its wording. There are also verses revealed with respect to a specific matter the verbal form of which is not general in nature. One example is provided by verses 17 and 18 of *sūrat al-Layl*: "Far removed from it shall be the one who is most fearful of God the one who spends his wealth for increase in self-purification", which is unanimously agreed to refer to Abū Bakr. The sense of these verses is definitely restricted to that one individual. Citing this verse in conjunction with verse 13 of *sūrat al-Ḥujurāt* (". . . the most noble of you in the sight of God is the one most fearful of God . . ."), Fakhr al-Dīn al-Rāzī has concluded that Abū Bakr is the best of all men after the Prophet, peace and blessings upon him.

Supposing the verse to be general in meaning, some people have believed that it can be extended to cover anyone who acts as Abū Bakr acted, in conformity with a general rule. They are mistaken, because nothing in the wording of this verse implies generality. The *alif-lam* conveys generality only when it precedes a relative pronoun or a definite noun in the plural (some would add, a definite noun in the singular, on condition that the article is not used to indicate previous knowledge). Now the *alif-lam* in *al-atqā* ("he who is most fearful of God") is not a relative pronoun, because, as is universally agreed, a relative clause cannot be introduced by an elative. *Al-atqā* is also not a plural; it is a singular noun, and used with it is a definite article indicating previous knowledge. Considering the fact that the elative paradigm *afʿāl* always conveys distinctness and serves to separate from others the one it designates in his possession of certain qualities, the view that this verse is general in meaning is, therefore, false, and the opposite view – that it is specific – is definitely correct. Its meaning is restricted to the one concerning whom it was revealed, namely Abū Bakr.

The third matter arises in connection with verses revealed with reference to a given event or occasion:

We have already said that the specificity of the occasion for the revelation of a verse is included within the general force of its wording. It sometimes happened that verses were revealed in response to particular occasions and causes but were placed appropriately, amidst verses of a general nature in order to conform to the beautiful pattern and arrangement of the Qurʾān. The result is that verses pertaining to specific concerns and having specific occasions of revelation acquire a general applicability because of the context in which they are placed.

Hence al-Subkī is of the opinion that there is a special class of verse intermediate between those that have a specific occasion of revelation and those that do not. One example is verse 51 of *sūrat al-Nisaʾ*: "Have you seen those who were given a portion of the Book? They believe in sorcery and evil . . .". This refers to Kaʿb b. al-Ashraf and others like him among the scholars of the Jews. When they went to Mecca after the Battle of Badr and saw the dead of the polytheists, they urged and encouraged them to seek vengeance and to do battle with the Prophet, peace and blessings upon him. When they asked the Jews, "Whose path is closer to right guidance, ours or that of Muḥammad and his Companions?" the Jewish scholars answered, "Your path is closer to true guidance." This was despite the fact that they had seen the attributes of the Prophet – peace and blessings be upon him – mentioned in their own books, and they were certain that those attributes applied to him. Moreover, a covenant had been taken from them not to conceal the truth, a covenant the fulfilment of which was obligatory and a trust. The answer they gave to the polytheists was motivated by envy of the Prophet, peace and blessings upon him.

The verse in question therefore threatens them and at the same time implicitly commands them to do the opposite of what they were doing – that is, to fulfil their trust by proclaiming that the attributes of the Messenger of God – peace and blessings upon them – were the same as those found in their books. This corresponds to verse 58 of *sūrat al-Nisā*ʾ ("Verily God commands you to return trusts to their owners . . ."), a verse which is general in meaning and relates to trusts of all kinds. Verse 51, by contrast, relates to a particular kind of trust, the proclamation of the attributes of the Prophet, peace and blessings upon him. Verses of a general nature always come after those of a specific nature, in the arrangement and writing down of the Qurʾān, as well as being revealed later than them. This in itself indicates that the meaning intended by a verse specific in nature is included in the meaning of the verse that is general in nature.

Thus Ibn al-ʾArabī says in his commentary on the Qurʾān: "The reason for the ordering of these verses is the following. First God related how the People of the Book concealed the attributes of Muḥammad – peace and blessings be upon him – and told the polytheists that their path was closer to true guidance, which was a treacherous act on their part; and then the discussion was broadened to cover trusts of all kinds."

Some people have said, "The objection that the verse concerning trusts was revealed about six years later than the earlier verse is misplaced, because time relates only to the occasion of revelation, not to the mutual congruity of verses. The purpose of establishing congruity is that a verse should be placed in its proper context. The verses were revealed in accordance with their various occasions, and then the Prophet – peace and blessings be upon him – ordered that they should be put in the places where God had told him they belonged."

The fourth matter arises in connection with verses revealed with reference to a given event or occasion:

Al-Wāḥidī says: "It is not permissible to discuss the occasions of revelation except on the basis of traditions stemming from persons who witnessed or saw the revelation of the verses in question, who were aware of the occasions of revelation, and who studied this branch of knowledge."

Muḥammad b. Sirīn says: "I asked ʿUbaydah concerning a certain verse of the Qurʾān. He replied: 'Fear God and speak truly. Those who knew the occasions concerning which the Qurʾān was revealed have departed this world . . .'."

Another person said: "Establishing the occasion for revelation of a verse was feasible for the Companions, given their knowledge of the context in which it was revealed. But even they were often uncertain and could not say that this, and this alone, was the occasion for revelation; they would therefore say, 'I believe that this verse was revealed with reference to this occasion.'"

Abd-Allah b. al-Zubayr is related in the Six Books to have said: "Al-Zubayr had a dispute with one of the Anṣār concerning an irrigation channel crossing a stony plot of ground. They took their disagreement to the Prophet – peace and blessings be upon him – and he said to al-Zubayr, 'First water your won field, and then release the water to your neighbour.' The man from the Ansār then objected, 'O Messenger of God, did you rule this because he is your cousin?' Thereupon, the colour of the Prophet's face changed."

Ibn al-Zubayr continues: "I believe that none other than this episode was the occasion for the revelation of verse 65 of *sūrat al-Nisāʾ*: 'By your Lord! They will certainly not be believers until they make you their arbiter . . .'."

Al-Ḥākim says in his *ʿUlūm al-Ḥadīth*: "Whenever a Companion who was a witness to the coming of revelation says of a given verse of the Qurʾān that it was revealed concerning a certain topic, his utterance is to be taken as a reliable tradition."

Ibn al-Ṣalāh and others agree with this statement. By way of example they cite a tradition of Jābir, reported by Muslim: "The Jews used to say that if someone copulated with his wife in the vulva but approaching her from behind, his child would be born squint-eyed. Then this verse was revealed: 'Your women are tilth for you, so approach your tilth however you will' (verse 223, *al-Baqara*)."

Ibn Taymiyah makes the following clarification: "When people say that a certain verse was revealed concerning such-and-such a subject, sometimes they do indeed mean that the subject was the occasion for the revelation of the verse. At other times, however, they mean that a ruling or ordinance concerning that subject is contained in the verse, being the occasion for its revelation. In the latter case, it is as if they were saying: 'this was the intention of the verse'. Scholars differ concerning sayings of the Companions to the effect that a certain verse was revealed concerning such-and-such a subject. Do such sayings count as traditions that go back to the Prophet, peace and blessings be upon him, and should they be taken as specifying the occasion for the revelation of the verse under discussion? Or are they to be treated as belonging to the category of interpretation, and not therefore as traditions going back to the Prophet, peace and blessings be upon him? Al-Bukhārī regards them as traditions going back to the Prophet, peace and blessings be upon him, while others do not; accordingly they are not included in the collections of tradition entitled *Musnad* that have been compiled by Aḥmad b. Ḥanbal and others. This is in contrast with those traditions in which a cause is mentioned that was followed by the revelation of a verse; such traditions are unanimously regarded as going back to the Prophet, peace ad blessings be upon him."

Al-Zarkāshī says the following in *al-Burhān*: "According to the conventions of the Companions and the Followers, if one of them said, 'This verse was revealed concerning such-and-such a topic', what he meant was that the verse contains a ruling on that topic, not that the topic was the occasion for the revelation of the verse. Such sayings belong therefore to the category of deducing a ruling from a verse, not to that of transmitting information concerning something that has occurred."

I wish to remark the following: What can be said by way of defining the occasion for the revelation is that it is a matter or event during the days of the occurrence of which a verse was revealed. What al-Wāhidī says concerning *sūrat al-Fīl* – that the occasion for its revelation was the bringing of the elephants by the Abyssinians – would therefore be discounted. That event was not the occasion for the revelation of the *sūrah*; it was simply a past event narrated in the *sūrah*, comparable to the stories of Noah, Ād and Thamūd, the building of the Kaʿba, and so forth. It is likewise obvious that God's mention of the reason for His taking Abrāhām as friend ("and God took Abrāhām as friend . . .", verse 125, *sūrat al-Nisāʾ*) does not count as the occasion for the revelation of the verse in which this mention occurs.

Note

If what counts in the case of a Companion as a tradition going back to the Prophet – peace and blessings upon him – is related by a follower, it is treated as *marfūʿ* and *mursal* (that is, its chain of transmission is incomplete). If the chain of transmission of the Follower is sound; if, moreover, he is one of the authorities on the interpretation of the Qurʾān who learned from the Companions – people like Mujāhid, ʿIkrimah, and Saʿīd b. Jubayr; and finally, if his saying is reinforced by another *mursal* tradition – if all this obtains, his statement is to be accepted.

The fifth matter arises in connection with verses revealed with reference to a given event or occasion:

It often happens that the commentators mention numerous occasions of revelation for the same verse. In such cases, the reliable method is to examine the wording of the sayings that have been transmitted. If one of them says, "The verse was revealed concerning such-and-such a subject", and another says the same, while mentioning a different subject, what is intended will be the purport or intention of a verse, not the occasion for its revelation. Hence there will be no contradiction between the two sayings, on condition that the wording of the verse in question is indeed capable of referring to both subjects. This will be discussed in detail in Chapter seventy-eight.

If, however, one of the traditions says, "This verse was revealed concerning such-and-such a subject", and another tradition clearly assigns to the verse in question an occasion of revelation which is incompatible with that subject, the latter tradition is to be relied on, for the former is purely deductive in nature. An example is provided by this tradition from Ibn ʿUmar, recorded by al-Bukhārī: "The verse, 'Your women are tilth for you . . .' was revealed concerning copulation with women in their anuses." As we have already seen, there is a tradition from Jābir clearly stating an occasion for the revelation of the verse which contradicts Ibn ʿUmar's assertion; it is to be relied on as preferable, for it is the narration of something that happened while Ibn ʿUmar's statement is purely deductive in nature. Ibn ʿAbbās also regards his statement as speculative, and has a tradition to the same effect as that of Jābir; it is recorded by Abū Dāwūd and al-Ḥākim.

If one tradition mentions one occasion for the revelation of a verse and another tradition mentions a different occasion, the tradition with the sound chain of transmission counts as authentic and is to be relied on. An example of this is provided by the following two traditions. Al-Bukhārī and Muslim report Jundab as saying: "The Messenger of God – peace and blessings be upon him – fell sick and for one or two nights he did not rise for the supererogatory prayer of *tahajjud*. A woman came to his presence and said, 'O Muḥammad, your demon has deserted you.' Then God revealed *sūrat al-Ḍuḥā*: 'By the morning light and the night when it is still, your Lord has not forsaken you nor is He displeased . . .'."

By contrast, al-Ṭabarānī and Ibn Shaybah record Ḥafs b. Maysarah as reporting his mother, who was a servant in the household of the Prophet – peace and blessings be upon him – to have said: "A puppy entered the house of the Messenger of God – peace and blessings be upon him – and hid beneath the couch where it later died. For four days thereafter, no revelation came to him, and he said, 'Khaulah, what has happened in the house of the Messenger of God so that Gabriel no longer comes to me?' I told myself that I would do well to sweep and tidy the house. When I swept beneath the couch, the dead puppy emerged. Then the Prophet – peace and blessings be upon him – came, and his beard was trembling as it always did when revelation was coming, for now God was revealing to him the first five verses of *sūrat al-Ḍuḥā*."

Ibn Hajar says in his commentary on al-Bukhārī: "The episode of Gabriel's delaying his coming on account of the puppy is well-known, but it is anomalous to regard it as the occasion for the revelation of these verses. Moreover, the person whose name occurs in the chain of transmissions is quite unknown. Therefore the other, authentic tradition which relates to this verse is to be relied on as preferable."

A further example is provided by the next set of traditions.

Ibn Jarīr and Ibn Abī Ḥātim, on the authority of Alī b. Ṭalḥah, report Ibn ʿAbbās to have said: "When the Prophet – peace and blessings be upon him – migrated to Medina, God commanded him to turn in the direction of Jerusalem, and the Jews rejoiced. For several months he prayed in the direction of Jerusalem, but he desired that *qiblah* of Abrāhām and he called upon God, looking to the heavens. Then God revealed the verse, '. . . turn your faces toward it (the Kaʿba) . . .' (verse 150, *al-Baqara*). The Jews were grieved by this and asked what had caused him to abandon their *qiblah*. Then God revealed the verse, 'Say: "God's is the East and the West"' (verse 142, *al-Baqara*), and He said too, 'Wheresoever you turn, there is the face of God'" (verse 115, *al-Baqara*).

Now al-Ḥākim and others report Ibn ʿUmar to have said that "Wheresoever you turn, there is the face of God" was revealed to make permissible the performance of a supererogatory prayer while mounted on an animal in whatever direction the animal might turn.

Al-Tirmidhī relates this tradition from ʿĀmir b. Rabīʿah, classifying it as weak: "On a dark night during a journey we did not know in which direction the *qiblah* lay. We therefore each prayed in a certain direction. When morning came, we informed the Prophet – peace and blessings be upon him – of what had happened and this verse was revealed."

Al-Dārqutnī relates a similar tradition from Jābir, with a weak chain of transmission. He also quotes from Ibn Jarīr this tradition of Mujāhid: "When the verse, 'Call on Me; I will answer your prayer' (verse 60 *Ghāfir*), as revealed, they asked, 'In what direction should we make our petition?' and this verse was revealed." This tradition has gaps in its chain of transmission.

In yet another tradition, Qatāda related that the Prophet – peace and blessings be upon him – said to the Companions: "One of your brethren has died; come and pray over him." They said, "He did not pray in the direction of the *qiblah*", whereupon this verse was revealed. However, this tradition is highly anomalous and problematic.

Thus five different occasions have been mentioned for the revelation of the same verse. The last of the traditions cited is the weakest, on account of its problematic character. Then comes the tradition preceding it, because of its weakness and the defective nature of its chain of transmission, followed by the tradition coming before it, because of the weakness of its narrators. The second tradition cited is authentic, but it says about the verse that it was revealed concerning a certain subject, without clearly specifying that subject to be the occasion for revelation. As for the first tradition cited, its chain of transmission is authentic and it explicitly mentions the occasion for revelation of the verse; it is therefore to be preferred to all the others and to be relied on.

A further example is provided by the next two traditions.

A tradition of Ibn ʿAbbās is reported by Ibn Mardawayh and Ibn Abī Ḥātim on the authority of Ibn Iṣhāq, who had it from Muḥammad b. Abī Muḥammad, who had it from ʿIkrimah (or Saʿīd): "Umayyah b. Khalaf and Abū Jahl b. Hishām came to the presence of the Messenger of God – peace and blessings be upon him – and said: 'O Muḥammad, show lenience to our gods, and we will enter your religion.' The Prophet – peace and blessings be upon him – wished for his people to become Muslim, and he felt moved by their state, whereupon God revealed this verse, 'And they were about to tempt you away from that which We have revealed to you . . .' (verse 73, *sūrat al-Isrāʾ*)."

But Ibn Mardawayh related, on the authority of al-Aufī, another tradition of Ibn ʿAbbās: "The tribe of Thāqif came to the Prophet – peace and blessings be upon him – and said, 'Give us a respite of one year for gifts to be given to our gods so we may take possession of them, and then we will become Muslims.' The Prophet – peace and blessings be upon him – was about to grant them their respite when this verse – 'They were about to tempt you away . . .' – was revealed."

The second tradition necessitates that the verse was revealed in Medina, and its chain of transmission is weak. The first tradition necessitates that the verse was revealed in Mecca, and its chain of transmission is good; according to Saʿīd b. Jubayr, as cited by Abū l-Shaykh, it may even be ranked as fully sound. It is therefore to be relied on as preferable.

A further possibility is that two differing traditions have chains of transmission equal in authenticity. In such a case, the tradition the narrator of which was present at the occasion of revelation or which enjoys some other kind of distinction is to be preferred. An example of this possibility is provided by the following two traditions.

The first is this tradition of Ibn Masʿūd, recorded by al-Bukhārī: "I was walking with the Prophet – peace and blessings be upon him – in Medina, and he was leaning on a stick made from the wood of the date palm. Some Jews passed by, and one of them said, 'It would be good to ask him something.' They agreed to ask him concerning the spirit. He stood still for an instant and raised his head, and I knew that revelation was coming to him. After the revelation was complete, he recited, 'Say: the spirit belongs to the affair of my Lord, and you are given but little knowledge' (verse 85 *sūrat al-Isrā'*)."

The second is a tradition of Ibn ʿAbbās, reported by al-Tirmidhī and designated by him as fully authentic: "The Quraysh said to the Jews, 'Teach us something which we can ask this man.' The Jews answered, 'Ask him about the spirit.' They therefore posed him a question on the subject and the verse concerning the spirit was revealed."

The second tradition necessitates that the *sūrah* was revealed in Mecca, which is contradicted by the first tradition. It is said, moreover, that whatever al-Bukhārī relates is more authentic than what others relate, and in addition Ibn Masūd was a witness of what he describes.

Fifth: Another possibility is that, as in the case of the verse just discussed, two or more occasions of revelation are attributed to the same verse and that the time which elapsed between the occurrence of the occasions on the one hand and the revelation of the verse on the other hand is unknown, making a definite attribution impossible. An example of this possibility is provided by the following two traditions.

The first is a tradition of Ibn ʿAbbās, reported by al-Bukhārī on the authority of ʿIkrimah: "Hilāl b. Umayyah accused his wife, in the presence of the Prophet – peace and blessings be upon him – of committing adultery with Shurayk. b. Sahmā'. The Prophet – peace and blessings be upon him – then said to him: 'Either produce proof, or undergo scourging.' Hilāl then said: 'O Messenger of God, if one of us sees another man closeted with his wife, is it then necessary for him to go seeking proofs?' God thereupon revealed verses 6 to 9 of *sūrat al-Nūr*: 'As for those who accuse their wives, having no witnesses but themselves . . .'."

The second is this tradition of Sahl b. Saʿd, related by al-Bukhārī and Muslim: "ʿUwaymir came to Āṣim b. ʿAdiy and said, 'Ask the Messenger of God whether a man who finding another man in the company of his wife kills him should be put to death, and if not, how he should be dealt with.' ʿĀṣim put this question to the Messenger of God – peace and blessings be upon him – in the absence of Uwaymir, and then conveyed the answer to him. Uwaymir said: 'By God, I will go myself to the Messenger of God and put the question to him.' So he went to the Prophet – peace and blessings be upon him – who told him, 'Some verses have been revealed concerning you and your wife' (meaning verses 6 to 9 of *sūrat al-Nūr*)."

These two traditions have been reconciled with each other by identifying Hilāl as the first person who found himself in the situation described. Then ʿUwaymir chanced to come to the Prophet – peace and blessings be upon him – soon after and posed him the same question. Thus it can be said that the verses were revealed in connection with both Hilāl and Uwaymir. This is the solution to which al-Nawawī inclined, and before him al-Khaṭīb had already said: "Perhaps this situation occurred for both men at the same time."

Al-Bazzāz reports Hudhayfah to have said: "The Messenger of God – peace and blessings be upon him – asked Abū Bakr, 'If you saw another man with Umm Rumān, what would you do to him?' He replied, 'Something evil.' He asked a similar question of ʿUmar, and he answered, 'I would say, curses be on the wretch too feeble to kill the man under such circumstances.' Then these verses (verses 6–9 of *sūrat al-Nūr*) were revealed."

In the opinion of Ibn Hajar, there is no harm if multiple occasions of revelation are attributed to the same verse.

Sixth: If it is not possible to reconcile different traditions concerning the occasion for the revelation of a verse, this should be attributed to a multiple or repeated revelation of the verse. One example of such a case is furnished by the following three traditions.

The first is this tradition of al-Musayyib, reported by al-Bukhārī and Muslim: "When the death of Abū Ṭālib drew near, the Messenger of God – peace and blessings be upon him – came to see him, and Abū Jahl and Abd-Allah b. Umayyah were also present. He said to Abū Ṭālib, 'O uncle, say "There is no god but God" so that I may present it to God as evidence in your favour.' But Abū Jahl and ʿAbdullah said, 'O Abū Ṭālib, will you turn away from the religion of ʿAbd al-Muttalib?' They continued talking to him until he said, 'I follow the religion of ʿAbd al-Muttalib.' The Prophet – peace and blessings be upon him – then said, 'I shall seek forgiveness for you as long as I am not forbidden to do so.' Thereupon this verse was revealed: 'It is not fitting for the Prophet and for those who believe to seek forgiveness for the polytheists, even if they be kinsfolk . . .' (verse 113, *al-Taubah*)."

The second tradition is one narrated from ʿAlī by al-Tirmidhī and classified by him as *ḥasan*: "I heard a man seeking forgiveness for his father and mother, who were polytheists. We asked him, 'Are you seeking forgiveness for your father and mother, even though they are polytheists?' He said, 'Abrāhām sought forgiveness for his father, who was a polytheist.' I told the Prophet – peace and blessings be upon him – what happened, and this verse (verse 113, *al-Taubah*) was revealed."

Finally, al-Ḥākim and others report Ibn Masʿūd as saying: "One day the Prophet – peace and blessings be upon him – went to the graveyard and sat next to a grave engaged in supplication. Then he wept and said, 'The grave I am sitting next to is the grave of my mother. I asked God for permission to pray for her, but He refused me and revealed this verse to me, 'It is not fitting for the Prophet and those who believe to seek forgiveness . . .'."

We reconcile these three traditions by concluding that the same verse was revealed several times.

A similar case emerges from the following two traditions.

Abū Hurayrah is reported by al-Bayhaqī and al-Bazzāz to have said: "When Hamzah was martyred and his body mutilated, the Prophet – peace and blessings be upon him – stood over him and said, 'I will mutilate seventy of their bodies in vengeance for you.' Then Gabriel came as the Prophet – peace and blessings be upon him – was still standing there and revealed to him the concluding verses of *sūrat al-Naḥl* ('If you punish, then punish with the like of that with which you were afflicted')."

The apparent meaning of the second tradition is that the revelation of the verse in question was postponed until the conquest of Mecca, while the first tradition places its revelation in the aftermath of the Battle of Uhud. Ibn al-Haṣṣār says that it is possible to reconcile the two traditions by asserting that the verse was revealed first in Mecca, before the Hijra, together with the rest of *sūrat al-Nahl* (for it is a Meccan *sūrah*); then for a second time on the Uhud; and finally for a third time on the day of the conquest of Mecca. The purpose of such repeated revelation would have been to remind men of the content of the verse.

Ibn Kathīr regards this verse on the spirit (verse 85, *al-Isrā'*) as belonging to the same category of verses revealed on more than one occasion.

Note

It sometimes happens that a tradition contains the words "and he recited", which is erroneously taken to mean "and then was revealed" by the narrator of the tradition. Such is the case, for example, with this tradition of Ibn ʿAbbās related by al-Tirmidhī and regarded by him as sound: "A Jew passed by the Prophet – peace and blessings be upon him – and asked him, 'O Abū l-Qāsim, would it not have been better if God had fashioned the heavens in such-and-such a way, the earth in this manner, the waters in this way and the rest of creation in this fashion?' Then God revealed this verse: 'They do not estimate God justly . . .'. (verse 91, *al-Anām*)."

The same tradition is to be found in al-Bukhārī with the wording, "Then the Messenger of God – peace and blessings be upon him – recited this verse . . ." This is the correct version, because the verse was revealed in Mecca.

Another example is provided by this tradition of Anas, recorded by al-Bukhārī: "When Abd-Allah b. Salam heard that the Prophet – peace and blessings be upon him – had arrived in Medina, he came to see him and said, 'I will ask you three things that only a prophet can know: what are the first indications of resurrection, what is the first food that will be given to the people of paradise, and what will a child be more like, its father or mother?' He replied, 'Gabriel has already given me the answer to these questions.' 'Gabriel?' asked ʿAbdullah; 'Yes,' said the Prophet. Then ʿAbdullah said, 'Gabriel is one of the angels hostile to the Jews.' Thereupon the Prophet – peace and blessings be upon him – recited these verses, 'Say: whoever is an enemy to Gabriel, for he brings down the revelation to your heart, by God's leave . . . God is an enemy to the unbelievers.' (verses 97–98, *al-Baqara*)."

In his commentary on al-Bukhārī, Ibn Ḥajar remarks that the wording in this tradition suggests that the Prophet – peace and blessings be upon him – recited these verses in refutation of what the Jews said, which does not necessitate that the verses were revealed at that moment. He continues: "This is indeed the correct view (that is, that the verses were not revealed at that moment), because we have an authentic tradition indicating that the verse was revealed in connection with an episode other than that involving Ibn Salam."

Note

It may conversely be the case that the same occasion for revelation is attributed to more than one verse. This does not present any problem, because sometimes numerous verses, distributed over different *sūrahs*, have been revealed concerning the same event.

An example is provided by the following three traditions, all from Umm Salamah.

In the first tradition, she is reported by al-Tirmidhī and al-Ḥākim to have said: "O Messenger of God, I have not heard of God mentioning anything about the migration of women. Then God revealed this verse: 'God responded to their prayer by saying, "I will not permit to be lost the deed of any among you, male or female"' (verse 195, *Āl ʿImrān*)."

In the second tradition, Umm Salamah is reported by al-Ḥākim to have said to the Prophet – peace and blessings be upon him: "The men go to war, and we do not, and we receive only half of the share in legacies. Thereupon God revealed two verses: 'And do not desire that which God has given more plentifully to some of you than to others . . .' (verse 32, *al-Nisāʾ*) and 'For Muslim men and Muslim women . . .' (verse 35, *al-Aḥzāb*)."

In the third tradition, Umm Salamah is reported, again by al-Ḥākim, to have said: "O Messenger of God, you mention men but you do not mention women. Then two verses were revealed: 'For Muslim men and Muslim women . . .' and 'God responded to their prayer . . .'."

Another example is provided by two traditions of Zayd b. Thābit.

In the first, he is recorded by al-Bukhārī as saying: "The Prophet – peace and blessings be upon him – was in the process of dictating to me verse 95 of *sūrat al-Nisāʾ*: 'Not equal among believers are those who sit at home and those who fight in the cause of God . . .' Then Ibn Umm Maktūm, who was blind, came and said, 'O Messenger of God, if I were able to go forth in *jihād*, I would.' Then God revealed, 'Except the disabled' (which was inserted into the verse after 'those who sit at home')."

In the second tradition, Zayd b. Thābit is related by Ibn Abī Ḥātim to have said: "I was acting as scribe for the Messenger of God – peace and blessings be upon him – and I was about to place my pen behind my ear when the command to engage in war was revealed. The Prophet – peace and blessings be upon him – was waiting for the revelation to continue when a blind man entered his presence and said, 'What is to become of me, O Messenger of God, for I am blind?' Then the verse was revealed: 'There is no blame on those who are infirm or ill . . .' (verse 91, *al-Taubah*)."

A final example is provided by two traditions of Ibn ʿAbbās.

Ibn Jarīr records Ibn ʿAbbās to have said: "The Messenger of God – peace and blessings be upon him – was sitting in a shady part of his room and said, 'Someone is about to come who sees with the eyes of Satan.' Soon a man with blue eyes entered the room and the Prophet – peace and blessings be upon him – called out to him, 'Why do you and your friends vilify me?' The man went and came back with his friends, and they all swore that they had not vilified him, so he relented. Then God revealed this verse: 'They swear by God that they said nothing evil, but indeed they uttered blasphemy . . .' (verse 74, *al-Taubah*)."

The second tradition of Ibn ʿAbbās, related by al-Ḥākim and Aḥmad b. Ḥanbal, is identical with the first, except that it concludes with: "Then God revealed this verse: 'On the day that God raises them all up for judgement, they will swear to Him as they swear to you . . .' (verse 18, *al-Mujādilah*)."

* * *

Note

Ponder well all that I have mentioned in this chapter and hold firmly to it, for I have written it not simply in accordance with my own thoughts but through gathering and examining all that the leading authorities have said in their diverse compositions. None has preceded me in such a venture.

Chapter ten

VERSES OF THE QURʾĀN REVEALED IN CONFORMITY WITH THE SAYINGS OF CERTAIN OF THE COMPANIONS

Properly speaking, this topic belongs together with the discussion of the occasions for revelation. It is based primarily on the verses that were revealed in conformity to utterances of ʿUmar. A number of people have written separate works on this subject.

Al-Tirmidhī related from Ibn ʿUmar that the Messenger of God – peace and blessings be upon him – said: "God has placed the truth in the heart and on the tongue of ʿUmar." Ibn ʿUmar also said: "Whenever something happened to people, and they said one thing concerning it and ʿUmar said something else, the revelation that came concerning it was close to what ʿUmar had said."

Mujāhid is related by Ibn Mardawayh to have said: "ʿUmar would express a certain opinion and then verses of the Qurʾān would be revealed in confirmation of it."

Al-Bukhārī and others relate Anas to have quoted ʿUmar as saying: "Three sayings of mine turned out to be in conformity with what God revealed. Once I said, 'O Messenger of God, shall we take the Station of Abrāhām as a place of prayer?' and the verse, 'Take the Station of Abrāhām as a place of prayer' (verse 125, *al-Baqara*) was revealed. On another occasion I said, 'O Messenger of God, all kinds of people, the virtuous and the wicked, enter the presence of your wives; should you not order them to veil themselves?' and the verse concerning veiling (verse 59, *al-Ahzāb*) was revealed. The third occasion came when the wives of the Prophet – peace and blessings be upon him – began vexing him with their jealousy, and I told them, 'It may be that if he divorces you, his Lord will give him in your stead wives better than you.' Then this verse was revealed: 'It may be that if he divorces you his Lord will give him in your stead wives better than you' (verse 5, *al-Tahrīm*)."

Muslim reports on the authority of Ibn ʿUmar that ʿUmar said: "My view on three matters turned out to be in conformity with the intention of my Lord: the veiling (of the Prophet's wives); the captives of Badr; and the Station of Abrāhām."

Ibn Abī Ḥātim relates on the authority of Anas that ʿUmar said: "My view on four matters turned out to be in conformity with the intention of my Lord. When the verse, 'Verily We created man from a quintessence of clay . . .' (verse 12, *al-Muʾminūn*) was revealed, I said, 'Glorified be God, the best of creators', and the verse, 'Glorified be God, the best of creators' (verse 14 *al-Muʾminūn*) was revealed."

It is related by ʿAbd l-Raḥmān b. Abī Layla that a Jew met ʿUmar and said: "This Gabriel whom your friend mentions is an enemy of ours." Then ʿUmar said, "Whoever is an enemy to God, His angels and His messengers, to Gabriel and Michael – God is an enemy to the unbelievers." ʿAbd-al-Raḥmān then adds: "God thereupon revealed verse 97 and 98 of *sūrat al-Baqara* (which contain an identical wording)."

In his *tafsīr*, Sunaid reports on the authority of Saʿīd b. Jubayr that when Saʿd b. Muʾādh heard the accusation that had been raised against Āʾishah he said: "Glory to God! This is a great calumny." Then verse 16 of *sūrat al-Nūr* was revealed, with exactly the same wording.

Ibn Akhī Mimi narrates in his *Fawāʾid* this tradition from Saʿīd b. al-Musayyib: "Whenever they heard the accusation against Āʾishah being discussed, two of the Companions would always say, 'Glory to God! This is a great calumny'; then a verse was revealed containing exactly the same wording. The two Companions in question were Zayd b. Hārithah and Abū Ayyūb."

Ibn Abī Ḥātim reports Ikrimah to have said: "When the news of what had happened at Uhud was late in reaching the women, they came out of their homes to search for information. They met two men riding on a camel, and one of the women asked, 'How is the Messenger of God?' 'Alive,' came the reply. 'In that case, I care not,' she said, 'if God takes martyrs from among His slaves.' Then a verse of the Qurʾān was revealed containing the words, 'and he may take martyrs from among you' (verse 40, *Āl ʿImrān*)."

Ibn Saʿd related in his *Ṭabaqāt*: "Al-Wāqidī told me that Ibrāhīm b. Muḥammad b. Shurahabīl al-Abdarī informed him that his father had said: 'Musʿab b. ʿUmayr was holding the banner of Islam in his hand on the day of Uhud. Then his right hand was severed, so he held the banner in his left, saying meanwhile, "Muḥammad is only a messenger; many messengers passed away before him. If he dies or is killed, will you turn back on your heels?" Then his left hand was severed, and he bent down, clasping the banner against his chest in his arms. All the time he kept on repeating, "Muḥammad is only a messenger . . ." until finally he was killed and the banner fell to the ground.' Muḥammad b. Shurahabīl remarked: "The verse containing the exact words Musʿab had been repeating – verse 144 of *sūrat Āl ʿImrān* – had not yet been revealed; in fact, it was revealed after this incident."

Addendum

A category of verses close to those we have been examining consists of verses in which (from a formal point of view) the speaker is not God but others – the Prophet – peace and blessings be upon him – Gabriel, or the angels – without the words being explicitly attributed to them or being introduced with the imperative, "Say".

An example is verse 104 of *sūrat al-Anām* ("Now there have come to your proofs from your Lord to open your eyes . . ."); the fact that it concludes with "I am not a guard over you" indicates that here revelation uses the words of the Prophet, peace and blessings be upon him. The same is the case with "Shall I seek other than God for judge?" (verse 114, *al-Anām*).

As for "We descend not save by the command of the Lord" (verse 64, *Maryam*), this verse reproduces the words of Gabriel. Verses 164–166 of *sūrat al-Sāffāt* ("Not one among us but has a place appointed; verily we are ranged in ranks, and we are those who proclaim His glory") were revealed using the words of the angels.

Likewise, verse 5 of *sūrat al-Fātiḥah* ("Thee alone do we worship and to Thee alone do we turn for help") represents the words of God's servants, although it is possible to assume an implied "Say" at the beginning of the verse. A similar assumption may be made with the respect to the first two verses of the *sūrah*, but not with respect to the third and the fourth.

Chapter eleven

VERSES REVEALED MORE THAN ONCE

Both early and late scholars have clearly stated that certain verses of the Qur'ān were revealed more than once. Ibn al-Hassār says: "The same verse was sometimes revealed more than once, as a reminder and an admonition." He then lists the last part of *sūrat al-Nahl* and the first part of *sūrat al-Rum* as examples. Ibn Kathīr also assigns the verse on the spirit to this category. Some people are of the opinion that *sūrat al-Fātiḥah* was revealed more than once, as was verse 113 of *sūrat al-Taubah* ("It is not fitting for the Prophet and those who believe . . .").

Al-Zarkāshī says in the *Burhān*: "Sometimes a verse might be revealed twice not only in order to magnify its worth but also to serve as a reminder for men (whenever an occasion for revelation recurred) and as a guarantee against its being forgotten." He then cites the verse on the spirit as an example, as well as verse 114 of *sūrat Hūd* ("Establish prayer at both the ends of the day . . .").

Al-Zarkāshī says in addition: "*Sūrat al-Isrā'* and *sūrat Hūd* are both Meccan *sūrahs*, but the occasions for their revelation indicate that they were revealed in Medina. This has seemed problematic to some people, but in fact no problem exists because each of the *sūrahs* was revealed twice. The same is true of *sūrat al-Ikhlās*: it served as a response first to the polytheists in Mecca and then to the People of the Book in Medina. Verse 113 of *sūrat al-Taubah* was also revealed more than once."

The reason for such repeated revelation was that sometimes an occasion would occur – either a question or an event – which necessitated the revelation of a verse when a verse appropriate to the matter had already been revealed. The same verse was therefore revealed anew to the Prophet – peace and blessings be upon him – as a reminder to the Muslims and as an indication that the verse applied also to the new situation that had arisen.

Note

It is possible that the variant readings of some letters in the Qur'ān (two or more in each instance) may also be connected with this category of verses. This is suggested by a tradition reported by Muslim on the authority of Ubayy: "The Messenger of God – peace and blessings be upon him – said, 'My Lord sent me the command to recite the Qur'ān in accordance with a single reading. I sent Him a response with the request to make the recitation of the Qur'ān easy for my people. I repeated the request, whereupon he sent command to recite it in accordance with two readings. I repeated the request. Thereupon He sent me the command to recite it in accordance with seven readings.'" This tradition proves that the Qurʾān was not revealed all at once but in successive segments.

After citing the view that *sūrat al-Fātiḥah*, was revealed twice, al-Sakhāwī says in *Jamal al-Qurrāʾ*:

"If it be asked what was the benefit in its being revealed twice, my answer is that it may have been revealed the first time with no variant readings, and the second with all the variant readings – *mālik* as well as *mālīk*, *al-sirāt* as well as *al-sirāt* and so on."

Note

Some people deny that any part of the Qurʾān was revealed more than once. I saw this view reflected in the book *al-Kafīl bi Maʿānī al-Tanzīl*, where it is argued that such repeated revelation would be redundant and useless. This view is, however, to be rejected, considering the benefits of repetition that we have cited above. It is also argued that repetition would necessitate that whatever was revealed in Mecca would also have to be revealed in Medina, but this argument, too, does not hold, because such a necessity does not exist. Finally, it is claimed that the meaning of revelation is that Gabriel brought to the Messenger of God – peace and blessings be upon him – a part of the Qurʾān he had not previously brought and recited it to him. In refutation of this it has been said that it is not part of the definition of revelation that the verses brought by Gabriel should not have been brought by him before.

With respect to *sūrat al-Fātiḥah*, it is sometimes suggested that what is meant by its repeated revelation may be that Gabriel descended at the time the *qiblah* was being changed and informed the Messenger of God – peace and blessings be upon him – that the recitation of *sūrat al-Fātiḥah* was still an obligatory part of the prayer as it had been in Mecca. It was then imagined that *sūrat al-Fātiḥah* had been revealed anew. Another possibility sometimes advanced is that Gabriel recited it to the Prophet – peace and blessings be upon him – in Medina with a different reading from that which he had used in Mecca, which again led to supposition that the *sūrah* was revealed twice.

Chapter twelve

VERSES WHICH ANTICIPATED THE PROMULGATION OF AN ORDINANCE AND VERSES WHICH WERE ANTICIPATED BY THE PROMULGATION OF AN ORDINANCE

It sometimes happened that a verse was revealed before the promulgation of the ordinance it contains. Such is the case with verses 14–15 of *sūrat al-Aʾlā*: "Certainly he who purifies himself (*tazakkā*), invokes the name of his Lord and prays, shall prosper", which according to a tradition Ibn ʿUmar related by al-Bayhaqī and others was revealed concerning *zakāt*. A similar tradition, classified as defective in its chain of transmission, is narrated by al-Bazzāz.

A certain scholar has remarked: "I do not know what is the justification for this interpretation, for this *sūrah* is Meccan, and in Mecca there was no question of the *ʿīd*, of *zakāt*, or of fasting." al-Bayhaqī answers this by suggesting that these verses were revealed before the promulgation of the ordinance concerning fasting.

Similar is the case of verses 1–2 of *sūrat al-Balad*: "I call to witness this city, and you are free to act in this city." This is a Meccan *sūrah*, but the effect of the Prophet's freedom to act in Mecca became apparent on the day of the conquest of the city when he proclaimed: "For one hour of this day it is permitted me to enter the city without *ihrām*."

A further example is provided by verse 45 of *sūrat al-Qamar* ("Soon will their multitude be put to flight and they shall turn their backs"). ʿUmar b. al-Khattāb said: "I asked, 'Which multitude will be put to flight?' Then, on the day of the Battle of Badr, the Quraysh took to flight, I looked at the Prophet – peace and blessings be upon him. He was pursuing them with his sword unsheathed and reciting, 'Soon will their multitude be put to flight . . .' It thus became clear that the verse had been revealed concerning the Battle of Badr." Al-Ṭabarānī reports this tradition in *al-Ausaṭ*.

Another case is provided by verse 11 of *sūrat Sād*: "There will be put to flight a host of confederates." Qatāda says: "God promised the Prophet – peace and blessings be upon him – while he was in Mecca that he would defeat a host of the polytheists. The interpretation of the verse in which the promise was made became apparent on the day of the Battle of Badr." This tradition is reported by Ibn Abī Ḥātim.

Yet another example is furnished by God's saying, "Say, 'Truth has come, and falsehood neither created nor restores anything'" (verse 49, *Sabaʾ*). Ibn Abī Ḥātim relates Ibn Masʿūd to have said concerning this verse: "What is meant here by the truth is the sword. We know that this verse is Meccan and that it was revealed before *jihad* was made incumbent." This interpretation of Ibn Masʿūd is confirmed by another tradition of his reported by al-Bukhārī and Muslim: "The Prophet – peace and blessings be upon him – entered Mecca on the day of its conquest. There were three hundred and sixty idols installed around the Kaʿba. He struck them down with the staff he was holding and said, "Truth has come and falsehood has vanished; certainly falsehood was destined to vanish", (verse 81, *al-Isrā'*) and "Truth has come, and falsehood neither created nor restores anything."

Ibn al-Hassār says: "God has made frequent mention of *zakāt* in the Meccan *sūrahs*, either directly or by way of implication, as an indication that God Almighty would fulfil his promise by preserving His religion and making it triumph in such a way that prayer, *zakāt* and other duties and ordinances would become obligatory. At the same time, there is no doubt that *zakāt* was never levied elsewhere than in Medina."

One of the Meccan verses referring to *zakāt* is verse 141 of *sūrat al-An'am* (". . . pay what is due on it the day it is harvested"). Verse 20 of *sūrat al-Muzammil* contains references to *zakāt* ("establish prayer and pay the *zakāt* . . .") as well as to *jihad* ("and others who fight in the path of God . . ."), although this had not yet been legislated.

As for verse 33 of *sūrat Fussilat* ("Who is better in speech than the one who calls to God and performs a good deed?"), this was revealed concerning muezzins, according to Ā'ishah, Ibn ʿAmr and several others, although the verse is Meccan and the call to prayer was first instituted in Medina.

As for verses which were anticipated by the promulgation of an ordinance, one example of this category is the verse on ablution. Ā'ishah is reported by al-Bukhārī to have said: "As we were entering Medina, I noticed that I had left one of my necklaces behind at al-Baydā'. So the caravan stopped, and the Messenger of God – peace and blessings be upon him – dismounted. Placing his head in my lap, he went to sleep. Then Abū Bakr came and struck me hard, saying, 'You are delaying people on account of a necklace!' Then the Prophet – peace and blessings be upon him – woke up as dawn was beginning to break. He went in search of water but found none. Thereupon this verse was revealed: 'O you who believe, when you rise up for prayer, wash your faces . . .' (verse 6, *al-Mā'idah*)." This verse is unanimously agreed to be Medinan, although ablution had already been made obligatory, together with prayer, in Mecca.

Ibn ʿAbd al-Birr says: "It is well known to all those who have studied the life of the Prophet – peace and blessings be upon him – that he never performed prayer without ablution; only the ignorant or the obstinate would deny this." Then he adds: "The reason for the revelation of the verse concerning ablution, at a time when ablution was already being practised, was to conjoin its obligatory nature with the recitation of a relevant verse."

Someone else said: "It is probable that the beginning of the verse was revealed at the same time that ablution was made obligatory, and that the remainder of it

– in which mention is made of dry ablution (*tayammum*) – was revealed in connection with this episode."

A similar example is furnished by the verse concerning Friday prayer (verse 9, *al-Jumuʿah*); it is Medinan, while the Friday prayer had already been made obligatory in Mecca.

Ibn al-Faras maintains that Friday prayer was never performed in Mecca, but this is refuted by the following tradition of ʿAbd-al-Raḥmān b. Kaʿb b. Mālik, related by Ibn Mājah: "When my father lost his eye, I took him by the hand and we went to the Friday prayer. Whenever he heard the sound of the call to prayer, he prayed for forgiveness for Abū Umāmah Asʾad b. Zarārah. I said, 'O father, I see that whenever you hear the call to Friday prayer you invoke blessings on Asʾad b. Zarārah; why is this?' He answered, 'Son, he was the first person who led us in Friday prayers before the arrival of the Prophet – peace and blessings be upon him – from Mecca.'"

A further example is provided by "alms are for the poor and the needy . . ." (verse 60, *al-Taubah*), which was revealed in the ninth year of the Hijra, although *zakāt* had already been made obligatory soon after the Hijra.

Ibn al-Haṣṣār says: "It is possible that the classes of people on whom *zakāt* was to be spent were already known, but there was no verse of relevance to be recited on the subject, just as in the case of ablution, which was practised even before a verse was revealed in confirmation of it."

Chapter thirteen

SŪRAHS THAT WERE REVEALED IN SUCCESSIVE SEGMENTS AND *SŪRAHS* THAT WERE REVEALED AS A WHOLE

Most *sūrahs* belong to the first of these two categories. Among the shorter *sūrahs* of the Qurʾān, examples are provided by *al-ʿAlaq*, of which the first five verses were revealed separately, and *al-Duhā*, of which again the first five verses were revealed separately, according to a tradition recorded by al-Ṭabarānī.

Among the shorter *sūrahs* which were revealed in their entirety on a single occasion are *al-Fātiḥah*, *al-Ikhlās*, *al-Kauthar*, *Tabbat*, *al-Qiyāmah*, *al-Naṣr* and the two *sūrahs* of refuge (*al-Falaq* and *al-Nās*), which were revealed at the same time.

One of the longer *sūrahs* to be revealed in its entirety at the same time is *al-Mursalāt*. Ibn Masʿūd is recorded in the *Mustadrak* to have said: "We were in a cave together with the Prophet – peace and blessings be upon him – when *sūrat al-Mursalāt* was revealed to him. I thus learned it from him as he recited it for the first time. I cannot recall with which verse he concluded the *sūrah*: 'In what message after that will they, then, believe?' (verse 50) or 'When they are told to bow, they do not do so' (verse 48)."

Another long *sūrah* revealed in its entirety at the same time is the *sūrat al-Saff*, as is apparent from the relevant tradition cited in Chapter one of this work.

Similar is the case of *sūrat al-Anʾam*, for Ibn ʿAbbās is recorded by Abū ʿUbayd and al-Ṭabarānī to have said: "*Sūrat al-Anʾam* was revealed at night in Mecca, surrounded by seventy thousand angels." al-Ṭabarānī relates the following tradition of Ibn ʿUmar, with a chain of transmission that goes back from Yūsuf b. Aṭiyyat al-Saffār (who is regarded as *matrūk*) to ʿAun b. Nāfiʿ: "The Messenger of God – peace and blessings be upon him – said, '*Sūrat al-Anʾam* was revealed to me in its entirety at the same time, accompanied by seventy thousand angels.'" Al-Ṭabarānī also records Mujāhid to have said, "*Sūrat al-Anʾam* was revealed in one piece, accompanied by five hundred angels", and ʿAtāʾ to have said, "*Sūrat al-Anʾam* was revealed as a whole accompanied by seventy thousand angels." All these traditions reinforce each other.

Ibn al-Ṣalāh says in his collection of *fatwas*: "We narrate the tradition concerning the revelation of *sūrat al-Anʾam* in its entirety at the same time through a chain of transmission originating with Ubayy b. Kaʿb and containing some weakness; we have not encountered any sound chain of transmission in support of it. Moreover, there are traditions which contradict it, asserting that it was not revealed together at the same time and that some of its verses – three, six or some other figure – were revealed in Medina."

God knows best.

Chapter fourteen

PARTS OF THE QUR'ĀN THAT WERE REVEALED ACCOMPANIED BY ANGELS AND PARTS THAT WERE REVEALED UNACCOMPANIED

Ibn Ḥabīb and, following on from him, Ibn al-Naqib have said: "Parts of the Qur'ān were revealed accompanied by angels. They are *sūrat al-An'am*, which was accompanied by seventy thousand angels; *sūrat al-Fātiḥah*, which was escorted by eighty thousand angels; *āyat al-Kursī* (verse 255, *al-Baqara*), which was accompanied by thirty thousand angels; and 'Ask those of Our messengers whom We have sent before you' (verse 45, *al-Zukhruf*), which was accompanied by twenty thousand angels. All the rest of the Qur'ān was brought by Gabriel alone, unaccompanied by any angel."

We have just discussed *sūrat al-An'am* and the various traditions concerning it. There are two additional traditions to be cited. The first is that of Anas b. Mālik, reported by al-Bayhaqī in his *Shu'ab* and by al-Ṭabarānī with a weak chain of transmission: "*Sūrat al-An'am* came down accompanied by a host of angels that filled the horizons from the east and to the west; the earth trembled with the reverberation of their proclamations of God's glory and sanctity."

The second is this tradition of Jābir, reported by al-Hakim and al-Bayhaqī: "When *sūrat al-An'am* was revealed, the Messenger of God – peace and blessings be upon him – glorified God and said: 'Countless angels, filling the horizons, have accompanied this *sūrah*.'" After relating this tradition, al-Hakim remarks: "According to Muslim, this tradition is sound." However, al-Dhahabī says: "There are lacunae in it, and in my opinion it is forged."

As for *al-Fātiḥah*, *Yāsīn*, and verse 45 of *al-Zukhruf*, I have not encountered traditions to the effect that they were accompanied by angels. In the case of *āyat al-Kursī*, as well as the rest of *sūrat al-Baqara*, there is this tradition of Maʿqal b. Yasar, reported by Aḥmad b. Ḥanbal in his *Musnad*: "The Prophet – peace and blessings be upon him – said, '*Al-Baqara* is the pillar and the summit of the Qur'ān; with each of its verses eighty thousand angels descended.' As for 'There is no god but He, the Living, the Eternally Self-Subsisting' (*āyat al-Kursī*), it was brought forth from beneath the throne to be joined to this *sūrah*."

Saʿīd b. Manṣūr relates in his *sunan* the following tradition of Dahhāk b. Muzāhim: "When Gabriel brought the final verses of *sūrat al-Baqara* he was accompanied by angels beyond number."

There are other *sūrahs* of this type, including *sūrat al-Kahf*. Ibn al-Durays says in his *Faḍā'il*: "On the authority of Ismaʿīl b. Ayyāsh, Yāzīd b. ʿAbd al-ʿAzīz al-Tayālisī reports Ismaʿīl b. Rāfiʿ to have said: 'We have heard that the Prophet

– peace and blessings be upon him – said, "Shall I not inform you of a *sūrah* the splendour of which filled the space between the heavens and the earth and which seventy thousand angels accompanied? It was *sūrat al-Kahf*."'"

Note

It remains to be seen how all the traditions cited so far in this chapter are to be reconciled with the following tradition of Saʿīd b. Jubayr, reported by Ibn Abī Ḥātim with a sound chain of transmission: "Whenever Gabriel brought part of the Qurʾān to the Prophet – peace and blessings be upon him – four angels accompanied him as guards and protectors." Similarly, Ibn Jarīr reports al-Dahhāk to have said: "Whenever the angel (Gabriel) was sent to the Prophet – peace and blessings be upon him – other angels were sent with him to guard him on all sides and to prevent Satan from assuming the guise of Gabriel."

Ibn al-Durays says: "Mahmud b. Ghaylān reports Yāzīd b. Hārūn to have said that Walīd – that is, Ibn Jamīl – told him on the authority of Qāsim that Abū Umāmah had said: 'Four parts only of the Qurʾān were revealed from the treasury of the Throne: the Mother of the Book (*sūrat al-Fātiḥah*), *āyat al-Kursī*, the closing verses of *sūrat al-Baqara* and *sūrat al Kauthar*.'"

As for *al-Fātiḥah*, al-Bayhaqī relates in his *Shuʾab* the following tradition of Anas, with a chain of transmission that is defective: "The Prophet – peace and blessings be upon him – said, 'One of the favours God has bestowed upon me is that He told me, "I have given you one of the treasures of My Throne – *sūrat al-Fātiḥah*."'" Again with a defective chain of transmission, al-Hakim reports Maʿqal b. Yasar to have related that the Prophet – peace and blessings be upon him – said, "I was given *sūrat al-Fātiḥah* and the closing verses of *sūrat al-Baqara* from beneath the throne." In his *Musnad*, Ibn Rahawayh relates that Alī was asked concerning *sūrat al-Fātiḥah*. He replied: "The Prophet – peace and blessings be upon him – told us that it was brought down from a treasury beneath the Throne."

As for the concluding verses of *sūrat al-Baqara*, al-Darimī reports in his *Musnad* that Ayfaʾ al-Kalāʾī said: "Someone asked the Prophet, peace and blessings be upon him, 'O Messenger of God, which verses do you wish to be given to yourself and your community as their distinctive portion?' He said, 'The concluding part of *sūrat al-Baqara*, for it comes from the treasury of Mercy which is beneath the Throne.'" Aḥmad b. Hanbal and others relate a tradition from ʿUqbah b. Āmir (with a defective chain of transmission) to the effect that the Prophet – peace and blessings be upon him – said: "Recite these two verses (verses 285–286, *al-Baqara*), for my Lord has given them to me from beneath the Throne."

Hudhayfah recounts that the Prophet – peace and blessings be upon him – said: "These verses at the end of *sūrat al-Baqara* were given to me from a treasury beneath the Throne; no prophet before me was given them." Abī Dharr relates the same tradition in almost identical wording; it has been narrated, in fact, with numerous chains of transmission, going back to ʿUmar, ʿAlī, Ibn Masʿūd, and others.

As for *āyat al-Kursī*, the relevant tradition of Maʿqal b. Yasār has already been quoted. In addition, Ibn Mardawayh reports Ibn ʿAbbās to have said: "Whenever the Prophet – peace and blessings be upon him – recited *āyat al-Kursī*, he would laugh and say, 'It comes from the treasury of the Compassionate One, which lies beneath the Throne.'" Abū ʿUbayd records Alī to have said: "*Āyat al-Kursī* was given to your Prophet from the treasury of the Throne, and no prophet before him was given it."

As for *sūrat al-Kauthar*, I have not come across any relevant tradition. The saying of Abū Umāmah on the subject has a defective chain of transmission; it is recorded by Abū l-Shaykh b. Ḥayyān, al-Daylamī, and others, with one chain of transmission that goes back from Muḥammad b. Abd al-Mālik to Yāzīd b. Hārūn as well as another one – defective, as already mentioned – that goes back to Abū Umāmah.

Chapter fifteen

THE VERSES THAT WERE REVEALED TO SOME OF THE PROPHETS AND THE VERSES THAT WERE REVEALED ONLY TO THE PROPHET (PEACE AND BLESSINGS BE UPON HIM)

To the second category belong the *Fātiḥa* (*sūrah* 1) and the Throne Verse (Q2, 255) and the last two verses of *Surat al-Baqara* (2), as will be shown in the *ḥadīths* a bit below.

Muslim[1] related on the authority of Ibn ʿAbbās: "An angel came to the Prophet (peace and blessings be upon him) and said: 'Rejoice for the two lights given to you which were not revealed to any prophet before.' The Fātiḥa and the final two verses of *Surat al-Baqara*."

Al-Ṭabarānī reported on the authority of ʿUqba Ibn ʿĀmir,[2] that they were not sure about the two verses at the end of *Surat al-Baqara* (Q2, 244) ". . . the Messenger believes . . . until the end (of the *sūrah*)", for indeed God singled out Muḥammad [to reveal them to]."

Abū ʿUbayd reported in his Faḍaʾil, on the authority of Kaʿb: "Muḥammad (peace and blessings be upon him) was given four verses that were not revealed to Moses; and Moses was given one verse that was not given to Muḥammad." He (continued) "The verses that were given to Muḥammad are (Q2, 284) "To God belongs all that is in the heaven and the earth . . ." (to the end of the *sūrah*). These comprise three verses; the fourth is the Throne Verse.[3] The verse that was revealed to Moses is: "O God! Do not let Satan enter into us; deliver us from him. For yours is the Kingdom and the Power and the Governance and the Possession and the Praise and the earth and the heavens, now and forever, for ever and ever, Amen and Amen."[4]

Al-Bayhaqī[5] reported in his Shuʿab on the authority of Ibn ʿAbbās, who said: "The seven longest *sūrahs* were not given to anyone but the Prophet (peace and blessings be upon him).

Moses was given two of them.

Al-Ṭabarānī reported on the authority of Ibn ʿAbbās in a sound [*marfuuʿ*] *ḥadīth*: "My Nation has been given for cases of emergency what no other nation has been given, namely 'We are God's and to Him we return'" (Q2, 156).

Belonging to the first category (that is, those verses revealed only to the Prophet) are those reported by al-Hakim[6] on the authority of Ibn ʿAbbās, who said: "When the verse 'Praise the name of your Lord on High!' (Q82, 1) was revealed, the Prophet (peace and blessings be upon him) said: 'All of it appears in the books of Abrāhām and Moses.' When 'By the star when it sets' (Q53, 1) to 'And by Abrāhām who fulfilled' (Q53, 37) then (God) said: '(fulfilled:) that no bearer of burdens can bear another's burden' (Q53, 38) up to the point where (God says in Q53, 56) 'This is a Warner of the Warners of old' were revealed, (the Prophet repeated that they appeared also in the books of Abrāhām and Moses)."

Saʿīd Ibn Manṣūr said: "Khālid Ibn ʿAbdullah related to us a *ḥadīth* on the authority of ʿAta Ibn al-Sa'ib, on the authority of ʿIkrimah, on the authority of Ibn ʿAbbās, saying: 'This *sūrah* (*53) appears in the books of Abrāhām and Moses.'"

Ibn Abī Ḥātim reported in a similar formulation: a repeat of what is in the books of Abrāhām and Moses.

It is reported on the authority of al-Suddi, who said: "This *sūrah* appears in the books of Abrāhām and Moses, just as it was revealed to the Prophet (peace and blessings be upon him)."

Al-Firyani said: "Sufyān informed us on the authority of his father, on the authority of ʿIkrimah: Indeed, this appears in the first books (Q87, 18) refers to these verses (under discussion)."

Al-Ḥakim reported, by way of al-Qāsim, on the authority of Abī Umama who said: "Of that which God revealed to Muḥammad that he also revealed to Abrāhām are: 'The worshipping repenters . . .' to '. . . and inform the believers'[7] and 'The believers have verily succeeded . . .' to 'they dwell forever in it'[8] and 'Indeed, the male Muslims and the female Muslims . . . (to the end of the verse).[9] Concerning: 'Those who are steadfast in their prayers . . .' up to '. . . they endure'[10] no one but Abrāhām and the Prophet (peace and blessings be upon him) were ever granted it."

Al-Bukhārī[11] related on the authority of ʿAbdullah Ibn ʿAmr Ibn al-ʿĀs: "He, that is, the Prophet (peace and blessings be upon him) is described in the Torah by some of his Qur'ānic epithets 'O Prophet! We have sent you as a witness, and as a bearer of good tidings and a warner'[12] and as a refuge for the unlettered . . . (to the end of the *ḥadīth*)."

Ibn al-Durays and others related, on the authority of Kaʿb, that "The Torah begins with 'Praise be to God who created the heavens and the earth and made darkness and light, yet those who disbelieve in their Lord hold others as equal (to Him).'[13] (The Torah) ends with 'Praise be to God who begets no son . . .' to '. . . magnify Him in His greatness'."[14]

It was also reported on (Ibn al-Durays's) authority (that the Prophet said: "The beginning of the Torah is (the same as) the beginning of Sūrat al-An'ām (*6) 'Praise be to God who created the heavens and the earth and made darkness and light' and the peroration of the Torah (is the same as) the peroration of Sūrat Hūd (*11) 'So worship Him, and put your trust in Him, your Lord is not unmindful of what you do.'"[15]

From another source we are informed that (the Prophet) said: "The first part of what (God) revealed in the Torah comprises the ten verses of Sūrat al-An'am (*6) from 'Say: come I will recite to you what your Lord prohibited you from . . .'[16] to the end of the verse."

Abū ʿUbayd reported that (the Prophet) said: "The first part of what (God) revealed in the Torah comprises ten verses from Sūrat al-Anʾām (*6) 'In the name of God the Compassionate, the Merciful. Say: come, I will recite to you what your Lord has really prohibited you from . . .'[17] to the end of the *sūrah* . . .". Some (of the authorities) hold that these verses comprise the ten verses that God wrote to Moses, at the beginning of God's writing down of the Torah, namely (strict) monotheism, prohibition of polytheism, (prohibition of) the false oath, disrespecting parents, murder, fornication, theft, giving false witness, coveting (lit. extending one's eye to what is in another's hand), and the commandment to honour the Sabbath.

Al-Dāraquṭnī reported from a *ḥadīth* on the authority of Burayda, that the Prophet (peace and blessings be upon him) said: "I will certainly teach you a verse which was not revealed to any prophet after Solomon except me: 'In the name of God, the Compassionate, the Merciful.' "

Al-Bayhaqī related on the authority of Ibn ʿAbbās: "(The Prophet) said: People have overlooked a verse in the Book of God never revealed to anyone before the Prophet (peace and blessings be upon him) but Solomon the son of David. (This verse is) 'In the name of God, the Compassionate, the Merciful' " (Q1, 1).

Al-Hakim reported on the authority of Ibn Maysara: "This (Qurʾānic) verse is written in the Torah (within) seven hundred verses: 'All that is in the heavens and the earth constantly praise God, the King, the Holy, the Omnipotent, the Wise', which is at the beginning of Sūrat al-Jumʿa (*42)."

* * *

Knowledge to be gained

What Ibn Abī Ḥātim reported on the authority of Muḥammad Ibn Kaʿb al-Quraẓī is relevant here: "Joseph was shown three verses of God's Book to protect him (in his trial of temptation)[18] (1) 'Indeed, there are guardians above you honorable scribes; they know what you do.'[19] (2) 'Whatever you may be occupied with, and whatever part of the Qurʾān you may recite . . . (to the end of the verse).'[20] (3) 'Is then He who knows what every soul does . . . (to the end of the verse).' "[21]

Some added another verse: "Do not (even) come close to adultery . . .".[22]

In addition, Ibn Abī Ḥātim reported on the authority of Ibn ʿAbbās (concerning the verse) ". . . had he (Joseph) not seen God's proof . . .".[23] (Joseph) saw a verse from God's Book engraved in the wall of the palace, which prohibited him (from committing adultery).

Chapter sixteen

ON THE MANNER OF (THE QURʾĀN'S) REVELATION

There are problems concerning this matter. First, God said: "The month of Ramaḍān in which the Qurʾān was revealed"[1] and "Verily, We have revealed it on the Night of Power".[2]

Authorities differ on the method of (the Qurʾān's) being brought down from the Preserved Tablet[3] in three different ways.

The best and most authoritative of these is that on the Night of Power, God brought (the Qurʾān) in its totality down to the lowest heaven, then He revealed it (to the Prophet) in instalments over a period of twenty years, twenty-three years or twenty-five years; the difference occurs because of the various views on how many years (the Prophet) (peace and blessings be upon him) resided in Mecca after his Call.[4]

Al-Ḥakim, al-Bayhaqī and others relate by way of Manṣūr, on the authority of Saʿīd Ibn Jubair, on the authority of Ibn ʿAbbās that (the Prophet) said: "The Qurʾān was brought down in its entirety on the Night of Power, and it was among the spheres of the stars. God then revealed it to His Emissary (peace and blessings be upon him) piece after piece."

Al-Ḥakim and al-Bayhaqī also related (as did al-Nasāʾī) by way of Dawud Ibn Abī Hind, on the authority of ʿIkrima, and the authority of Ibn ʿAbbās, that (the Prophet) said: "On one night the Qurʾān was brought down to the lowest heaven. (This is) the Night of Power, after which it was revealed over (a period) of twenty years." Then he recited, "And no question do they bring to you but we reveal to you the truth and the best interpretation"[5] and "It is a Qurʾān which we have divided so that you might recite it to men at intervals; we have revealed it in stages."[6]

Ibn Abī Ḥātim reported the same thing in this regard; at its end: whenever the polytheists came up (with a challenging question), God would provide them with the (appropriate) answer.

Al-Ḥakim and Ibn Abī Shayba reported by way of Ḥasan Ibn Ḥurayth, on the authority of Saʿīd Ibn Jubair, on the authority of Ibn ʿAbbās that (the Prophet said), "The Qurʾān was separated from the *Dhikr* (previous scriptures),[7] and was placed in the Abode of Glory[8] in the lowest heaven, then Gabriel began to reveal it to the Prophet (peace and blessings be upon him)." All of the *isnāds* of the relevant *ḥadīths* are sound.

Al-Ṭabarānī reported, using a different isnād going back to Ibn ʿAbbās, that (the Prophet) said: "The Qurʾān was brought down on the Night of Power in the month of Ramaḍān. Then it was revealed in instalments." *Isnād* of this tradition is not reproachable.[9]

Al-Ṭabarānī and al-Bazzāz reported a different tradition going back to Ibn ʿAbbās that the Qurʾān was revealed in its entirety and put in the abode of Glory in the lowest heaven. Then Gabriel revealed it to the Prophet (peace and blessings be upon him) in answer to the questions and action of people.

Ibn Abī Shayba, in his Faḍaʾil al-Qurʾān, reports on the authority of Ibn ʿAbbās (although through a different *isnād*) that (the Prophet) said: "It was given to Gabriel on the Night of Power in its totality, and he put it in the Abode of Glory"; then he began to bring it down (to the Prophet) in instalments.

Ibn Marduwayhi and al-Bayhaqī reported in *al-Asmaʾ wa- al-Sifat* (The Names and the Attributes) by way of al-Suddi, on the authority of Muḥammad, on the authority of Ibn Abī al-Mukhālid, on the authority of al-Qāsim, on the authority of Ibn ʿAbbās, that (the latter) asked ʿAṭiyya Ibn al-Aswad (about this). He answered that he was in doubt about this because:

1 "The month of Ramaḍān in which the Qurʾān was revealed"[10] and "Verily we have revealed it on the Night of Power."[11] But this was revealed in (the months of) Shawal, Dhu al-Qaʿida, Dhu al-Ḥijja, al-Muḥarram, Ṣafar and the month of Rabīʿ. Ibn ʿAbbās answered him: "It was brought down in its totality on the Night of Power in the month of Ramaḍān, then it was brought down in instalments to the spheres of the stars with deliberation[12] through the months and days."

Abū Shāma said: "By 'with deliberation' (Ibn ʿAbbās means) 'with extreme care' and by 'to the spheres of the stars' he means 'to their setting positions', in the sense that (the Qurʾān) was brought down in instalments, one part following another, slowly and with deliberation."[13]

The second opinion has it that (the Qurʾān) was brought down to the lowest heaven on twenty Nights of Power, or on twenty-three, or on twenty-five; on each night God brought down what He had determined (He was to reveal to the Prophet) each year; then He brought it down in instalments each year. The Imām Fakhr al-Dīn al-Rāzī[14] expressed this opinion as a hypothesis (bahthan) adding: "It is probable that He would bring down on each Night of Power the revelation the likes of which mankind needed from the Preserved Tablet to the lowest heaven; then He stopped." Is this opinion more worthy of consideration than the first!

Ibn Kathīr said: "This that (al-Razī) calls a probability was transmitted by al-Qurtubiyy on the authority of Muqatil Ibn Ḥayyān, who related that the consensus is that (the Qurʾān) was brought down as a totality from the Preserved Tablet to the Abode of Glory in the lowest heaven."

I (Suyūṭī) say: "Among those who support the opinion of Muqatil are al-Ḥalīmī and al-Māwardī.[15] Ibn Shihāb also agrees on this that the last part of the Qurʾān to come from the Throne is the Debt Verse."[16]

The third opinion is that (the Qurʾān's) revelation began on the Night of Power, then it was revealed in instalments on different occasions, until the final one; so holds al-Shaʿbi.

Ibn Hajar said in (his) commentary on al-Bukhārī: "The first (opinion) is clearly the true one; al-Māwardī also expressed a fourth opinion, namely, that (God) brought it down in its entirety from the Preserved Tablet, and that the guarding angels partitioned it out to Gabriel over a period of twenty nights, and Gabriel partitioned it out to the Prophet (peace and blessings be upon him) over twenty years. This also is unlikely; the most authoritative view is that Gabriel used to revise with the Prophet in the month of Ramaḍān the revelation that (the Prophet) received throughout an entire year."

Abū Shama said (about this fourth opinion): "It is as if the one who holds this view wanted to combine the first with the second opinion."

I (Suyūṭī) say: "This that al-Māwardī reported was already reported by Ibn Abī Ḥātim, by way of Ibn ʿAbbās, (who reported: the Prophet) said: 'The Qurʾān was revealed in its entirety from the Presence of God to the Preserved Tablet, (and then) to the noble (angel) scribes who do their scribing in the lowest heaven; then the (angel) scribes would partition it out to Gabriel over a period of twenty nights, and then Gabriel would partition it out to the Prophet (peace and blessings be upon him) over a period of twenty years.' "

Points of note

1 The secret of (the Qurʾān's) being brought down to the (lowest) heaven is (the Qurʾān's) exaltation and the exaltation of Him to whom it was revealed, by informing the dwellers of the seven heavens that this is the last Book (revealed) to the Seal of the Prophets, for the most noble of Nations: "We have brought it near to them in order to reveal it to them." Were it not for the Divine Wisdom, that necessitated its being revealed in parts according to the events, it would have been brought down to the earth in its totality like the previous revealed Books. But God made a difference between the Qurʾān and previous revealed Books by giving the Qurʾān the two situations: revealed in its entirety once and then revealed in instalments, to honour him to whom it was revealed. Thus holds Abū Shama in his *al-Murshid al-Wajiz* (the Abridged Guide).

2 Al-Ḥakim al-Tirmidhī (reported that) the Qurʾān was revealed in its totality to the lowest heaven to deliver to the Nation from it what is most prominent in their destiny, that is, Muḥammad's (peace and blessings be upon him) Mission; this is on account of that his Mission is Mercy;[17] when Mercy went out at the opening of the door, it brought Muḥammad (peace and blessings be upon him) and the Qurʾān; it placed the Qurʾān in the Abode of Glory in the lowest heaven so that it would penetrate the boundary of the lower world; and (the Mercy) put Prophecy in Muḥammad's heart; then Gabriel revealed the Message (*al-risaalah*) and the Revelation (*al-waḥy*); it is as if (He), He is forever exalted, stretched out to bestow the Mercy which is the Destiny of this Nation (directly) from God to the Nation.

Al-Sakhawī said in his *Jamal al-Qurraʾ* (Reciters' Beauty): "Concerning (the Qurʾān's) being brought down in its entirety: this is to honour and glorify human beings by the angels, and to inform them of God's care for them and His mercy on them; this is the import of (His) ordering seventy thousand angels to escort *Surat al-Anʿam* (verse 6), and the import of (His), He is forever to be praised, order to Gabriel to dictate it to the noble (angel) scribes, and their scribing it and reciting it to (Gabriel). Also, (this means that) there is equality between our Prophet (peace and blessings be upon him) and Moses (peace and blessings be upon him) in the matter of the revelation of his Book as a totality; but the preference is to Muḥammad, whose revelations came down in instalments, so that He could memorize them."

Abū Shāma said: "If you were to ask concerning (Q97, 1) 'Verily, We revealed it on the Night of Power' (could it mean) a part of the totality that was brought down as a totality or not? For if it were not a part, then what was brought down as a totality? And if it were a portion, then what in truth is the meaning of this expression?"

I (Suyūṭī) say: "There are two aspects to this question. The first is that the meaning of (God's) speech is: 'Verily, We have decided to bring it down (in its entirety) on the Night of Power (and We have done so)'; and 'We have determined (its text) for eternity'; the second (aspect) is that its wording is the wording of the past tense, but it refers to the future, that is, 'We will reveal it (as a totality) on the Night of Power.'" End (of my opinion.)

Second, Abū Shāma also said: "It is clear that (the Qurʾān's) revelation as a totality to the lowest heaven (occurred) before the appearance of His (peace and blessings be upon him) prophecy." (He added:) "It is also possible that it happened afterwards."

I (Suyūṭī) say: "This second (opinion) is correct: the *isnāds* of the above-mentioned *ḥadīths* going back to Ibn ʿAbbās clearly indicate this."

Ibn Hajar said in his commentary on al-Bukhārī: "Aḥmad, and al-Bayhaqī in his Shuʿab, reported on the authority of Waʾila Ibn al-Asqaʿ that the Prophet (peace and blessings be upon him) said: 'The Torah was revealed after the six first days of Ramaḍān; the Evangel was revealed after the first thirteen days (of Ramaḍān); and the Zabur (Psalms) after the first eighteen days, and the Qurʾān was revealed on the twenty-fourth day of Ramaḍān.'"

According to another report: "The Books of Abrāhām are for the first night." This agrees well with "The month of Ramaḍān in which the Qurʾān was revealed"[18] and 'Verily, We have revealed it on the Night of Power.'[19] Thus it is possible that the Night of Power that year was that night, and (the Qurʾān) was brought down in its totality to the lowest heaven, then it was first brought down to earth on the fourteenth day, beginning with: 'Recite in the Name of Your Lord.'"[20]

I (Suyūṭī) say: "But there is a problem with the well-known report that (the Prophet) (peace and blessings be upon him) was called[21] (to His Mission) in the month of Rabīᶜ (sic); this (apparent difficulty) is solved (by the fact that the authorities) record that He was first informed of His Prophecy in a dream in the month of His birth (Rabīᶜ al-Awwal 12), then, (about six months later), He received Revelation while awake." This agrees with what al-Bayhaqī and others reported.

But there is really a problem with the previous *ḥadīth* because of what Ibn Abī Shayba reported in his *Faḍaʾil al-Qurʾān* (Excellencies of the Qurʾān) on the authority of Abī Qullaba: "The totality of all the Books were revealed on the night [eve?] of the twenty-fourth of Ramaḍān."

The third (opinion), also noted by Abū Shāma: "If you were to ask: 'What is the secret in (the Qurʾān's) being brought down in instalments; why wasn't it revealed as a totality like the rest of the (Heavenly) Books?' "

We (Suyūṭī and other authorities) say: "God has already answered this question, by His saying 'Those who reject faith say: "Why was not the Qurʾān revealed to the Prophet (peace and blessings be upon him) all at once . . .?" '[22] Indicating the manner in which previous Emissaries were given Revelation; and God, He is exalted, answered them: '. . . thus . . .'[23] (that is, thus We have revealed it in pieces) '. . . that we may strengthen your (that is, Muḥammad's) heart with it,'[24] that is, we will fortify your heart."

If (Revelation) were renewed in each instance, it would be more firmly embedded in (Muḥammad's) memory, and more considerate to the one given it; this requires a plethora of the Angel's visits, and renewing the contact with Him and (the Revelation) previously given Him by the Omnipotent Presence (*al-janaab al-ᶜAzīz*), such that He would feel an inexpressible joy. Thus, because of the plenitude of His meetings with Gabriel, Ramaḍan is the most propitious time.

Another opinion is that the meaning of ". . . to strengthen Your heart . . ."[25] is: "We will make You memorize it" because (He) (peace and blessings be upon him) was unlettered – that is, He could neither read nor write; thus, unlike the case with other Prophets, (Gabriel) partitioned it for Him to facilitate His memorization, for other prophets were able to read and write, and he was able to memorize it in its entirety.

Ibn Furak said: "(Some authorities hold that) the Torah was revealed in its entirety, because it was revealed to a prophet who could read and write, namely Moses; but God brought down the Qurʾān in unwritten instalments to an unlettered Prophet."

Another opinion holds that it was not brought down as a totality because of the abrogating and abrogated (*al-naasikh wa-l-mansuukh*) verses it contains, and this would be impossible were it revealed all at one time. And some of it contains (both) the answer to a question and the response to the denial to some thing said or acts committed. Ibn ᶜAbbās has made this point well: "Gabriel brought down (the Qurʾān) to (Muḥammad) to give answers about the believers' words and deeds"; and (Ibn ᶜAbbās) interpreted "And no question do they bring you but We reveal the Truth to you . . ."[26] This was reported on the authority (of Ibn ʿAbbās) by Ibn Abī Ḥātim.

Addenda

Concerning the preceding reports that the rest of the (Heavenly) Books were revealed as a totality: the most valid of the authorities' words and speech almost make it the consensus; but I (Suyūṭī) have seen that some of the most excellent (scholars) of this age deny this by claiming that there exists no proof of it, and that (the rest of the Books) were revealed in instalments like the Qurʾān.

I (Suyūṭī) say: "The truth (is in) the first (view); the verse quoted above from *Surat al-Furqan* (*25) is one of the proofs of this."

Ibn Abī Ḥātim, by way of Saʿīd Ibn Jubayr, on the authority of Ibn ʿAbbās reported that (the Prophet) said: "The Jews would say: 'O Father of al-Qāsim (that is, the Prophet)! Would that the Qurʾān be brought down as a totality as the Torah was brought down to Moses!' Then this verse (Q25, 32) was brought down."

The same meaning was transmitted on a *ḥadīth* with a different *isnād* going back to Ibn ʿAbbās using the words "the polytheists would say"; similar reports were issued by Qatada and al-Suddi.

Were you to claim that there is no clear mention of this in the Qurʾān, and that its truth is merely implied (*ʿala taqdiir thubuuti-hi*), I would respond that this is what the unbelievers say!

I (Suyūṭī) say that God's Exalted silence in its response to them in preference to giving the appropriate response against them on this, for guidance toward the clarification of His wisdom is a proof of its truth.

If all the (Heavenly) Books were brought down in instalments, then it would be sufficient to answer them with: "This is God's way (*sunna*) to bring down Books to the previous prophets, as He answered them in similar way when they said: 'What is the matter with this Emissary: He eats and drinks and walks in the streets,'[27] with His saying: 'Has God sent a man as an Emissary?'[28] and also 'Before You We have sent only men to whom We have given Revelation.'[29] They also used to say: 'How can there be an Emissary who thinks of nothing but women?' (God) answered: 'We have sent Emissaries before you who had wives and children . . . (to the end of the verse).' "[30]

Another proof of this is His, He is exalted, saying concerning the bringing down of the Torah to Moses on the Day of the Thunderclap (*yawm al-saʿaqa*): "Take what I give you, and be among those who are thankful . . .[31] We wrote laws for him in all matters in the tablets, both commanding and explaining all things. Take and hold these with firmness . . ."[32] and ". . . He cast down the tablets . . ."[33] and "When Moses' anger had subsided, he took up the tablets: in them is Guidance and Mercy . . ."[34] and "When We shook the Mount (Sinai) over them, as if it had been a canopy, and they thought that it was going to fall on them, (We said:) 'Hold firmly to what We have given you.'"[35] All of these verses prove that the Torah was brought down as a totality.

Ibn Abī Ḥātim reported by way of Saʿīd Ibn Jubayr on the authority of Ibn ʿAbbās that (the Prophet) said: "(He) gave the Torah on seven emerald tablets to Moses; in it was the clarification of all things and prohibitions, and when (Moses) brought it (to His people) He saw them in a crowd worshipping the (Golden) Calf, He threw the Torah to the ground and it was smashed; God took up (to heaven) from it six-sevenths, leaving only one-seventh."

It was also related, by way of Jaʿfar Ibn Muḥammad, on the authority of his father, on the authority of his grandfather: "He took it up"; that is, the tablets which were brought down to Moses were composed of (wood from) the Garden (of Eden)'s lote-trees; the height of the tablet was twelve cubits.

Al-Nasaʾi and others related on the authority of Ibn ʿAbbās concerning the *ḥadīth* of the temptation: "After (Moses') anger had subsided, he took the tablets, and he commanded them concerning the tasks which God had assigned for them, and they left those that were difficult for them, and they refused to accept them, so God held up the mountain over them as if it were a canopy, and (He) brought it so close to them that they feared that it would fall on them, so they accepted (their tasks)."

Ibn Abī Ḥātim related on the authority of Thābit Ibn al-Hajjāj that (the Prophet) said: "The Torah came to them in its entirety, but it was hard for them (to accept it) so they rejected it. Then God held the Mountain overshadowing them until they accepted it."

The (above-mentioned) *ḥadīth*s concerning the bringing down of the Torah as a totality are sound and clear; one may infer from the last *ḥadīth* another bit of wisdom concerning the bringing down of the Qurʾān in instalments: for when it is brought down gradually it calls out for acceptance, which is not the case were it brought down as a totality; (in the latter instance) more people would refrain from accepting it, because of the plethora of positive and negative commandments contained in it.

Al-Bukhārī clarifies this in a report on the authority of Āʾishah; she said: "The first thing revealed in the final quarter of the Qurʾān (*al-mufassal*)[36] is the *sūrah* in which there is mention of Paradise and hellfire; to the point in time that people would repent and accept Islam there was then revealed the Allowed and the Prohibited (*al-ḥalal wa-l-ḥaram*). Had the first thing to be revealed been 'Don't drink wine', they would have said that they never abandoned drinking wine; and had (the first thing) to be revealed been 'Don't commit adultery' they would have claimed that they never abandoned that too." Later, I (Suyūṭī) found this (gem of) wisdom explained clearly in *al-Makkī's al-Nāsikh wa-l-Mansūkh* (The Abrogating and the Abrogated Verses).

Section

What we can infer from the sound *ḥadīths* and from other (material) is that the Qurʾān was brought down according to necessity, five or ten, or more or less, verses at a time; because the ten verses about the Story of the Lie (*qissat al-ʿifk*)[37] were revealed as a totality; and so were the first ten verses of *Surat al-Muʾminin* (*23); the verse (Q4, 95) "... (those believers who) receive no hurt ..." was revealed as a singleton, and it is only one among others: "And if you fear poverty ..." (to the end of the verse).[38] (Indeed,) this (mid-portion of the verse) was revealed after the beginning of the verse, as we (Suyūṭī) have published (*Ḥarrar -naa- hu*) it in (our) *Asbab al-Nuzul* (Occasions of Revelation); this is only one of several verses (which have been revealed as singletons).

Ibn Ashtah reported in his *Kitāb al-Maṣāḥif* (Book of Qurʾān Manuscripts), on the authority of ʿIkrama, in his discussion of "... the setting (of the stars) ...":[39] (God) brought down the Qurʾān in instalments of three verses, four verses, and/or five verses.

Al-Nakzawī said in his *Kitāb al-Waqf* (Book of (Qurʾānic) Pauses) that the Qurʾān was revealed one verse at a time, two verses at a time, three verses at a time four verses at a time, and so on.

Ibn ʿAsākir reported by way of Abū Nudra, who said: "Abū Saʿid al-Khudri would teach us the Qurʾān five verses in the afternoon, and five verses at night; he informed us that Gabriel would bring down the Qurʾān five verses at a time."

Concerning al-Bayhaqī's report in his *al-Shuʿab* (Branches (of Knowledge)):

By way of Abū Khalada, on the authority of ʿUmar: (the Prophet) said: "Study the Qurʾān. Five verses at a time, because Gabriel would bring down the Qurʾān five verses at a time to the Prophet (peace and blessings be upon him);" and, based on a *ḥadīth* with a weak isnād going back to ʿAlī, (the Prophet) said: "The Qurʾān was revealed five verses at a time except for *Surat al-Anʾam* (verse 6); and by memorizing (the Qurʾān) five verses at a time, one won't forget it."

In fine, the import of this – if correct – is that the delivery to the Prophet (peace and blessings be upon him) was of this length so that He memorize it; sometimes (Gabriel) would bring down (to the Prophet) the remainder in instalments of other than five verses. Al-Bayhaqī clarifies this even further when he reports on the authority of Khālid Ibn Dinar, who said: "Abū al-ʿAlīya told us: 'Learn the Qurʾān five verses at a time, because the Prophet (peace and blessings be upon him) used to receive it five verses at a time from Gabriel.'"

* * *

The second question concerns the manner of the Revelation (*al-ʿinzāl*) and the Inspiration (*al-waḥy*).

Al-Aṣfahāni said at the beginning of his Qurʾān commentary: "The People of the Sunna and the Consensus agree that God's Speech (that is, the Qurʾān) was brought down; but they differ on the definition of 'revelation/bringing down (ʿ*inzāl*)'. Some take it as 'displaying the recitation', while others say: 'God, He is exalted, inspired (ʾalhama) Gabriel with His speech while (Gabriel) was in heaven above the place (*al-makaan*) (on earth of the first Revelation) when (God) taught (Gabriel the Qurʾān's) recitation; then Gabriel brought it down to the place (*al-makān*) (of the first Revelation to the Prophet).' There are two methods of transmission: the first is that the Prophet (peace and blessings be upon him) was transformed from human to angelic form, and then He received (Revelation) from Gabriel; the other[40] is that the Angel was transformed into human form so that (the Qurʾān) could be communicated to the Emissary from Him; the first (possibility) is more problematic." End (of al-Aṣfahāni's remark).

Al-Ṭayyibi said: "Perhaps the bringing down of the Qurʾān to the Prophet (peace and blessings be upon him) was that the Angel would receive (the Qurʾān) spiritually directly from God; or that (Gabriel) would memorize it from the Preserved Tablet, and then He would bring it down to the Emissary, and teach it to Him."

The *Quṭb* ("Pole" "great scholar") al-Rāzī[41] said in his *Hawashi al-Kashshāf* (Marginal Notes on al-Zamakhsharī's Qurʾān Commentary) that ʿ*inzāl* (bringing down/revelation), the same as (*īwāʾ*), is a technical term which indicates the movement of something from above to below; but neither term actually fits (God's) Speech, for in it (the term ʿ*inzāl*) is used metaphorically. Whoever claims that the Qurʾān itself stands in for God's (He is exalted) Essence must hold that its ʿ*inzāl* means that He creates the words and the letters which point out this meaning; He has affixed them to the Preserved Tablet. Whoever claims that the Qurʾān is equivalent to its words (themselves) must hold that its ʿ*inzāl* means exclusively its inscription on the Preserved Tablet. This latter view agrees with the Qurʾān's being transmitted in the manner expressed by each of the two technical terms. It is also possible that the meaning of its ʿ*inzāl* is (the Qurʾān's) firm placement in the lowest heaven, after its firm placement on the Preserved Tablet; this (also) is in accordance with the second view; the meaning of the ʿ*inzāl* of the (Heavenly) Books to the Emissaries is that the Angel would teach from God spiritually; He would keep (the Heavenly Books) on the Preserved Tablet, and (then) bring them down (to the Emissaries) and teach them. End (of this al-Rāzī section).

Others related three views on the bringing down (of the Qurʾān) to the Prophet (peace and blessings be upon him): (1) that it is both the words and the meanings: Gabriel memorized the Qurʾān from the Preserved Tablet, and brought it down. Others claim that the letters of the Qurʾān are on the Preserved Tablet, each letter of which is bigger than Qāf Mountain, and that beneath each letter are meanings that can be comprehended only by God. (2) Gabriel brought down only the specific meanings, and then (Muḥammad) (peace and blessings be upon him) learned their meanings and then expressed them in the language of the Arabs; one who claims this bases his opinion on: "the trustworthy spirit

(Gabriel) brought down[42] upon Your heart . . .".[43] (3) Gabriel gave (the Prophet) the meanings, and (the Prophet) expressed them in the language of the Arabs; the heavenly host would recite it in Arabic; then (Gabriel) would bring it down to (the Prophet) piece by piece.

Al-Bayhaqī stated: "We brought (the Qurʾān) down on the Night of Power"[44] means (and God only knows (if it's true)): We caused the Angel to hear and understand it, (then) We had the Angel bring down what He heard; thus the Angel would transfer it from above to below."

Abū Shama said: "This interpretation of *ʿinzāl* is applicable when referring either to the Qurʾān or to any part of it; the believing people of the Sunna believe in the co-eternity of the Qurʾān, and that it is an attribute standing in for the Essence of God (He is exalted)."

I (Suyūṭī) say: "From sound (marfuuʿ) *ḥadīth* from al-Nawas Ibn Sanʿān cited by al-Ṭabarānī, it is clear that Gabriel taught (the Prophet) orally from God (He is exalted): (The Prophet said:) 'When God utters words of inspiration (*al-wahy*), the earth trembles violently out of fear of God; and when the host of heaven hears it, they are stunned and fall on their faces in prostration; the first to raise his head is Gabriel, and God utters the words of His inspiration (*waḥyi-hi*) He wants to give (Gabriel), who in turn gives Inspiration to the other Angels. All the time that (Gabriel) passes through the heavens, its host asks Him: "What does our Lord say?" (Gabriel) answers: "The Truth," until He reaches the point to where (God) ordered him to stop.' "

Ibn Marduwayh reported a *ḥadīth* (whose *isnād*) was traced back to the Prophet (*rafaʿa-hu*) by Ibn Masʿūd: (The Prophet said:) "When God speaks words of Inspiration (*al-wahy*) the host of the heavens hears it as the pealing of a chain beaten on a smooth rock; they are terrified because they recognize it as one of the Events of (the Final) Hour." The original (version of this *ḥadīth*) is found in the *Ṣaḥīḥ* (Collection of Sound Traditions (author unstated)).

From the Qurʾān Commentary (*tafsīr*) of ʿAlī Ibn Sahl al-Nisābūrī:

"A group of scholars (*ʿulamaaʾ*) claimed that the Qurʾān was brought down as a totality on the Night of Power from the Preserved tablet to an Abode they call 'the Abode of Glory'; then Gabriel memorized it, and the host of the heavens fainted at the sublimity of God's Speech. Then Gabriel passed among them, and they awakened and said: 'What does Your Lord say?' He[45] answered: 'The Truth, that is, the Qurʾān; this is the meaning of His saying: ". . . when terror is removed from their hearts . . ." '[46] So Gabriel brought (the Qurʾān) down to the Abode of Glory, and dictated it to the writing scribes, that is, the angels; this is the meaning of His (He is exalted) saying: '(Written) by the hands of scribes, honorable and pious.' "[47]

Al-Juwaynī said: "God's revealed Speech is of two parts: In one part He said to Gabriel: 'Say to the Prophet to whom you are sent: "God says: 'Do such and such.' " ' Gabriel understood what His Lord said, then He would bring it down to that Prophet what God had said; but (Gabriel's) expression would not be in the same words as when God would tell (Gabriel) 'Say (such-and-such) to someone (in particular) "The Angel tells you: 'Strive to serve; gather your troops for battle . . .'" for the Emissary might say: "The Angel tells me not to ignore my service, and not to leave my troops scattered about, and that I should roust them into battle . . .".' This can in no way be interpreted as tainted either by falsification or abridgement."

The other[48] part is when God tells Gabriel: "Recite this Book to the Prophet", upon which Gabriel would recite the words verbatim and without alteration, as when a king dictates a letter and entrusts it to a loyal secretary. God would say: "Dictate this to so-and-so, and (Gabriel) would change neither a word nor a letter of it." End (of al-Juwaynī quotation).

I (Suyūṭī) say: "The second part refers to the Qurʾān; the first is the *Sunna*, according to the reports that Gabriel would bring down the *Sunna* the same way He would bring down the Qurʾān. From this it follows that one is permitted to transmit the Sunna according to its meaning (rather than verbatim), because Gabriel transmitted it according to its meaning. But it is not possible to transmit recitation by meaning, because Gabriel transmitted it verbatim; also, God did not allow (Gabriel) to inspire (*iihaaʾi-hi*) (the Prophet) according to the meaning: the secret in this is that what is intended is worship with God's own words, with the miraculous inimitability (*al-ʿiʿjaaz*) therein; for it is impossible for anyone to invent expressions that could substitute for it, and because underneath every letter of it there are meanings that the multitudes will never comprehend; and no one can produce anything which comprises what it comprises; it is also a facilitation for the Nation that their Revelation came down to them in two parts: one part they see as inspired Words; and one part they understand in meaning. Had all of it been brought down to be related verbatim, that would indeed be onerous. Had (all of it been brought down according to) meaning, it would not have been believed because of alterations and corruptions (in the wording); consider!" And I (Suyūṭī) have seen what supports Juwaynī words from past scholars.

Ibn Abī Ḥātim reported, by way of ʿUqayl, on the authority of al-Zuhri, that when (the Prophet) was asked about Inspiration (*al-wahy*), he said: "Inspiration is what God inspires a certain prophet with; He plants it firmly in his heart; He speaks to him and dictates to him; this is God's Speech. (The Prophet) neither speaks it nor dictates it to anyone, neither does he order its being written down; but he converses about it with people, and clarifies to them that God ordered him to explain it to the people, and to deliver it to them."

Section

The Scholars (*al-ʿulamāʾ*) discussed the different manners of Inspiration (*al-waḥy*). One of the views is that the Angel brought it like the ring of a bell as it is related in the *Ṣaḥīḥ*. In the *Musnad of Aḥmad*, on the authority of ʿAbdullah Ibn ʿUmar: "(Someone) said: 'I asked the Prophet (peace and blessings be upon him): "Do you feel the Inspiration?" (The Prophet) answered: "I hear ringing, then I become quiet; yet Inspiration has never come to me but that I expect my soul to shatter."'" Al-Khattābī said: "This means that the sound would come down in bursts which He would hear but at first were not explained to Him; later, He would explain it to (the Prophet). Another view holds that the sound was the beating of the Angel's wings; the wisdom in (the Angel's) doing this is for (the Prophet) to hear the Inspiration (exclusively), leaving room for no other sound. It is also related in the *Ṣaḥīḥ* that this was the most excruciating part of the Inspiration for (the Prophet). Another opinion holds that this would happen when a verse concerning the Threat (of hellfire) or menace was being brought down.

2 (Gabriel) would breathe the Words into (the Prophet's) soul (*rawʿ*), as (the Prophet) (peace and blessings be upon him) said: "The Holy Spirit (*al-ruuh al-qudus*) breathed into my soul." This was reported by al-Hakim; these returns (us) to the first situation, or the one after it, that (Gabriel) would bring it to (the Prophet) in one of the two ways, and would breathe it into his soul.

3 (Gabriel) would come to him in the form of a man and would speak to him, as it is reported in the *Ṣaḥīḥ*: (The Prophet said:) "Sometimes the Angel would take the form of a man and speak to me and I would internalize all of it." In his Ṣaḥīḥ, Abū ʿAwāna added (the words) ". . . and this was the easiest upon him."

4 (Gabriel) would come to (the Prophet) while he was asleep. Some people included *Surat al-Kawthar* (*108) in this; see above.[49]

5 God would speak directly to (the Prophet) while he was awake, as during the Night of the Ascension;[50] or while he was asleep, as in this *ḥadīth* related by Muʿadh: (The Prophet said:) "My Lord came to me and said: 'What does the High Host (*al-malaʾ al-aʿla*) disagree about . . . (until the end of the *ḥadīth*).'"

As far as I (Suyūṭī) know, there is nothing in the Qurʾān of this type; it is true that it is possible that one might consider the last two verses of *Surat al-Baqara* (*2) (as discussed just above) as such, and part of *Surat al-Ḍuḥa* (*93); and also (the *sūrah* of) A-lam Nashraḥ (*94).

Ibn Abī Ḥātim reported one of ʿUdayy Ibn Thābit's *ḥadīths*: The Emissary of God said: "I asked my Lord a question I wish I hadn't asked, namely: 'O My Lord, You took Abrāhām as a Friend (*khalil*), and You spoke directly to Moses . . . (to the end of the *ḥadīth*).' God answered: 'O Muḥammad! Did[51] I[52] not find you an orphan and give You shelter;[53] and wandering, and I gave you guidance;[54] and poor, and I enriched you?;[55] and[56] have I not expanded your chest (for acceptance of the Message) and lifted your burden from you;[57] and have I not raised your fame, so that whenever I am mentioned you are mentioned with me!'"

Points to be learned

The Imām Aḥmad reported in his History by way of Dawūd Ibn Abī Hind, on the authority of al-Shaʿbi, who related that Prophecy was brought down to the Prophet (peace and blessings be upon him) when he was forty years old. (The Angel) Isrāfil was involved in the (transmission of) the Prophecy for three years during which (Isrāfil) would teach him the Word and the Meaning (*al-shayʾ*), but He would not bring down the Qurʾān to (the Prophet's) tongue. After three years had passed, Gabriel became involved with the Prophecy and transmitted the Qurʾān to the Prophet for twenty years.

Ibn ʿAskar related that the wisdom in the assignment of Isrāfil is because He is responsible for the Trumpet which will herald the destruction of creation and the coming of the (Final) Hour; (the Prophet's) Prophecy announces the imminence of the Hour and the end of Inspiration (*al-wahy*). Just as Alexander the Great (*Dhū al-Qarnayn*) was entrusted to Rayafil who covers the earth and Khālid b. Sinan was entrusted to Mālik the guardian of hellfire.

Ibn Abī Ḥātim related on the authority of Ibn Sābiṭ, who said that in the Archetype of the Book (*ʾumm al-kitab*) everything in existence until the Day of Resurrection is written down. God entrusted three of the angels to guard it:[58] He entrusted to Gabriel the Books and the Inspiration (*al-wahy*) to the Prophets, victory in war with the eradication of (entire) peoples, if that be God's wish. (God) entrusted Michael with rain water (lit: "drops", *al-qutr*) and plants. He assigned the Angel of Death with seizing souls. When the Day of Resurrection comes, they will compare what they have memorized with what the Archetype of the Book contains, and they will find it to be the same (*fa-yajidūna-hu sawāʾan*).

(Ibn Abī Ḥātim) also related, on the authority of ʿAtaʾ Ibn al-Ṣaib, who said: "The first one to be considered is Gabriel, because He was God's faithful communicator to (God's) Emissaries."

Second thing to be learned

Al-Ḥakim and al-Bayhaqī related, on the authority of Zayd Ibn Thābit, that the Prophet (peace and blessings be upon him) said: "The Qurʾān was revealed in *tafkhim* (velarized, or emphatic pronunciation), as it is (*ka-hayʾati-hi*)[59] 'justification or warning'[60] 'the two mountain passes;'[61] 'Isn't His the Creation and the Command?' "[62] And similar (verses)." I (Suyūṭī) say that it is true what Ibn al-Anbārī related in his *Kitab al-Waqf wa-l-Ibtidaʾ* (Book of Where One Pauses and Where One Begins (in reciting the Qurʾān)) based on a *ḥadīth* which he had traced back to the Prophet, according to which the marfuʿ of the Qurʾān was revealed in *tafkhim*, and the other parts of it were revealed in ordinary language; this is based on a report from ʿAmar Ibn ʿAbd al-Mālik, a certain *ḥadīth* relator.[63]

Another thing to learn

Ibn Abī Ḥātim related, on the authority of Sufyān al-Thawrī: "Inspiration (*wahy*) came down only in Arabic, then it was translated by each Prophet for his people."

Another thing to learn

Ibn Saʿd related that Āʾishah said: "Whenever the Prophet (peace and blessings be upon him) received Inspiration (*al-wahy*), his head would twitch, he would foam at the sides of his mouth, he would feel cold in his incisors, and he would break into a sweat until it flowed down like pearls."

The third inquiry: the seven *aḥruf* (plural of *ḥarf*) readings in which the Qurʾān was revealed

I (Suyūṭī) say that the *ḥadīth*: "The Qurʾān was revealed in seven ahruf" was related by a large group of Companions: Ubayy Ibn Kaʿb, Anas (Ibn Mālik), Hudhayfa Ibn al-Yaman, Zayd Ibn Arqam, Samūra Ibn Jundab, Sulayman Ibn Surad, Ibn ʿAbbās, Ibn Masʿud, ʿAbd-al-Raḥmān Ibn ʿAuf, ʿUthmān Ibn Affan, ʿUmar Ibn al-Khaṭṭāb, ʿAmr Ibn Abī Salamah, ʿAmr Ibn al-ʿĀs, Muʿadh Ibn Jabal, Hishām Ibn Ḥakim, Abū Bakra, Abū Juham, Abū Saʿīd al-Khudri, Abū Talḥa al-Anṣāri, Abū Hurayra, and Umm Ayyūb. These are the twenty-one Companions; Abū ʿUbayd has specified that this is an often repeated Tradition.

Abū Yaʿlā related in his *musnad*: "I remember, by God [Ib. has /Allāh/here, which I take for a misprinted *wa-llaahi*], a man heard the Prophet (peace and blessings be upon him) say: 'Verily, the Qurʾān was revealed in seven *ahruf*, each one of which is perspicuous and sufficient.'[64] When he stood up, the people stood up until they couldn't be counted, and they gave witness to this, and he said: 'I give witness with them.' "

The difference in views concerning the Qurʾān's being revealed in seven *aḥruf*[65]

I (Suyūṭī) will survey the necessary (authoritative) material conveyed. I maintain that there are about forty differences concerning the meaning of this *ḥadīth*.

1 This is one of the problematic questions that can never be answered: *ḥarf* may be a technical term for a letter of the alphabet; or a word; or a meaning; or a proposition (*jihah*). So said Ibn Saʿdān the grammarian.

2 "Seven" does not mean "seven" in the literal sense of the numeral; its intention is rather to simplify, facilitate and generalize. The expression "seven" expresses a plethora within the single digits, just as "seventy" does for the decades and "seven hundred" for the hundreds: the specific numeral is not the intention. ʿAyyāḍ and his followers leaned towards this view. Ibn ʿAbbās, in a *ḥadīth* reported

in both the *Ṣaḥīḥs* (of al-Bukhārī and Muslim), countered this: "The Emissary of God (peace and blessings be upon him) said: 'Gabriel dictated (the Qurʾān) to me in one *harf*, then I would repeat it; we continued in this manner until He concluded with the seventh *harf*.'" According to a *ḥadīth* related by Ubayy in Muslim ('s *Ṣaḥīḥ*: the Prophet said:) "Verily, my Lord sent me to recite the Qurʾān in a *harf*; I asked that He be more lenient to my Nation, so He sent me to recite it in two *harfs*; then I asked Him again to be more lenient to my Nation, so He sent to me to recite it in seven *harfs*."

In a formulation from (the Prophet) in al-Nasāʾī ('s *sunan* – Collection of sound *ḥadīth*s, the Prophet said:) "Verily, Gabriel and Michael approached me; Gabriel sat on my right and Michael on my left. Gabriel said: 'Recite the Qurʾān in one *ḥarf*.' Michael said: 'Add one to that,'" and He continued thus until He reached seven *ḥarfs*.

And from a *ḥadīth* transmitted by Abū Bakra: "(The Prophet added). 'So I gazed at Michael and I became silent. For I realized that He had finished adding (*harfs*).'"

3 The (meaning of this term) is that there are seven (variant) readings; but this is contradicted by the fact that there are but few such words e.g. ". . . worshipped idols . . ."[66] ". . . do not say to (your parents): 'uffin'".[67]

4 I (Suyūṭī) would answer that the intention is that each word can be read in one, two, three or more ways up to seven; the difficulty with this is that some words can be read in even more ways; this can count as the fourth view.

5 Qutayba related that what is meant by (seven *harfs*) is the type of change that may occur in each expression. First: we may have a change in vowel with no corresponding change in either form or meaning, as in: "let no harm be done to or by any scribe"[68] reading either *yu Darra* or *yu Darru*. Second: we may have a change in a verb, like "lengthen" (*baaʿid*)"[69] or *baaʿada* ("He lengthened"), expressing either the past tense (*bāʿada*), or the imperative (*al-Ṭalab*): (*bāʿid*). Third, we can have a change in expression (specifically, the verb form) as in: "We will raise (the dead bones)"[70] with either (form IV) *nunshizu-haa*; or (form I) *nanshuru-hā*.[71] Fourth, we can have a change of one letter with another with a close articulation point: "clusters of banana fruit"[72] with either *Ṭalḥin* or *Ṭalʿin manḍūdin*. Fifth, we can have a switch in (two successive) words: "and when the agony of death justly takes them"[73] by switching the last two words *al-mawti* and *bi-l-Haqqi*. Sixth, changes can be made by adding and subtracting (words): "By Him that created the male and the female . . ."[74] we may omit the first two words *wa-mā khalaqa*; and change the reading of the third word from *al-dhakara* to (the oath form) *al-dhakari*. Seventh: we may substitute one (synonymous) word for another: "(mountains) like tufts of carded wool . . .[75] (for

the first word in) *ka-l-ʿihni al-manfūsh* we may substitute *ka-l-Ṣūfi* (with no perceptible change in meaning).

Qāsim Ibn Thābit objected to this licence; most (of the Arabs of the Prophet's) time knew neither how to write nor to trace (*al-rasm*); they merely knew the sounds and how to pronounce them (lit: the letters and their points of articulation). I (Suyūṭī) would reply to this that this does not in any way detract from Qutayba's view, because of the possibility that the aforementioned limitation is an agreed-upon position, and is thus deserving of further research.

6 Abū al-Faḍl al-Rāzī said in his *al-lawaʾiḥ* that there are only seven aspects of differences in speech. First: the difference in nouns, singular, dual, or plural; and (gender), masculine or feminine. Second: the difference (in the "tenses") of the verbs, perfect, imperfect and (positive) imperative (*al-ʿamr*). Third: desinence (declension, final case vocalization). Fourth: subtracting and adding. Fifth: moving (a word or an expression) forward or backward. Sixth: permutation (*ʾibdāl*). Seventh: various pronunciations, e.g. (*al-ʿimālah*) – that is, the inflection of *a* and *aa* towards that of *i* and *ii*; ordinary pronunciation as opposed to (*tafkhiim*) velarized ("emphatic") pronunciation; assimilation as opposed to unassimilated pronunciation, etc. This is (the end of) the sixth view.

7 Some of the authorities hold that it is the manner of speech in transmission, as to whether the pronunciation was with assimilation or without it; in normal speech or in velarized ("emphatic") speech; whether it was with *ʾimaalah* or without (that is, with *ʾishbaaʿ* – "impletion"); with the full pronunciation of the lenghthened *alif* or not; with or without abbreviation, with or without consonant doubling (gemination), with or without consonant softening (*talyīn*). This is the end of the seventh view.

8 Ibn Jazarī said that he had studied the various readings: sound, false, weak and objectionable. They all have to do with seven aspects, to which there is no exception: whether it be a difference in the vowels without changing either the meaning or the form, e.g. "niggardly"[76] read in four different permutations, namely: (*al-bukhli*; *al-bukhuli*; *al-bakhli*; *al-bakhali*); or, changing only the meaning, as in "Ādam received the names from God . . ."[77] (the last word of which may be read *kalimaatun* or *kalimaatin*; or a change of letter, retaining the consonantal skeleton of the word (*al-Surah*), but changing the meaning, as in ". . . (what the soul) has done . . .",[78] that is, one may read either *tabluu* or *tatluu* ("followed"); or the reverse of this, as in spelling ". . . (straight) path"[79] (*al-Sirāṭ*) either with a *saad* or a *Siin*; or substituting for ". . . go (where you are commanded) . . ."[80] (*wa-mDuu* (the synonymous) *wa-sʿaw*);[81] or one may switch the word order as in ". . . then they kill and are killed . . ."[82] (to: ". . . then they are killed and kill"); or by adding or subtracting, as in ". . . (Abrāhām) . . .

enjoined (the Faith on his children . . .)", that is, one may add an initial *alif* (to the form II verb) *waSSa* (to form the form IV synonym) *ʾawSa*; there are no exceptions to these seven types of differences. He added that differences regarding readings with or without assimilation; with or without vowel coloration (*ʾishmaam*) or slurring of the final vowel (*al-rawm*); pronouncing fully or not; transmission or permutation (*ʾibdāl*); none of these produce variants that change the expression or the meaning; for they are all different ways of carrying out (the Recitation); no exceptional case exists.

Thus end (the comments of al-Jazarī). This is the eighth view. An example of switching the order (of words) is the generally accepted reading of ". . . thus does God stamp the heart of every doubting transgressor",[83] where Ibn Masʿud exchanged the order of the words "every" and "heart".

9 The meaning (of "seven *ḥarfs*") is the seven connotations of synonymous meanings using different expressions, as in the following expressions for "come (here)": *ʾaqbil*, *taʿāla*, *halumma*, *ʿajjil* (Ib. has an additional *shadda* here, incorrectly), *ʾasriʿ*. Sufyān Ibn ʿUyayna, Ibn Jarīr (al-Tabari), Ibn Wahb and others leaned towards this view. Ibn ʿAbd al-Barr attributed this view to the majority of the scholars (*al-ʿulamāʾ*). This view is strengthened by Aḥmad and al-Ṭabarānī's presenting one of Abū Bakra's *ḥadīth*s: "(The Prophet said:) 'Verily, Gabriel said: "O Muḥammad! Recite the Qurʾān with one *ḥarf*"; Michael said: "Add (one) to it . . . until (the Prophet) arrived at seven *ḥarfs*." (The Prophet) said: 'Each *ḥarf* is clearly sufficient:[84] no punishment verse concludes with mercy, and no mercy verse concludes with punishment; it is as one may say (the synonyms for "come here"): *taʿāla*, *ʾaqbil*, *halumma*, *adhab*, *ʾasriʿ*, or *ʿajjil*.' " This wording was related by Aḥmad; its *isnād* is good. Aḥmad and al-Ṭabarānī relates a similarly worded *ḥadīth* on the authority of Ibn Masʿūd. According to Abū Dawūd on the authority of Ubayy: "(The Prophet) said: 'I say the words "Hearing", "Knowing", "Omnipotent" and "Wise" (appropriately), so as not to confuse a punishment verse with a mercy verse, nor to confuse a mercy verse with a punishment verse.' "

Aḥmad relates a *ḥadīth* on the authority of Abū Hurayra: "(The Prophet said:) 'The Qurʾān was revealed in seven *ḥarfs*: "Knowing, Wise, Forgiving and Merciful." ' " He also reported on the authority of ʿUmar, (that the Prophet said:) "The entire Qurʾān is true, as long as one doesn't misinterpret forgiveness as punishment, nor punishment as forgiveness." The *isnāds* of these *ḥadīths* are valid.

Ibn ʿAbd al-Barr said that what is meant by this is to give examples of the *harfs* in which the Qurʾān was revealed, meanings which agree in their concepts but differ in their sounds, where no meaning may contradict itself, for example, mercy and punishment which are opposites and contradictory. Then he related a *ḥadīth* on the authority of Ubayy Ibn Kaʿb that he would read ". . . as long as it gives light, they walk (*mashaw*) in it",[85] he might substitute for "walk in it",[86] "go in it (*saʿaw fi-haa*)." Ibn Masʿūd was wont to recite ". . . (will say) to the believers: 'Wait for us . . . (*inẓirūnā*)'," and substitute for "Wait for us . . .", "Slow down for us (*ʾamhiluu-naa ʿakhkhiruu-naa*)."

Al-Ṭaḥāwī said that this is merely a permission given at a time when for many of them recitation using (exactly) the same words was difficult due to their lack of knowledge and the pressure of exact memorization; later, this was abrogated when conditions changed (lit: "the excuse was no longer in effect") as writing and memorization became easier.[87] Thus held Ibn ʿAbd al-Barr and al-Baqalani, among others.

In Abū ʿUbayd's Faḍāʾil, he reports a *ḥadīth* by way of ʿAwn Ibn ʿAbdullah: "Ibn Masʿud dictated to a fellow: 'Verily, the tree of Zaqqum is the food of the sinner (*al-ʿathiim*) . . .'.[88] But the man (who lisped) recited: '. . . the food of the orphan (*al-yatiim*).' Ibn Masʿud tried to correct him, but the man's tongue was not up to it. (Finally) Ibn Masʿūd asked the man, can you recite '. . . the food of the fornicator (*al-fājir*)?' and was answered in the affirmative. Ibn Masʿūd said to him 'Do so' ".

10 The meaning of ("seven *ḥarfs*") is seven Arabic dialects. This is the view of Abū ʿUbayd, Thaʿlab, al-Azharī and others. Ibn ʿAṭiyya objected to this, and he was supported in this by al-Bayhaqī in his Shuʿab. The difficulty is that the (pre-Islamic) Arabic dialects number more than seven. I (Suyūṭī) would argue that what is meant here is the (seven) most eloquent of them. We have a *ḥadīth* on the authority of Abū Sālih, on the authority of Ibn ʿAbbās, that (the Prophet said:) "The Qurʾān was revealed in seven dialects; five of them from the clan of ʿAjuz of the tribe of Hawāzin.[89] Saʿd Ibn Bakr, Jusham Ibn Bakr, Naṣr Ibn Muʿāwiya and Thaqif were all members of this clan; they were called 'the Elite (*ʿulyaa*) of Hawāzin.' Abū ʿAmr Ibn al-ʿAlāʾ used to say that the Elite of Hawāzin and the dregs of the Tamīm (tribe) – that is, the clan of Banu Daram – were the most eloquent of Arabic speakers."[90]

Abū ʿUbayd reported from a different source, on the authority of Ibn ʿAbbās, that (the Prophet) said: "The Qurʾān was revealed in the dialect of the two Kaʿbs, Kaʿb (Ibn Luʾayy, the grandfather of)[91] Quraysh and Kaʿb (Ibn ʿAmr, the grandfather of)[92] Khuzaʿa." He was asked: "How so?" He replied: "They were one integral abode: the Khuzaʿa were neighbours of the Quraysh, and this made their dialect easier for them."

Abū Ḥātim al-Sijistānī said that (the Qurʾān) was revealed in the dialects of Quraysh, Hudhayl, Tamīm, Azd, Rabīʿ, Hawāzin and Saʿd Ibn Bakr. Ibn Qutayba rejected this, claiming that it was revealed (only) in the dialect of Quraysh. He supported this by quoting "We have sent Emissaries only in the language of their people."[93] Thus the "seven dialects" refers to those of the sub-clans of Quraysh. This is the opinion of Abū ʿAlī al-ʿAhwāzī.

Abū ʿUbayd said that the intention is not that every word can be recited in the seven dialects, but that the seven dialects are dispersed in it: some of them are in the dialect of Quraysh, some in the dialect of Hudhayl, some in the dialect of Hawāzin, some in the dialect of al-Yaman, etc. He added that some dialectal (pronunciations) were more felicitous and more fortunate.

Some held that (the Qurʾān) was revealed in the dialect of Mudar specifically, basing this on ʿUmar's claim: "The Qurʾān was revealed in the dialect of Mudar." (In his *al-Tamhīd li-mafī al-Muwaṭṭaʾ min al-Maʿānī wa-l-Asānīd*, Abū ʿUmar)[94] Ibn ʿAbd al-Barr reported that the seven Mudarites Hudhayl, Kinana, Qays, Dabba, Taym, Ribab, Asad Ibn Khuzayma and Quraysh, were named specifically. These are the tribes of Mudar, and they comprise seven dialects.

Abū Shama transmitted, on the authority of some of the elders (*al-shuyuukh*), that (the Prophet) said: "The Qurʾān was revealed at first in the language of Quraysh, and the more eloquent Arabs were able to recite it; later, it was permitted to the Arabs to recite it in their own dialects familiar to them through usage, despite the differences in phrasing and final vocalization (that would result). No one was asked to change from his own dialect to another, due to the extreme difficulty involved. When they were especially zealous, they would ask for a simplification to understand the meaning."

Another authority added to this that the permission just mentioned does not imply arbitrariness, lest anyone change (any) word to its synonym in his dialect; rather what is required is knowledge gained from actually hearing the recitation from the Prophet (peace and blessings be upon him).

Some of the authorities pointed out a difficulty in this: Gabriel would have to have pronounced the same expression seven times! I (Suyūṭī) would answer that he would have to do this only if all seven *ḥarfs* could be conflated into one expression, but we have said that Gabriel came each time with one *ḥarf*, (and add one to it), until there were seven. This view is also refuted by the report of ʿUmar Ibn al-Khaṭṭāb and Hishām Ibn Hakim, both to whom spoke in the Qurayshiy dialect and were of the same Qurayshiy tribe, that their respective recitations (of the Qurʾān) differed; it is absurd to believe that ʿUmar did not know his own dialect: this proves that the meaning of the "seven *ḥarfs*" cannot be the dialects.

11 This view is refuted by the foregoing *ḥadīths*: it is that the "seven *ḥarfs*" are the seven types of speech (*sinf*); those who hold this view differ on which they are. They were named: (positive) commandment and prohibition, allowed and forbidden, the "unambiguous" Qurʾānic verses and the "ambiguous ones (*al-muhkamat wa-l-mutashabihat*)" and parables. Al-Ḥākim and al-Bayhaqī support this view when they report, on the authority of Ibn Masʿūd, that the Prophet (peace and blessings be upon him) said: "The first part of the Book came down from one Gate (of Heaven) and in one *ḥarf*, and then the remainder of the Qurʾān came down from seven Gates and in seven *ḥarfs*: scolding and commanding, allowing and prohibiting, the 'unambiguous' and the 'ambiguous', etc . . .".

Some authorities reject this, because the reference is not to the seven *ḥarfs* mentioned above that are referred to in other *ḥadīths* because the context excludes this; but it is clear the intention is that a word may be recited two, three, and up to seven ways, in order to simplify and facilitate. One thing may not be both allowed and prohibited in the same verse.

Al-Bayhaqī said that the meaning of the "seven *ḥarfs*" here is the ways (*al-ʾanwāʿ*) in which (the Qurʾān) was revealed, and in the other *ḥadīths* what is meant are the dialects in which it may be recited. Someone else objected that whoever interprets (*ʾawwala*) the seven *ḥarfs* thus is mistaken: it is impossible that one *ḥarf* be prohibition, and not all the others; or that one *ḥarf* be permitting, and not all the others; and it is not possible that the Qurʾān be recited entirely as permitting, or entirely as prohibiting, or as entirely consisting of parables.

Ibn ʿAṭiya called this view weak because the consensus (*al-ʿijmaaʿ*) is that meaning cannot be stretched to include forbidding what is permissible, nor to permitting what is forbidden, without changing the accepted meaning of these words.

Al-Māwardī held that this is wrong: (The Prophet) (peace and blessings be upon him) implied permission to recite (the Qurʾān) in all seven *ḥarfs*, and the exchange of one *ḥarf* with another. Muslims are agreed that it is not permitted to substitute a legal verse with a parabolic verse.

Abū ʿAlī al-Ahwazī and Abū al-ʿAla al-Hamadani said that when (the Prophet) said: ". . . scolding and commanding . . ." etc., it was a continuation of another statement, namely that "it is scolding", meaning the Qurʾān. Thus the interpretation (*tafsīr*) of the "seven *ḥarfs*" is not relevant – people only imagined this because of the agreement in number. In support of this (there exist *ḥadīths*) transmitted through different ways that quote ". . . scolding and commanding . . ." in the accusative case; the implication is that this is the manner in which (the Qurʾān) came down in the seven types of commands.

Abū Shama said that it is possible that the above-mentioned interpretation (*al-tafsīr*) is of the "types" and not of the "*ḥarfs*". That is to say that these are seven of the types of speech and its parts – that is, God brought down (the Qurʾān) in these seven types (*sinf*); it is not to be abridged in any one type like the other (Revealed) Books.

12 Others hold that (the expression "the seven *ḥarfs*") refers to the absolute and the limited, the general and the particular, the text and its interpretation (*al-muʾawwal*), the "abrogating" verses and the "abrogated" verses, the general and the specific (*al-mufassar*), the exception and its parts (*wa-ʿaqsāmu-h*). Shaydhala reported this from the legists (*al-fuqahāʾ*). This is the twelfth view.

13 Others hold that ("the seven *ḥarfs*") refers to elision and syndesis (connecting words with particles), switching of order, metaphor, repetition, metonymy and truth and metaphor, the general and the specific, the obvious and the strange. This[95] is related on the authority of the grammarians. This is the thirteenth view.

14 Others hold that the meaning (of the "seven *ḥarfs*") is masculine and feminine, protosis and apodosis (the two parts of a conditional sentence), diptocy and triptocy (final vowels, without or with nunation), oaths and their answers, plural and singular, diminutiveness and maximization, and the differing usage of particles. He related this on the authority of the grammarians; this is the fourteenth (view).

15 Another view is that it means rules for seven kinds of behaviour: asceticism and contentment with absolute conviction; service with humility and nobility; perseverance in poverty; striving and self-reflection with fear and ease; humility and begging forgiveness with satisfaction and gratitude; patience with contemplation and love; desire with watchfulness; He told this on the authority of the *Sūfis*. This is the fifteenth (view).

16 That, (the "seven *ḥarfs*) refers to the seven sciences: the science of creating and becoming; the science of Unicity (God's Oneness) and dissociation of God's Oneness from all taint, the science of the attributes of God's Essence; the science of the attributed actions (towards God),[96] the science of forgiveness and punishment, the science of the Final Mustering and the Judgement, and the science of the Prophecies.[97]

* * *

Ibn Hajar said that al-Qurtubiyy mentioned, on the authority of Ibn Habban[98] that the differences in the views about the meaning of the "seven *ḥarfs*" reached thirty-five, of which al-Qurtubiy mentioned only five. I (Suyūṭī) did not come across what Ibn Habban said although I looked into all the possible sources for it.

I say: Ibn al-Naqib said, in the introduction to his *tafsīr*, on the authority of (Ibn Ḥabban), by way of the al-Sharf al-Muzni al-Mursī: "Ibn Habban said concerning the 'seven *ḥarfs*' that the scholars had thirty-five differing views. Some of them hold that it refers to scolding and commanding, permitting and forbidding, 'unambiguous' (verses) and 'ambiguous' (verses), and parables."

2 Others hold that it refers to permitting and forbidding, commanding, prohibiting, and scolding, information on what is already in existence, and parables.

The third group hold that it refers to the Promise (of Heaven) and the Threat (of hell), permitting and prohibiting, exhortations and parables.

The fourth group: command and prohibition, giving glad tidings and warning, stories, and parables.

5 "Unambiguous" (verses) and "ambiguous" verses, abrogating (verses) and abrogated (verses), the particular and the general and parables.

6 Command and scolding, frightening and terrifying, strife and narrative, and parables.

7 Command and prohibition, definition and science, (mystical) secrets, exoteric (surface) and esoteric (deeper) insight (into the meaning of the text).

8 Abrogating and abrogated, Promise and Threat, restraint and discipline, and warning.

9 Permitting and forbidding, introducing and narrative virtues, and punishments.

10 Positive commands, scoldings, parables and information (*ʾanbaaʾ*); remonstration, admonishment and narrative.

11 Permitting, prohibiting and parables; specificity (*manṣūṣ*); narrative and allowances (permissions).

12 Exoteric (meanings) and esoteric (meanings), individual duties and lament; the specific and the general and parables.

13 Positive and negative commandments, the Promise and the Threat, licence, permissions, guidance and lessons (*al-ʿiʿtibaar*).

14 The previous and the subsequent, individual duties and *Huduud* (that is, based on Islamic Law) punishments, admonishments, the "ambiguous" (verses) and parables.

15 Particular and general (*mujmal*); judged, regret, and (acceptance of the *qādī*'s) decision (*Ḥatm*) and parables.

16 The command to accept the *qadi*'s judgement and the command to regret; (cases in which there is a) prohibition of the same; information and permissions.

17 Commanding the individual, and prohibiting the acceptance of the *qadi*'s decision; the command to lament, and the prohibition of a guide; the Promise and the Threat; and narrative.

18 Words have only seven aspects: the "particular" to mean the "particular"; the "general" to mean the "general"; or, the "general" to mean the "particular"; or the expression "particular" to mean "general". A revealed word is in no need of interpretation (*tanzīl*); a word's meaning may be unknown to all but the scholars (*al-ʿulamāʾ*), and another word may not be understood correctly except by those firmly grounded in knowledge.

19 Demonstration of Lordship, consolidation of Unicity, Glorifying the Godhead, worshipping God, eschewing polytheism, longing for (Final) Reward, and being terrified of punishment.

20 Seven dialects: five from Hawāzin, and two from the rest of the Arabs.

21 Seven different dialects from among all the Arab (tribes), each *ḥarf* from each dialect from a well-known tribe.

22 Seven dialects: four from the (clan) of ʿAjz Hawāzin: Saʿd Ibn Bake, Jushm Ibn Bakr, and Naṣr Ibn Muʿāwiya; and three from Quraysh.

23 Seven dialects: the dialect of Quraysh, one of the dialects of al-Yaman, the dialect[99] of Jurhum, one of the dialects of Hawāzin, the dialect of Quḍāʿa, one of the dialects of Tamīm, and one of the dialects of Tayy.

24 The dialect of the two Kaʿbs, Kaʿb Ibn ʿAmr and Kaʿb Ibn Luʾay, theirs being seven dialects.

25 The differing dialects of all the Arab tribes where terms are synonymous, e.g. "come (here)" is *halumma*, *hāti*, *taʿāla*, and *ʾaqbil*.

26 The seven readings of seven of the Companions: Abū Bakr, ʿUmar, ʿUthmān, ʿAlī, Ibn Masūd, Ibn ʿAbbās, Ubay Ibn Kaʿb – may God (He is forever exalted) be pleased with them.

27 The glottal stop, *imālah*, short vowels *a* and *i*, emphatic (velarized) recitation, extension and abbreviation.

28 Diptocy and verbal nouns, exceptional scansion and rhymed prose (*sajʿ*), and the various dialects where they have synonyms.

29 One word vocalized seven ways, resulting in one meaning even if the pronunciation is different.

30 The most important of the letters of the alphabet (lit: "the mothers of the letters"): the *alif*, *bāʾ*, *jīm*, *dāl*, *rāʾ*, *sīn* and *ʿayn*, for around them circulate the speech of the Arabs.

31 They are the Lord's names, e.g. "The Forgiving, the Merciful"; "The Hearer, the Seer"; "The Knowing, the Wise".

32 It is a verse about the attributes of (God's) Essence; a verse whose interpretation (*tafsīru-hā*) is in another verse; and a verse whose clarification (*bayaanu-haa*) is in the true *Sunna*. Also, a verse in the story of the prophets and emissaries, and a verse about creation of the world (lit: "of things"), a verse describing the Garden, and a verse describing hellfire.

33 A verse concerning the Maker (*al-Sāniʿ*), a verse about the verification of His Unicity, a verse about His attributes, a verse about the verification of His emissaries, a verse about the verification of His Books, a verse about the verification of Islam, and a verse negating unbelief.

34 Seven aspects of the attributes of the Essence of God, which are inexplicable (*llatī lā yaqaʿu ʿalay-hā*[100] *al-takyīfu* – lit. "about which one cannot ask: How?").

35 Belief in God, demonstrating the inconsistency (*al-mubāyanah*) of polytheism, validation of the positive commandments, avoiding being scolded, steadfastness in Belief, prohibiting what God has prohibited, and obeying His Emissary.

Ibn Habban summed up: "These are the thirty-five views of the scholars and grammarians concerning the meaning of the concept 'the bringing down of the Qurʾān in seven *ḥarfs*'. Some of these views resemble one another; all are possible, as are other views."

Al-Mursī objected: "Some of these views are confused (*mutadākhilah*): I know neither their *isnāds* nor from whom they were transmitted. I don't know why each view was singled out to apply to the 'seven *ḥarfs*,' despite the fact that each one of them is found in the Qurʾān. And I have no clue as to (the reason for this) choice! Truly, I don't understand the meaning of some of them; and most of them are opposed by the *ḥadīth* about ʿUmar and Hishām Ibn Hakim which is in the *Ṣaḥīḥ*; for neither of them differed in (the Qurʾān's) interpretation (*tafsīr*) nor in its legislation – they differed only in the reading/recitation (*qiraʾah*) of its *ḥarfs*. Many of the common people suppose that (the seven *ḥarfs*) refers to the seven variant readings[101] (*al-qiraʾāt*) – this is just vile ignorance.

* * *

Note

There is a difference of opinion as to whether the "ʿUthmanic codices"[102] are complete in regard to the seven harfs. Large groups of jurisprudents, Qurʾān readers, and philosophers (*al-mutakallimuuna*) held this view. They pointed out that it is not possible for the Nation to neglect any part of its tradition. The Companions had formerly agreed that the "ʿUthmanic codices" derived directly from the codices that Abū Bakr had written down, and they agreed to reject all other (versions of the Qurʾānic text).

The overwhelming majority of the first generation and later generations (*al-salaf wa-l-khalaf*)[103] and the Muslim *imāms* agree that it contains only what resembles in writing the seven *harfs*; with all that come in the last reciting which Gabriel brought down to the Prophet (peace and blessings be upon him). It is complete: no *harf* is missing.

Ibn Jazarī said that this appears to be the case.

One may answer concerning the first (view) with what Ibn Jarīr (al-Tabari) said: reading/reciting in all seven *harfs* is not incumbent on the Nation. It is merely allowable for them to do so, because when the Companions saw that the Nation would become disparate and would differ if they did not agree on one *harf*, they made a widespread agreement on this. They are infallible (*maʿsuumuuna min al-Dalaalah*); there is no neglecting of obligation nor of doing anything prohibited here. There is no doubt but that the (text of) the Qurʾān was (in part) abrogated (*nusikha*) and changed in the final recitation (by Gabriel); thus the Companions agreed that they would record what was verified as the fixed (text of) the Qurʾān at the time of the final Revelation, and they rejected everything else.

Ibn Ashta in his Masahif and Ibn Abī Shayba in his *Faḍāʾil*, related, by way of Ibn Sirin, on the authority of ʿUbayda al-Salmani: that the reading revealed to the Prophet (peace and blessings be upon him) in the year in which he died is the same reading as we do today.

Ibn Ashta also related, on the authority of Ibn Sirin: "Every year in the month of Ramaḍan, Gabriel used to recite the Qurʾān with the Prophet (peace and blessings be upon him).[104] In the year of his death Gabriel read the Qurʾān with the Prophet (peace and blessings be upon him) twice; it is seen that this, our (present) reading, is the same as (the recitation at the) time of the final occasion of reciting the Qurʾān."

Al-Baghawi said in his *Sharh al-Sunna* (Explanation of the *Sunna*): "It is related that Zayd Ibn Thābit[105] witnessed the final reciting of Revelation, where it was explained what was to be abrogated (*nusikha*) and what was to remain, and he recorded it for the Emissary of God (peace and blessings be upon him), and he recited it to him. He would recite it to the people until he died. Thus Abū Bakr and ʿUmar endorsed Zayd b. Thābit's appointment for its collection; later, ʿUthmān entrusted him to write the codices."

Chapter seventeen

THE NAMES OF THE QURʾĀN AND OF THE *SŪRAHS*

Al-Jāḥiẓ said that God named His Book in a manner different from that by which the Arabs named their speech as a whole or in its parts. Its entirety is called "Qurʾān" just as (the Arabs) would call (a collection of poems) a "diwan"; and a part (of the Qurʾān) a "*sūrah*" (just as part of a *diwan* is called) a "*qaṣīda* (ode)"; and part of (a *sūrah* is called an "*aya* (verse)", just as part of a *qasida* is called a "*bayt* (line of poetry)"; and the end (of an *aya* is called) a "*fasila* (separating pause)", (just as the end of a line of poetry is called) a "*qafiya* (rhyme)".[1]

Abū al-Maʿali ʿAzizi[2] Ibn ʿAbd al-Mālik, known as "Shaydhala"[3] (God bless him) in (his) Burhān[4] reported that God named the Qurʾān with fifty-five names.

1 He called it: "a book" and "clear" as in "Ḥaʾ Mim. By the clear Book".[5]

2 and: "a Qurʾān", and "noble", as in "Verily, it is a noble Book."[6]

3 and: "speech", as in ". . . until he hears God's speech".[7]

4 and: "a light", as in "We have brought down to you a clear light."[8]

5 and: "a guidance and a Mercy", as in ". . . a guidance and a Mercy for the believers".[9]

6 and: "a discriminator (*furqān*)", as in "He brought down the Discriminator for his slave."[10]

7 and: "a healing", as in "We bring down the Qurʾān which is a healing."[11]

8 and: "an admonition", as in "An admonition has come to you from your Lord, and a healing for what is in your breasts."[12]

9 and: "a *dhikr*[13] (Remembrance)" and "blessed", as in "This blessed Remembrance – We have revealed it."[14]

10 and: "sublime (*ʿaliyyun*)", as in "It is with us in the Mother of the Book, truly sublime."[15]

11 and: "Wisdom", as in ". . . profound Wisdom."[16]

12 and: "Wise", as in "These are the verses of the Wise Book."[17]

13 and: "guarding", as in ". . . confirming the Scripture that came before it, and guarding it . . .".[18]

14 and: "rope", as in ". . . hold fast to God's rope."[19]

15 and: "Straight Path", as in ". . . that this is My Straight Path."[20]

16 and: "straight", as in ". . . straight, that He may heed the godless . . .".[21]

17 and: "decisive", as in ". . . verily, it is decisive Speech."[22]

18 and: "a powerful proclamation (*al-nabaʾ*)", as in "Concerning that which you ask about – it is a powerful proclamation."[23]

19 and: "the best of Speech (*ḥadīth*)", "*mathani* ('oft-repeated'), and *mutashabih* ('consistent within itself; unambiguous')", as in "God has brought down the best of *ḥadīth* – a Book which is *mutashabih* and *mathani*."[24]

20 and: "Revelation", as in "Verily, it is the Revelation from the Lord of the Worlds."[25]

21 and: "Spirit", as in "We have inspired (*ʿawHay-naa*) You with a Spirit by Our permission."[26]

22 and: "Inspiration (*waHy*)", as in "We warn you only through inspiration."[27]

23 and: "Arabic", as in ". . . an Arabic Qurʾān . . .".[28]

24 and: "lights (*basāʾir*)", as in "These are lights (from your Lord) . . .".[29]

25 and: "a Declaration (*balāgh*)", as in "This is a Declaration for mankind . . .".[30]

26 and: "Knowledge", as in ". . . after the Knowledge that came to You . . .".[31]

27 and: "True (*ḥaqq*)", as in "Verily, this is the True Narrative . . .".[32]

28 and: "Guiding", as in "Verily, this is a Qurʾān that is guiding . . .".[33]

29 and: "Miraculous", as in ". . . a Miraculous Qurʾān . . .".[34]

30 and: "a Message (*tadhkirah*)", as in "Verily, it is a Message . . .".[35]

31 and: "a firm hand-hold", as in ". . . grasp the firm hand-hold . . .".[36]

32 and: "Truth (*sidq*)", as in " . . . which brought Truth . . .".[37]

33 and: "Justice", as in ". . . Your Lord's words have concluded in Truth and Justice."[38]

34 and: "Command", as in ". . . this is God's Command; He brought it down to you . . .".[39]

35 and: "Call", as in ". . . We have heard a herald with a Call to Belief (*al-ʿīmān*)."[40]

36 and: “Good News”, as in “. . . Guidance and Good News . . .”.[41]

37 and: “Glorious”, as in “Nay it is a Glorious Qurʾān”.[42]

38 and: “Psalms (*zabur*)”, as in “We had inscribed previously in the Psalms . . .”.[43]

39 and: “a bringer of Good News and a Warner”, as in A Book whose verses are differentiated; an Arabic Qurʾān for a people who understand. A bringer of Good News and a Warner . . .”.[44]

40 and: “of exalted power”, as in “. . . verily, it is a Book of exalted power.”[45]

41 and: “a Message (*balāgh*)”, as in “This is a Message for mankind.”[46]

42 and: “narrative”, as in “. . . the best of narratives.”[47]

(God) further named the Qurʾān with four more names, all from the same verse: “On Noble Pages (*Suhuf mukarrama*), Exalted and Pure (*marfuʾah mutahhara*).”[48] End (of section).

* * *

As for (God’s) calling (the Qurʾān) “a Book”, (the root meaning KTB)[49] conveys the same meaning as “to gather together (root: *JMʿ*)”, because it[50] gathers together various types of sciences, narratives and information in the most eloquent way. “Book” is synonymous with “collection”.[51]

(As for the Qurʾān’s being called) *al-mubìn* (“discerning”), it is because it clarifies – that is, it discriminates[52] between the Truth and falsehood.

(As for the Qurʾān’s being called) “Qurʾān”, there are differing opinions. One group (of scholars) held that it is a non-derived proper noun, applied specifically to God’s Speech, and was pronounced without the glottal stop (as (*quraan*) as opposed to (*qurʾaan*)). Thus read Ibn Kathir, based on the view of al-Shāfiʿī. Al-Bayhaqī, al-Khaṭīb and others related, also based on a view of al-Shāfiʿī, held that he would pronounce “I read (*qaraʾ-tu*)” with the glottal stop, but he would pronounce *quraan* without it. Another view is that *quraan* has no glottal stop, because it is not derived from the same root as “I read (*qaraʾtu*)” (that is, *QRʾ*),[53] but rather it is the name of God’s Book, like “the Torah” or the “New Testament (*al-ʿinjiil*)”.

Al-Ashari, among others, claimed that “Qurʾān” was derived from the root *QRN*, with the meaning “to connect something with something else”, because (the Qurʾān) connects the *sūrahs*, the verses and the words (*ḥarfs*) in it.

Al-Farrāʾ derives (the word “Qurʾān”) from “*qarā*” (in pairs), because the verses validate one another and resemble one another: thus they are “pairs”. Both these views are held in the case in which the glottal stop is not present; its root contains the radical nuun (that is, the root is *QRN*).

Al-Zajjāj said that this was an oversight; the truth is that the glottal stop is omitted to ease pronunciation, because there is a phonetic zero preceding it.[54]

Other (scholars) have said that the glottal stop there is different. Al-Liḥyāwī and his ilk held (that the word "Qurʾān") was a verbal noun like "*rujhān*"[55] preponderance (from the root *RJH* plus suffix *-an*) and "*ghufrān*" – forgiveness, (from the root *GH F R* plus the suffix *-aan*). "The Book" was also called "the *recited-al-makruuʾ* (with final glottal stop), as one may use the passive participle for the verbal noun.

Al-Zajjāj and others of his ilk held that (the word "Qurʾān") is an adjective on the morphological pattern of *FuMLaan* (where *F* = first radical, *M* = middle radical and *L* = last radical), derived from the root *KRʾ* meaning "to collect together".[56] Thus one says "*qaraʾ-tu* (I carried) water from the pool", in the sense of "I gathered it up".

Abū ʿUbayda held that it was called ("Qurʾān") because it collected the *sūrahs* one after the other.

Al-Rāghib said that not every collection is called "a Qurʾān", neither is a collection restricted to speech. It is called "Qurʾān" because it is a collection of the fruits of all the former Heavenly Books. Another view is that it contains all the varieties of knowledge.

Quṭrub related that it is called "a Qurʾān" because the reader (*al-qaariʾ*) displays (*yuzhiru-hu*)[57] and clarifies it from his mouth. The Arabs were wont to say: "The she-camel never gave birth to (*qaraʾ-at*) a toothless (baby camel) (*sallan*)" – that is, she did not have offspring; (in other words), she never gave birth; (which is to say), she never had become pregnant. The reader recites the Qurʾān orally, and sends it forth (to others), and thus it was called "a Qurʾān".

I (Suyūṭī) hold to al-Shāfiʿī's opinion.

(The Qurʾān is called) "Speech" (*al-kalam*) because it is derived from the word (*al-kalm*), meaning "impression" (and "wound"), because it leaves an impression in the mind of the hearer, which is a new benefit to him.[58]

(The Qurʾān is called) "the Light" because by it one penetrates the secrets of the permitted and the forbidden.[59]

It is called "Guidance" because it points out the Truth; grammatically, (*hudan*) is a verbal noun substituting for an active participle, to give the word emphasis.[60]

It is called "the Discriminator" (*al-Furqān*) because it discriminates between truth and falsehood. Mujāhid pointed this out, as reported by Ibn Abī Ḥātim.[61]

It is called "the Healing" because it cures some spiritual illnesses, e.g. unbelief, ignorance, and malice; (it cures) corporeal illnesses, also.[62]

It is called "the Remembrance" (*al-dhikr*) because of its admonitions (based on) the fate of bygone nations. *Dhikr* also means "honour": God, He is exalted, said: "Verily, it is a *Dhikr* for you and for your people"[63] – that is, it is an honour that He communicated it to them."[64]

It is called "the Wise" (*al-Ḥakīm*) because its verses are perfected (*ʾuHkimat*) in the most wonderful arrangement and eloquence of meanings; they are perfected also from rejecting substitution, textual corruption, differences and disparity.[65]

It is called "guarding" (*muhaymin*)[66] because it is a witness to all the (revealed Holy) books, and to bygone peoples.[67]

It is called "the Rope" (*al-Ḥabl*) because whoever takes hold of it arrives at the Garden or to Guidance. *Al-Ḥabl* is a synonym of *al-sabab* (originally "tent-pole) rope". (Now used mostly to express "reason".)[68]

It is called "the Straight Path" because it is the way to the Garden, straight, with no deviations.[69]

It is called "oft-repeated" (*al-mathāni*) because in it are the accounts of bygone peoples; for it is second (*thaanin*) (that is, subsequent) to (the Books) that preceded it. Another opinion is that it is called thus because of its repetition of the stories and the admonitions in it. A third opinion, as related by al-Kirmānī in his *Ajaʾib* (Wonders), is that it was brought once only in meaning, then once again with words and meanings;[70] as God said: "Verily, this is in the first Books."[71]

It is called the "internally consistent" (*al-mutashābih*) because each part of it is consistent with every other part in Goodness and Truth.[72]

It is called "the Spirit" (*al-rūh*) because through it hearts and souls are brought to life.[73]

It is called "the Glorious" (*al-mājid*) by dint of its nobility.[74]

It is called "of exalted power" (*al-aʾzīz*) because it overwhelms anyone who attempts to oppose it[75] (by attempting to imitate it).[76]

It is called "the Message" (*al-balāgh*) because it communicates to mankind what it is permitted to do, and what it is forbidden to do. Or: because it contains more eloquence and sufficiency than other (writings).[77]

In one of his writings, al-Silafiy[78] wrote that he had heard Abū al-Karam al-Ṭaḥawī claim that he had heard Abū al-Qāsim al-Tanukhī say that he had heard Abū al-Ḥasan al-Rumaniy answer the question: Every book has a particular by-name (*tarjamah*) – what is the by-name of God's Book? He answered by citing "This is a Message (*balāgh*) for mankind that they be warned by it."[79]

Abū Shama[80] and others cited His, He is exalted, saying "The nourishment (*rizq*) that God gives you is better and longer-lasting",[81] (which demonstrates that rizq is another name for) the Qurʾān.

Lessons to be learned

In his Taʾriikh (history), al-Muzaffari[82] said that when Abū Bakr collected the Qurʾān, he said: "Give it a name." Some people answered: "Call it 'Good News (*ʿinjīl*)'," but others were not pleased with this. Others suggested: "Call it (the Hebrew word for 'book') 'sifr'," but they rejected this because it came from the Jews. Ibn Masūd interjected: "In Ethiopia I saw a book (*kitāb*) which they call (in Geʾez, or Old Ethiopic) *maṣḥaf* so they called the (collected Qurʾān) *Maṣḥaf*."[83]

I (Suyūṭī) say: In his *Kitāb al-Maṣāḥif* (Book of the Codices), Ibn Ashta[84] claims, by way of Mūsā Ibn ʿUqba, on the authority of Ibn Shihab, who said: "When they collected the Qurʾān, they wrote it on paper. (Then) Abū Bakr asked them to give it a name. Some suggested 'the *sifr*'; others suggested 'the *mashaf*', because the Ethiopians call (a book) 'a *maṣḥaf*'. So Abū Bakr consulted the people who collected God's Book together, and decided to call it 'the *Maṣḥaf*'. Later (Ibn Ashta) confirmed this report via another route, namely from Ibn Burayda; this will be mentioned in the next Naw."[85]

Another thing to be gleaned

Ibn Durays[86] and others related, on the authority of Kaʿb, who said: "In the Torah is the verse 'O Muḥammad I am bringing down to you a new Torah which will open blind eyes, deaf ears and wrapped hearts.' "

Ibn Abī Ḥātim reported, on the authority of Qatada, who said: "When Moses received the Tablets, he said: 'O my Lord! I find in the Tablets a Nation whose "Good News" (*ʾanaajiilu-hum*) is in their hearts, so make them my Nation.' (God) answered: 'This (refers to) Aḥmad's (that is, Muḥammad's) Nation.' "

In the above two *ḥadīths* (*al-ʿathar-ayni*), the Qurʾān is called "Torah" and "Good News"; nevertheless, it is not permissible to us these terms thus today. The Torah had been referred to by "the Discriminator" (*al-Furqān*) in His saying "When We gave Moses the Book (*al-kitāb*) and the *Furqān* . . ."[87] (The Prophet) (peace and blessings be upon him) also called the "Psalms" (*al-zabūr*) "Qurʾān" when he said: "(God) made the Qurʾān easy for David."

Section: Concerning the *Sūrahs*' names

Al-Qutaybi[88] said the word "*sūrah*" may be pronounced with or without the glottal stop (that is, as either *suurah* or *suʾrah*). If one pronounces it with the glottal stop, it must be derived from *ʾasʾar-tu* – that is, *ʾafdal-tu* (I left a little in the cup – that is, from *suʾr* which indicates the remainder of drink in a vessel (that is, it is from the root *SʾR*), as if a *suʾrah* were a section of the Qurʾān. If one pronounces it suurah without the glottal stop, he produces the same meaning, although he omits the glottal stop.

Others link the word with *sūr al-bināʾ* (a building's wall) – that is, a piece of it, or one level above another.

Another opinion is that it is linked to *suur al-madiinah* (a city wall), because of its being enclosed[89] in its verses and groups (of verses), just like a house among other houses. From this is derived the *suwār* (armband), which encloses the arm.

Another opinion is that (it is called "*sūrah*") because of its loftiness: because it is God's lofty Speech, the *sūrah* (which He) brought down. Al-Nabigha said[90]: "Have you not seen that God has given you a *sūrah*; you will see every king jinkering around it."

Another opinion is that (it is called a "*sūrah*") because they are all interconnected, as one says *al-taswur* (climbing over a wall), with the sense of escalation and being piled up, as in ". . . Behold they climbed over the wall of the private chamber."[91]

Al-Jaʿbarī[92] said that "*sūrah*" can be defined by a "Qurʾān" (recitation) which includes verses, having a beginning and an end, the shortest of which contains three verses.[93]

Someone else claimed that "*sūrah*" is a *taʾnafah*, established as a fixed by-name – that is, named with a particular by-name by the Prophet (peace and blessings be upon him).[94]

The names of the *sūrahs* have been firmly fixed in the *ḥadīths* and histories (*al-ʿaḥadīth wa-l-ʿathar*). Were it not for fear of being too wordy, I (Suyūṭī) would clarify the details of this for you here.

Ibn Abī Ḥātim brought some supporting evidence for this on the authority of I'krama, who said that the polytheists would say: "The *sūrah* of the Cow! The *sūrah* of the Spider . . ." mocking them. Then He brought down: "For sufficient are we against those who scoff."[95]

Some (of the previous authorities) disliked calling *sūrahs* by their names, according to al-Ṭabarānī's and al-Bayhaqī's reports, on the authority of Anas (Ibn Mālik) (by way of a *ḥadīth* whose *isnādis* traced all the way back to the Prophet, who said): "Do not say: 'the *sūrah* of the Cow', or 'the *sūrah* of the family of ʿImrān', or the '*sūrah* of Women', and so on for the rest of the Qurʾān, but say rather: 'the *sūrah*, in which the Cow is mentioned', 'the *sūrah* in which the family of ʿImrān is mentioned', and so on for all the Qurʾān." (This *ḥadīth*'s) *isnād* is weak; Ibn al-Jawzī believed (this *ḥadīth*) to be spurious.

Al-Bayhaqī claimed that this *ḥadīth* had been interrupted at the point where (ʿalā) Ibn ʿUmar becomes a link in the *isnād*, but then (al-Bayhaqī) reported the same *ḥadīth* on the authority (of Ibn ʿUmar) with a sound *isnād*. Other *ḥadīths* with totally sound *isnāds* going back to (the Prophet) (peace and blessings be upon him) have allowed saying "the *sūrah* of the Cow", etc.

In the *Ṣaḥīḥ*, it is reported that Ibn Masūd said: "This is the place in which 'The *sūrah* of the Cow' (*sūrat al-Baqara*) was revealed to Him", demonstrating clearly that this is common usage.

Section

A *sūrah* may have only one name, which is very common. It may have two names or more; thus the *Fātiḥa* (*1) has been given some twenty-odd names, which points out its nobility: a plethora of names demonstrates the nobility of the thing named.

1 Ibn Jarīr (al-Tabari) mentioned *Fātiḥat al-Kitāb* (the Opening of the Book). He based this on a *ḥadīth* by way of Ibn Abī Dhiʾb, on the authority of al-Muqbari, on the authority of Abū Hurayra, on the authority of the Prophet, who said: "(The *Fātiḥa*) is the 'Mother of the Book', 'The Opening of the Book', and 'The seven *mathānī*' (oft-repeated)." It is called this because it begins every codex, every lesson and every recitation during prayer. Another opinion is that it (is called this) because it is the first *sūrah* to be revealed. Another opinion is that (it is called this) because it is the first *sūrah* to be inscribed on the Preserved Tablet. Al-Mursī reported the latter opinion and added that this needs support (*yahtaaju ʿilā naql*). Another view is that "praise" (*al-Ḥamd*) precedes all discourse. Another view has it that it is at the beginning of every book. Al-Mursī also related this, but qualified it (*r a u dda*) by adding that every book begins with "the praise *al-Ḥamd*" (that is, the phrase *al-Hamdu li-llaahi* – Praise be to God) only, not the entire (first) *sūrah*; and it is clear that the word "Book" here refers only to the Qurʾān, not books in general. (Al-Mursī) said that it is related that one of (the Fātiḥa's) names is "The Opening of the Book" and that "Book" can refer only to the Qurʾān here.

2 (The *Fātiḥa*) is called *Fātiḥat al-Qurʾān* (the Opening of the Qurʾān)," as al-Mursī has also pointed out.

3 and 4 (The *Fātiḥa* is called) *Umm al-Kitāb* (the Mother of the Book), and *Umm al-Qurʾān* (the Mother of the Qurʾān). Ibn Sirin objected that it be called *the Mother of the Book*; and al-Ḥasan objected that it be called *the Mother of the Qurʾān*. Baqi Ibn Mukhlad agreed with them: (in his opinion) "the Mother of the Book" refers to the Preserved Tablet. (God), he is exalted, said: "With Him is the Mother of the Book . . ."[96] and "Verily, it is in *the Mother of the Book*."[97] (*The Mother of the Book*) is also equated with verses concerning the prohibited and the allowed: "The unambiguous verses are *the Mother of the Book*."[98] Al-Mursī added that there is an unsubstantiated *ḥadīth* which says: "(The Prophet said:) 'Let not one of you call (the *Fātiḥa*) "the Mother of the Book", but rather call it "the Opening of the Book".' "

I (Suyūṭī) hold that there is no support for this view in the books of *ḥadīth* (collections); Ibn Durays reported (this *ḥadīth*) with this wording on the authority of Ibn Sirin and al-Mursī was confused on this. Indeed many sound *ḥadīths* attest (to the fact that the *Fātiḥa* may be called "the Mother of the Book"). Al-Daraqatni called (this *ḥadīth*) sound, (based on an *isnād*) on the authority of Abū Hurayra, who reported: "(The Prophet said:) 'When you recite "al-Hamd (the praise)," recite also: "In the Name of God, the Compassionate, the Merciful"; because (the *Fātiḥa*) is "the Mother of the Qurʾān", "the Mother of the Book", and "the seven *mathānī* (oft-repeated)".' "

There were differences of opinion concerning why it was thus named. One view is that one begins any codex by writing it, and one recites it in prayer before the *sūrah*. Abū ʿUbayda published this view in his *Majāz* (Metaphor). In his *Ṣaḥīḥ*, al-Bukhārī agreed wholeheartedly with him. The difficulty in this is that it is appropriate to call (the *Fātiḥa*) "the Opening of the Book", and not "the Mother of the Book". I (Suyūṭī) would argue that this is because the mother is the beginning of the child. Al-Māwardī said that it is called thus because it precedes and all else follows, because it – *ʾamma-t-hu* – that is, it precedes it; thus one calls the war banner "mother (*ʾumm*)" because it precedes and the army follows. A person's by-gone years are also called "mother" because they preceded (the present). Mecca is nicknamed "the Mother of Cities" because of its precedence over all the other cities. Another view is that something's "mother" refers to its origin; and (the *Fātiḥa*) is the origin of the Qurʾān because it contains within it all of the purposes, sciences, and rules (contained in the Qurʾān), as I will explain in more detail in Nawʿ seventy-three. Another view is that it is called this because it is the most excellent of *sūrahs*, as one may call the leader of a people "the mother of the people". Another view is that it is inviolable (*hurmah*) just as the entire Qurʾān is inviolable. Another opinion that it is called thus is because people of faith are roused to rally[99] around it, just as they do around a flag because the army rallies[100] to it. Another view is that it is called this because it is "unambiguous (*muḥkam*)", and the "unambiguous (verses)" are "the Mother of the Book".

5 (The *Fātiḥa*) is called "the Mighty Qurʾān (*al-qur'ān al-ʿazīm*)" according to a *ḥadīth* reported by Aḥmad, on the authority of Abū Hurayra: "The Prophet (peace and blessings be upon him) said: '(The *Fātiḥa*) is[101] "the Mother of the Qurʾān", "the seven *mathānī*" and "the Mighty Qurʾān"'; it was called thus because it contains all the meanings (*maʿaani*) contained in the entire Qurʾān."

6 (The *Fātiḥa*) is called "the seven *mathani* (oft-repeated)" in a very well-known *ḥadīth*, and in many other *ḥadīths*. As for its being called "seven": it has seven verses. Al-Dāraquṭnī reported this on the authority of ʿAlī. Another view is that it is called this because there are seven "disciplines (*ʾādāb*)", each verse being a "discipline". This is unlikely (*wa-fi-hi buʿd*). Another view is that it is called this because it omits seven letters (*ḥarf-s*): the *tāʾ*, *jīm*, *khāʾ*, *zāy*, *shīn*, *Ẓāʾ* and the *fāʾ*. This is even more feeble than the previous view because one names something for what it has, not what it lacks. As for the *mathani*, it is possible that it is derived from *thanāʾ* (praise), because (the *Fātiḥa*) praises God, He is exalted. It is also possible that it is derived from *thunyaa* (exception), because God made an exception (of giving the *Fātiḥa*) to this Nation. It is also possible that it is derived from *tathniyah* (to repeat), because one repeats it with each genuflection (*rakʿah*). This view is supported by Ibn Jarīr (al-Tabari) who reported (a *ḥadīth*) with a good *isnād*, on the authority of ʿUmar, who said that "the seven *mathani*" refers to "the Opening of the Book", because one repeats it with every genuflection. Another opinion is that it is followed by (*tuthannā*)

another *sūrah*. Another view is that (it is called this) because it was revealed twice. Another opinion is because it contains two parts, praise (*thanā᾽*) and supplication. Another view is because whenever (God's) slave recites one verse (of the *Fātiḥa*), God follows it (*thanā-hu*) by giving information about (the slave's) actions, as it is reported in the *ḥadīth*. Another opinion is because (the *Fātiḥa*) includes the eloquence of the *mathani* and the rhetorical brilliance (*faṣāhat al-mathānī wa-balāghat al-mᶜānī*)[102] of (the entire Qur᾽ān). There exist other opinions, also.

7 (The *Fātiḥa*) was also called "*al-wafiyah* (the sufficient)". Sufyān Ibn ᶜUyayna used to call it this because it comprehensively contains all of the meanings (*maᶜani*) of the entire Qur᾽ān. (Al-Zamakhsharī) mentioned this in his *Kashshaf*. Al-Thaᶜlabī said (that the *Fātiḥa* is called this) because it does not admit of bisection,[103] for every (other) *sūrah* of the Qur᾽ān may be recited in halves, the first with the first genuflection and the second half with the second genuflection; except for the *Fātiḥa* (as all of it has to be read) (*la-jaza bi-khilafi-ha*). Al-Mursī said (that it is called this) because it distinguishes between what is God's and what is (His) slave's.

8 (The *Fātiḥa*) is called "the Treasure (*al-kanz*)": it came first in "the Mother of the Book". (Al-Zamakhsharī) said so in his *Kashshāf*. Its being called this is mentioned in the *ḥadīth* of Anas, mentioned above[104] in Nawᶜ 14.

9 (The *Fātiḥa* is called:) "the Sufficient (*al-kāfiyah*)" because during prayer it is sufficient in itself; no other (*sūrah*) is.

10 (The *Fātiḥa*) is called "the Foundation (*al-᾽asās*)" because it is the root of the Qur᾽ān and the first *sūrah* in it.

11 (The *Fātiḥa* is called:) "the light (*al-nūr*)".

12 and 13 (The *Fātiḥa* is called:) "the *sūrah* of Praise (*al-Ḥamd*)" and "the *sūrah* of Gratitude (*al-shukr*)".

14 and 15 (The *Fātiḥa* is called:) "the First *sūrah* of Praise" and "the Concise *sūrah* of Praise".

16, 17, and 18 It is called "the Incantation (*al-ruqyah*)", "the Healing (*al-shifā᾽*)" and "the Healer (*al-shāfiyah*)". See the *ḥadīths* below in the Nawᶜ concerning "Particular topics (*al-khawāṣ*)".

19 It is called "the Prayer *sūrah*" because prayer cannot be without it.

20 It is also called "Prayer". There is a *ḥadīth* (*Qudsi*) to the effect that (God) said: "I have divided prayer in two; one half for me and one half for My Servant)."[105] (By "prayer" He means) "the *sūrah*" (that is, the *Fātiḥa*). Al-Mursī said that (the reason the *Fātiḥa* is called "prayer" is that the *Fātiḥa*) is one of the requirements (of prayer). At times a thing is named for something that requires it; this is its twentieth name.

21 It is called "the Supplication (*al-duʿāʾ*)" because it contains the plea *ihdina* ("lead us (to the Straight Path)").[106]

22 It is called "the *sūrah* of Entreaty (*al-suʾal*)" for the same reason. The Imām Fakhr al-Dīn (al-Razī) noted this.

23 It is called "the *sūrah* which teaches one how to entreat (God) (*taʿlīm al-masʾalah*)". Al-Mursī said that this is because the etiquette of entreaty (is included in the *Fātiḥa*) because (the body) of it is preceded by praise (*thanāʾ*) (that is, verse 2: "Praise be to God . . .").

24 The *Fātiḥa* is also called "the *sūrah* of the Call for Redemption" because in it (God's) slave calls for redemption from his Lord: "You it is we worship, and to you we call for help."[107]

25 It is also called "the *sūrah* of Authorization (*al-tafwīḍ*)" for this idea is included in "You it is we worship, and to you we call for help."[108]

These are the names by which the *Fātiḥa* has been called. They have never been collected together in one book before this.

Apropos: (Concerning) the *Sūrat al-Baqara* (*2): Khālid Ibn Maʿdan used to call it "the Qurʾān's Fortress (*fusṭāṭ*)". This was related in a *ḥadīth* whose *isnād* is traced all the way back to the Prophet which is found in *al-Firdaws Musnad*. This is because of (*Sūrat al-Baqara*'s) magnificence, and because of the laws mentioned exclusively in it. In a *ḥadīth* in the *Mustadrak* (it is called) "the Summit (*al-sanam*)" because this is what one calls anything's high point. (*Sanam*) means originally "camel's hump".)

(Concerning) *Sūrat* al ʿImrān (*3): In his *Sunan*, Saʿīd Ibn Manṣūr on the authority of al-Attaf the name Āl ʿImrān is in the Torah, thus it is a good (name for the *sūrah*). In his *Ṣaḥīḥ*, Muslim (says that the *sūrah* and *Sūrat al-Baqara* (together) are called "the two Resplendent (*sūrahs*)".

(Concerning) *Sūrat al-Māʾidah* (*5): It is called also "the Contracts (*al-ʿuqūd*)" and "the Saviour (*al-munkidhah*)". Ibn al-Ghars said that this is because it saves the one who has learned it from the angels of punishment.

(Concerning) *Sūrat al-Anfāl* (*6): Abū al-Sheikh reported, on the authority of Saʿd Ibn Jubair, that the latter asked Ibn ʿAbbās (about the name of this *sūrah*), and he answered "the *sūrah* of (the Battle of) Badr".

(Concerning) *Sūrat Barāʾa* (*9): It is called also "*Sūrat al-Tawba* (Repentance)" because it contains the phrase "God has forgiven the Prophet . . . (to the end of the verse)."[109] (It is also called) "the Accuser (*al-fāḍiḥah*)". Al-Bukhārī reported, on the authority of Saʿīd Ibn Jubair, on the authority of Ibn ʿAbbās, who said (that the *sūrah* was called both) "the Repentance" and "the Accuser" because while (the words) "some of them (will be punished)", we were all afraid that each one of us (would be included) here. Abū al-Sheikh also reported, on the authority of ʿIkrama, on the authority of ʿUmar, who said: "(God) had not completed the Revelation before each one of us (the Companions) feared that he would be included."

It is called "the Accuser" and "the *sūrah* of Punishment". In his *Mustadrak*, al-Hakim reported, on the authority of Hudhayfa, (the Prophet said) "The *sūrah* one calls '*sūrah* of Repentance' is 'the *sūrah* of Punishment'." Abū Sheikh reported on the authority of Saʿīd Ibn Jubair, who said that whenever ʿUmar Ibn al-Khaṭṭab heard "the *sūrah* of Innocence (*baraʾah*)" mentioned to him as "the *sūrah* of Repentance (*al-tawbah*)", he would say that "(the *sūrah* of) Punishment" would be more appropriate: it renounces nearly all mankind, and leaves no one out.

(It is also called "the *sūrah* of the) Scarring (*almuqashqishah*)". Abū al-Shaykh reported on the authority of Zayd Ibn Aslam that a man told Ibn ʿUmar (that it is called) "the *sūrah* of Repentance". Ibn ʿUmar then asked: "Then which one is 'the *sūrah* of Repentance'?" The man answered "(the *sūrah* of) Innocence." Ibn ʿUmar responded: "Had any thing taken people to task, except it." The only name we would call it by is "(the *sūrah* of) Scarring" – that is, the healing over of hypocrisy.

(It is also called "the *sūrah* of) the Borer (*al-munaqqirah*)". Abū Shaykh (reported) on the authority of ʿUbayd Ibn ʿUmayr that ("the *sūrah* of) Innocence" would be called ("the *sūrah* of) the Borer" because it bored into and removed what was in the polytheists' hearts.

(It is also called "the *sūrah* of) *al-baḥūth*, with a short *a* after the *baaʾ*, (the *sūrah* of the) Inquirer)."[110] Al-Hakim reported this on the authority of al-Miqdād that some one said to him "Perhaps you do not go to war this year?" He said "'the *sūrah* of the Inquirer'," that is, the (*sūrah* of) Innocence, has come to us."

(It is also called "the *sūrah* of) the Digger (*al-Ḥafirah*)", because it digs into the hearts of the hypocrites. So reported Ibn al-Ghars.

(It is also called "the *sūrah* of) the Provoker (*al-muthīrah*)". Ibn Abī Ḥātim, on the authority of Qatāda, who said that this *sūrah* is called "the Accuser" – that is, the accuser of the polytheists – said it is also called "the Provoker" because it points out their defects and shameful deeds (*aʾwrati-him*, lascivious deeds).

Ibn al-Ghars also reported that one of its names is "(the *sūrah* of) the Dispenser (*al-mubaʾthirah*)", but he assumed that this was a scribal error for "(the *sūrah* of) the Borer (*al-munaqirah*)". If so, then these would total ten names (for *sūrah* *9). He had seen it written in the handwriting of al-Sakhāwī of the book *Jamal al-Qurra*ʾ (The Reciters' Beauty) thus: *al-mubaʾthirah* (with an *ʿayn*), and had said that (this *sūrah* is called this) because it disperses and dispels (*aʿthara-t*) the polytheists' secrets.

Other names for this *sūrah* have been reported: ("the *sūrah* of the) Humiliator (*al-mukhziyah*), Deterrer (*al-munakkilah*), Dispeller (*al-musharidah*) and Growler (*al-mudamdimah*)".

(Concerning) *Sūrat al-Naḥl* ("the *sūrah* of the Bees", *16): Qatāda said that it is called "the *sūrah* of the Bounties (*al-niʾam*)". Ibn Abī Ḥātim reported, on the authority of Ibn Ghars, that this is because in it God enumerated His bounties for his slaves.

(Concerning *Sūrat*) *al-Isrāʾ* ("Night Journey", *17): It is also called "the *sūrah* of Intense Praise (*subhan*)," and "the *sūrah* of The Children of Israel (*banī ʿIsrāīl*)".

(Concerning "the *sūrah* of) the Cave (*al-Kahf*)" (*18), it is also called "the *sūrah* of the Companions of the Cave (*ashab al-Kahf*)". Thus reported al-Marduwayhi; al-Bayhaqī, on the authority of Ibn ʿAbbās, in a *ḥadīth* whose *isnād* is traced to the Prophet, reported that it is called the "Intercessor (*al-Haʾilah*)" because it comes between the reader and hellfire. Others rejected this *ḥadīth* as spurious.

(Concerning "the *sūrah* of) Ṭaʾ haʾ" (*20): In his *Jamal al-Qurra*ʾ, al-Sakhāwī mentioned that it is also called "(the *sūrah* of) the one directly spoken to (that is, Moses) (*al-kalim*)".

(Concerning "the *sūrah* of) the Poets (*al-Shuʿarāʾ*)" (*26): In his *tafsīr*, the Imām Mālik mentioned that it is also called "the *sūrah* of the Gatherer (*al-jamiʾah*)".

(Concerning "the *sūrah* of) the Ants (*al-Naml*)" (*27): it is also called "the *sūrah* of Solomon".

(Concerning "the *sūrah* of) the Prostration" (*al-Sajda*) (*32): it is also called "the *sūrah* of the couches (*al-maḍajiʾ*)".

(Concerning "the *sūrah* of) the Creator (*al-Fāṭir*)" (*35): it is also called "the *sūrah* of the Angels".

(Concerning "the *sūrah* of) *Yāsīn*" (*36) (The Prophet) (peace and blessings be upon him) called it "the heart of the Qurʾān". Al-Tirmidhī reported this in a *ḥadīth* on the authority of Anas.

Al-Bayhaqī reported in a *ḥadīth* on the authority of Abū Bakr, who quoted the Prophet as saying: "In the Torah, the *sūrah* of Yāsīn is called 'the Conflator (*al-muʾimmah*)' because it combines the Goodness of this world and the Hereafter; it is also called 'the Defender (*al-dafiʿa*)' and 'the Decider (*al-qaadiyah*)' because it defends whoever has it (memorized) from all evil, and it decided every matter in his favour. Others consider this *ḥadīth* to be counterfeit.

(Concerning "the *sūrah* of) the Crowds (*al-Zumar*)" (*39): it is also called "the *sūrah* of the Chambers (*al-ghuraf*)".

(Concerning "the *sūrah* of) the Forgiver (*al-ghāfir*)" (*40): it is also called "the *sūrah* of Might (*al-Tawl*)" and ("the *sūrah* of) the Believer (*al-Mu᾿mīn*)" (the latter because of its containing in verse 28 "A believing man said . . .").

(Concerning "the *sūrah* of) the Expounder (*fuṣṣilatt*)" (*41): it is also called ("the *sūrah* of) the Prostration (*al-sajdah*)" and (the *sūrah* of) the Lamps (*al-maSaabih*)".

(Concerning "the *sūrah* of) the Kneeling (*al-jathiya*)" (*45): it is called ("the *sūrah* of) the Islamic Law (*al-Sharīʿa*)" and ("the *sūrah* of) Everlastingness (*al-Dahr*)". Thus reported al-Kirmānī in his Aja᾿ib.

(Concerning "the *sūrah* of) Muḥammad" (*47): it is also called "(the *sūrah* of) the Battle (*al-qital*)".

(Concerning "the *sūrah* of) Qāf" (*50): it is also called ("the *sūrah* of) the Lofty Ones (*al-basiqāt*)".

(Concerning "the *sūrah* of) 'Has come close (*iqtarabat*)'" (*54): it is also called ("the *sūrah* of) the Moon (*al-Qamar*)". Bayhaqī reported, on the authority of Ibn ʿAbbās, (that the Prophet said:) "In the Torah, (this *sūrah*) is called 'the Whitener (*al-mubaida*)' because he who has it (memorized) will have his face whitened (with joy), while the faces (of the unbelievers on the Last Day) will be blackened." Other authorities consider this *ḥadīth* to be false.

(Concerning "the *sūrah* of) the Beneficent (al-Raḥmān)" (*55): it is called the Bride of the Qur᾿ān; al-Bayhaqī recorded this on a sound (*marfu᾿*) *ḥadīth* on the authority of ʿAlī.

(Concerning "the *sūrah* of) She who pleads (*al-Mujādila*)" (*58): in Ubay's codex it is called "al-Ẓihār" (a pre-Islamic method of divorce)".

(Concerning "the *sūrah* of) the Mustering (*al-Ḥashr*)" (*59): Al-Bukhārī reported, on the authority of Ibn Jubair, that the latter has inquired of Ibn ʿAbbās, who answered that (the Prophet) said: "Call it 'the *sūrah* of the Banu Nadir'." Ibn Ḥajar explained that (the Prophet) did not want it called "the *sūrah* of the Mustering" because one might think that the intention was at the Day of Resurrection. But the intended reference of the word here is the expulsion of the Banu Nadir.

(Concerning "the *sūrah* of) the Examiner (*al-Mumtaḥana*)" (*60): Ibn Hajar explained that the usual usage was to pronounce this word with (a penultimate vowel) *a*, but that one may pronounce it with *i* instead. The difference is that the first pronunciation indicates the adjective which applies to the woman who was the cause of this *sūrah*'s being brought down; the second pronunciation is an adjective describing the *sūrah* itself, as on may call ("*sūrah*, *9) al-Bara᾿ah (Innocence)" "*al-Fāḍiḥa* (Accuser)". In the *Jamāl al-Qurra᾿* it is also called "the *sūrah* of the Test (*al-imtihan*)" and "the *sūrah* of Friendship (*al-mawadda*)".

(Concerning "the *sūrah* of) the Battle Array (*al-Ṣaff*)" (*61): it is also called "the *sūrah* of the Apostles (*al-Ḥawariyīn*)".

(Concerning "the *sūrah* of) Divorce (*al-Ṭalāq*)" (*65): it is also called "the extremely brief *sūrah* of Women (*sūrat al-Nisaʾ al-qusrā*)". Al-Bukhārī and others reported that Ibn Masūd called it this. Al-Māwardī denied it, saying that he doesn't find the words *qusrā* or *Sughrā* ("extremely little") appear at all in the Qurʾān (*Mahfouz*), nor is any *sūrah* called by either word. Ibn Ḥajar reported that this is an answer to sound *ḥadīths* reported without *isnāds*; and that "shortness" and "length" are relative terms. Al-Bukhārī reported, on the authority of Zayd Ibn Thābit, (that the Prophet said:) "The height or of the two highest peaks (*Tuli al-Tula-yayni*)." He was referring to "the *sūrah* of the Heights (*al-Arāf*)" (*7).

(Concerning "the *sūrah* of) the Prohibition (*al-Taḥrīm*)" (*66): it is also called "the *sūrah* of the Prohibited (*al-mutaḥairrim*)" and "the *sūrah* of 'it was not prohibited (*lam tuharram*)'."

(Concerning "the *sūrah* of) 'Blessed be' (*tabaraka*)" (*67): it is also called "the *sūrah* of Dominion (*al-Mulk*)". Al-Hakim and others reported, on the authority of Ibn Masūd, that it is (called "the *sūrah* of) the Preventer (*al-mānīʾah*)" because it prevents one from suffering the Torments of the Tomb. Al-Tirmidhī reported, on the authority of Ibn ʿAbbās (that the Prophet said:) "It is the Preventer – the saviour that saves (the believer) from the Torments of the Tomb." According to a *ḥadīth* in ʿUbayd's *Musnad*:

(The Prophet said:) "It is the saviour and the pleader (*al-mujaadila*) because on the Day of Resurrection it pleads with its Lord for the sake of its reciter."

In Ibn ʿAsākir's History, he records one of Anas' *ḥadīths*: "(The Prophet (peace and blessings be upon him) said:) '(Sura *67)'s name is "the Saviour".'" Al-Ṭabarānī reported, on the authority of Ibn Masūd, who said: "In the time of The Prophet (peace and blessings be upon him) we used to call it 'the Preventer'." (It is recorded) in the Jamal al-Qurraʾ that it was also called "the Protector (*al-waaqiyah*)" and "the Certain Preventer (*al-mannaaʿah*)".

(Concerning "the *sūrah* of) 'He asked' (*saʾala*)" (*70): it is also called "the Ways of Ascent (*al-maʾārij*)" and "the Actual (*al-wāqiʿ*)".

(Concerning "the *sūrah* of) About what? (*ʿam-ma*)" (*78): it is also called "the Great News (*al-nabaʾ*)" "the Disputing (*al-tasāʾul*)"[111] and "the Clouds (*al-muʾsirāt*)".[112]

(Concerning "the *sūrah* of) 'Were not going to' (*lam yakun*)" (*98): it is also called "the People of the Book": thus in Ubay's codex. In the Jamal al-Qurraʾ it is called "the *sūrah* of the Resurrection (*al-qiyaamah*) of the Wilderness (*al-bariyah*); and the Secession (*al-infikāk*)".

(Concerning "the *sūrah* of) 'Have you seen?' (*ʾa-raʾay-ta*)" (*107): it is also called "the *sūrah* of the Religion (*al-din*)" and "the *sūrah* of the Neighbourly Assistance (*al-maʿun*)".

(Concerning "the *sūrah* of) the Unbelievers (*al-kafirūn*)" (*109): Ibn Abī Ḥātim, on the authority of Zarara Ibn Awfa, reported that it is called "the Scarrer (*al-muqashqishah*)". In the Jamal al-Qurraʾ it is also called "the *sūrah* of Worship (*al-iʿbādah*)".

(Concerning "the *sūrah* of) Help (*al-Naṣr*)" (*110): it is also called "the Farewell (*al-tawdīʿ*)" because of the reference it contains about (the Prophet)'s (peace and blessings be upon him) death.

(Concerning "the *sūrah* of) 'May they perish (*tabba-t*)'" (*111): it is also called "the *sūrah* of the palm leaf fibre (*al-masad*)".[113]

(Concerning "the *sūrah* of) the Purity of Faith (*al-ʿIkhlāṣ*)" (*112): it is also called "the Foundation (*al-ʿasās*)" because it mentions God's Unicity, which is the Foundation of the Religion.

(Concerning "the *sūrahs* of) the Daybreak (*al-falaq*)" (*113) and "Mankind (*al-Nās*)" (*114): they are called "the two Pleadings for Refuge (*al-muʿawithatān* with a short *a* as the antepenultimate vowel)". They are also called "the two sententious ones (*al-mushaqshiqat-aan*)" because of the Arabic usage "a sententious preacher (*khaṭīb mushaqshiq*)".

Note

In his Burhān, al-Zarkashī reported that the enumeration of these names requires investigation: is it fixed (*tawqifi*) or do the names appear according to the circumstances? If it be the latter, then the disagreements (about the names) will never[114] cease, because one may infer many meanings from the names of each *sūrah*, requiring even the etymological derivations of each of the *sūrah's* names; and this is far-fetched.

(Al-Zarkashī)[115] said that one must examine the particularity of each *sūrah* by how it is named. It is certain that the Arabs would notice that many names were applied to things because of one of the rare or strange characteristics[116] or attributes that identify it. In order to understand the reason for something's name, one must understand that it may be accompanied by something wiser, larger, or precedent[117] to it. (The Arabs) call a sentence (*al-jumlah*, lit: "a complete one") and a lengthy ode (*al-qasidah al-Tawiila*, lit: "fat[118] and long (a technical term for a poetic metre)" because of their most salient feature. Thus were the *sūrahs* of the Qurʾān named: "The *sūrah* of the Cow" (*2) was named because it narrates the story of the well-known (Golden Cow), and the wondrous wisdom contained therein. "The *sūrah* of Women" (*4) was named this because it contains a wealth of laws relating to women. "The *sūrah* of the Cattle" (*6) was called this because of the plethora of these animals' circumstances that is found depicted therein. It is true that the word "cattle" occurs in many other *sūrahs*; but only in this *sūrah* do the verses "Of the cattle are some for burden and some for meat . . . or were you witnesses . . ."[119] occur. Analogously, the word "women" appears in several *sūrahs*, but the laws pertaining to them are neither expounded nor repeated, except in "The *sūrah* of Women". Likewise with "The *sūrah* of the Table" (*5): the word "table" is not repeated in any other *sūrah*, thus this *sūrah* is named by this particular characteristic.

It might be said that in "The *sūrah* of Hūd" (*11) the names of Noah, Ṣālih, Abrāhām, Lot, Shuʿayb and Moses are mentioned; Hūd's name is not particularly prominent. In fact, the story of Noah in this *sūrah* is longer and has more of a presence in it. I (Suyūṭī) would reply that these narratives appear in "The *sūrah* of the Heights" (*6) "The *sūrah* of Hūd" (*11) and "(The *sūrah* of) the Poets" (*26) more prominently than they appear in (other *sūrahs*). In these three *sūrahs* the name "Hūd" is not repeated as much as it is in his (that is, Hūd's)[120] *sūrah*. It is repeated in four places in it; repetition, as we have noted, is one of the strongest reasons (for naming a *sūrah*).

One might object that Noah's name appears in six places in this *sūrah*, (And this is more times than Hūd is mentioned).[121] But the story of Noah and his people was singled out in (*Sūrat Nūḥ*, *71) in its entirety, and it treats of no other subject. Thus this *sūrah* was more worthy to be called by (Noah's) name, rather than (*Sūrat Hūd*), which contains the story of Noah and others. (As for *Sūrat Hūd*, it was the first to be named after him (peace and blessings be upon him).)[122] End (of al-Zarkishi section).

I (Suyūṭī) hold that if you were to say that *sūrahs* in which the stories of the prophets are narrated are named for them, e.g. "the *sūrah* of Noah", "the *sūrah* of Hūd", "the *sūrah* of Abrāhām", "the *sūrah* of Jonah", "the *sūrah* of Al ʿImrān", "the *sūrah* of TS Solomon", "the *sūrah* of Joseph" (*12), "the *sūrah* of Muḥammad" (*47), "the *sūrah* of Maryam" (*19), "the *sūrah* of Luqmān" and "the *sūrah* of the Believer", likewise with the stories of various peoples, e.g. "the *sūrah* of the Children of Israel", "the *sūrah* of the Companions of the Cave", "the *sūrah* of al-Hijr" (*15), "the *sūrah* of Sheba", "the *sūrah* of the Angels", "the *sūrah* of the Jinn", "the *sūrah* of the Hypocrites", and "the *sūrah* of the Dealers in Fraud" (*83). Yet despite the numerous times Moses is mentioned in the Qurʾān, no *sūrah* has been named for him. Some people cavilled that almost the entire Qurʾān was about Moses, and that the first *sūrah* that should be named after him is "the *sūrah* of Taʾ Haʾ" (*20), or "the *sūrah* of the Narrations" (*28), or ("the *sūrah* of) the Heights" (*7), because they contain the most frequent mentioning of him. Likewise with Ādam: although he is mentioned in several *sūrahs*, none are named after him – it is as if "the *sūrah* of the Man" (*76) fulfilled (the "requirement" that a *sūrah* should be named for Ādam). Likewise with the story of "the (son of Abrāhām) intended for sacrifice", one of the most miraculously beautiful stories yet the *sūrah* called "the *sūrah* of Those Arranged in Ranks" (*37) was not named after him". The story of David occurs in "the *sūrah* called (the Letter) *Sad*" (*38), and it is not named after him. Consider the wisdom in this: after writing the above lines, I (Suyūṭī) discovered in al-Sakhawi's *Jamal al-Qurraʾ* that "*sūrah* Ṭaʾhaʾ" (*20) is also called "the *sūrah* of the One to Whom God spoke to directly (viz. Moses)" and in his *Kamil al-Hudhali* he called it "the *sūrah* of Moses" and he called "the *sūrah* of Sad" "the *sūrah* of David". I also saw in the writings of al-Jaʿbarī that "the *sūrah* of Those Arranged in Ranks" is called "the *sūrah* of the (son of Abrāhām) intended for sacrifice". But the *ḥadīths* these views are based upon need supporting *isnād*.

Section

Just as one *sūrah* may have many names, some *sūrahs* have only one name, like the *sūrah* called "*ALM*" or "*ALR*". This view is based on the acceptance of the "mysterious letters (preceding some *sūrahs*)" to serve as the *sūrah's* name.

The value of understanding the final vocalization of the *sūrahs'* names

In his *Sharh al-Tashīl* (The Explanation of the Facilitation), Ibn Ḥayyān said that a fragment such as "say, He inspired (*awha*)" or "God's order came" may be called "a sentence (*jumlah*)". A verb whose inherent pronoun is not expressed is given the final vocalization of zero, except when it begins with a consonant cluster (lit. "With *hamzat al-waṣl*"): in that case, its glottal stop will be pronounced (that is, it will become *hamzat al-qatʿ*). At the end of a verse, a final *taa' marbutah* will be pronounced as a *haa'*, and will be written as a *hāa'*. Thus I would read *iqtarabat* (with a final *taa' marbuutah*) at the end of a verse as *iqtarabah*. As for the final inflectional vowels, they have become nouns, and nouns are constructed according to a fixed morphological pattern. As for pronouncing the glottal stop (lit: "changing the *hamzat al-wasl* to *hamzat al-qaṭʿ*"), it does not occur in nouns except for frozen forms that have no analogue. As for the change of the final *taa' marbutah* to *haa'*, this is the grammatical rule concerning the feminine ending of nouns. And as for the writing of this final letter, this is due to the fact that writing generally follows pronunciation.

What is called a noun may be one letter of the alphabet to which you have added a *sūrah*. Ibn ʿUṣfur holds (that such "mysterious letters" that precede *sūrahs*) are read without final vocalization – that is, they end with a phonetic zero. Al-Shalawbin[124] holds that there are two possibilities: with or without vocalization. As for the first, called the narration (*al-Ḥikaya*) it is because they are separate letters to be pronounced as they are. As for the second, one considers the letters to be nouns, and thus they are vocalized accordingly; they may be considered as either masculine or feminine nouns. If individual letters have no *sūrah* occurring after them, neither expressly nor implicitly, then you may include or exclude (the letters') final vocalization. In case it was more than one letter, then if it was like non-Arabic nouns such as *Ṭasīn* and *Ḥamīm*, whether a *sūrah* was connected to it or not one can follow the narrations. Vocalization is not allowed whether it sounded like *Qabil* and *Habil* or not. If it was not like *Qābīl* and *Hābīl* and not combined like *Ṭāsīnmīm* and a *sūrah* was connected to it then one can narrate or vocalize, be it combined as in *Ḥaḍramūt* or when it is related vocalized or not, considering it to be either masculine or feminine. If no *sūrah* is added then narration is the rule, non-vocalization like *khamsatashar*. If it is not combined then non-vocalization is the rule, whether a *sūrah* is added or not, like *kat ha ya aynsad*, *Ḥāmīm sin ayn qaf*. Vocalization is not permitted became there is nothing like it in vocalized nouns. Neither is this combination like that of connecting two nouns; not many nouns are connected like that. However, Yunis permitted vocalization.

For a *sūrah* which is given a name which is not a letter of the alphabet, there are two possibilities: if the name of the *sūrah* has the definite article, then it is pronounced in the genitive, as in (sūrat) al-Anfāl, (sūrat) al-Aʿrāf, and (sūrat) al-Anʾam. If, on the other hand, the name of the *sūrah* is a diptote, and you omit the word "*sūrah*" preceding it, then you pronounce it in the nominative case – that is, "this (*sūrah*) is Hūd u", "this (*sūrah*) is Nūḥ u", etc – and you also say: "I recited (the *sūrah* of) Hūd a", "I recited (the *sūrah* of) Nūḥ a", etc. But if you add the word "*sūrah*" what is reported above is operative: a diptote is declined as such, e.g. "I recited *sūrat Yunis*"; if not, it is fully declined as a triptote, e.g. "I recited *sūrat Nūh in*", "I recited *sūrat Hūd in*", etc. End of synopsis.

Conclusion

The Qurʾān is divided into four parts, and a name was given to each part. Aḥmad and others related a *ḥadīth* on the authority of Wāʾila Ibn al-Asqaʿ reporting that the Prophet (peace and blessings be upon him) said: "was given in place of the Torah the Seven Long (*sūrahs*); in place of the Psalms the *sūrahs* containing approximately two hundred verses; in place of the Evangel the seven 'oft-repeated ones (*al-mathānī*)'; and esteemed above all by the sectioned[125] (last) quarter of the Qurʾān. God willing, I will add some words on this topic in a *nawʾ* below."

It is reported in the *Jamāl al-Qurraʾ* that some of the early Muslims said that the Qurʾān contains meadows, orchards, exclusive enclaves, brides and silk brocades. Its meadows are its (*sūrahs* beginning with) "*ALM*"; its orchards are (the *sūrahs* beginning with) "*ALR*"; its exclusive enclaves are (the *sūrahs* of) praise; its brides are (its *sūrahs*) that glorify (God); and its brocades are "*AL*" and "*Haaʾ Mim*" and the "Garden of the Mufassal (the fourth quarter of the Qurʾān)". (According to others, its silk brocades are the *Ṭawāsīm*; the *Ṭawāsīn*; *AL-Ḥa mīm*; or the *Ḥawamim*.)

I (Suyūṭī) hold to what al-Ḥākim reported on the authority of Ibn Masʿūd, who said that the *Ḥawāmīm*[126] are the silk brocade of the Qurʾān. Al-Sakhāwī held that the "Qurʾān's Stingers (*al-qawaarīʾ*)"[127] are the verses by which the (believer) takes refuge and fortifies himself; they were named this because they sting Satan, thus defending themselves against him and driving him off – e.g. the Throne verse and the final two *sūrahs* of the Qurʾān, etc.

I (Suyūṭī) hold by the sound *ḥadīth* reported by Aḥmad in his Musnad, on the authority of Muʾadh Ibn Anas: the "Verse of Power" is "Praise be to God who never fathered a son . . . (To the end of the verse)".[128]

Chapter eighteen

ON THE QURʾĀN'S COLLECTION AND ARRANGEMENT

In his *Fawaʾid*, al-Dayyir ʿĀqūlī said that Ibrāhīm Ibn Bashshār reported, on the authority of Sufyān Ibn ʿUyayn, on the authority of al-Zuhri, on the authority of Zayd Ibn Thābit, that the Prophet died before the Qurʾān was collected.

Al-Khaṭṭābī remarked that this only related to it being written down in a codex, because of his explanation that some may still be revealed to him which might abrogate some *ahkam* (laws) or recitations. When Revelation ended with the Prophet's death, God *alhama* (inspired) the first four rightly guided caliphs in this, in accordance with God's promise to preserve the Qurʾān for this Nation. This began under the rule of the *siddiq*, the absolutely trustworthy Friend, namely Abū Bakr, with the advice of ʿUmar.

Concerning Muslim's reporting the Tradition on the authority of Abū Saʿīd: The Prophet (peace and blessings be upon him) said: "Do not write down anything concerning me except the Qurʾān (to the end of the *ḥadīth*)." This, however, does not negate the foregoing, because it speaks about a specific writing down in a special. Also, the entire Qurʾān had already been written down during the lifetime of the Prophet (peace and blessings be upon him), but it was not collected all in the same place nor had its *sūrahs* been arranged.

Concerning the collection of the Qurʾān three times

In his *Mustadrak*, al-Hakim said that the Qurʾān was collected three times. The first time was in the Prophet's (peace and blessings be upon him) presence. This is related in a sound Tradition reported in both *Ṣaḥīḥs*. Zayd Ibn Thābit said: "We were in the presence of the Prophet (peace and blessings be upon him) arranging the fragments upon which parts of the Qurʾān were written . . . (to the end of the *ḥadīth*)." Al-Bayhaqī said that what is intended here is that separated fragments of the Qurʾānic text from various *sūrahs* were being arranged under the direction of the Prophet (peace and blessings be upon him).

Second, in the presence of Abū Bakr; in his *Ṣaḥīḥ* al-Bukhārī relates that Zayd Ibn Thābit said: "At the time of the Battle of Yamama, Abū Bakr sent for me, and I met him and ʿUmar Ibn al-Khaṭṭāb was with him. Abū Bakr said to me: 'Verily, ʿUmar has approached me, and told me that the death toll of those who had memorized the Qurʾān had heavily increased, and I fear that it will result in the severe loss of Qurʾān memorizers in the Islamic centres of population, resulting in the loss of much of the Qurʾān. Thus ʿUmar saw fit that he order the collection of the Qurʾān. Abū Bakr asked ʿUmar how could he do something that even the Emissary of God (peace and blessings be upon him) did not do, but ʿUmar swore that it was the proper thing to do. ʿUmar insisted on this until God opened his heart to accept it, because he realized what ʿUmar had realized.'" Zayed added: "Abū Bakr told me that I was an intelligent youth who was above suspicion: and that I had written down the *wahy* (inspiration) for the Emissary of God (peace and blessings be upon him). He ordered me to research and collect the Qurʾān. By God had I been ordered to move mountains, it would have been an easier task than the collecting of the Qurʾān which he had demanded of me. So I asked him: 'How can you two possibly do something that the Prophet (peace and blessings be upon him) refused to do?' Abū Bakr insisted on this until God opened my heart the way he did with Abū and ʿUmar. So I researched and collected fragments of the Qurʾān from palm leaves, smooth white stones, and the memories of men. I discovered the final part of *Surat al-Tawba* in the possession of Abū Khuzaima al-Anṣāri; he was the only one who had 'Now has come unto you a Messenger . . .' (until the end of *Surat al-Barāʾa*). Abū Bakr kept the codices until his death, upon which they were passed on to ʿUmar, and then to ʿUmar's daughter Hafṣa."

In his *al-Maṣahif*, Ibn Abī Dāwūd reported, in a sound Tradition, on the authority of ʿAbd Khayr, that the latter had heard ʿAlī say: "Abū Bakr is the person most worthy of reward for preserving the codices of the Qurʾān. May God have mercy on Abū Bakr! He was the first man to collect God's Book." On the other hand, I. A. Dawūd also reported, by way of Ibn Sirin, who claimed that ʿAlī said: "When the Emissary of God (peace and blessings be upon him) died, I swore that I would not get dressed except for the Friday prayers, until I collected the Qurʾān." Then he collected it.

Ibn Ḥajar said that this is a weak Tradition with a non-continuous *isnād*. Yet it is true intention, because it implies that "collecting the Qurʾān" means "memorizing it".

What ʿAbd Khayr reported above is the more trustworthy and authoritative view.

I (Suyūṭī) say: In this *faḍaʾil*, Ibn Al-Ḍurays reported it through a different *isnād*: "Bishr Ibn Mūsā reported, on the authority of Hawdha Ibn Khalifa, on the authority of ʿAwn, on the authority of Muḥammad Ibn Sirin, on the authority of Ikrama, who said: 'After the swearing of allegiance to Abū Bakr, ʿAlī Ibn Abī Ṭālib sat in his home. (It was said to Abū Bakr said that ʿAlī disliked the swearing of allegiance to you), so he sent for ʿAlī, and asked him if he did not like to swear allegiance to him. ʿAlī vehemently denied this. Abū Bakr then asked what may have kept him away from him, and ʿAlī answered that people had been making unwarranted additions to God's Book, and thus ʿAlī had sworn not to dress (to go out) except for the Friday Prayers until he had collected the entire Qurʾān. Abū Bakr then commended ʿAlī's act. Muḥammad Ibn Sirin then said that I told ʿIkrama that they arranged the Qurʾān chronologically. ʿIkrama then replied that if all mankind and all the jinn would cooperate in such an effort to correctly arrange the Qur'ān chronologically, they would never be able to achieve it (as has been arranged).' "

In his *al-Maṣaḥif*, Ibn Ashitta reported another tradition, with a different *isnād* yet traced back to the authority of Ibn Sirin saying that he had written in his codex the abrogating and abrogated verses; and that Ibn Sīrīn had said that he had searched for such a codex as far as Medina, but did not succeed in finding one.

Ibn Abī Dāwūd reported by way of al-Ḥasan, that ʿUmar inquired about a verse in God's Book, and was told that it was with someone who had been killed on the day of the battle of Yamama. ʿUmar then exclaimed: "We are God's!" and he then ordered the collection of the Qur'ān; he was the first to have it written down in codices. The *isnād* on which this Tradition is based is non-continuous; yet it is true in intention: "ʿUmar was the first to have it written down" means that he directed its collection.

I (Suyūṭī) say: One of the strange narratives about the first person to have the Qur'ān collected was reported by Ibn Ashittah in his *Masahif*, by way of Kahmas, on the authority of Burayda, who claimed that the first collector of the Qur'ān in a complete codex was Salim, Abū Hudhayfa's slave, who swore that he would never get dressed until he had collected the Qur'ān; so he did it. The authorities conferred, and they inquired of this codex's name. Some said: "Let's call it 'the *Sifr*' "; this is what the Jews call it, so they rejected it. Others said they had seen the likes of it in Ethiopia, and it is called "the *Maṣḥaf*", so they agreed to call it by this latter name. The *isnād* is acceptable because he was one of the collectors who acted on Abū Bakr's orders.

Ibn Abī Dāwūd reported, by way of Yaḥyā Ibn ʿAbd-al-Raḥmān Ibn Ḥaṭib, who said ʿUmar came and ordered that anyone who had heard any of the Revelation from The Emissary of God (peace and blessings be upon him) should bring it to him. They used to record it on pages, and stones, and palm-leaves. ʿUmar would not accept any piece of the Qur'ān unless it were certified by two witnesses; this shows that Zayd would not write down any piece from written records unless it were witnessed by someone who had heard it personally from the Prophet, in addition to Zayd having memorized it previously; this was done out of an abundance of caution to prevent any extraneous or erroneous material from entering the Qur'ānic text.

Ibn Abī Dawud also reported, by way of Hishām Ibn ʿUrwa, on the authority of his father, that Abū Bakr said to ʿUmar and to Zayd: "Sit by the mosque gate, and whenever two witnesses bring you a piece of God's Book, write it down." The Tradition this is based upon has a non-continuous *isnād*, but the individual links in the chain of transmission are trustworthy.

Ibn Hajar remarked that it is as if the term "two witnesses" here refers to "the memorization and the written down".

In his *Jamāl al-Qurrā*, al-Sakhawi said that the two of them give witness to the fact that the piece to be written down by Zayd had previously been dictated and written down in the presence of the Emissary of God (peace and blessings be upon him), who had approved it; or, that the two of them bear witness to one of the *wujuh* (ways) by which the Qur᾽ān was revealed.

Abū Shama commented that the intention here is that only those parts which had been dictated and written down in the presence of the Emissary of God (peace and blessings be upon him) would be accepted; memorization alone was not sufficient. He added that for this reason he said at the end of *Surat al-Tawba*: "I did not find it with the others" – that is, he did not find it written down with others, because memorization without being written down is not sufficient.

I (Suyūṭī) say that "the two bear witness" that the verses in question were from what had been recited for the Prophet (peace and blessings be upon him) referred to in the year of his death, as can be inferred from the information above at the end of the sixteenth chapter.

In his *al-Maṣaḥif*, Ibn Ashitta reported, on the authority of al-Layth Ibn Saʿd, who said that Abū Bakr was the first to collect the Qur᾽ān; he had Zayd write it down. Men would approach Zayd Ibn Thābit, who would not record a single *aya* (verse) unless it had been attested to by two reliable witnesses; and that the end of *Surat al-Barā᾽a* would not now exist were it not for Khuzayma Ibn Thābit. Zayd said "Write it down, for verily, the Emissary of God (peace and blessings be upon him) approved his authenticity as equal to that of two trustworthy men"; thus was it written down. And verily, ʿUmar brought Zayd *ayat al-rajm* (the "stoning verse") to include in the codex, but Zayd did not include it, because ʿUmar was the only witness.

In his *Kitāb Fahm al-Sunan*, al-Ḥarith al-Ḥāsibi said that the writing down of the Qur᾽ān is not an innovation, because the Prophet (peace and blessings be upon him) ordered that it be written down; but scattered in fragments that were dispersed on scraps of leather, the dried scapula of camels and palm-leaves. Thus the Ṣiddīq (Abū Bakr) ordered them collected from their various sources; they were copied down in one place in the form of paper found in the Emissary of God's home, within which the as-yet-to-be arranged Qur᾽ān was also found. It was collected together and put in order, and then it was firmly bound so that nothing could be lost from it.

One might then inquire about how the trustworthiness of the owners of these fragments and those who had it in their chest (that is, memory) was determined. The answer is that they would all bring forward the miraculous arrangement and exact syntax, which they had personally heard the recitation of from the Prophet (peace and blessings be upon him) over a period of twenty years; this was a guarantee against any kind of forgery. The only worry was the possibility of loss from any of the *suhuf* (leaves).

We have mentioned above one of Zayd's Traditions saying that he had collected the Qur᾽ān from palm-leaves and smooth stones; and in another one, from pieces of leather; in another, from pieces of dried animal skin; in another; from the dried scapula of camels; in another from ribs; in another, from saddle-planks. *ʿUsub* is the plural of *ʿasib*, which is the palm-leaf; the Arabs would remove the stem, and write on the broad leaf. *Likhaf*, with a short *I* following the *lam*, and a *kha* with a diacritical point above it, and *fa*ʾ at the end is the plural of *lakhfa*, which, with a short *a* following the *lam* and the *kha*ʾ followed by a phonetic zero, means "smooth stones". Al-Khaṭībi said it means "slabs of stone". *Ruqa* is the plural of *raqʾa*, which may be a piece of skin, parchment or paper. *Aktaf* is the plural of *katif* which is the bone of a camel or a sheep, which the Arabs would write on after it had dried up. *Aqtab* is the plural of *qatab*, which is a piece of wood used as a camel saddle.

In his *Muwaṭṭa*, Ibn Wahb reported, on the authority of Mālik, on the authority of Ibn Shihab, on the authority of Salim Ibn ʿAbd Allāh Ibn ʿUmar, who said that Abū Bakr requested that Zayd collect the Qurʾān on sheets of paper, but Zayd refused until he was further urged to do so by ʿUmar.

In his *Maghāzī*, Mūṣa Ibn ʿUqba reported, on the authority of Ibn Shihāb, who said that when the Muslims suffered heavy casualties at the Battle of Yamama, Abū Bakr became overcome with anxiety, fearing that part of the Qurʾān would be lost. Then people came with those parts of the Qurʾān they had memorized or had written down, until the entire Qurʾān was collected on paper during the reign of Abū Bakr. Thus was Abū Bakr the first to collect the Qurʾān on *suhuf* (leaves).

Ibn Ḥajar reported that a Tradition of ʿAmāra Ibn Ghāziyya contained the statement that Zayd Ibn Thābit had said that Abū Bakr had ordered him to write down the Qurʾān on pieces of dried skin and palm-leaves; ʿUmar succeeded Abū Bakr after the letter's death, upon which Zayd wrote the entire Qurʾān in one *ṣaḥīfa* (codex), which ʿUmar kept.

Ibn Hajar said that first report is correct: first were the pieces of skin and the palm-leaves, before the entire Qurʾān was collected during the reign of Abū Bakr. Later it was collected in the mashaf (codex) during Abū Bakr's time, just as reported in the various sound and successive Traditions.

The third collection

According to al-Ḥakim, the third collection refers to the arrangement of the *sūrahs* during the reign of ʿUthmān. Al-Bukhārī related, on the authority of Anas, that Hudhayfa Ibn al-Yaman approached ʿUthmān and told him that while campaigning with the Syrians for the conquest of Armenia and with the Iraqis for the conquest of Azerbayjan, he had been non-plussed at the differences in the Qurʾān recitations of the two groups. He advised ʿUthmān to enlighten the Muslim Nation before they would have to suffer all of the scriptural disputations of the Jews and the Christians. ʿUthmān then requested that his daughter Hafsa send him the *suhuf* (leaves) which had been copied into the *masahif* (codices); he added that he would later return them to her. She did so.

ʿUthmān then ordered Zayd Ibn Thābit, ʿAbd Allāh Ibn al-Zubayr, said Ibn al-ʿĀs, and ʿAbd-al-Raḥmān Ibn al-Ḥārith Ibn Hishām to copy it all in the *maṣāḥif* (codices). ʿUthmān told the group of the three Qurayshis if they and Zayd differed on a reading, they should write it in the dialect of Quraysh because the Qurʾān was revealed in their dialect; they did so, copying all the *suhuf* (leaves) into the *maṣāḥif* (codices). ʿUthmān returned the leaves to Hafsa.

ʿUthmān then sent to all the corners of his empire the standard copies he had made, and ordered that any extraneous *sahifa* (leaf) or *maṣḥaf* (codex) be burned.

Zayd reported that he had missed a verse into *Surat al-Aḥzab* when copying the codex, after having heard the emissary of God (peace and blessings be upon him) recite it.

We searched for it, and found it in the possession of Khuzayma Ibn Thābit al-Ansāri: "Among the believers are men who have been true to their covenant with God." So we added it in its proper place in the codex.

Ibn Ḥajar said that this happened in the year twenty-five; he added that some of our contemporaries are ignorant of this, and assume that it occurred in about the year thirty, but there is no authoritative support for this. End of Ibn Hajar's remarks.

Ibn Ashitta reported, by way of Ayyub, on the authority of Abū Qullaba, who said that someone from the Banu Āmir named Anas Ibn Mālik said that in the time of ʿUthmān people differed about the reciting of the Qurʾān, so much so that teachers and students scuffled. ʿUthmān Ibn ʿAffān was astonished that while they who were so close by he demanded that they lie and misread the Qurʾān, then those far away from him will be even worse. ʿUthmān declared: "O Companions of Muḥammad! Come together and inscribe for the people an *Imām* (official standard codex)." So they did. Whenever they differed or argued about any verse, they would agree that "this is the way that the Emissary of God dictated it to so-and-so". They would search him out, and have him testify in the presence of three Medinan men that "the Emissary of God (peace and blessings be upon him) dictated such-and-such a verse, in such-and-such a manner". They would write it down, and then insert it in the codex in its proper place.

Ibn Abī Dāwūd reported, by way of Muḥammad Ibn Sirin, on the authority of Kathir Ibn Aflaḥ, who said that when ʿUthmān had decided to record the codices, he summoned twelve men of Quraysh and the Ansār (Helpers), and they sent for the chest for keeping Qurʾān codices that was in ʿUmar's home, and it was delivered to them.

ʿUthmān used to surprise them whenever they disagreed and they would delay any decision on it. Muḥammad Ibn Sīrīn added that he assumed that they wanted to delay any decision in order to determine who was most recently acquainted with the lost revelation (version) of the Prophet (peace and blessings be upon him), so they wrote it all down according to his version.

Ibn Abī Dāwūd reported a sound Tradition, on the authority of Suwayd Ibn Ghafala, who reported that ʿAlī said: "Don't say anything but good about ʿUthmān. By God! He dealt with the codices with the authority of many of us. He

(ʿUthmān) said, 'What do you say about this reading? I have been informed that someone would say to another: "My reading is better than your reading."'"

Now, this is practically unbelief! We said, "What do you think we do about it?" ʿUthmān said that all men should be united in having only one *mashaf* (codex), so that there be neither differences nor disputations. We agreed and said: "Verily what you have recommended is correct."

Ibn al-Tin and others reported that the difference between the collections of Abū Bakr and ʿUthmān is that in the former case the collection was done out of fear that a fragment might become lost from the Qurʾān's entirety, because it had never been collected in one place, so he had it collected on *ṣaḥāʾif* (leaves) arranged according to the verses of its *sūrahs*, according to the readings that the Prophet (peace and blessings be upon him) had told them to.

ʿUthmān's collection came about after the plethora of variant readings had been discovered, to the point that people were reciting the Qurʾān in all of their various and widely diverse dialects! This would cause some to think that others were in error, and ʿUthmān feared the adverse compounding effect of this, so he had those *suhuf* (leaves) copied into one *maṣḥaf* (codex) arranged according to the Qurʾān's *sūrahs*; he removed all the dialectal readings except those of Quraysh because the Qurʾān was revealed in that dialect. This was so although in the beginning (to make it easy) recitation in other dialects was widespread and people were very tolerant of variant dialectal readings. But ʿUthmān realized that the need for this leniency was no longer relevant, and so he limited recitation to the one dialect.

The Judge Abū Bakr al-Baqillani reported in his Intisar that ʿUthmān did not intend to collect the same text of the Qurʾān that Abū Bakr had completed "between the two book covers (*al-lawhany*); he intended rather to bring together all of the authoritatively correct reading that came directly from the Prophet (peace and blessings be upon him) and to exclude all others. They would then place it in a *maṣḥaf* (codex), in correct order and no *taʾwīl* (interpretation) which had become attached to the verse text. Also excluded were any abrogated from recital, despite its having been written down with verses the recitation and memorization of which were ordained. All this was one to guard against any corruption or suspicion on the part of later generations.

Al-Ḥārith al-Ḥasibī reported that popular belief holds that ʿUthmān was the collector of the Qurʾān, yet this is not the case. ʿUthmān rather made the people recite in one way which was determined by him together with those present from the Muhajirun (emigrants) or the Ansār (Helpers). This was done out of fear of the anarchy that would reign given the disputes between the Iraqis and the Syrians concerning the *ḥarfs* (letters, sound) of the recitation. Formerly, the *masahif* (codices) contained some arbitrary readings based on the seven *ḥarfs* in which the Qurʾān was brought down; ʿUthmān's predecessor in collecting the entirety of the Qurʾān was the Ṣiddīq (Abū Bakr). ʿAlī said: "Had I been in power at that time, I would have done with the *masahif* exactly what ʿUthmān did." End.

Note

There were some differences concerning the number of codices that ʿUthmān sent out to the far corners of his empire. The most well known is that they were five: Ibn Abī Dāwūd reported by way of Ḥamza al-Zayyat, who claimed that ʿUthmān had sent out four codices, and that he had heard Abū Ḥātim al-Sijistānī say that seven codices had been written, which ʿUthmān had dispatched to Mecca, Syria, Yemen, al-Baḥrayn, Baṣra and Kufa; one was kept in Medina.

Section

The consensus and all succeeding traditions is that the arrangement of all the verses is (divinely) ordained; there isn't the least doubt in this. A number of scholars have cited Traditions to this effect, among them al-Zarkashī in his *Burhān*, Abū Jaʿfar Ibn al-Zubayr in his *Munasabat*. This is expressed by saying that the arrangement of the verses in their *sūrahs* was determined by the Prophet (peace and blessings be upon him), who commanded the first generation of Muslims not to change anything.

I will cite below some of the authorities' writings in support of this.

Concerning the texts, we have cited one of Zayd's Traditions above: "We were arranging fragments of the Qurʾān in the presence of the prophet (peace and blessings be upon him)."

Aḥmad Abū Dāwūd al-Tirmdhi, al-Nisāʾī, Ibn Ḥibban and al-Ḥakim all reported on the authority of Ibn ʿAbbās that the latter had asked ʿUthmān why he had appended *Surat al-Anfal* (it being one of the *mathani* (oft-repeated ones), to *Surat al-Barāʾa* (it being one of the *sūrahs* of about two hundred verses) and connected the first to the second without inserting the line "In the Name of God, the Compassionate, the Merciful"; and then inserted *Surat al-Barāʾa* into the seven longest *sūrahs* in the Qurʾān. ʿUthmān responded that the Emissary of God (peace and blessings be upon him) would receive *sūrahs* with many verses; when a piece would come down to him, he would call to whoever was writing it down and say: "Put these verses in the *sūrah* in which such-and-such is mentioned." *Surat al-Anfal* was one of the first *sūrahs* to be revealed in Medina, while *Surat al-Barāʾa* was from the last part of the Qurʾān to be revealed. Since their contents were similar, ʿUthmān thought they should go together. The Emissary of God (peace and blessings be upon him) passed away without informing us that it belonged to it. For that I (ʿUthmān) joined them together, without having to insert the line "In the Name of God, The Compassionate, the Merciful" between them, and I inserted it within the seven longest *sūrahs* of the Qurʾān.

Aḥmad reported on the basis of a sound Tradition, on the authority of ʿUthmān Ibn Abī al-ʿĀs, who said that he was sitting with the Emissary of God (peace and blessings be upon him), when He raised his eyes and then looked down and said: "Gabriel came to me and commanded me to put this verse in this place in this *sūrah*: 'God commands Justice and loving-kindness and Generosity towards relatives . . .'."

Al-Bukhārī reported on the authority of Ibn al-Zubayr, who recited the following verse to ʿUthmān: "Those of you who die and leave behind wives . . ." and then noted that this verse had been abrogated by another one. He then asked ʿUthmān why he should write it or leave it out. ʿUthmān answered: "O my cousin! I will never change any verse's position in the text."

Muslim reported on the authority of ʿUmar, who said that he never asked the Prophet (peace and blessings be upon him) about anything more than he had asked him about the *kalāla* (a person who had left no descendants). The Prophet (peace and blessings be upon him) stuck his finger in ʿUmar's chest, and told him: "The verse revealed in the summer (of that year) which occurs at the end of *Surat al-Nisaʾ* should suffice you."

Of them are also Traditions relating to the final verses of *Surat al-Baqara*.

Muslim reported a sound Tradition on the authority of Abū al-Dardāʾ; "The Prophet said: 'Whoever memorizes ten verses from the beginning of *Surat al-Kahf* is protected from the Dajjāl (Anti-Christ).'" Abū al-Dardāʾ has a variant of this tradition which replaces "the beginning" of the *sūrah* to "the end".

Many other texts also support this position. They attest to the Prophet's own reciting of several *sūrahs*, e.g. *Surat al-Baqara*, *Surat al-Imran* and *Surat al-Nisaʾ*; all of this found in Hudhayfa's Traditions. In his *Ṣaḥīḥ*, al-Bukhārī reports the same concerning *Surat al-Aʿrāf*; the Prophet recited it at the *Maghreb* (Evening) prayer. Al-Nisāʾī related that the Prophet would recite *Surat Qad Aflaḥa* during the Morning Prayer, from the first verse up to the forty-fifth verse in which Moses and Aaron are mentioned. At that point, the Prophet had a coughing spell, and genuflected. Al-Ṭabarānī reported that the Prophet would recite *Surat al-Rum* during the Morning Prayer. According to both shaykhs, al-Bukhārī and Muslim, the Prophet would recite *Surat al-Tanzīl* and *Surat* Has There Come to Mankind, during the Friday Morning Prayers. In his *Ṣaḥīḥ*, Muslim reports that the Prophet would recite *Surat Qaf* during the Friday sermon. In the *Mustadrak* and elsewhere, it is reported that the Prophet would recite *Surat al-Raḥmān* to the Jinn. In the *Ṣaḥīḥ* it is reported that the Prophet recited *Surat al-Najm* to the unbelievers in Mecca, then prostrated himself at its conclusion. Muslim also reports that the Prophet recited *Surat Iqtarabat* and *Surat Qāf* together during ʿĪd (Korban and Ramaḍān Biram) and Friday prayers; and that he would recite *Surat al-Munafiqin* during the Friday prayers. In the *Mustadrak*, it is related on the authority of ʿAbd Allāh Ibn Salām that the Prophet (peace and blessings be upon him) recited *Surat al-Ṣaff* at the moment it was revealed to him, from start to finish. The companions witnessed the Prophet's (peace and blessings be upon him) recitation of several *sūrahs* in the final quarter of the Qurʾān; the order of the verses was always ordained. None of the Companions would change the order of the Prophet's (peace and blessings be upon him) order of recitation of the verses. This universally accepted. It is true that some doubt about this might arise from what Ibn Abī Dawud reported in the Masahif by way of Muḥammad Ibn Isḥāq, on the authority of Yaḥya Ibn ʿIbad Ibn ʿAbd Allāh Ibn Zubayr, that his father said: "Al-Ḥarith Ibn Khuzayma brought two verses from the end of *Surat al-Barāʾa*, claiming that he had heard the Emissary of God (peace and blessings be upon him) recite them, so he had memorized them." Then ʿUmar said: "I give witness: I also heard them recited by the Prophet." ʿUmar then added: "Had they been three verses instead of two, I would have made them a *sūrah* unto itself. Look at the chronologically last *sūrah* of the Qurʾān; and attached these two verses at its conclusion."

Ibn Ḥajar noted: "This may seem that they used to arrange the verses of the *sūrahs* according to their *ijtihād* (independent rational judgement); all Traditions attest to the fact that they did not do anything like that except according to the fixed and unchangeable order."

I (Suyūṭī) say this is also opposed in Ibn Abī Dāwūd, by way of Abū al-ʿAliya, on the authority of Ubayy Ibn Kaʿb, who claimed that when collection of the Qurʾān had been completed at ". . . then they turned aside. God turned their hearts, for they are a people who do not understand", they supposed that this was the final part of the Revelation, but Ubayy said that the Emissary of God (peace and blessings be upon him) recited to him the following two verses; "an Emissary has come to you . . . (to the end of the *sūrah*)".

Makki and others have reported that the arrangement of the verses in their *sūrahs* was fixed by order of the Prophet (peace and blessings be upon him); when he did not give the order, as at the beginning of *Surat al-Barāʾa*, it was left without the usual preface, "In the Name of God, the Compassionate, the Merciful."

In his *Intiṣār*, the judge Abū Bakr al-Baqillani said that the arrangement of the verses in their *sūrahs* is in a fixed order; it is a firm rule: Gabriel used to say to the Prophet: "Put such-and-such a verse in such-and-such a position." He added that his school of thought holds that when God brought down the entire Qurʾān He determined the order of the verses in their *sūrahs*: neither the text nor the recitation had been changed since that time; what we now possess between the *daffatyn* (two book covers) is the entire Qurʾān just as it had been recorded in ʿUthmān's codex. There is neither anything added nor subtracted from it; its arrangement and order are fixed according to God's (He is exalted) determination. His Emissary arranged it accordingly; he neither placed a verse before nor after its fixed position in the text. The Islamic Nation preserved the Prophet's (peace and blessings be upon him) arrangement and position of the verses of each *sūrah*, and was aware of the exact nature of the entire text. It also preserved his exact readings and recitation. It is also possible that the Emissary (peace and blessings be upon him) did his own arrangement of the *sūrahs*, and assigned to the Nation to complete it for themselves after his death. Indeed, this latter view is more probable.

Ibn Wahb reported that he had heard Mālik say that the arrangement of the Qurʾān was accomplished solely on the basis of what the people heard the Prophet (peace and blessings be upon him) recite.

In his *Sharḥ al-Sunna*, al-Baghawi said that the Companions (May God be pleased with them) collected the entire Qur'ān between the *daffatayn* (book covers) exactly as God had revealed it to His Emissary; they neither added to it nor subtracted from it, fearing that part of it may become lost due to the demise of the Qur'ān-memorizers. Thus they wrote it down exactly as they heard it from the Emissary of God (peace and blessings be upon him), without moving a verse before or after its fixed position; they did not make any arrangement save that which they took from the Prophet (peace and blessings be upon him) of God's arrangement. Rather, the Emissary of God (peace and blessings be upon him) would instruct and teach his Companions the Qur'ān portions which had been revealed to Him; this is what we now have in our *maṣāḥif* (codices). Thus had Gabriel fixed the arrangement, and had taught the Prophet at the time of Revelation which verse follows another verse, and thus they should be inscribed in their *sūrah* in their proper position. Thus did the companions strive to collect the entire Qur'ān in one place, if not in its proper order: for, verily, the Qur'ān is inscribed in its proper order on the *lawh al-mahfuz* (Preserved Tablet). God had brought it down in its entirety to the lowest Heaven, then He would bring down sections of it according to need – that is, when the occasion demanded it; thus the order of the original Revelation is not the same as its recitation today.

Ibn al-Ḥaṣṣār said that the *sūrahs*' arrangement and the verses' positioning were achieved only through *wahy* (inspiration); the certainty of the continuous tradition in this order is due to the facts that the Emissary of God (peace and blessings be upon him) recited it in this way, and that the Companions arranged it in this order in the *mashaf* (codex).

Section

As to the present order of the *sūrahs*: are they also fixed by God or is their present order due to the Companions' *ijtihad* (independent rational judgement)? Although there remain differences of opinion, the great majority of the ʿulamaʾ (scholars) hold the second view; among them are Mālik and the Judge Abū Bakr al-Baqillānī in one of his two opinions.

Ibn Fāris claimed that the collection of the Qur'ān was of two types: the first is the order of the *sūrahs*, e.g. "seven long ones" precede the *sūrahs* of about two hundred verses each, because the latter chronologically follow the former. This is what the Companions did in the *sūrahs*. This is fixed (that is, ordained) by the Prophet (peace and blessings be upon him) as he was informed of it by Gabriel, at His Lord's command. This one may infer from the difference in the arrangement of *sūrahs* in the codices of the first Muslim. ʿAlī's codex was arranged chronologically according to the sequence of Revelation; first to appear is Surat Iqraʾ, then Surat al-Mudathir, Surat Nūn, Surat al-Muzamil, Surat Tabbat, Surat al-Takwīr, and so on until the end of the Meccan and Medinan *sūrahs*. In Ibn Masʿūd's codex, Surat al-Baqra comes first, then Surat al-Nisā,

Surat al-ʿImrān – this is quite a difference! Likewise for the personal codices of Ubayy and others.

In this Masahif, Ibn Ashittah reported, by way of Ismaʾil Ibn ʿAyyāsh, on the authority of Ḥabbān Ibn Yaḥyā, on the authority of Abū Muḥammad al-Qurashī, who said: "ʿUthmān commanded the companions to place the seven long *sūrahs* first, and to follow them with *Surat al-Anfāl* and *Surat al-Tawbah*, not separating the last two with the preface inserted before every other *sūrah* of the Qurʾān": In the name of God, the Compassionate, the Merciful.

The vast majority of the scholars hold with the first view; one of these is the judge Abū Bakr in one of his two statements above.

Abū Bakr Ibn al-Anbārī reported that God brought down the entire Qurʾān to the lowest heaven, and then divided it into some twenty-odd sections. Each *sūrah* was then revealed according to the proper circumstance, and each verse was revealed to impart new information. Gabriel would determine for the Prophet (peace and blessings be upon him) the positioning of each verses and every *sūrah*; all of the *sūrahs*, verses and individual letters are in absolutely harmonious co-ordination – all of this is directly by way of the Prophet (peace and blessings be upon him). Whoever moves a *sūrah* forwards or backwards from its fixed position in the text has thereby desecrated and violated the organizational integrity of the Qurʾān.

In this *Burhān*, al-Kirmānī reported that the present arrangement of the *sūrahs* is in accordance with the way God inscribed them on the *al-Lawh al-Mahfuz* (Preserved Tablet). Thus would the Prophet (peace and blessings be upon him) arrange it every year after collecting the material that Gabriel would reveal to him during that year, and show it to Gabriel. In the year of his death, the Prophet showed Gabriel his final arrangement twice. The last verse to be revealed is "Fear the day on which you will be returned to God"; Gabriel told him to place it in between the "Usury verse" and the "Debt verse".

Al-Ṭayyibī reported that God first brought down the entirety of the Qurʾān to the lowest Heaven, then revealed it in instalments according to necessity, then He Himself confirmed its permanent order and arrangement in the *masahif* (codices) according to what He had inscribed on the *al-Lawh a-Mahfuz* (Preserved Tablet).

In his *Burhān*, al-Zarkashī reported that the difference between the two views is semantic: the second view is held by those who see in it that the Prophet (peace and blessings be upon him) indicated to his Companions to do that because of their knowledge of the "occasions of its revelation" and the arrangement of its words. That is why Mālik said that the Companions only arranged the Qurʾān according to the way in which they heard the Prophet (peace and blessings be upon him) recite it while saying that the final arrangement was really done through their own *ijtihad* (effort). The difference is seen tied up in whether this is a question of fixed wording or merely special pleading, giving them room to wriggle. Abū Jaʿfar Ibn Zubayr preceded them in his.

In his *Madkhal*, al-Bayhaqī said that in the time of the Prophet (peace and blessings be upon him) the Qur'ān had its present order except for *Surat al-Anfāl* and *Surat al-Barā'a*, in accordance with ʿUthmān's Tradition above. Ibn ʿAṭiyya was inclined towards the view that the final arrangement of most of the *sūrahs* had already been accomplished during the Prophet's (peace and blessings be upon him) lifetime, e.g. the "seven long *sūrahs*", "the Hawamim" and the final quarter of the Qur'ān. It is possible that he left the remainder to the Islamic Nation to arrange after his death.

Abū Jaʿfar Ibn Zubayr said that the Traditions testify to more than Ibn ʿAṭiyya alluded to: there is very little that allows room for argument. As Muslim reported, the Prophet said: "Recite the *zahrawayn* (the 'two resplendent ones') namely *Surat al-Baqara* and *Surat al-Imrān*." According to a Tradition of Saʿīd Ibn Khālid, the Emissary of God used to recite the "seven lengthy *sūrahs*" in a *rak'a* during prayer. This was also reported by Ibn Abī Shayba in his *Musannaf*. In the same work is a Tradition that the Prophet (peace and blessings be upon him) used to recite the entire fourth quarter of the Qur'ān in one *rak'a* during prayer.

Al-Bukhārī reported on the authority of Ibn Mas'ud that the Prophet said concerning the *sūrahs Isra'il*, *al-Kahf*, *Maryam ta'ha'* and *al-Anbiya'* that "These are the *ʿitaq* (those of noble lineage); they are my very birthright." He mentioned them in the order we now possess.

Al-Bukhārī reports also that the Prophet, when retiring every night, would bring his hands together, blow in them, and would recite: "Say: 'He is one . . . (to the end of *sūrah* 112), and the final two *sūrahs* (113 and 114).' "

Abū Jaʿfar al-Naḥḥas said that the present arrangement of the *sūrahs* derives directly from the Emissary of God (peace and blessings be upon him) according to Waʿila's Tradition saying "The seven long (*sūrahs*) are in place of the Torah . . . (to the end of the Tradition)." He adds that this Tradition indicates that the present arrangement of the Qur'ān is taken from the prophet (peace and blessings be upon him) in his time. We have a unanimous consensus concerning the *Mashaf* because of this Tradition related in the Emissary of God's (peace and blessings be upon him) own words concerning the redaction of the Qur'ān.

Ibn al-Hassar reported that the arrangement of the *sūrahs* and the positioning of the *āyas* in their proper places was accomplished solely through divine decree.

Ibn Ḥajar reported that the arrangement of the *sūrahs* in separate groupings does not imply that their order is not divinely ordained. He added that further support for this view that the arrangement of the *sūrahs* is divinely ordained is that Ahmed Ibn Hanbal and Aws Ibn Abī Aws reported that Hudhaifa al-Thaqafī said: "I was in a delegation of the Thaqafīs that converted to Islam . . . (to the end of the Tradition)." This Tradition contains the words: ". . . then the Emissary of God (peace and blessings be upon him) told us that 'Suddenly a *hizb* (portion) of the Qur'ān comes to me, and I do not want to come out until I receive it completely.' " We asked the Companions of the Emissary of God (peace and blessings be upon him): "How do you apportion the Qurʾān?" They answered: "We apportion it in groups of three *sūrahs*, five *sūrahs*, seven *sūrahs*, nine *sūrahs*, eleven, thirteen and the last quarter of the Qurʾān which contains the *sūrahs Qaf* until the end. Hudhaifa added that this indicates that the order of the *sūrahs* presently in the *Maṣḥaf* is according to the determination made by the Emissary of God (peace and blessings be upon him). He added that it was also possible that what was arranged then was exclusively the final quarter of the Qurʾān unlike the remainder of it.

I (Suyūṭī) hold that further evidence that the order of the *sūrahs* is divinely ordained is the fact that the Hawamim – that is, *sūrahs* 40–46, which begin with the "mysterious letter" *Ḥaʾmīm*, are arranged together; likewise the *Tawasin* – that is, *sūrahs* 26–28. Yet the *Musabbihat* – that is, *sūrahs* that begin with Praise of God – do not follow one another in succession, but rather are dispersed throughout the Qurʾān. As for *sūrah* 26 (The Poets), which begins with *Taʾ Sin* and *sūrah* 28 (The Narrations), which begins with the same three letters – they are separated by *sūrah* 27, which begins with *Ta*, *Sin*, despite the fact that this latter *sūrah* is shorter than the other two. Now had this arrangement been due to someone's individual effort rather than being divinely ordained, then the *Musabbihat* (*sūrahs* of Praise) would also follow one another in succession, and *sūrah* 27 would follow *sūrah* 28.

Al-Bayhaqī gives further support in his discussion of *sūrah* 94 (The Expansion of the Breast), where he states that all of the *sūrahs* are arranged according to divine decree except for *Surat Barāʾa* and *Surat al-Anfāl*. It is not necessary to demonstrate that the present order is divinely ordained by means of the Emissary of God's (peace and blessings be upon him) own recital: by doing so we would deny the Tradition that he (peace and blessings be upon him) would recite *sūrah* 4 (Women) before *sūrah* 3 (Āl ʿImrān), because the recitation of the *sūrahs* in their usual order is not obligatory; perhaps he (peace and blessings be upon him) recited thus to demonstrate this latitude.

In his *Kitāb al-Maṣaḥif* (Book of Codices) Ibn Ashta reported, by way of Ibn Wahab, on the authority of Sulayman Ibn Bilāl, who said that he had heard Rabīʿ ask why the *sūrahs al-Baqara* and *al-Imran* were placed before some eighty-odd *sūrahs* which had been revealed previously in Mecca, and *sūrahs al-Baqara* and *al-Imran* were revealed later in Medina. The response was that the Qurʾān was arranged by following sound Traditions; these two *sūrahs* were placed in their order by those who arranged the Qurʾān by relying on the testimony of reliable scholars of tradition and their consensus in this matter. This is the final, irrefutable conclusion.

Conclusion

Concerning "the seven long *sūrahs*": the first is *Surat al-Baqara* and the last is *Surat Barāʾa*, according to the general consensus. But al-Hakim, al-Nisāʾī and others report, on the authority of Ibn ʿAbbās, who said that "the seven long *sūrahs*" are *al-Baqara*, *Āl ʿImrān*, *al-Nisaʾ*, *al-Maʾida*, *al-Anʿam* and *al-Aʿraf*. Al-Rāwi noted that Ibn ʿAbbās mentioned "seven", but al-Rāwi himself had forgotten the name of the seventh. There is a sound Tradition on the authority of Ibn Abī Ḥātim and others, on the authority of Saʿīd Ibn Jubayr, which states that the "seventh" referred to is *Surat Yūnus*; we have given a similar report on the authority of Ibn ʿAbbās above in Chapter one. Al-Ḥākim also records the view that the "seventh" refers to *Surat al-Kahf*.

Concerning the *Miʾūna* ("Hundreds"): these *sūrahs* are so called because each of them either approximates or exceeds one hundred verses.

Concerning the *Mathānī*: they follow the "Hundreds", because they succeed them – that is, they come after them. They are secondary to the "Hundreds", which are their predecessors. Al-Farrāʾ said that the *Mathānī* are the *sūrahs* whose verses are fewer than one hundred because they are repeated more often than the "seven Long Ones" and the "Hundreds". Another opinion is that they are called the *Mathānī* because of the stories' lesson to be learned in the parables they repeat; so related al-Nakzawī.

In his *Jamāl al-Qurrāʾ*, al-Sakhawī reported that the *Mathānī* refers to those *sūrahs* that repeat the "accounts of bygone peoples". As already noted, *al-Mathānī* may refer to the entire Qurʾān or to the Fātiḥa only.

Concerning the *Mufaṣṣal*: this term refers to the short *sūrahs* which follow the *Mathānī*. They are called this because of the numerous times the *bismalla* which separates them is recited. Another opinion is that their name is due to the paucity of abrogated verses in them; for this reason it was also called the *Muhkam* (unambiguous), as al-Bukhārī related on the authority of Saʿīd Ibn Jubayr, who said: "What they call the '*Mufaṣṣal*' is the '*Muḥkam*'. It is unanimously agreed that it concludes with *Surat al-Nās*."

There are twelve differing opinions concerning which was its first *sūrah*: (1) *Qaf*, according to Aws' Tradition quoted a bit above. (2) *al-Hujurat*. Al-Nawawī considers the Tradition on which this is based to be sound. (3) *Muḥammad*. Al-Māwardī ascribed this view to many. (4) *al-Jāthiya*. The Qadiʿ Ayyaḍ reported this. (5) *al-Ṣāffat*. (6) *al-Ṣaff*. (7) *al-Mulk*. Thus reported the three traditions of Ibn Abī al-Sayyif in his *al-Nuʿkat ala al-Tanbīh*. (8) *al-Fath*. Thus reported al-Kamal al-Dhamarī in his *Sharḥ al-Tanbīh*. (9) *al-Raḥmān*. Thus reported Ibn al-Sayyid in his *Amāli ʿalā al-Muwaṭṭa*. (10) *al-Insan*. (11) *al-Aʿla*. This is reported by Ibn al-Firkah in his comments from al-Marzuqi. (12) *al-Duha*. This is reported by al-Khaṭṭābī, who instructed the reader to separate these *sūrahs* by reciting the *takbīr*.

In his *Mufradat*, al-Rāghib said that the *Mufaṣṣal* refers to the last seven *sūrahs* of the Qurʾān.

Note

Ibn Maʿn said that the *Mufaṣṣal* contains long, medium and short *sūrahs*: its long ones are the *sūrahs* up through the end of *Surat al-Nabʾ*; its medium ones are through *Surat al-Duha*; and its short ones are the ones that conclude the Qurʾān. This is the most probable view in this matter.

Caution

In his *Kitāb al-Maṣāḥif*, Ibn Abī Dāwūd says, on the authority of Nāfiʿ, on the authority of Ibn ʿUmar, who said, "And which of the Qurʾān is not *Mufaṣṣa*, but you should say rather 'a short or a small *sūrah*'?"

This view was rejected by a large group including Abū al-Aʾliya; others, however, allowed it. So reported Ibn Abī Dāwūd.

Ibn Sīrīn an Abū ʿĀliya reported that one should not say "a *sūrah*" because God said: "We will send you a ponderous saying; say rather 'an easy *sūrah*'."

Gleaning: On the arrangement of the codices of Ubayy and Ibn Masʿūd

In his *Kitāb al-Maṣāḥif*, Ibn Ashta reported that Muḥammad Ibn Yaʾqub told us, on the authority of Abū Dawud, that Abū Jaʿfar al-Kufi said that the arrangement of Ubayy's codex was as follows: *Surat al-Fātiḥa*, then *al-Baqara*, *al-Nisāʾ*, *Āl ʿImrān*, *al-Anʿām*, *al-Aʿraf*, *al-Māʾida*, *Yūnus*, *al-Anfāl*, *al-Tawba*, *Hūd*, *Maryam*, *al-Shuʿarāʾ*, *al-Ḥajj*, *Yūsuf*, *al-Kahf*, *al-Naḥl*, *al-Aḥzāb*, *Banū Isrāʾil*, *al-Zummar* (beginning with the letters *Ḥamīm*), *ṬaʾHaʾ*, *al-Anbiyāʾ*, *al-Nūr*, *al-Muʾminun*, *Sabaʾ*, *al-ʿAnkabūt*, *al-Muʾmin*, *al-Raʿd*, *al-Qaṣas*, *al-Naml*, *al-Ṣāffāt*, *Ṣad*, *Yasīn*, *al-Ḥijr*, *al-Shurā*, *al-Rūm*, *al-Ḥadīd*, *al-Fatḥ*, *Muḥammad*, *al-Ẓihar*, *Tabaraka* (*Alladhī bi-yadi-hi*) *al-Mulk*, *al-Sajda*, (Inna Arsalna) *Nuḥ*, *al-Aḥqāf*, *Qāf*, *al-Raḥmān*, *al-Wāqiʿa*, *al-Jinn*, *al-Najm*, *Saʾala Saʾil*, *al-Muzammil*, *al-Mudathir*, *Iqtarabat*, *Ḥamīm*, *al-Dukhan*, *Luqmān*, (*Ḥamīm*) *al-Jāthiya*, *al-Ṭūr*, *al-Dhāriyāt*, *Nūn*, *al-Ḥāqqa*, *al-Ḥashr*, *al-Mumtaḥina*, *al-Mursalāt*, *ʿAmma Yatsaʾaluna*, (*La Uqsimu bi-Yawm*) *al-Qiyāma*, *Idha al-Shams Kuwwirat*, *Ya Ayyuha al-Nabi*, *Idha Talaqtum al-Nisaʾ*, *al-Naziʿāt*, *al-Taghbun*, *ʿAbasa*, *al-Muṭaffifūna*, *Idha al-Samāʾ Inshaqqat*, *Wal-Tīn wal-Zaytūn*, *Iqraʾ bi-Smi Rabbika*, *al-Ḥujarat*, *al-Munafiqūna*, *al-Jumʿa*, *Lima Tuḥarrim*, *al-Fajr*, (*La Uqsimu bi-hadhihi*) *al-Balad*, *wa-l-Layli*, *Idha al-Samaʾ Infaṭarat*, *wa-l-Shamsi wa-Ḍuḥaha*, *wa-l-Samaʾi wa-Tāriqi*, *Sabbiḥ Ism Rabbi-ka*, *al-Ghāshia*, *al-Ṣaff*, *Surat Ahl al-Kitāb* (which is also called *Lam Yakun*,) *al-Duḥā*, *A-lam Nashraḥ*, *al-Qariʿa*, *al-Takāthur*, *al-ʿAṣr*, *Surat al-Khalʿ*, *Surat al-Ḥafd*, *Wayl li-Kull Humaza*, *Idha Zalzalat*, *al-Adiyat*, *al-Fil*, *li-Ilaf*, *A-Raʾayta*, *Inna Aʿtaynaka*, *al-Qadr*, *al-Kafirūna*, *Idha Jaʾa Naṣr Allāh*, *Tabbat*, *al-Ṣamad*, *al-Falaq*, and *al-Nās*.

Ibn Ashta also related that Abū al-Ḥasan Ibn Nāfiʿ related that Abū Jaʿfar Muḥammad Ibn ʿAmr and Ibn Mūsā told them that Muḥammad Ibn Ismʿaīl Ibn Sālim said that ʿAlī Ibn Mihrān al-Ṭāʾi told us that Jarīr Ibn ʿAbd al-Ḥamīd said that this is the arrangement of ʿAbd-Alla Ibn Masʿūd's codex.

The "Long *sūrahs*" refers to *al-Baqara*, *al-Nisā*ʾ, *Āl ʿImrān*, *al-Aʿrāf*, *al-Anʿām*, *al-Māʾida* and *Yūnus*.

The "Hundreds" refers to *Barāʾa*, *al-Naḥl*, *Hūd*, *Yūsuf*, *al-Kahf*, *Banū Israʾīl*, *al-Anbiyāʾ*, *Ṭaʾ Haʾ*, *al-Muʾminūna*, *al-Shuʾarāʾ* and *al-Ṣāffat*.

The *Mathānī* refers to *al-Aḥzāb*, *al-Ḥajj*, *al-Qaṣaṣ*, (*Tāʾ Sīn*) *al-Naml*, *al-Nūr*, *al-Anfāl*, *Maryam*, *al-ʿAnkabūt*, *al-Rūm*, *Yāsin*, *al-Furqān*, *al-Ḥijr*, *al-Raʿd*, *Sabaʾ*, *al-Malāʾika*, *Ibrāhīm*, *Ṣād*, *Alladhina Kafaru*, *Luqmān*, *al-Zummar*, *al-Ḥawāmīm*, *Hamīm al-Muʾmin*, *al-Zukhruf*, *al-Sajda*, *Hamīm ʿAyn Sīn Qaf*, *al-Ahqaf*, *al-Jathiya*, *al-Dukhan*, *Inna Fatahna Laka*, *al-Hashr*, *Tanzil al-Sajda*, *al-Ṭalaq*, *Nūn*, *al-Qalam al-Ḥujurat*, *Tabaraka*, *al-Taghabun*, *Idha Jāʾaka al-Munāfiqun*, *al-Jumʿa*, *al-Ṣaff*, *Qul Uhiya*, *Inna Arsalna*, *al-Mujādila*, *al-Mumtaḥina* and *Ya Ayyuha al-Nabi Lima Tuḥarrim*.

The *Mufassal* contains *Surat al-Raḥmān*, *al-Najm*, *al-Ṭur*, *al-Dhariyāt*, *Iqtarabat al-Sāʿa*, *al-Wāqiʿa*, *al-Naziʿāt*, *Saʾala Saʾil*, *al-Mudathir*, *al-Mazammil*, *al-Muṭaffifūna*, *ʿAbasa*, *Hal Ataka*, *al-Mursalāt*, *al-Qiyāma*, *ʿAmma Yatasaʾilūna*, *Idha al-Shams Kuwwirat*, *Idha al-Samāʾ Infaṭarat*, *al-Ghāshiya*, *Sabbiḥ*, *al-Layl*, *al-Fajr*, *al-Buruj*, *Idha al-Samaʾ Inshaqqat*, *Iqraʾ Bi-Smi Rabbika*, *al-Balad*, *al-Ḍuha*, *al-Ṭāriq*, *al-ʿĀdiyat a-Raʾayta*, *al-Qāriʿa*, *Lam Yakun*, *al-Shams wa-Ḍuḥāha*, *al-Tin*, (*Way li-Kull Humaza*) *a-lam Tara Kayfa*, (*Li-ʿIlāf*) *Quraysh*, *Alhākum Inna Arsalnāhu*, *Idha Zulzilat*, *al-ʿAsr*, (*Idha Jāʾa*) *Naṣr Allāh*, *al-Kawthar*, (*Qu Yā Ayyuhā*) *al-Kafirūn*, *Tabbat*, *Qul Huwa Allāh Aḥad*, *a-lam Nashraḥ*; Ibn Masʿūd's codex omits the *Fātiḥa* and the last two *sūrahs* (of refuge).

Chapter nineteen

CONCERNING THE NUMBER OF *SŪRAHS*, VERSES, WORDS AND LETTERS

There are, according to the accepted consensus, one hundred and fourteen *sūrahs* in the Qurʾān. Another opinion is that there are one hundred and thirteen, if one combines *al-Anfāl* and *Barāʾa* into one *sūrah*. Abū al-Shaykh reported that Abū Rawq said that *al-Anfāl* and *Barāʾa* comprise one *sūrah*. Abū Rajāʾ reported that he asked al-Ḥasan whether *al-Anfal* and *Barāʾa* constitute one or two *sūrahs*, and he replied that they were two discrete *sūrahs*. We have statements similar to Abū Rawq's on the authority of Mujāhid; and Ibn Abī Ḥātim reported the same on the authority of Sufyān.

Ibn Ashitta reported, on the authority of Ibn Luḥayʾa, that *Barāʾa* is to be considered an integral part of *al-Anfal* because one does not write the *bismalla* at the beginning of *Barāʾa*. This opinion is based on the similarity of the two *sūrahs*, and the absence of the *basmala* between them. This opinion is refuted by the fact that the Prophet (peace and blessings be upon him) named each of them as discrete *sūrahs*.

The author of the Iqna reported a tradition that the *basmala* was present in Ibn Masʿūd's codex, but one could not rely on this report.

Al-Qushayri said that the truth is that the *basmala* was not in it because Gabriel (may God bless him) did not reveal it in that *sūrah*.

A tradition going back to Ibn ʿAbbās in the Mustadrak related that he asked ʿAlī Ibn Abī Ṭālib: "Why wasn't 'In the name of God, the Compassionate, the Merciful' included in *Barāʾa*?" He answered: "Because it (the *basmala*) is security; the *sūrah Barāʾa* (Immunity) was revealed with the sword."

Mālik reported that when the first part of *Barāʾa* was omitted, the *basmala* was omitted with it. It was confirmed that it was equal to *al-Baqara* in length.

There were one hundred and twelve *sūrahs* in Ibn Masʾud's codex, because the *Muʾawwidhatan* (the final two *sūrahs*) were not written in it. There were one hundred and sixteen in Ubayy's codex, because he added at its end the *sūrahs* of *al-Ḥafd* and *al-Khal*.

Abū ʿUbayd reported on the authority of Ibn Sīrīn, who said that Ubayy Ibn Kaʿb wrote in his codex the *Fātiḥa* and the *Muʾawwidhatan* and "by God, We beseech your aid", and by "God you it is we worship"; Ibn Masʾud omitted these, and ʿUthmān wrote from them only the *Fātiḥa* and the *Muʾawwidhatan*.

In his *al-Duʿāʾ*, al-Ṭabarānī reported, by way of ʿAbbād Ibn Yaʾqūb al-Asadī, on the authority of Yaḥyā Ibn Yaʾlā al-Aslami, on the authority of Ibn Lahiʿa, on the authority of Ibn Hubayra, on the authority of ʿAbd Allāh Ibn Zubayr al-Ghāfiqī, who said that ʿAbd al-Mālik Ibn Marwān told him: "I know of your love for Abū Turāb – that is, ʿAlī, even through you are an uncouth Bedouin." Al-Ghāfiqi answered: "I memorized the Qurʾān before your parents met, and ʿAlī Ibn Abī Ṭālib had taught me two *sūrahs* which the Emissary of God (peace and blessings be upon him) had taught him, and which neither you nor your father know: (1) 'O God, we beseech Your help and Your forgiveness; we praise You, and do not disbelieve You. We repudiate and ostracize those who sin against You'; (2) 'O God You it is we worship and to You we pray. We prostrate ourselves to be near to You. We hasten to serve You in longing for Your mercy, and we fear Your punishment; indeed, Your punishment is for the unbelievers.' "

Al-Bayhaqī reported, by way of Sufyān al-Thawrī, on the authority of Ibn Jurayj, on the authority of ʿAṭaʾ, on the authority of ʿUbayd Ibn ʿUmayr, that after the *rukūʿ*, Ibn al-Khaṭṭāb humbled himself before God, saying: "In the name of God, the Compassionate, the Merciful. Verily, we beseech You and ask Your help; we praise You, and do not disbelieve in You; we repudiate and ostracize those who sin against You. In the name of God, the Compassionate, the Merciful. O God! You it is we worship, and to You we pray and prostrate ourselves; to You we hasten to serve You in longing for Your mercy; we fear Your revenge. Verily Your punishment is for the unbelievers."

Ibn Jurayj reported that the reason for the presence of the *basmala* here is that these are two discrete *sūrahs*, in codices of some of the Companions.

In his *Kitāb al-Ṣalāt* (Book of Prayer), Muḥammad Ibn Naṣr al-Marwazī reported, on the authority of Ubayy Ibn Kaʿb, that he would humble himself by reciting these two *sūrahs*, and that he had written them down in his codex.

Ibn Durays reported that Aḥmed Ibn Jamīl al-Marwazi told him, on the authority of ʿAbd Allāh Ibn al-Mubārak, on the authority of al-Ajlaḥ Ibn ʿAbd Allāh Ibn al-Raḥmān, who said that his father told him that Ibn ʿAbbās' codex contained the reading of Ubayy and Abū Mūsā:

"In the name of God, the Compassionate, the Merciful. O God! We ask Your help and Your forgiveness; we give praise to You in the best way, and we do not disbelieve in You. We renounce and ostracize those who sin against You." And: "O God! You it is we worship, and to You we pray and prostrate ourselves, and You we hasten to serve. We fear Your punishment, and long for Your mercy. Verily, Your punishment is for the unbelievers."

Al-Ṭabarānī reported, on the basis of a sound *isnād*, that Abū Iṣhāq said: "Umayya Ibn ʿAbd Allāh Ibn Khālid Ibn Usayd led us in prayer in Khurasan, and he recited these two *sūrahs*: 'Verily, we beseech your help and your forgiveness . . .' "

Al-Bayhaqī and Abū Dāwūd in his *Marāsīl* reported, on the authority of Khālid Ibn Abī ʿImrān, that Gabriel brought this down to the Prophet (peace and blessings be upon him) when he was praying and had reached the verse ". . . not for you is the decision . . . (to the end of the verse)"; when he humbled himself before God, praying for the curse to fall on the tribe of Muḍar.

Caution

Thus some transmitted concerning Ubayy's codex that it contained one hundred and sixteen *sūrahs*. The truth, however, is that it contained one hundred and fifteen *sūrahs*:

Surat al-Fīl and *Surat Li-ʾĪlāfi Quraysh* are conflated in it into one *sūrah*. This was transmitted on the authority of al-Sakhawi in his *Jamāl al-Qurrāʾ*, on the authority of Jaʾfar al-Ṣādiq and Abū Nahik also.

I (Suyūṭī) say: al-Hakim and al-Ṭabarānī related something from one of Umm Hani's Traditions that denies this: the Emissary of God (peace and blessings be upon him) said: "God endowed the Quraysh with seven . . . (to the end of the *ḥadīth*)" in which he said: "Verily, God revealed a *sūrah* about them in which only they were mentioned, viz. *Li-ʾĪlāfiQuraysh*."

In al-Hudhali's *al-Kāmil*, it is related on the authority of one of the Companions, who said: "The *sūrahs al-Duḥā* and *al-lam Nashraḥ* comprise one *sūrah*." This is related by the Imām al-Rāzī in his *tafsīr*, on the authority of Ṭāwūs and ʿUmar Ibn ʿAbd al-ʿAzīz.

Gleanings

It was said that the wisdom in dividing the Qurʾān into *sūrahs* is the realization that the *sūrah* itself is one of God's signs, and an indication that each *sūrah* has its own form. Thus *Surat Yūsuf* is characterized by its narrative about his story; *Surat Barāʾa* is characterized by the hypocrites' situations and secrets, etc. The *sūrahs* are classified as long, of middle length, or short, in order to indicate that length is not a condition for inimitability: so *Surat al-Kawthar* consists of three verses, and its inimitability is no less than that of *Surat al-Baqara*.

The wisdom in this is seen in teaching and grading children; one begins with the short *sūrahs* and progresses on to longer ones: this is facilitation from God to His worshippers in memorizing His Book.

In his *Burhān*, al-Zarqashī asked: "Wasn't this the case with the previous revealed books?" I (Suyūṭī) would answer: "There are two aspects to this question: (1) they were not inimitable from the standpoint of their form and arrangement; and (2) memorization. In this *Kashshāf*, al-Zamakhsharī produced evidence to negate both these views, saying: 'The value in dividing the Qurʾān into many discrete *sūrahs* is that God revealed the Torah, the Evangel and the *Zabūr* (Psalms) in this manner; He did reveal it to His prophets in *sūrahs*, and the collectors redacted them into chapters of separate types, with appended explanations, upon publication. Thus when the type would have sub-types and sub-sections this is a better and more praiseworthy way than to publish it as a single chapter: when the reader finishes a *sūrah* or a chapter of the book, then goes on to the next section he will be fully prepared to learn it; and will be more dedicated to learn from it than if he were to continue to the end of the book. This is similar to a situation in which a traveller traverses a mile or a *farsang* and arrives at the highest point of a wilderness, for now he can be refreshed and be eager for more travel. Thus was the Qurʾān partitioned into thirtieths and fifths, so that when the memorizer masters a *sūrah*, he believes that he has taken a discrete and independent part from God's Book, and he would greatly value the part he has memorized.' "

A propos is Anas' Tradition: "When man recites *Surat al-Baqara* and *Surat al ʿImrān* he gains respect with us." Thus the recitation of a *sūrah* during prayer is preferable; and the division groups together the appropriate forms and synonyms so that the meanings and sounds chime; and there are other advantages of this as well.

What Zamakhsharī says about the division into *sūrahs* of the other books is sound or correct. Ibn Abī Ḥātim related, on the authority of Qatada, who said: "We used to say that the *Zabūr* was composed of one hundred and fifty *sūrahs*, all of which contain admonitions and praise rather than the permitted and the forbidden, or obligations and *ḥudūd* punishments. They also mentioned that the Evangel contained a *sūrah* entitled 'Proverbs'."

Section on the number of verses

A group of some of the reciters gave individual attention to this subject. Al-Jaʾfarī said that a verse (*Āya*) is a sentence component (though it be virtual) of the Qurʾān, having a beginning and an end, and included in a *sūrah* (chapter) with the function of a sign, e.g. "Verily, it is a sign of his authority . . .; because it is an indication of bounty and truth; or because of the group as it is a group of words."

Someone else said that a verse is part of the Qurʾān which is separated from what comes before it and from what comes after it.

Another said that it is one of the countable units of a *sūrah*. It is called "a sign" because it is an indication of the truth of him who brings it, as opposed to the fecklessness of him who would try to imitate it.

Another said it is a sign because it is an indication of the separate natures of what precedes and what follows it.

Al-Wāḥidi said: "One of our Companions said: 'In opposition to the latter view, one might call a part of a verse an *āya* (a verse) but for the fear that they were divinely ordained as they are now.' "

Abū ʿAmr and al-Dani said: "I don't know of any verse consisting of only one word except for *Mudhāmmatān*, 'two dark green ones'."

Another scholar took exception to this view, saying there are others, e.g. *Wal-Najm* ("by the star!"), *Wal-Ḍuḥā* ("By the dawn!"), *Wal-ʿAṣr* ("By the afternoon!") This is also the case with those who consider the "abbreviated letters" at the beginning of some *sūrahs* discrete verses.

Another held that the truth of the matter is that the verse is known by an ordinance from God (*al-Shāriʿ* = the Law Giver), in the way the *sūrah* is known.

He said: "The verse comprises a group of letters of the Qurʾān, the point of separation of which is known by its position by ordinal – that is, at the words that follow it in the first part of the Qurʾān and the words which precede it in the last part of the Qurʾān. What precedes it and what follows it are not included in it." He added: "Thus does a *sūrah* emerge."

Al-Zamakhsharī said that the verses comprise a divinely ordained science in which there is no room for analogy. Thus *Alīf-Lām-Mīm* was considered one verse wherever it occurred; likewise with *Alīf-Lām-Mīm-ṣād*. They did not consider *Alīf-Lam-Mim-Raʾ* or *Alīf-Lām-Raʾ* as a verse. They did count *Ḥā-Mīm* as a verse in those *sūrahs* that begin with this; likewise *Ṭaʾ-Haʾ* and *Ya-Sīn*; but not *Ṭaʾ-Sīn*.

I (Suyūṭī) say: In his *Musnad*, Aḥmed reported something by way of ʿĀṣim Ibn Abī al-Najūd, on the authority of Zirr, on the authority of Ibn Masʿūd, that supports the view that the science of verses is divinely ordained: "The Emissary of God (peace and blessings be upon him) recited to me one of the *sūrahs* which contain about thirty verses – that is, *sūrahs* 40–46 which begin with the 'abbreviated letters' *Ḥāmīm*." He added: "Those *sūrahs* with a few verses more than thirty are still called one of the 'Thirties' . . . (to the end of the *ḥadīth*)."

Ibn al-ʿArabī said that the Prophet (peace and blessings be upon him) mentioned that *al-Fātiḥa* consists of seven verses and that *Surat al-Mulk* consists of thirty verses. It is true that he recited the ten final verses of *Surat Āl-ʿImrān*. He added that the counting of the verses is one of the difficulties of the Qurʾān; it has long and short verses, and verses which end at the end of a sentence, and some that don't.

Another said that the reason for the difference in the early Muslims' counting of the verses is that the Prophet (peace and blessings be upon him) would pause at the beginning of each verse, and when the location in the text became clear, he would continue to the end. But the hearer might then think there had been no pause.

Ibn Durays reported, by way of ʿUthmān Ibn ʿAtāʾ, on the authority of his father, on the authority of Ibn ʿAbbās, who said that the total number of the Qurʾān's verses is six thousand, six hundred verses, and the total number of its letters is three hundred and twenty three thousand, six hundred and seventy-one.

Al-Dānī reported that there is a consensus that the number of the Qurʾān verses is six thousand. There is a difference of opinion on what to add to this. Some claimed there is nothing to add, and others claimed that one must add two hundred and four; another opinion is two hundred and fourteen; or two hundred and nineteen; or two hundred and twenty-five; or two hundred and thirty-six.

I (Suyūṭī) say: In his *Musnad al-Firdaws*, al-Daylamī reported, by way of al-Fayḍ Ibn Wathīq, on the authority of Furat Ibn Salmān, on the authority of Maymūn Ibn Mihran, on the authority of Ibn ʿAbbās, that the Prophet (peace and blessings be upon him) said: "The steps of the Garden are like the verses of the Qurʾān: for each verse there is a step, so there are six thousand, two hundred and sixteen verses; between each step is the distance of heaven from the earth. Concerning al-Fayḍ, Ibn Muʿīn said that he was a vile, inveterate liar.

In his *Shuʿab*, al-Bayhaqī reports a Tradition from ʿĀʾishah: "The Prophet said: 'The number of steps of the Garden is equal to the number of the Qurʾān verses. Anyone among the people of the Qurʾān (that is, who memorizes it) who enters the Garden has no step above him.'" Al-Ḥākim said that this Tradition has a sound *isnād*, but the Tradition is peculiar. In his *Ḥamālat al-Qurʾān*, al-Ājirī reported tradition accompanied by another, albeit interrupted, *isnād*.

In his commentary on his Righteous ode on the Numbering, Abū ʿAbd Allāh al-Mawṣilī said that they disagreed on the number of Qurʾānic verses in Medina, Mecca, Damascus, Basra and Kufa, There are two different numberings by the people of Medina: (1) that of Abū Jaʾfar Ibn Yazīd Ibn al-Qaʾqaʿ and Shayba Ibn Naṣṣāh; and (2) that of Ismaʿīl Ibn Jaʾfar Ibn Abī Kathīr al-Ansāri. Concerning the numbering by the people of Mecca: it is given on the authority of ʿAbd Allāh Ibn Kathīr, on the authority of Mujāhid, on the authority of Ibn ʿAbbās, on the authority of Ubayy Ibn Kaʿb; concerning the numbering of the people of Damascus, that was given by Hārūn Ibn Mūsā al-Akhfash and others, on the authority of ʿAbd Allāh Ibn Dhakwān, Aḥmed Ibn Yazīd and others on the authority of Hishām Ibn ʿAmmār. Ibn Dhakwān and Hishām reported, on the authority of the Qurʾān reciter Ayyūb Ibn Tamīm, on the authority of Yaḥyā Ibn al-Ḥārith al-Dhimārī, who said that this was the numbering of the people of Damascus as the elders reported it to them from the Companions; ʿAbd Allāh Ibn ʿĀmir al-Yaḥṣabī and others relate the same on the authority of Abū al-Dardaʾ. Concerning the numbering of the people of Baṣra: the sources of this revolve around ʿĀṣim Ibn al-ʿUjaj al-Juhdrai. Concerning the numbering of the people of Kūfa: it came from Ḥamza Ibn Ḥabīb al-Zayyāt and Abū al-Ḥasan al-Kisaʾi and Khalaf Ibn Hishām. Ḥamza said that he was informed of this by Ibn Abī Layla, on the authority of ʿAbd-al-Raḥmān al-Sullami, on the authority of ʿAlī Ibn Abī Ṭālib.

* * *

Al-Mawṣilī said that the Qurʾān's *sūrahs* are of three varieties: (1) those about which there is no difference of opinion regarding either the whole *sūrah* or the number of its verses; (2) those on which there is agreement regarding the whole *sūrah* but difference regarding the number of its verses; and (3) those on which there is difference of opinion, regarding both the *sūrah* and the number of its verses.

The first group is comprised of forty *sūrahs*. *Yūsuf*, one hundred and eleven; *al-Ḥijr*, ninety-nine; *al-Naḥl*, one hundred and twenty-eight; *al-Furqān*, seventy-seven; *al-Aḥzāb*, seventy-three; *al-Fatḥ*, twenty-nine; *al-Ḥujurāt* and *al-Taghābun*, eighteen; *Qāf*, forty-five; *al-Dhariyat*, seventy; *al-Qamar*, fifty-five; *al-Ḥashr*, twenty-seven; *al-Mumtaḥina*, thirteen; *al-Ṣaff*, fourteen; *al-Jumʾa*, *al-Munafiqūn*, *al-Ḍuḥā* and *al-ʿĀdiyāt*, eleven; *al-Taḥrīm*, twelve; *Nūn*, fifty-two;

al-Insān, thirty-one; *al-Mursalāt*, fifty; *al-Takwīr*, twenty-nine; *al-Infiṭār* and *Sabbiḥ*, nineteen; *al-Taṭfīf*, thirty-six; *al-Burūj*, twenty-two; *al-Ghāshiya*, twenty-six, *al-Balad*, twenty; *al-Layl*, twenty-one; *A-lam Nashrah*, *al-Tin* and *Alha-kum*, eight; *al-Humaza*, nine; *al-Fīl*, *al-Falaq* and *Tabbat*, five; *al-Kāfirūn*, six; and *al-Kawthar* and *al-ʿAṣr*, three. The second group had four *sūrahs*; *al-Qaṣaṣ*, eighty-eight; the people of Kūfa counted *Ṭaʾ-Sīn-Mīm* as a verse; the rest regarded the verse fragment "there were a group of men watering their flocks" as a complete verse (in place of *Ṭaʾ-Sīn-Mīm*).

Al-ʿAnkabūt, sixty-nine; the people of Kūfa counted *Alīf-Lām-Mīm* as a verse. In Baṣra, they counted instead ". . . making their devotion sincerely to Him . . .". In Damascus, they counted ". . . and cut off the highway . . ." instead.

Al-Jinn, twenty-eight. Al-Makkī counted ". . . no one can deliver me from God . . .". The others counted ". . . nor should I find refuge except in Him".

Al-ʿAṣr, three. Al-Madanī counted the last verse fragment ". . . of patience and constancy", rather than the first verse "By the time through the ages!"

The third group consists of seventy-three *sūrahs*.

1 *Al-Fātiḥa*, seven by general consent. The Kūfans and the Meccans counted the *bismalla* as a verse, but not ". . . who you have favoured . . .". The others did the opposite. Al-Ḥasan said it had eight verses, so he added the two of them; others, who said six, did not add the two of them. Another said nine, so he added two more, in addition to the verse fragment ". . . and you it is we worship". The first view is supported by what Ahmed, Abū Dawud, al-Tirmidhī, Ibn Khuzayma, al-Ḥākim, al-Dāraquṭni and others reported on the authority of Umm Salamah (the Prophet's (peace and blessings be upon him) wife): the Prophet (peace and blessings be upon him) used to recite: "(1) In the name of God the Compassionate, the Merciful. (2) Praise be to God, Lord of the worlds. (3) The compassionate, the Merciful. (4) The Possessor on the Day of Judgement. (5) You it is we worship, and from you we beseech help. (6) Lead us to the straight path; (7) the path of those whom you have favoured, those whose portion is not wrath, and those who go not astray." Thus he would divide it verse by verse, as do most Arabs. He counted "In the name of God, the Compassionate, the Merciful" as a verse, but not "(favoured) them". Al-Dāraquṭni reported, based on a sound *isnād*, on the authority of ʿAbd Khayr, who said: "ʿAlī was questioned about the seven *mathani*, and he replied: 'Praise be to God the Compassionate, the Merciful . . .'. He was told that this was only six verses, and he answered: '"In the name of God, the Compassionate, the Merciful" is a verse.'"

2 *Al-Baqara*, two hundred and eighty-five; or six, or seven.

3 *Al ʿImrān*, two hundred; or, one hundred and ninety-nine.

4 *Al-Nisāʾ*, one hundred and seventy-five; or six, or seven.

5 *Al-Mā'ida*, one hundred and twenty, or one hundred and twenty-two, or three.

6 *Al-Anʿām*, one hundred and seventy-five, six, or seven.

7 *Al-Aʿrāf*, two hundred and five, or six.

8 *Al-Anfāl*, seventy-five, six, or seven.

9 *Barā'a*, one hundred and thirty, or one fewer.

10 *Yūnus*, one hundred and ten, or one fewer.

11 *Hud*, one hundred and twenty-one, two, or three.

12 *Al-Raʿd*, forty-three, four, or seven.

13 *Ibrāhīm*, fifty-one, two, four, or five.

14 *Al-Isrā'*, one hundred and ten, or eleven.

15 *Al-Kahf*, one hundred and five, six, ten, or eleven.

16 *Maryam*, ninety-nine, or eight.

17 *Ṭa' ha*, one hundred and thirty-two, four, five, or (one hundred and) forty.

18 *Al-Anbiyā'*, one hundred and eleven, or twelve.

19 *Al-Ḥajj*, seventy-four, five, six, or eight.

20 *Qad Aflaḥa*, one hundred and eighteen, or nineteen.

21 *Al-Nūr*, sixty-two, or four.

22 *Al-Shu'arā'*, two hundred and twenty-six, or seven.

23 *Al-Naml*, ninety-two, four, or five.

24 *Al-Rūm*, sixty, or one fewer.

25 *Luqmān*, thirty-three, or four.

26 *Al-Sajda*, thirty, or one fewer.

27 *Saba'*, fifty-four, or five.

28 *Fāṭir*, forty-six, or five.

29 *Ya' Sīn*, eighty-three, or two.

30 *Al-Ṣaffāt*, one hundred and eighty, or one hundred and eighty-two.

31 *Ṣād*, eighty-five, six, or eight.

32 *Al-Zumar*, seventy-two, three, or five.

33 *Ghāfir*, eighty-two, four, five, or six.

34 *Fuṣṣilat*, fifty-two, three, or four.

35 *Shūrā*, fifty, or fifty-three.

36 *Al-Zukhruf*, eighty-nine, or eight.

37 *Al-Dukhān*, fifty-six, seven, or nine.

38 *Al-Jāthiya*, thirty-six, or seven.

39 *Al-Aḥqāf*, thirty-four, or five.

40 *Al-Qitāl*, forty, or one, or two fewer.

41 *Al-Ṭūr*, forty-seven, eight, or nine.

42 *Al-Najm*, sixty-one, or two.

43 *Al-Raḥmān*, seventy-seven, six, or eight.

44 *Al-Waqiʿa*, ninety-nine, seven, or six.

45 *Al-Ḥadīd*, thirty-eight, or nine.

46 *Qad Samiʿa*, twenty-two, or one.

47 *Al-Ṭalāq*, eleven, or twelve.

48 *Tabāraka*, thirty, or thirty-one, counting "They will say: 'Yes indeed; a Warner did come to us . . .'" as a verse. Al-Mawṣilī said that the first view is correct. Ibn Shanbūdh said that no one could possibly object to this view, given the support it has in Tradition. Aḥmad and the authors of the *Sunan* collections reported, and al-Tirmidhī considered authentic, a Tradition on the authority of Abū Hurayra that the Emissary of God (peace and blessings be upon him) said: "Verily, a *sūrah* of the Qurʾān of thirty verses will intercede for the benefit of its Memorizer, so that he is forgiven his sins; 'Blessed be he in whose hands is Dominion.'" Al-Ṭabarānī reported a Tradition with a sound *isnād*, on the authority of Mālik Ibn Anas, who reported that the Emissary of God (peace and blessings be upon him) said: "*a sūrah* (chapter) of the Qurʾān, only thirty verses will plead for its memorizer until he is entered into the Garden; it is *Surat Tabāraka*."

49 *Al-Ḥaqqa*, fifty-one, or two.

50 *Al-Maʿārij*, forty-four, or three.

51 *Nūḥ*, thirty, or one, or two fewer.

52 *Al-Muzammil*, twenty, or one, or two fewer.

53 *Al-Mudaththir*, fifty-five, or six.

54 *Al-Qiyāma*, forty, or one fewer.

55 *ʿAmma*, forty, or forty-one.

56 *Al-Naziʿāt*, forty-five, or six.

57 *ʿAbasa*, forty, forty-one, or two.

58 *Al-Inshiqāq*, twenty-three, four, or five.

59 *Al-Ṭāriq*, seventeen, or sixteen.

60 *Al-Fajr*, thirty or one fewer; or thirty-two.

61 *Al-Shams*, fifteen, or sixteen.

62 *Iqraʾ*, twenty, or one fewer.

63 *Al-Qadr*, five, or six.

64 *Lam Yakun*, eight, or nine.

65 *Al-Zalzala*, nine, or eight.

66 *Al-Qariʿa*, eight, ten, or eleven.

67 *Quraysh*, four, or five.

68 *A-raʾayta*, seven, or six.

69 *Al-Ikhlāṣ*, four, or five.

70 *Al-Nās*, seven or six.

Constraints

In one of the seven *ahruf* (modes of reciting), the *bismalla* was revealed along with the *sūrah*. Whoever recites in the *harf* it was revealed in, counts it as a verse: whoever recites in one of the other *harfs* does not count it as a verse.

The kūfans counted *Alīf-Lām-Mīm* as a verse wherever it occurs; likewise *Alīf-Lām-Mīm-Ṣād*, *Ṭaʾ-Ha*, *Kaf-Haʾ-Yaʾ-ʿAyn-Ṣad*, *Ṭaʾ-Sīn-Mīm*, *Yasīn* and *Ḥaʾ-Mīm*; they counted *Ḥaʾ-Mīm-Ayn-Sīn-Qāf* as two verses. All the others did not count any of these a verse.

The scholars of numbering are in agreement that one should not count *Alīf-Lām-Rāʾ* as a verse wherever it occurs. Likewise *Alīf-Lām-Mīm-Rāʾ*, *Ṭaʾ-Sīn*,

Ṣād, *Qāf* and *Nūn*. Some of them later allowed a more traditional counting. In this matter one cannot resort to analogy. Some of them said that one should not count *Ṣād*, *Nūn* and *Qāf* because they consist of only one letter; and not *Ta'-Sin*, because it differs from its two counterparts with *Ṭā'-Sīn-Mīm*, and because it resembles a singular on the morphological pattern of *Qābil*. And not *Yā'-Sīn*, albeit on this same morphological pattern: its first letter is a *yā'* and thus resembles a plural, and there is no singular noun is Arabic that begins with a *ya'*, They did not count *Alīf-Lām-Rā'* as opposed to *Alīf-Lām-Mīm*, because the latter sounds like the former in pauses; thus they counted "O you wrapped up in a mantle!" as a verse because of its resemblance to the pauses after it; they differ on "O you folded in garments!"

Al-Mawṣilī said that they counted ". . . then he looked around . . ." as a verse; there is no verse of the Qur'ān shorter than this; but similar are "Amma", "Wal-Fajr" and "Wal-Ḍuḥā".

Addition

ʿAlī Ibn Muḥammad al-Ghālī composed an Urjūza poem "*Al-Qara'in wal-Akhawāt*" in which he included the *sūrahs* with an equal number of verses, e.g. *al-Fātiḥa* and *al-Maʿūn*, *al-Raḥmān* and *al-Anfāl*, *Yūsuf*, *al-Kahf* and *al-Anbiyā'*, but this known from what preceded.

Gleanings

There are laws of jurisprudence that fix the order of knowledge and numbering of, and pauses between, the verses.

One of them concerns the expression of them by one who does not know the *Fātiḥa*: he must learn seven other verses.

Another is their expression in the Friday sermon; this requires the recitation of a complete verse. One may not abridge it, even if it is long – and this ruling applies to the reciting of a long verse by the general public. There is a difference of opinion concerning the end of a verse as to whether its recitation suffices in the Friday sermon. This problem deserves further inquiry; I am not aware that anyone has mentioned this before.

Another concerns a *sūrah*, or its substitute, that is recited during prayer; it is mentioned in the *Ṣaḥīḥ* that the Prophet (peace and blessings be upon him) used to recite sixty to one hundred verses every morning.

Another is their expression in recitation in the supererogatory nocturnal prayers. We have some Traditions: (1) "Whoever recites ten verses will not be considered one of the neglectful." (2) "Whoever recites fifty verses in one night will be counted among the memorizers." (3) "Whoever recites one hundred verses is counted among the observant." (4) Whoever recites two hundred verses is counted among the winners." (5) "Whoever recites three hundred verses is promised munificent reward"; and (6) "Whoever recites one thousand five hundred or seven hundred verses . . . (to the end of the *ḥadīth*)." These Traditions are reported by al-Dārami in separate locations in his *Musnad*.

Another concerns locations of pause, as we will see below.

In his *Kāmil*, al-Hudhali said that some people were ignorant of the importance of the numbering; al-Zaʾfaranī even said that the numbering is not a science; some scholars exploit the topic merely to enhance their position. Al-Hudhali denied this, saying that there are benefits in it and in knowledge about pauses, because the consensus is that a prayer is not acceptable by reciting half a verse. He added that a group of the scholars say one verse is enough; others say three verses, while others insist on seven. Inimitability cannot occur without a verse; and counting has magnificent benefits.

Another gleaning

The verses are mentioned in the Traditions countless times, e.g. the Traditions about the *Fātiḥa*, the first four verses of *Surat al-Baqara*, the Throne verse, the last two verses of the same *sūrah*, and the Tradition on the Great Name of God in the following two verses: (1) "And your God is one God, there is no god but He, the Compassionate, the Merciful; and (2) "*Alīf-Lām-Mīm.* Allāh there is no god but He, the Living, the Self-subsisting, Eternal. In *Bukhārī* there comes, on the authority of Ibn ʿAbbās, who said: "If it delights you to know about what the ignorant of the Arabs learn, then recite the verses that follow the one hundred and thirtieth verse of *Surat al-Anʾ am*, from 'Lost are they who slayed their children . . .' to '. . . guidance'."

In his *Musnad*, Abū Yaʾlā reported, on the authority of al-Miswar Ibn Makhrama, who said: "I said to ʿAbd-al-Raḥmān Ibn Auf, 'O Uncle! Tell us your story of the Day of Uhud.' He answered: 'If you read the verses that follow the hundred and twentieth verse from *Surat Āl ʿImrān*, you will find our story. "Remember that morning you did leave household (early) to post the faithful at their stations for battle . . .".'"

Section

People numbered the words of the Qurʾān as seventy-seven thousand, nine hundred and thirty-four words. Another opinion is seventy-seven thousand, four hundred and thirty-seven: or seventy-seven thousand, two hundred and seventy-seven words. There are other opinions as well.

It is said that the reason for the differences in numbering the words is that each word has its own truth, metaphoric value, expression and writing; expressing each of them is possible, and each scholar expressed a possibility.

Section

The numbering of the letters of the Qur'ān was reported by Ibn ʿAbbās as mentioned before and there are others' reports. There is no use in dealing with each one of these matters: Ibn al-Jawzī has dealt with this in his *Funun al-Afnan*; he counted the halves, the thirds, up to the tenths and he expanded on this subject so one can follow it there. Our Book is intended for serious subjects, not such fruitless pursuits.

Al-Sakhāwī reported that he didn't see an advantage in counting the words or the letters of the Qur'ān, for any advantage would flow from the possibility of increasing or decreasing the number; this is not possible with the Qur'ān.

Al-Tirmidhī reported a tradition on the topic of counting the letters contained in the Qur'ān. It is based on the authority of Ibn Mas'ud, who reported that the Prophet (peace and blessings be upon him) said; "Whoever reads one *harf* of God's Book benefits from it, and this one benefit is multiplied by ten. I do not count *Alīf-Lām-Mīm* as one *ḥarf*; I count *Alīf* as one *harf*, *Lam* as one *harf*, and *Mim* as one *harf*."

Al-Ṭabarānī reported, on the authority of ʿUmar Ibn al-Khaṭṭāb, that the Prophet (peace and blessings be upon him) said: "The Qur'ān contains one million and twenty thousand letters, and if you read it patiently and deeply you will have one wife of the dark-eyed houris of Paradise for every *harf*." The links in this Tradition's *isnād* consist of reliable and pious scholars, except for al-Ṭabarānī's shaykh Muḥammad Ibn ʿĀbid Ibn Ādam Ibn Abī Iyās, of whom al-Dhahabī wrote concerning this Tradition. Abū Iyās is also blamed for corrupting some of the Qur'ānic text; the total number is now clearly different.

Cleaning

One of the Readers said that the Glorious Qur'ān expressions consist of halves; the half with the *huruf* is the nun, from *nukr* ("an un-heard of thing") in *Surat al-Kahf*, and *ḥurūf kaf* are in its second half.

Some said it is with words from the letter *da*, from *wal-julūd* ("skins") in *Surat al-Ḥajj*, and the second half from the expression *wa-lahum maqamiʿ* ("they have maces of iron").

With the verses half is *ya'fiqun* ("they fake") from *Surat al-Shu'ara'*, and the second half is from *fa-ulqiya al-sahara* ("then did the sorcerers fall down").

Half according to the counting of the *sūrahs* is after *Surat al-Ḥadīd*, and *Surat al-Mujādala* is in the second half.

These are ten partitions. Another opinion is that a half is with the *kaf* of *nukr*; others say with the *fa'* in *wal-yatalaṭṭaf* ("and let him behave with care and courtesy").

Chapter twenty

THE QURʾĀN'S MEMORIZERS AND NARRATORS

Al-Bukhārī reported, on the authority of ʿAbd Allāh Ibn ʿAmr Ibn al-ʿĀs, who said that he heard the Prophet (peace and blessings be upon him) say: "Take the Qurʾān from four men: from ʿAbd Allāh Ibn Masʿūd, Salim, Muʾadh and Ubayy Ibn Kaʿb; that is to say: learn it from them." Of the four mentioned, the first two are of the Muhajirūn; the other two are from the Ansār. Salim is Ibn Maʾqil, the client of Abū Hudhayfa, and Muʾadh is Ibn Jabal. Al-Kirmāni reported that it is possible that the Prophet (peace and blessings be upon him) intended to make known what would occur after his death – that is, that these four would remain unsurpassed.

What followed is that they were not unique, but those who specialized and excelled in Qurʾānic *tajwīd* in the generation after the Prophet (peace and blessings be upon him) were very many. Sālim, the client of Abū Hudhayfa, was slain in the battle of Yamāma, and Muʾadh died during ʿUmar's caliphate. Ubayy and Ibn Masʿūd died during the caliphate of ʿUthmān; Zaid Ibn Thābit remained to become the author in Qurʾānic recital; he outlived them by a long while. It is clear that the order to take the Qurʾān from these four was meant for the time the order was given. This does not mean that no others shared with them memorization of the Qurʾān at the time: but the fear is some of the companies did memorize more than the said four did. It is reported in the *Ṣaḥīḥ*, that at the Battle of Biʾr Maʾuna, those Companions killed in it were called the "Reciters". They were seventy men.

Al-Bukhārī also reported, on the authority of Qatāda, who said that he asked Mālik Ibn Anas: "Who collected the Qurʾān during the time of the Emissary of God (peace and blessings be upon him)?" He answered that four men, all of them of the Anṣār, did: Ubayy Ibn Kaʿb, Muʾādh Ibn Jabal, Zayd Ibn Thābit and Abū Zayd. Qatada then asked Anas: "Who is Abū Zayd?" and Anas answered: "One of my paternal uncles."

Al-Bukhārī also reported a Tradition with a different *isnād*, on the authority of Anas, who said: "At the time of the death of the Prophet (peace and blessings be upon him) only four men had collected the Qurʾān: Abūʾl-Dardaʾ, Muʾadh Ibn Jabal, Zayd Ibn Thābit and Abū Zayd. This Tradition differs from that of Qatada in two ways: one of them clarifies the limitation to four, and the other mentions Abūʾl-Dardaʾ instead of Ubayy Ibn Kaʿb. A majority of the *imāms* (leading scholars) reject this limitation to four men.

Al-Mazirī said that Anas' words "others had not collected it" do not necessitate the conclusion that the fact of the matter is thus, because at bottom, Anas was not aware of any others. How could he follow the great number of the Companions and their dispersion in so many lands? This could only happen if he had encountered each of them in his isolation, and admit that he had not completed the collection of the Qurʾān during the Prophet's (peace and blessings be upon him) lifetime. Ordinarily, this would be the height of improbability, but even if untrue, it represents the limit of his knowledge concerning the reality of the situation.

Al-Bukhārī said that a majority of the heretics took hold of these words of Anas, yet they have no justification for doing so. We do not consider its real import to be its superficial interpretation. How in the world can they believe this to be the last word in the matter! Even so! It is not necessarily true that the entire vast majority memorized the Qurʾān, but a majority in fact did so. That every individual memorize the Qurʾān in its entirety is not a necessary condition for its faithful transmission; but if it was all memorized, even a portion by each would be enough.

Al-Qurṭubī said that seventy Readers were killed on the day of Yamama, and in the lifetime of the Prophet (peace and blessings be upon him) a similar number perished at Biʾr Maʿuna. It is only because of his strong connection to the above-mentioned four that Anas mentioned them specifically; or, because he had only them in mind.

Al-Qaḍī Abū Bakr al-Baqillānī said that there are several aspects to refuting Anas: (1) He did not understand, so others may have memorized; (2) the intention is that only these four memorized it in all its aspects and readings; (3) only these four collected what was written down after being recited by the Prophet (peace and blessings be upon him); (4) his intention was that only these four memorized directly from the Emissary of God, peace and blessings be upon him, as opposed to others who it is possible memorized part of it from an intermediary; 5) they took upon themselves the task of reciting and teaching the Qurʾān and became famous for this, while others who knew as they did were not equally known to those who know the former so they only referred to them. But this is not precisely true; (6) "Collection" means "writing down". Anas does not deny that others might have learned the Qurʾān by heart; the four he mentioned collected it in writing, as well as learning it by heart.

(7) The intention is that no one stated clearly that he had collected it, in the sense that he had memorized it completely in the time of the Emissary of God (peace and blessings be upon him), except these four men. This was not made clear because others had not memorized it completely until after the death of the Emissary of God (peace and blessings be upon him) when the last verse was revealed. Perhaps this last verse and its like were not heard by any but these four, out of all of those who had collected all of it previously; though many who had not collected the Qurʾān were present at the time it was revealed. (8) "Collection" means "hearing and obeying, doing what is required by it". In his *al-Zuhd*, Aḥmad reported by way of Abūʾl-Ẓāhiriya, that a man approached Abūʾl-Dardaʾ and

told him that his son had collected the Qur'ān. Abū'l-Darda' replied: "O God, grant forgiveness! It is only the one who hears it and obeys it that 'collects' it."

Ibn Hajar said that in all these possibilities there is officiousness, especially in the last one. He said also that there appeared to him another possibility, and that it was meant for the Khazraj in relation to the Aws only. This does not imply that Muhajirun other than these two Ansar tribes (Aws and Khazraj) had collected the Qur'ān because he reported this on an incident of boasting between the Aws and the Khazraj. Ibn Jarīr al-Tabari reported, by way of Sa'īd Ibn Abī 'Aruba, on the authority of Qatada, on the authority of Anas, who said: "Both tribes, the Aws and the Khazraj, boasted; Aws said that four men were from them; they claimed that the Throne shook for Sa'd Ibn Mu'adh; the man whose word as witness was worth two others is Khuzayma Ibn Thābit; the man whom the angels cleansed is Khanzala Ibn Abī Āmir; and the man whose skull was protected by bees is 'Asim Ibn Abī Thābit. The Khazraj claimed that four of their members collected the Qur'ān, and no one else; then they named them."

Ibn Hajar said that what emerges from copious Traditions is that Abū Bakr had memorized the Qur'ān during the lifetime of the emissary of God (peace and blessings be upon him). According to the *Ṣaḥīḥ*, he built a mosque in the courtyard of his house in which he would recite the Qur'ān. This is taken to mean all that was revealed of the Qur'ān at that time. Ibn Hajar added that this is irrefutable in light of Abū Bakr's zeal in receiving the Qur'ān from the Prophet (peace and blessings be upon him), and his total deference to him while they were in Mecca, and in consideration of their mutual closeness to one another – to the extent that Ā'ishah said that the Prophet's (peace and blessings be upon him) family would be visited by him day and night. The Tradition says that: "The people should be led by those who are most diligent in reciting God's Book." When he fell ill, the Prophet (peace and blessings be upon him) appointed him *imām* for the Muhajirun and the Ansār, an indication that he was the best in recitation. (End of Ibn Hajar's comments.)

Ibn Kathir reported this first.

But I (Suyūṭī) say that Ibn Ashta, in his *Masahif*, related a tradition with a sound *isnād* on the authority of Muḥammad Ibn Sirin, who said that when Abū Bakr died, the Qur'ān had not yet been collected; and when 'Umar was killed, the Qur'ān had not been collected. Ibn Ashta added that some authorities took this to mean that the entire Qur'ān was not yet recited from memory; others held that "Collected" here refers to the codices.

Ibn Hajar said that, according to 'Alī, he memorized the Qur'ān conforming to the chronological order of revelation soon after the death of the Prophet of God (peace and blessings be upon him). Ibn Abī Dawud recorded this tradition.

Al-Nisā'ī recorded a Tradition with a sound *isnād*, on the authority of 'Abd Allāh Ibn 'Umar, who said; "I memorized the Qur'ān, and I used to recite it every evening. Once the Prophet of God (peace and blessings be upon him) came me (while I was reciting), and said: 'Recite it in a month . . . (to the end of the *ḥadīth*).' "

Ibn Abī Ḥasan reported a Tradition with a good *isnād*, on the authority of Muḥammad Ibn Kaʿb᾽ al-Qurāzī, who said: "Five of the Anṣār memorized the Qur᾽ān during the lifetime of the Emissary of God: Mu᾽adh Ibn Jabal, ʿIbada Ibn al-Samit, Ubayy Ibn Kaʿb, Abū᾽l-Darda᾽ and Abū Ayyūb al-Anṣāri.

In his *Madkhal*, al-Bayhaqī reported, on the authority of Ibn Sirin, who said that during the lifetime of the Emissary of God (peace and blessings be upon him) there was no objection to the fact that four men memorized the Qur᾽ān: Muʿādh Ibn Jabal, Ubayy Ibn Kaʿb, Zayd and Abū Zayd. The authorities differ about two or three: Abū᾽l-Darda᾽ and ʿUthmān. Others say: ʿUthmān and Tamīm al-Dari.

Both al-Bayhaqī and Abū Dāwūd report, on the authority of al-Sha᾽bi who said: "During the lifetime of the Prophet (peace and blessings be upon him) six men memorized the Qur᾽ān: Ubayy, Zayd, Muʿādh, Abū᾽l-Darda᾽, Saʿd Ibn ʿUbayd and Mujammi᾽ Ibn Jāriya; the last memorized all but two or three *sūrahs*.

In his *Kitāb al-Qirā᾽āt* (Book of Reading), Abū ʿUbayd mentioned that the Reciters from the Prophet of God's (peace and blessings be upon him) Companions were from among the Muhajirun; he counted the first four Rightly-guided caliphs along with Talḥa, Saʿd, Ibn Mas᾽ud Hudhayfa, Salim and Abū Hurayra, ʿAbd Allāh Ibn al-Ṣā᾽ib, al-ʿIbadila, ʿĀ᾽ishah, Hafṣa and Umm Salamah. Among the Anṣār, he counted ʿIbāda Ibn al-Ṣāmiṭ and Muʿādh (whose honorific was Abū Ḥalima), Mujammi Ibn Jāriya, Faḍāla Ibn ʿUbayd and Maslama Ibn Mukhallad. Abū ʿUbayd made clear that some of them completed the task after the Prophet of God's (peace and blessings be upon him) demise; he did not reject the above-mentioned limitation in Anas' Tradition. Ibn Abī Dāwūd counted among them Tamīm al-Dārī and ʿUqba Ibn ʿĀmir.

According to Abū ʿAmr al-Dānī, Abū Mūsā al-Ashʿarī also memorized it.

Caution

The authorities differed about the name of the Abū Zayd mentioned in Anas' Tradition. One opinion is that he is Saʿd Ibn ʿUbayd Ibn al-Nuʿmān, one of the Banū ʿAmr Ibn ʿAwf tribe. This view is to be rejected because he was a member of the Aws tribe, while Anas was a member of the Khazraj tribe. Another opinion is that he was one of Zayd's paternal uncles; as previously mentioned, al-Shaʿbī counted both Zayd and Abū Zayd among those who memorized the Qur᾽ān, indicating that Abū Zayd was someone else.

Abū Aḥmad al-ʿAskari said that no one from among the Aws collected the Qur᾽ān except Saʿd Ibn ʿUbayd. In this Muḥabbar, Ibn Habīb reported that Saʿd Ibn ʿUbayd was one of those who memorized it during the lifetime of the Prophet of God (peace and blessings be upon him).

Ibn Ḥajar said that Ibn Abī Dāwūd mentioned that among those who memorized the Qur᾽ān was Qays Ibn Abī Ṣaʿṣa, a member of the Khazraj tribe, whose by-name was Abū Zayd; perhaps this is he. He also mentioned Saʿīd Ibn al-Mundhir Ibn Aws Ibn Zuhayr, who was also a khazrajite. Yet I (Suyūṭī) do not see any clarification in the fact that his by-name was Abū Zayd.

Ibn Ḥajar added that he later found in the possession of Ibn Abī Dawud material that settled the matter. In a Tradition holding to al-Bukhārī's standards of authenticity for an *isnād*, it was related to Thumama, on the authority of Anas, that the Abū Zayd who memorized the Qurʾān was named Qays Ibn al-Sakan. He added: "He was a man from among us – that is, the clan of the Banu Ubayy Ibn al-Najjār, one of my paternal uncles who died without leaving a descendant. We were his inheritors."

Ibn Abī Dāwūd reported that Anas Ibn Khālid al-Anṣārī told him that he was Qays Ibn al-Sakan Ibn Zaʾawra, from the Banū ʿUdayy Ibn al-Najjār clan; he added that he died, unknown, at about the time of the Emissary of God's (peace and blessings be upon him) death. No traditions were related by him: he was an ʿAqabī and a Badrī. Among the personal names attributed to him were Thābit, Aws and Muʿādh.

Gleaning

I (Suyūṭī) have become aware of a woman from among the Companions of the Prophet (peace and blessings be upon him) who had memorized the Qurʾān, with whom none of those who have dealt with this matter have mentioned. In his *al-Ṭabaqāt*, Ibn Saʿd reported that al-Faḍl Ibn Dukayn said that al-Walīd Ibn ʿAbd Allāh Ibn Jamiʿ said that his grandmother told him about Umm Waraqa bint ʿAbd Allāh Ibn al-Ḥārith, that the Emissary of God (peace and blessings be upon him) used to visit her, and he would call her the "Martyr (*shahida*)".

She had indeed memorized the Qurʾān. When the Emissary of God (peace and blessings be upon him) embarked on the Badr campaign, she asked him if she could accompany him to care for the wounded and nurse the sick, so that perhaps God would guide her to martyrdom. The Prophet (peace and blessings be upon him) responded that God was indeed leading her to martyrdom. He (peace and blessings be upon him) would also have her lead the prayer for those in her household. She used to have a *muezzin*. A slave-boy and slave-girl of hers were angered by her. They killed her during ʿUmar's caliphate. ʿUmar said: "The Emissary of God (peace and blessings be upon him) was correct; he used to say: 'Let's go and visit the Shāhida.'"

Section on the former reciters

Seven men of the Companions of the Prophet (peace and blessings be upon him) became famous for their Qurʾān recitation: (1) Uthmān; (2) ʿAlī; (3) Ubayy; (4) Zayd Ibn Thābit; (5) Ibn Masʾud; (6) Abūʾl-Dardaʾ; and (7) Abū Mūsā al-Ashʾarī. Al-Dhahabī mentioned them in his *Ṭabaqāt al-Qurrāʾ* (Classes of the

Reciters). A large number of the Companions recited according to Ubayy's recitation; among them are Abū Hurayra, Ibn ʿAbbās and ʿAbd Allāh Ibn al-Sāʾib. Ibn ʿAbbās took instruction from Zayd also. A number of the Tabiʾun (the second generation of Muslims) also took instruction from them.

Those Readers who were in Medina: Ibn Musayyab, ʿUrwa, Sālim, ʿUmar Ibn ʿAbd al-ʿAziz, Sulaymān and ʿAṭaʾ (sons of Yasār), Muʾadh Ibn al-Ḥārith (known as "Muʿādh the Reciter"), ʿAbd-al-Raḥmān Ibn Hurmuz al-Aʿraj, Ibn Shihāb al-Zuhrī, Muslim Ibn Jundab and Zayd Ibn Aslam.

Those in Mecca: ʿUbayd Ibn ʿUmayr, ʿAlaʾ Ibn Abī Rabāḥ, Ṭāwūs, Mujāhid, ʿIkrama and Ibn Abī Mulayka.

Those in Kūfa: ʿAlqama, al-Aswad, Masrūq, ʿUbayda, ʿAmr Ibn Sharahbil, al-Ḥārith Ibn Qays, Rabīʿ Ibn Khuthaym, ʿAmr Ibn Maymūn, Abū ʿAbd al-Raḥmān al-Sullami, Zirr Ibn Ḥubaysh, ʿUbayd Ibn Nudayla, Saʿīd Ibn Jubayr, al-Nakhaʿī, and al-Shaʿbī.

Those in Baṣra: Abū al-ʿĀlīya, Abū Rajaʾ, Naṣr Ibn ʿĀṣim, Yaḥyā Ibn Yaʾmar, al-Ḥasan, Ibn Sīrīn and Qatada.

Those in Syria: al-Mughīra Ibn Abī Shihāb al-Makhzūmi (ʿUthmān's friend), and Khalifa Ibn Saʿd (Abūʾl-Darda's friend).

Some people then isolated themselves to devote their most fervent energies to delving into and arriving at the correct recitation of the Qurʾān. They emerged as leaders to whom people travelled and whom they imitated. In Medina were Abū Jaʿfar Yazīd Ibn al-Qaʿqāʿ, then Shayba Ibn Naṣāḥ, then Nāfiʿ Ibn Naʾim. In Mecca were ʿAbd Allāh Ibn Kathier, Ḥamid Ibn Qays al-Aʾraj, and Muḥammad Ibn Muḥaysin. In Kūfa: Yaḥyā Ibn Waththab, Asim Ibn Abī al-Najud, Sulayman al-Aʾmash, then Ḥamza, then al-Kisaʾi. In Basra: ʿAbd Allāh Ibn Abī Isḥāq, ʿIsā Ibn ʿUmar, Abū ʿAmr Ibn al-ʿAlaʾ. ʿAṣim al-Juhdari, then Yaʾqūb al-Ḥaḍramī. In Syria: ʿAbd Allāh Ibn ʿĀmir, Atiya Ibn Qays al-Kulabi, Ismāʿīl Ibn ʿAbd Allāh Ibn al-Muhājir, then Yaḥyā Ibn al-Ḥārith al-Dhamārī, then Shuraykh Ibn Yazīd al-Ḥarami.

From among these, who became famous throughout the regions, were seven *imāms* (leading reciters): (1) Nāfiʿ: he reported on the authority of seventy of the Tabiʿūn, among whom is Abū Jaʿfar; (2) Ibn Kathīr: he reported from the Companion ʿAbd Allāh Ibn al-Sāʾib; (3) Abū ʿAmr: he reported from the Tabiʾun; (4) Ibn ʿĀmir: he reported from Abūʾl-Dardāʾ, and from ʿUthmān's friends; (5) ʿĀṣim: he reported from the Tabiʿūn; (6) Ḥamza: he reported from ʿAṣim, al-Aʿmash, al-Ṣabiʾi, Manṣūr Ibn al-Muʿtamar and others; and (7) al-Kisāʾī: he reported from Ḥamza and Abū Bakr Ibn ʿAyyāsh.

The various readings were then disseminated throughout the countries of the Islamic world, and were spread one generation after another. Among the narrators of all the methods of the seven readers, two stand out from each: (1) from Nāfiʿ: Qālūn and Warsh; and (2) from Ibn Kathīr: Qanbal and Bizzī, and from friends of the latter; (3) from Abū ʿAmr: al-Daūrī and al-Sūsī, by way of al-Yazīdī; (4) from Ibn ʿĀmir: Hishām and Ibn Dhakwān, from his friends; (5) from ʿAṣim: Abū Bakr Ibn Ayyāsh and Hafṣ; (6) from Ḥamza: Khalaf and Khallad, from Sālim; and (7) from al-Kisāʾi: al-Daūri and Abūʾl-Ḥārith.

Later, when the breach had become widespread, and falsehood had nearly overtaken the Truth, the Nation's experts arose to painstakingly ponder over and collect the words and readings. They set down the homonyms and the narrations, and determined what was sound and true and peculiar, according the principles they defined, and strictures they set out in detail.

The first man to classify the readings was Abū ʿUbayd al-Qāsim Ibn Salām, then Aḥmad Ibn Jubayr al-Kūfi, then Ismāʿil Ibn Isḥāq al-Maliki (Qalūn's friend), then Abū Jaʿfar Ibn Jarīr al-Ṭabarī, then Abū Bakr Muḥammad Ibn ʿUmar al-Dajuwānī, then Abū Bakr Ibn Mujāhid; later, men arose during the latter's lifetime and after it.

Collections of this type, comprehensive and partial, succinct and verbose, and the experts in the readings, are innumerable.

The Guardian of Islām, Abū ʿAbd Allāh al-Dhahabī, has classified these experts; so did the guardian of the Readings Abūʾl-Khayr Ibn al-Jazarī after him.

Chapter twenty-one

ON THE KNOWLEDGE – OF THE *ISNĀDS* – ʿĀLĪ

("High" – having very few links between the transmitter and the Prophet, and hence more reliable; or Nāzil – "Low" – having more links)

Be aware that search for the "height" of the *isnāds* is *sunna*; because it determines proximity to God (He is Exalted). The People of the Tradition divided this science into five parts, and I (Suyūṭī) present them to you as follows: (1) Proximity to the Emissary of God (peace and blessings be upon him), in regard to the number of transmitters in an *isnād* which is clean and not weak; this is the most excellent and splendid of the categories of "height".

At this time, the best possible Traditions are those which have *isnāds* that have fourteen authoritative tradents: and these come from Ibn Āmir's reading from Ibn Dhakwān's narration. Also, fifteen; these come from ʿAsim's reading, from Hafṣ' narration; and from Yaʾqub's recitation, from Ruways' narration.

2 The distinctions of "height" according to the Traditionists: proximity to one of the *imāms* of the Tradition, e.g. al-Aʾmash, Hushām, Ibn Jurayḥ al-Awzaʿī and Mālik. Parallel to this is proximity to one of the seven *imāms*. The Highest Tradition for scholars today is one connected by recitation to Nāfiʿ; these number twelve. Those related to ʿĀmir are also twelve.

3 According to the Traditionists: "height" is in reference to its narration in one of the "Six Books" (of reliable Traditions). What is narrated in one of these "Six Books" is assumed to have a sounder *isnād* than what is recorded elsewhere in other collections of Traditions. This is parallel to what is related in some of the authoritative books of Readings, e.g. the *Taysīr* or the *Shaṭibiya*. Here one is dealing with (*al-muwāfaqāt*) mutual agreements, (*al-abdal*) substitutions, (*al-musāwāt*) identicals, and (*muṣafaḥāt*) co-incidentals.

a Concerning the "Mutual Agreements": one of the authors of the books has a tradition concerning his teacher, whether it is with a short *isnād* or not. An example of this type is Ibn Kathir's reading of the al-Bizzī's narrative, by way of Ibn Banan, on the authority of Abū Rabīʾa, on Ibn Kathir's authority, which Ibn al-Jazarī relates from Abū Manṣūr Muḥammad Ibn al-Mālik Ibn Khayrūn's *Kitāb al-Miftāḥ*; and also from Abū al-Karam al-Shahrazūrī's *Kitāb al-Miftāḥ*.

Both of these authors recited under the tutelage of ʿAbd al-Sayyid Ibn ʿIttāb, narrating this type of transmission with one of its two *isnāds*; this is called "Mutual Agreement", following the technical terminology of the scholars of Tradition.

b Concerning the "Substitutes": if there is agreement in the *isnād* with that of his teacher's teacher, etc. The *isnād* here may also be short or not. An example of this is Abū ʿAmr's reading of al-Dūrī's narration by way of Ibn Mujāhid, on the authority of Abū Zaʿrāʾ, on al-Dūrīs authority. Ibn al-Jazarī narrated it from the *Kitāb al-Taysīr*; al-Dānī recited it under the tutelage of Abūʾl-Qāsim ʿAbd al-ʿAzīz Ibn Jaʾfar al-Baghdādī, and to Abū Ṭāhir, on the authority of Mujāhid. Abūʾl-Karam recited it from the *Miṣbāḥ* under the tutelage of Abūʾl-Qāsim Yaḥyā Ibn Aḥmad al-Sayyibī, and also under the tutelage of Abūʾl-Ḥasan al-Hammāmī, and also under the tutelage of Abū Ṭāhir. His narration of this by way of the *Misbāḥ* is a "Substitute" for al-Dānī concerning his teacher's teacher.

c Concerning the "Identicals": between the Prophet (peace and blessings be upon him) or the Companions or others and the narrator to the teacher of one of the book's authors, these have the same length *isnād* as between the author of one of the books and the Prophet (peace and blessings be upon him) or the Companions or someone else.

d Concerning the "Co-incidentals": these have one additional link in the *isnād*; it is as if the author of one of the books met another man, shook hands with him and related on that man's authority. An example of this is Nāfiʿ's reading, which al-Shatibi related on the authority of Abū ʿAbd Allāh Muḥammad Ibn ʿAlī al-Nafzi, on the authority of Abū ʿAbd Allāh Ibn Ghulam al-Faras, on the authority of Sulaymān Ibn Najāḥ and other, on the authority of Abū ʿAmr al-Dani, on the authority of Abūʾl-Fath Faris Ibn Ahmed, on the authority of ʿAbd al-Bāqī Ibn al-Ḥasan, on the authority of Ibrāhīm Ibn ʿUmar al-Muqriʾ, on the authority of Abūʾl-Ḥasan Ibn Buyān, on the authority of Abū Bakr Ibn al-Ashʾab, on the authority of Abū Jaʿfar al-Rabaʾi, known as Abū Nāshit, on the authority of Qālūn, on the authority of Nāfiʿ.

Ibn al-Jazarī also related it on the authority of Abū Bakr al-Khayyāṭ, on the authority of Abū Muḥammad al-Baghdādī and someone else, on the authority of al-Saʾigh, on the authority of al-Kamāl Ibn Fāris, on the authority of Abūʾl-Yaman al-Kindī, on the authority of Abūʾl-Qāsim Hibat Allāh Ibn Aḥmad al-Ḥarīrī, on the authority of Abū Bakr al-Khayyāṭ, on the authority of al-Faradi, on the authority of Ibn Buyān.

This is an "Identical" for Ibn al-Jazarī: there are seven links in the *isnād* from Ibn Buyān to him, and this is equal to the number of links between al-Shatibi and him. For those who receive Tradition from Ibn al-Jazarī, this is a "co-incidental" for al-Shatibi.

This differentiation by the men of the Tradition resembles the differentiation by the Readers of the status of Traditions: (*qirāʾa*), readings, (*riwāya*) narration, (*turuq*) ways (that is, *isnāds*) and (*wajh*) aspects. If the difference is related for one of the seven or ten *imāms*, or someone else of their status, and to a tradition that agrees with another in its narrative and ways, then it is accepted as a correct reading. If it is related to a narrator then it is accepted as a correct narrative.

If someone after him, etc., learns it with the same *isnād* then it is considered (*ṭarīq*) an accepted way. Then it is left to the preference of the reader (reciter); this is an accepted way of reading (reciting).

The fourth division of "height": the shaykh (teacher) dies before his colleague having been taught by the same shaykh. For example, the Traditions learned on the authority of al-Taj Ibn Maktūm are "higher" than the Traditions learned on the authority of Abūʾl-Maʿāli Ibn al-Labbān, and Traditions learned on the authority of Ibn al-Labban are "higher" than those from al-Burhān al-Shāmī, even though they are each learned on the authority of Abū Ḥayyān. The first died before the second, and the second before the third.

The fifth division: "height" in terms of the teacher's death, without any other change in the situation, or another teacher whenever it may occur. Some recent authorities say that an *isnād* has "height" if it is fifty years previous to the teacher's death; Ibn Mandah said: thirty.

Thus learning Traditions from Ibn al-Jazarī's companions is "high" from the year 863 AH: he was the last tradent whose *isnāds* are "high". It is now thirty years since the time of his death.

These are the rules of the Traditions, which I have clarified, and I have compared them with the rules of the Readings. I am the first to do this. Praise and gratitude are God's.

If a person knows about "heights" and its divisions, he knows the low; and vice versa. Wherever there is disdain for the low, that is when it is not compensated for by having the men in the links of his *isnād* more knowledgeable, more conservative, more perfect, more noble, more famous, or more pious, for if they were so, then it would be neither blameworthy nor of less merit.

Chapters twenty-two to twenty-seven

CONCERNING KNOWLEDGE OF THE MUTAWĀTIR (RECITATIONS TRANSMITTED BY SO MANY TRUSTWORTHY PERSONS AS TO BE BEYOND DOUBT): OF THE MASHHŪR (RECITATIONS TRANSMITTED BY MORE THAN TWO TRANSMITTERS, WHICH MAY OR MAY NOT THEREFORE BE AUTHENTIC): OF THE ĀḤĀD (RECITATIONS TRANSMITTED FROM TOO FẸW TRANSMITTERS TO MAKE THEM MUTAWĀTIR); OF THE SHĀDHDH (RECITATIONS WHICH ARE AT VARIANCE WITH ACCEPTED RECITATIONS); OF THE MAWḌŪʿ (FICTITIOUS RECITATIONS); AND OF THE MUDRAJ (RECITATIONS WITH UNACKNOWLEDGED INSERTIONS INTO THE TEXT OR THE *ISNĀD*)

Be aware that al-Qāḍī Jalāl al-Dīn al-Bulgīnī said that recitations are divided into *mutawātir*, *aḥad* and *shādhdh*. The *mutawātir* recitation consists of the seven authorized readings; the *aḥād* consists of the readings of the three authorities making the total ten on which the Companions relied; the *shadhdh* consists of recitations from the followers (that is, the generation after the Companions, e.g. al-Aʾmash, Yaḥyā Ibn Waththāb, Ibn Jubayr, etc.).

There are various opinions concerning this matter, as follows. The best person who ever discussed this matter is the *Imām* of the Readers of his generation, the teacher of our teacher, Abū al-Khayr Ibn al-Jazarī. At the beginning of his book, *(Kitāb) al-Nashr*, he said that every recitation which is in correct Arabic, even in only one aspect; and which agrees with a recitation in one of the *ʿuthmānic* codices, even just barely; and its *isnād* is sound – then it is an irrefutably correct recitation. In fact, it is one of the seven *ahruf* in which the Qurʾān was revealed; it must be accepted by everyone, whether it stems from one of the seven Readers, or from the ten, or from authoritative *imāms* other than them. If one of these three pillars is removed, then one lets loose a recitation which is *ḍaʿīfa* (weak), *shādhdha* (problematic), or *batila* (invalid), whether it is related on the authority of the seven, or even one greater than them. This is the correct view as held by the most meticulous *imāms* from among the predecessors and their followers. This was explicated by al-Dani, al-Makkī, al-Mahdāwī and Abū Shāma; it is the fixed view of the predecessors to which no one can make objection.

In his *Murshid al-Wajīz*, Abū Shāma said that one should not be deceived by every recitation ascribed to one of the seven, and call it a sound pronunciation or that thus was it revealed, unless it is examined and found to be meeting these rules: its transmission thus would relate that recitation to one of the Readers and not another, and that transmission will not be limited to them, but if one were to transmit a recitation on the authority of one of the other Readers, that would not prevent it from being sound. Reliance is on achieving a consensus with these features, and the one it is related to. For every recitation related to each of the seven Readers (and others) has within it the accepted and the problematic; nevertheless, because of the fame and the abundance of correct recitations of the seven Readers, one may trust their recitations more than those of others.

Then Ibn al-Jazarī said that concerning "quality text", "even if in only one aspect", which refers to a facet of Arabic grammar: be it very eloquent or eloquent, generally accepted or harmlessly debated, if it is a generally accepted reading which the *imāms* accept with a sound *isnād*, then it is a strong foundation and a mighty pillar. How many readings have the grammarians, or at least many of them, rejected! Their rejections should be discarded, e.g., (1) reading with a phonetic zero at Q2, 54 (reading *barīʾ-kum* for *barīʾikum*, "your creators"); and at (Q2, 67) (reading *yaʾmur-kum* for *yaʾmuru-kum*, "commands you"); (2) reading in the genitive case, as at Q4, 1 (reading *wal-arḥāmi* for *wal-arḥāma*, "and the wombs"); (3) reading in the accusative case, as at Q45, 16 (reading *li-yujzā qawm*^{an} for *li-yujzā qawm*^{un}, "that a people be recompensed"); (4) reading with *tmesis* – that is, with a noun inserted between the two members of a genitive construct (*iḍāfa*), as at Q6, 137 (reading *qatla awlād*^{i}*-him shurakāʾ-hum* as opposed to *qatla shurakā*^{i}*-him-awāld*^{i}*-him*, "their partner's" slaughter of their children"), etc.

Al-Dānī said that the imāms of recitation of the Qurʾān's *ḥarfs* are not concerned at all with the most common of the language nor analogies with the *Arabiyya*, but rather with the soundest of traditional recitations and those most reliable in transmission. If a narration is considered to be sound, it cannot be refuted by resort to analogous *ʿArabiyya* readings nor by popular usage: these are readings of the accepted *Sunna*; one must accept and follow them.

I (Suyūṭī) say that, in his *sunan*, Saʿīd Ibn Manṣūr reported, on the authority of Zayd Ibn Thābit, who said that recitation is accepted *Sunna*. Al-Bayhaqī said that our predecessors wanted to follow the *ḥarfs* of the accepted *Sunna*: one may not differ from the fixed codex which is the archetype (*imām*), nor can one differ from the generally accepted reading even if the alternative is of correct speech and is of more clarity.

Ibn al-Jazarī said that we mean by agreement with one codex what is present in some of them but not necessarily in all others, like Ibn ʿĀmir's reading of verse 116 *sūrah* 2, without the "*wāw*": "they say Allāh has taken a son"; or confirming the *ba* in verse 184, *sūrah* 3: "with the books and with the lighting scripture". This is present in the Syrian codex. Also like Ibn Kathīr's reading, adding "*min*" in verse 100 at the end of *sūrah* 9: "rivers flowing from under them . . .". This is present in the Meccan codex. And similar readings. If it is not in any of ʿUthmān codices, then it is odd because of departure from the generally accepted transcription.

By saying "even if probable" we mean what agrees even if by approximation like: "*malk yawm al-dīn*" because it is written in all codices without an *alif*. Reading without the *alif* agrees with the reality, while reading with the alif agrees with the approximation, because the *alif* is not written in the transcription for brevity such as in "*mālik al-mulk*" verse 26 *sūrah* 3.

Difference in recitation may agree with the reality of transcription such as "*ta'lamūn*" with the *ta* or *ya* or "*wa-yaghfir lakum*" with the *ya* or *nūn* and so on, which show that the letters were not dotted or annotated, either when omitted or included. This is despite the fact that the Companions were adepts in the science of spelling in particular and had piercing understanding in determining all sciences. See how they wrote *al-Sirat* with the *sad* that is changed from the *Sin* and left out the *Sin* which is the original. So when readings with *Sin* although the transcription is *sad*: the reading becomes of the original and thus they equalize. In this situation *Ishmam* reciting is possible, a thing which cannot be if it was written with the original *sin*. Re-editing in any manner other than the *Sin* is considered contrary to the transcription and the original. That is why there are differing opinions regarding the reciting of *basta* with *sad* (verse 69, *sūrah* 7) and not *basta* with *sin* (verse 247, *sūrah* 2) as the letter in *sūrah* 7 was transcribed as *sin* and that in *sūrah* 7 as *ṣād*! However, clear departure from the transcription in a letter which is *nudgham* (assimilated), *mubaddal* (changed); *thābit'* (fixed), *mahdūf* (omitted) or the like is not considered a contradiction to the morn if reciting in that manner has been confirmed and came in famous, profuse ways. That is why they did not consider the addition or omission of the *ya* in verse 70, *sūrah* 18, the *wāw* in verse 20, *sūrah* 63, or the *za* in verse 24, *sūrah* 83, and such as rejected or unacceptable departure from the transcription. Difference in such a situation is forgiven. That is because it is close and leads to one meaning. It is sanctioned by the correctness of the recitation as well its fame and acceptance. This is contrary to adding, omitting, putting forward or delaying a word; even if it was one single letter of the letters that have meaning. For the ruling is the ruling of the *kalmia* which allows for no variants in the text; this is the borderline between the truth of following the text or deviating from it.

Ibn al-Jazarī said that by the term "and the reading has a sound *isnād*" we mean this reading is on the authority of an impeccably reliable source, who received it from someone with the same qualifications. Thus for every link of the chain of transmitters to its end. It also must be acceptable to the *imāms* of this discipline who do not count any wrong in it nor deem it to be an odd reading.

He added that some of the moderns put a condition on this pillar of *tawatur*: that a sound *isnād* was not sufficient in itself, and they claimed that the Qur'ān could not have an authoritative reading unless it be through *tawatur*, and what came by way of the *aḥād* could not be an authentic Qur'ānic reading.

It is clear that if the *tawatur* is accepted, it has no need of confirmation by the latter two pillars, the text and the other. If the *harf* in dispute is derived from the Prophet (peace and blessings be upon him) by *tawātur*, it must be accepted as authoritative and unquestionable Qurʾān, whether it corresponds to the text or not. If we were to make *tawatur* compulsory for every reading under dispute, many of the disputed *ḥarfs* authorized by the seven Readers would be vitiated. Abū Shāma has said that what is on the tongues of the majority of modern readers and other Traditionalists is that all readings authorized by the seven are *mutawātir* – that is, each and every one of the readings narrated from them.

The decision that all these readings are revealed by God is necessary. We say this but we are speaking only about those readings with are transmitted with sound *isnāds*, according to the consensus, and which all parties unanimously adhere to. This is the least to ask for as a condition, when the *tawatur* is not found in some of them.

Al-Jaʿbarī said that the condition is one and the same: the soundness of the transmission. The other two conditions are necessary, for whoever determined the reliability of the authoritative tradents and is an authority in Arabic, and thoroughly scrutinized the text, for him the doubt is resolved.

Makki said that what is read in the Qurʾān is of three types.

1 That which is read; and whoever denies this is to be considered a disbeliever. This is what the most authoritative tradents taught; the language and writing of which agree with Arabic and the text of the *maṣḥaf*.

2 That which is narrated on the authority of individual tradents, which is in correct Arabic, but its pronunciation differs from the writing. Thus it is accepted, but one may not recite it for two reasons: because it differs from the commonly accepted reading and is not taken by the consensus of the community, but only by individual tradents; one may not accept it as Qurʾān, but the one who denies it is not to be counted a disbeliever. Woe to anyone who would deny it!

3 That which is related by an authoritative tradent, but is in ungrammatical Arabic, and that which is related by an unauthoritative tradent, is not to be accepted even if it agrees with the written text.

Ibn Jazarī said that readings of the first type are numerous: mālik (with the "*dagger alif*") and *malik*; *yakhdaʿūna* and *yukhādiʿūna* (with the "*dagger alif*); examples of the second type are (reading with Ibn Masʾud and others at Q92, 3): *wal-dhakar^{i} wal-unthā* ("I swear by the Male and the Female!") instead of *al-dhakar^{a} wal-unthā* (". . . ["I swear by the creation] of the male and female"), and Ibn ʿAbbās's reading at Q18, 79: *wa-Kana amama-hum malik^{un} yaʾkhudhu kulla safinat^{in} salihat^{in}* (". . . for in front of them was a king who seized every worthy ship.") for Q18, 79: *wa-kāna warāʾ-hum Malik^{un} yaʾkhudhu kulla safīnat^{an} ghasb^{an}* (. . . "for after them was a certain king who seized every boat by force"), etc. Ibn Jazarī added that the scholars of the Religion differ in these readings, the majority rejecting them because the *tawatur* is interrupted, even if the reading has a sound *isnād*; thus it is abrogated on account of the last reading of Gabriel to the Prophet, or by consensus of the Prophet's (peace and blessings be upon him) Companions about the ʿUthmānic codex.

There are many examples of what has been transmitted by unreliable persons in the odd-reading books. These are usually of very weak links (*isnād*). Among such is the reading related to Imām Abū Hanifa collected by Abū al-Faḍl Muḥammad b. Jaʾfar al-Khūzaʿī and transmitted from him by Abū al-Qāsim al-Hudhali. Among this is verse 28, *sūrah* 35 (*Fatir*) where Allāh is rendered in the nominative case when Allāh should be rendered in the accusative "verily those who fear Allāh most from among his servants are those who have knowledge". Al-Daraquṭnī and others wrote that his book is a fake and has no basis.

Examples of readings in ungrammatical Arabic transmitted by an authoritive tradent are so few as to be virtually non-existent. One that has been brought to light has been attributed to Nāfiʿ: *maʿaʾish* for the correct *maʿāyish* ("means for the fulfilment of your life") at Q7, 10 and Q15, 20.

Ibn al-Jazarī said that there remains a fourth unacceptable type, that is of a reading whose Arabic and writing agreement, but was never transmitted. In this type rejection is truer and prohibition is more vigorous; fabricating this type of reading is a heinous sin. According to Abūʾl-Miqsam, it was permitted; a meeting was held on account of this, and the consensus was to prohibit it. From that time the reading based on absolute analogy, and without foundation, is to be rejected as there is no basis on which one may act on it.

In the case of the ones that have valid base analogy is acceptable, such as the assimilation in, e.g. Q5, 23 *qāla rajulānⁱ* (read as *qarrajulānⁱ*, "two men said . . .") based on the pronunciation of Q18, 22 and Q28, 85 *qul rabbⁱ* (pronounced with a sandhi assimilation *qurrabⁱ* ("Say: 'My lord . . .' ") and likewise for where there is no difference in text, nor origin, nor will it be rejected by the consensus, even though such cases are extremely rare.

I (Suyūṭī) say that Ibn al-Jazarī has dealt thoroughly with this problem, and from him I have learned about various types of readings.

1 The *mutawātir* is the type that is of transmitted by a group of men when there is no possibility of their conspiring to lie about their authority, and by the likes of them to the end of transmission. Most readings are of this type.

2 The *mashhūr* is the one where the *isnād* is sound, but it does not reach the rank of a *mutawātir*; the Arabic agrees with the writing; it is common among the Readers, and is not considered ungrammatical nor peculiar. This is recitable according to the conditions set out by Ibn al-Jazarī, and the above-mentioned words of Abū Shāma will clarify them. An example of this are the differences

between what came from the seven Readers, some narrators transmitting what others did not transmit.

Examples of unique readings are plentiful in the plethora of the books of readings like the one mentioned above. The most famous of these classified collections are al-Dani's *Taysīr* (facilitation), and al-Shaṭibi's *Qaṣīda* (ode), and Ibn al-Jazarī's two works *Awʿiyat al-Nashr fī al-Qiraʾat al-ʿAshr* (Prose Vessels concerning the Ten Readings) and *Taqrīb al-Nashr* (Prose Propinquity).

The third type consists of the *aḥād* (recitations transmitted from too few transmitters to make them *mutawātir*), which are those readings supported by a sound *isnād*, but whose Arabic and writing conflict; or it was not accepted by a sufficient number of authorities. These are not to be recited. Al-Tirmidhī in his Jāmiʿ and al-Hakim in his *Mustadrak* devoted a chapter to it containing a large number of these with sound *isnāds*. One example is al-Kakim's reporting by way of ʿAsim, on the authority of al-Juhdarī, on the authority of Abū Bakra that the Prophet (peace and blessings be upon him) recited at Q55, 76: "Reclining on green cushions and rich carpets of beauty", using the plural word for "cushions" *rafārif*ᵃ, rather than the standard reading with the collective noun *rafraf*ⁱⁿ. He also recorded a report on the authority of Abū Hurayra saying that the Prophet (peace and blessings be upon him) would recite at Q32, 17: "Now no person knows what delights of the eye . . .", reading for "delights" *qurrat*ⁱ (a plural noun) for the standard reading *qurrat*ⁱ (in the singular). He reported on the authority of Ibn ʿAbbās that the Prophet (peace and blessings be upon him) would recite at Q9, 12: "Now has come unto you a Prophet from among yourselves . . .", reading for the last word *anfasi-kum* rather than the standard *anfusi-kum*.

In addition, he reported on the authority of Āʾishah that the Prophet (peace and blessings be upon him) would recite at Q56, 89: "(There is for him) rest and satisfaction . . .", reading for "rest" the form *ruh*ᵘⁿ rather than the standard *rawh*ᵘⁿ.

The fourth type is the peculiar (*shadhdh*) in which the *isnād* is unsound. Collections of this type exist – for example, Q1, 4: *malaka yawm*ᵃ *d-dīn*ⁱ ("He possessed/reigned on the Day of Judgement") instead of the accepted *maliki Yawm*ⁱ *d-din*ⁱ ("Master of the Day of Judgement"); and at Q1, 5: *iyya-ka yu'badu* ("You are worshipped") (in the passive voice) for the standard *iyya-ka na'budu* ("You we worship").

The fifth type is the fabricated type, like the readings of al-Khuzāʿī.

It appears to me that there is a sixth type which resembles the *mudraj* (recitations with unacknowledged insertions into the text or *isnād*) class of *ḥadīths*. These consist of additions to gloss the text as a hermeneutical strategy, for example Saʿīd Ibn Manṣūr's report of Saʿd Ibn Abī Waqqaṣ's reading at Q4, 12: ". . . but has left a brother or a sister from the same mother . . .", adding the last four words to the text. Similar is al-Bukhārī's report of Ibn ʿAbbās's reading of Q2, 198: "It is no crime in you if you seek the bounty of your lord during Pilgrimage . . .", where he inserts the last two words into the text.

Ibn Zubayr's reading of Q3, 104: "Let there arise out of you a band of people inviting to all that is good, enjoining what is right, and forbidding what is wrong, invoking the help of Allāh in what befell them", where he adds the final six words to the text. ʿUmar said that he did not know whether those words comprised a variant reading, or whether Ibn Zubayr was interpreting. Both Saʿīd Ibn Manṣūr and al-Anbārī reported this. The latter determined that additional words were indeed interpretation. He reported also, on the authority of al-Ḥasan, that Ibn Zubayr used to recite at Q19, 71: "Verily all of you will pass over it, that is, enter it . . ." Ibn al-Anbārī said that the last four words are al-Ḥasan's interpolation intended to gloss "pass over it (*warid*ᵘ*-ha*)". Some reciters erred and conflated it into the Qurʾān.

At the conclusion of his remarks, Ibn al-Jazarī said that it was possible that they would insert interpretations into the readings for clarification and explanation because they were determining what they had received from the Prophet (peace and blessings be upon him) as Qurʾān; they were free of all deceit, yet, perhaps some of them inserted the interpretation into the Qurʾān. Whoever claims that any of them permitted a reading determined by the meaning of the text rather than the actual wording, is a liar.

I (Suyūṭī) will devote a separate chapter to the topic of the *mudraj* (recitations with unacknowledged insertions into the text or the *isnād*).

Caveats

There is no disagreement that everything that is Qurʾān must be *mutawātir* (recitations transmitted by so many trustworthy persons as to be beyond doubt) in its foundation and all its parts. As for its *mahall* (desinential inflection; case ending) and its *wad*ʿ (position in the text) and its *tartib* (arrangement), these are also so determined by the people of the *Sunna's* verifiers. It is because this being the glorious miracle which is the foundation of the Eternal Religion and the straight Path all conditions were created concerning its transmission in toto and in detail.

Whatever was transmitted as an *āḥād* not having the status of a *mutawātir* was excised as being not part of the Qurʾān at all. Many of the *Uṣūlīs* (Early Traditionists) held that having the status of a *mutawātir* was a condition to verify what was the original Qurʾān; it was not conditional on its *mahall* (desinential inflection; case ending) or its *wad*ʿ (position in the text) or its *tartib* (arrangement). But the number of *aḥād* (recitations transmitted from too few transmitters to make them *mutawātir*) increased thereby. Al-Shāfiʿī's work was decisive in the matter of the inclusion of the *bismalla* before each *sūrah*.

This (Uṣūlī) method is to be rejected because it requires the condition that every reading must have *mutawātir* status because were it not required, it would allow many oft-repeated phrases of the Qurʾān to be expunged, and much of what is not authentically Qurʾān to be included. Concerning the former: had we not required the status of *mutawātir* in regard to its *mahall*, then many of the oft-repeated phrases of the Qurʾān would no longer have the status of *mutawātir*, for example: Q55 (a refrain repeated sixteen times): "For which is it of the bounties of your Lord that you and you deny?" Concerning the latter: if, on account of its *mahall*, part of the authentic Qurʾān does not have the status of *mutawātir*, then this part would qualify as one of the *āḥād*.

In his *Intiṣār*, the Qadi Abū Bakr said that some of the jurisprudents and the scholastic theologians have concluded that one may accept an *aḥād* type of transmission as equal to but not Qurʾān. The people of truth denied this, and abjured it. Some of the scholastic theologians said that one may rely on the application of independent judgement to verify a recitation, a *wajh* (sense of a word or phrase), or a *ḥarf*. If these *wajhs* are expressed in correct Arabic, even if the Prophet (peace and blessings be upon him) did not recite it the people of Truth reject and abjure this, and give the lie to anyone who accepts it. End (of Ibn Jazarī's remarks).

The Mālikis and others, who advocated removing the *bismalla* from the beginning of the *sūrahs*, relied on this foundation deciding that it did not have the status of a *mutawātir* at the beginnings of the *sūrahs*, and whatever does not have the status of a *mutawātir* is not part of the Qurʾān.

On our part, we reject the view that these recitations are not *mutawātir*, for many a recitation is considered *mutawātir* by some people yet rejected by others. Or they may be accepted or rejected at various times. It is sufficient for it to have the status of a *mutawātir* in one of the Prophet's (peace and blessings be upon him) Companions' codices; and it suffices that those who followed them copied codices in which it was prohibited to write what was not in the official ʿUthmānic version of the codex, for example the *sūrahs*' names, "Amen", and the division of the text into tenths. Were it not an integral part of the Qurʾān, it would not have been included in the text. This would put the Muslims in jeopardy, tempting them to believe in something which was not actually Qurʾān. One can hardly believe the Prophet's (peace and blessings be upon him) Companions to be capable of such a thing.

If one were to claim that the *bismalla* had been placed to separate the *sūrahs*, I would reply that this is deception; it could not have been constructed merely to separate the *sūrahs*, for if it were, it would appear between *sūrah* 8, *al-Anfal* and *sūrah* 9, *Barāʾa* (where, exceptionally, it does not occur).

The proof that the *bismalla* is an integral part of the revealed Qurʾān is found in a Tradition reported by Abū Dāwūd, al-Ḥākim and others, on the authority of Umm Salamah, one of the Prophet's (peace and blessings be upon him) wives, reporting that he would recite Q1, 1 "In the Name of Allāh, the Compassionate, the Merciful" and Q1, 2 "Praise is Allāh's . . ." to the end of the Tradition. It includes the fact that he counted "In the Name of Allāh, the Compassionate, the Merciful" as a Qurʾān verse, but did not count *ʿalay-him* – that is, Q1.7, as a separate verse.

In the Maʿrifa, Ibn Khuzayma and al-Bayhaqī reported a Tradition with a sound *isnād*, by way of Saʿīd Ibn Jubayr, on the authority of Ibn ʿAbbās, who said that Satan has stolen from the people the most glorious verse of the Qurʾān, namely "In the Name of Allāh, the Compassionate, the Merciful."

Al-Bayhaqī reported in his Shuʾab and Ibn Mardawayhi reported with a good *isnād* – by way of Mujāhid, on the authority of Ibn ʿAbbās, who said that the people neglected a verse of God's Book which was never revealed to any prophet except the Prophet (peace and blessings be upon him), unless it was Solomon, the son of David; that verse is "In the name of Allāh, the Compassionate, the Merciful."

Al-Dāraquṭnī reported – as did al-Ṭabarānī in his *al-Awṣat* with a weak *isnād* – on the authority of Burayda, who said that the Prophet (peace and blessings be upon him) said: "I will not exit the mosque until I inform you of a verse that was never revealed to any prophet after Solomon, the son of David, except to me." Then he said: "By what from the Qurʾān do you start with when you begin prayer?" I said: "In the Name of Allāh, the Compassionate, the Merciful." He said "It is, it is."

Abū Dawud, al-Hakim, al-Bayhaqī and al-Bazzar reported by way of Saʿīd Ibn Jubayr, on the authority of Ibn ʿAbbās, who said that the Prophet said: "Separation of the *sūrahs* was not known until the verse 'In the Name of Allāh, the Compassionate, the Merciful' was revealed." Al-Bazzar added that had it been revealed, then it would been known when a *sūrah* had ended, and another was anticipated, or another began.

Al-Ḥākim reported an additional Tradition, with a different *isnād*, on the authority of Saʿīd Ibn Jubayr, on the authority of Ibn ʿAbbās, who said that the Muslims did not know when to end a *sūrah* until "In the Name of Allāh, the Compassionate, the Merciful" was revealed. After it was revealed, they knew when to end the *sūrah*. The *isnād* of this Tradition meets the conditions of al-Bukhārī and Muslim for soundness.

Al-Hakim reported an additional Tradition, with a different *isnād*, on the authority of Saʿīd Ibn Jubayr, on the authority of Ibn ʿAbbās, who said that the Prophet (peace and blessings be upon him), whenever Gabriel came to him saying "In the Name of Allāh, the Compassionate, the Merciful", knew that a *sūrah* would follow.

Other authorities, and al-Bayhaqī in his *Shuʾab*, reported on the authority of Ibn Masʾud, who said; "We never knew when to separate two *sūrahs*, until 'In the Name of Allāh, the Compassionate, the Merciful' was revealed."

Abū Shāma said that this was probably when the Prophet (peace and blessings be upon him) first recited under the direction of Gabriel (that is, he would repeat what Gabriel revealed), and he would continue reciting until Gabriel ordered him to say the *bismalla*, upon which he would know that the *sūrah* had come to an end. And the Prophet (peace and blessings be upon him) expressed it in Qurʾānic phraseology, indicating that it was an integral part of the Qurʾān by introducing every *sūrah* reciting the *bismalla*. It is also possible that the meaning of this is that all the verses of all the *sūrahs* were revealed before the *bismalla* was; when the Prophet (peace and blessings be upon him) recited the verses, Gabriel would bring down the *bismalla* and display the *sūrah*, and thus the Prophet (peace and blessings be upon him) would know that it had concluded; nothing could then be added to it.

Ibn Khuzayma reported, as did al-Bayhaqī, a Tradition with a sound *isnād*, on the authority of Ibn ʿAbbās, who said that the seven *mathani* comprise the Opening of the Book (i.e. *sūrah* 1). When asked which was the seventh, Ibn ʿAbbās would answer: "In the Name of Allāh, the Compassionate, the Merciful."

Al-Dāraquṭnī reported a Tradition with a sound *isnād*, on the authority of ʿAlī, who when asked about the seven *mathani*, would recite Q1, 2: "Praise be the Allāh, Lord of the worlds." When someone would respond that *sūrah* 1 comprised only six, ʿAlī would reply that "In the Name of Allāh, the Compassionate, the Merciful" is a verse.

Al-Dāraquṭnī, Abū Nuʾaym and al-Ḥākim in his *History*, reported a Tradition with a weak *isnād*, on the authority of Nāfiʿ, on the authority of Ibn ʿUmar that the Prophet (peace and blessings be upon him) said: "Whenever Gabriel brought me *waḥy* (Revelation), the first he dictated to me was 'In the Name of Allāh, the Compassionate, the Merciful.'"

Al-Wahidi reported another Tradition with a different *isnād*, on the authority of Nāfiʿ, on the authority of Ibn ʿUmar, who said that "In the Name of Allāh, the Compassionate, the Merciful" was revealed in every *sūrah*.

Al-Bayhaqī reported a Tradition with a third *isnād*, on the authority of Nāfiʿ, on the authority of Ibn ʿUmar, who said that he used to recite "In the Name of Allāh, the Compassionate, the Merciful" in prayer, and whenever he finished reciting a *sūrah*, saying that it had been written down in the codex for the specific purpose of being recited.

Al-Dāraquṭnī reported a Tradition with a sound *isnād*, on the authority of Abū Hurayra, who said that the Prophet (peace and blessings be upon him) would say: "When you recite *al-Ḥamad* (that is, Q1, 2–7), recite also 'In the Name of Allāh, the Compassionate, the Merciful' because it is the Mother of the Book, and the Mother of the Book is the seven *mathānī*, one of whose verses is 'In the name of Allāh, the Compassionate, the Merciful.'"

Muslim reported, on the authority of Anas, who said that one day at noontime the Prophet (peace and blessings be upon him) took a nap, and upon awakening, said: "I have just received a *sūrah*" and then recited (Q108): "In the Name of Allāh, the Compassionate, the Merciful. To you we have granted the fount (of Abundance . . .)" . . . to the end of the Tradition.

These Traditions confer the status of semantic *mutawātir* to the fact that the *bismalla* is an integral part of the Qurʾān introducing the *sūrahs*.

One of the difficulties with this principle is, as the Imām Fakhr al-Dīn al-Rāzī noted, that some of the ancient books reported that Ibn Masʾud denied that the *Fātiḥa* (*sūrah* 1) and the final two *sūrahs*, *al-Falaq* (*sūrah* 113) and *al-Nas* (*sūrah* 114), are not part of the Qurʾān. This is extremely problematical, for if we were to claim that the *mutawātir* transmission was obtained during the era of the Prophet's (peace and blessings be upon him) Companions because it came directly from the Qurʾān, then this denial amounts to unbelief; if we were to claim that the Qurʾān was not obtained at that time, then we have to conclude that the Qurʾān is not originally *mutawātir*. Thus the Imām Fakhr al-Dīn al-Rāzī said that it is most reasonable to argue that relating this to Ibn Masʾud is false and this is the solution to the problem. The Qadi Abū Bakr said the same, adding that it has never been confirmed that he said that it was not part of the Qurʾān, nor has that been known of him. What Ibn Masʾud did was to erase and omit the three above-mentioned *sūrahs* from his codex denying their inclusion in the text, but not denying that they constituted Qurʾān, because it was his *sunna* (practice) not to write in his codex anything that the Prophet (peace and blessings be upon him) did not order to be inscribed in it. Ibn Masʾud did not witness the Prophet (peace and blessings be upon him) writing those three *sūrahs*, neither did he hear him ordering that it be done.

In his Commentary on the *Muhadhdhab*, al-Nawawī said that Muslims agree that *sūrahs* 1, 113 and 114 are an integral part of the Qurʾān, and that anyone who denies this is an unbeliever. What was transmitted on the authority of Ibn Masʾud is invalid, and not sound.

In his *Maḥalli*, Ibn Ḥazm said that this lie concerning Ibn Masʿūd is fabricated – what is true is that the recitation of ʿAsim on the authority of Zirr, on Ibn Masʾud's authority, is that *sūrahs* 1, 113 and 114 are an integral part of Qurʾān.

In his commentary on al-Bukhārī's *Ṣaḥīḥ*, Ibn Hajar al-ʿAskālanī said that it is correct that Ibn Masʿūd denied this. Aḥmad and Ibn Hibban reported, on the authority of Ibn Masʿūd, that he would not write *sūrahs* 113 and 114 in his codex.

In his Additions to the Musnad, ʿAbd Allāh Ibn Aḥmad-and al-Ṭabarānī and Ibn Marduwayhi reported by way of al-Aʿmash, on the authority of Abū Isḥāq, on the authority of ʿAbd-al-Raḥmān Ibn Yazīd al-Nakhaʿi who said that ʿAbd Allāh Ibn Masʿūd used to erase *sūrahs* 113 and 114 from his codex, saying that they were not parts of God's Book.

Al-Bazzār and al-Ṭabarānī reported a Tradition with a different *isnād* which reports that Ibn Masʿūd would erase *sūrahs* 113 and 114 from his codex, saying that the Prophet (peace and blessings be upon him) commanded only that they be recited in order to take refuge from Satan, but they were not to be recited as Qurʾān. The *isnād* of this Tradition is based on are sound.

Al-Bazzār said that not even one of the Companions of the Prophet (peace and blessings be upon him) followed Ibn Masʿūd in this; it is true that the Prophet (peace and blessings be upon him) used to recite these two *sūrahs* in prayer.

Ibn Ḥajar said that whoever claims this is a lie about Ibn Masʿūd should be given the lie. Doubting sound *riwayāt* (Traditions) without proof is to be rejected. The *riwayāt* (Traditions) (about Ibn Masʿūd) are however sound and *ta'wil* (explanation) is possible. Ibn Ḥajar added that among others, the Qaḍī Abū Bakr reported, on the basis of sound *isnāds*, that Ibn Masʿūd would not write the two *sūrahs* in his codex; this is based on Tradition with sound *isnāds*. But the sound *riwaya* (Tradition) which I (Suyūṭī) related above obviates this by saying, "Ibn Masʿūd said that *sūrahs* 113 and 114 are not part of God's book." Ibn Ḥajar added that the expression "God's Book" probably referred to Ibn Masʿūd's codex, so the above-mentioned *ta'wil* (explanations) are indeed valid, saying that anyone who ponders the *siyaq* (background connections) of the above-mentioned *turuq* (isnāds), will consider their *jamʿ* (being put into the same category) as improbable. He said in addition that Ibn al-Ṣabbāgh replied that he hadn't accepted this (*qatʿ*) categorically, but that later it was agreed upon, and he decided that *sūrahs* 113 and 114 were indeed *mutawātir* in his era, but they were not in Ibn Masʿūd's.

In his Mushkil al-Qur'ān, Ibn Qutayba said that Ibn Masʿūd thought that *sūrahs* 113 and 114 were not part of the Qur'ān because he saw the Prophet (peace and blessings be upon him) ask refuge from Satan for his grandsons Ḥasan and Ḥusayn, and he stood by his opinion. We do not say that he was correct in this and that the Muhājirūn and the Anṣār were wrong.

Ibn Qutayba added that, concerning Ibn Masʿūd's omitting the *Fātiḥa* from his codex, it wasn't Ibn Masʿūd's view that the *Fātiḥa* was not part of the Qur'ān, God forbid! Rather he was of the opinion that the Qur'ān was collected and written down between the *lawhayn* (two book-covers), out of fear of doubt, forgetting, increasing, or decreasing the text. He believed that, concerning *Surat al-Ḥamd* (that is, the *Fātiḥa*), this was safe because of its brevity and the obligation that everyone learn it by heart.

I (Suyūṭī) say that what Abū ʿUbayd reported in a Tradition with a sound *isnād*, viz. that Ibn Mas'ud omitted the *Fātiḥa* from his codex (as I reported at the beginning of Chapter nineteen), is true.

Second caveat

In his Burhān, al-Zarkashī said that the Qur'ān and the recitations are two discrete truths: the Qur'ān is the way (inspiration) revealed to the Prophet (peace and blessings be upon him) for *bayan* (clarity) and *iʿjaz* (inimitability). The recitations are the expressions of the above-mentioned inspiration in view of its harfs and quality, e.g. pronouncing a consonant as single or doubled, etc. The consensus of the community is that the seven recitations have the status of *mutawātir*, or, as others claim, *mashhur*.

Al-Zarkashī added that the opinion is that the seven recitations are *mutawātir* from the seven *imāms*, but there is difference of opinion concerning their being *mutawātir* from the Prophet (peace and blessings be upon him). The Tradition concerning the seven recitations, with its *isnād*, is found in the collections of variant readings. This *isnād* is composed of one individual on the authority of another sole individual.

I (Suyūṭī) say that these opinions will be described below. As reported above, Abū Shāma took exception to the disputed recitations related and did not regard them as being of the *qurrā'* (seven Readers).

Ibn al-Hajib took exception to Traditions concerning *al-ada*ʾ (actual performance of pronunciation), elongation of the *a* vowel, *imāla*, and the consonantal pronunciation of the glottal stop. Someone else said there is truly a firm basis to consider elongation and *imāla* to be *mutawātir*, but the underlying form is not *mutawātir* because of the difference of its quality. Thus said al-Zarkashī, who also said that all the various types of realizing the pronunciation of the glottal stop are *mutawātir*.

Ibn al-Jazarī said that we don't know of anyone who expressed this view before Ibn al-Hajib. All of it was granted *mutawātir* status by the original *imāms*, like the Qāḍī Abū Bakr and others – and this is true. For if the expression is valid, then so is the form of its execution: without the latter, we cannot have the former – it must be present and valid.

Third caveat

Abū Shāma said that some people suppose that the seven readings we have now are the same ones referred to in the *ḥadīth* (Tradition), but this is absolutely the reverse of what the consensus of the community holds; only the foolish believe this.

Abū ʿAbbās Ibn ʿAmmār said that whoever transmitted these seven Readers has done what he should not have done. What made things difficult for people by confusing all of those who have limited ability is that: these seven recitations are actually those mentioned in the *khabar* (Tradition). It would have been better to decrease their number or add to them to remove the doubt.

What also detracts from their worth is that when there are only two narrators from each *imām*, and one claims that he had heard a reading from a third narrator beside these two, then he nullifies the third narrator's reading. But this (third) reading may be the most genuinely *mashhūr*, *ṣaḥīḥ* (sound), and evident. He may even go to the extent of calling others sinners and disbelievers.

Abū Bakr Ibn al-ʿArabī said that the fact that these seven Readers are singled out for approved readings does not mean that others, the like of Abū Jaʿfar, Shayba, al-Aʿmash, and even more prominent authorities, cannot also do so. Many have held this view, e.g. Makkī, Abūʾl-Aʿla, al-Hamadhānī and other *imāms* of the Readers.

Abū Ḥayyān said that none of the readings in Ibn Mujāhid's book, and none of the readings related from his followers, is *mashhūr* except for a very few. Abū

ʿAmr Ibn al-Aʿlā became famous for transmitting from seventeen narrators whose names he mentioned. However Ibn Mujāhid's book had only al-Yazidi, who had only ten souls mentioned. So how can one rely only on al-Susi and al-Duri who are no better than anyone else, as all agree in the scruting, perfection and common source (Tradition). Ibn Ḥayyān added that he saw no reason for this Tradition, except for lack of knowledge.

Makkī said that whoever supposes that the readings of these Readers like Nāfiʿ and Asim are seven *ḥarfs* as related in the *ḥadīth* (Tradition) has made a grievous mistake. He added that what follows from this is that he reading other than those of the seven Imāms and has been confirmed by the authorities (*imāms*) and which agree with the written text in the codex would not be Qur'ān? This would be a great mistake. The original *imāms* who classified the readings, e.g. Abū ʿUbayd al-Qāsim Ibn Sallām, Abū Ḥātim al-Sijistānī, Abū Jaʿfar al-Tabari, and Isma'il al-Qadi, have narrated twice as many readings as the former. People in Basra at the end of the second century were on the readings of Abū ʿAmr and Yaʿqub, in Kufa, of Ḥamza and ʿĀṣim; In Damascus, of Ibn ʿĀmir; in Mecca of Ibn Kathīr; in Madīna, from Nāfiʿ. They continued like that and when they were at the end of the first three hundred years Ibn Mujāhid confirmed the name of al-Kisaʿī, and omitted that of Yaʿqūb. Makkī said that the reason for the condensation to seven Readers – despite the fact that the *imāms* of the recitations had among them some more glorious in ability, and the likes of the latter were different from the likes of the former – was that the narrators from the *imāms* were much more numerous. When people became less zealous they summarized the readings to those easy to memorize, and to pronounce precisely of those readings which agreed with the text of the codex. They looked into who was famous for reliability, exactitude and length of time in reciting his knowledge and the agreement to take from him (*akhdh*). They singled out one *imām* from each of the *amṣār* (famous cities, e.g. Medina, Kufa, Basra, Damascus, Cairo, etc.), although not omitting reading from other *imāms*, e.g. the readings of Yaʿqūb, Abū Jaʿfar, Shayba and others. He said that Ibn Jubayr al-Makkī had written a book of readings arranged according to topics before Ibn Mujāhid did. He limited himself to five, choosing one *imām* from each of the *amsar*. He limited himself thus because the codices which ʿUthmān sent to all the amsar numbered five. Another opinion is that he sent seven, these above-mentioned five plus one codex to Yemen and another to Bahrayn, but as no *khabar* (Tradition) was heard concerning these latter two codices, Ibn Mujāhid and others wanted to adhere to the number of codices, so they chose two readers from outside Yemen and Bahrayn to complete this number. This agreed with the number narrated in the Tradition. This resulted in those who did not know the basis of the problem, and who were without intelligence – to assume that "the seven *ḥarfs*" are "the seven Readings". The necessary principle is the soundness of the orally transmitted *isnād*, the determination of *wajh* (semantic authenticity) of the Arabic, and agreement with the written text. The soundest readings are based on Traditions with *isnāds* containing Nāfiʿ and ʿAsim; the ones in the most eloquent Arabic from Abū ʿAmr and al-Kisaʾi.

In his *al-Shāfiʿī*, al-Qarrāb said that insisting on the readings of the seven Readers and excluding others has no *athar* (basis in Tradition) nor any basis in the *Sunna*. It is merely the consensus of some of the later authorities which spread; it was assumed that none could be added to them, but no one said that.

Al-Kawāshī said that all Traditions with sound *isnāds* and which are in correct Arabic, and which agree with the writing in the *imām* (archetypical) codex are part of the seven *mansus* (*mutawātir* readings); if one of these conditions is not met, then that Tradition is *shadhdh* (peculiar).

The *imāms* (authorities) in this field stressed the rejection of the view of those who would restrict the number of recitations to the *mashhur* (acceptable) readings, for example as advocated in the Taysīr and the Shāṭibiyya. The last authority to declare this is the Shaykh Taqiʾ al-Dīn al-Subkī; in his *Sharḥ al-Minhāj* (Explaining the Way), some colleagues say that in prayer and elsewhere one may recite the seven readings, but not the peculiar ones; but this may lead some to think that readings other than the seven *mashhūr* readings are peculiar. Al-Baghawi transmitted his agreement with the readings of Yaʿqūb and Abū Jaʿfar together with the seven *mashhūr* readings, and this is correct. Al-Baghawī added that one should know that the exceptions to the seven *mashhūr* reading are of two types: (1) those which differ with the writing in the codex; there is no doubt that these are prohibited in prayer or elsewhere; and (2) those which do not differ with the writing in the codex, and whose usage has not spread, but only spring from a strange source, and are not dependable. They are clearly prohibited in recitation. Among these are some that spread from the authorities in this field, long ago and recently. This is no reason to prohibit them, e.g. the readings of Yaʿqub and others.

Al-Kawāshī said that al-Baghawi is the most trustworthy in this: he is a *muqriʾ* (teacher of Qurʾān recitation) who is a *faqīh* (jurisprudent), and learned in all the religious sciences. He added that concerning details of peculiar readings, within the seven Readings there are a large number of these. End of al-Kashawi's remarks.

In his *Manʿ al-Mawāniʿ* (Prohibition of the Prohibitions), al-Kashawī's son said what we said in our *Jamʿ al-Jawāmiʿ* (Collection of the Collections), namely that the seven are *mutawātir*, then we said concerning the peculiar and the sound that these come after the ten Readers; we did not say that the ten are *mutawātir*, because none differ from the seven as being *mutawātir* readings. First we mentioned the position of the *ijmaʿ* (consensus of the community), then we added the position of difference. Al-Kashawī's son said that the statement that the three additional readings are not *mutawātir* is to be rejected outright and that no one whose opinion in matters of religion can be trusted can say this, in that these readings do not differ from the writing in the codex; he added that he had heard his father strongly protest to some *qāḍis* (judges) because he had become aware that they had prohibited reciting from them. Some of our friends once asked him to allow him to teach reciting from the seven, and he said: "I allow you to teach reciting from the ten."

To a question asked by Ibn al-Jazarī, he answered that the seven recitations that al-Shāṭibī restricted himself to – and the three others by Abū Jaʿfar, Yaʿqūb, and Khalaf – are undeniably *mutawātir* in the religion by necessity, and every *ḥarf* held by any of the ten is part of the religion, for it was revealed to the Emissary of God (peace and blessings be upon him). No one but the stubbornly ignorant would deny this.

The fourth caveat

From differences in recitations there may occur difference in religious laws. Thus the jurisprudents allowed a man who had recently had intercourse not to perform the *wuḍū'* (partial ablution before prayer), or to do so based on Q4, 43: ". . . or if you have (*lamas-tum* or *lāmas-tum*) been in contact with women . . ." They also allowed coitus with a menstruating woman at the end of her period before the completion of her purification with ghusl (total ablution), or without it, based on Q2, 222: . . . "(so keep away from women in their courses, and do not approach them until) (*yathur-na* or *yaṭṭahhar-na*) they are clean. (But when they have purified themselves, you may approach them in any manner, time, or place . . .)" They told of a strange difference concerning a verse which can be recited with both forms. In his book *al-Bustān* (The Garden), Abū-I-Layth al-Samargandi said that: (1) God said them both; (2) God said only one, but He allows us to recite both. Then al-Samargandi chose to expand this principle: any reading of which there are two opposing interpretations, God pronounced them both; each reading has the status of a verse, e.g. Q2, 222: ". . . until they are pure . . ."; if the interpretations of two discrete readings are the same, e.g. Q2, 189 ". . . the houses . . ." read as either *al-buyūt* or *al-biyūt*, then God said only one; each tribe was allowed to pronounce it in its own particular way, as was their custom.

He added that if you were to claim that God pronounced only one of them, then which one of the two readings is it? We (Suyūṭī) would answer that it is the one which conforms to the dialect of Quraysh. End of Ibn al-Kawāshī's remarks.

Some of the *mutaʾakhkhirūn* (later Traditionists) said that there are benefits from the differences and types of variant readings: (1) for the Nation's simplification, facilitation, and ease in recitation; (2) the demonstration of its excellence and nobility to the other nations, because no scripture had ever been revealed to any of them, but that it had only one permissible reading; (3) increasing their reward, for they expend their energies to realize this, and to strive for rigour word by word, to the extent of determining the true execution of a long *a* vowel, or the attenuation of the *imāla* (vowel) a tending toward *i*, then pursuing the implications of these and deriving the *ḥikam* (lessons) and ahkam (rules) from the definition of each expression, and research to discover their *tawjih* (validation), *taʿlīl* (reasoning), and *tarjih* (preference in judgement); (4) the demonstration of God's secret in His Book, and his protecting it from arbitrary change or meaningful differences, despite its variant outward aspects; (5) increasing its *iʿjaz* (inimitability) by means of its succinctness, for the varations in its readings have the status of verses; if each definition of each word was made discrete verse, one would have to feel the resulting exaggeration, e.g. at Q5, 6: *wa-ʾarjul i/u/a-kum* (that is, this word may be recited with all three case vowels) "... your feet ...", which was revealed concerning the washing of the feet when preparing for prayer, and for wiping the soles of the feet – the word is the same, but the case ending vowels differ; (6) some of the readings clarify what may be unknown from others, e.g. at Q2, 222, the reading *yattahhar-na* clarifies the meaning of its variant *yathur-na* (see just above); and Ibn Masʿūd's reading of Q2, 9: ... *fa-mḍaw ila dhikri Allāh* ("... go to the Remembrance of Allāh ...") clarifies that the intention of the standard reading ... *fa-s'aw* ... ("... hasten earnestly to the Remembrance of Allāh ...") is "earnestly going" and not merely "ambling quickly".

In his *Faḍāʾil al-Qurʾān* (Excellencies of the Qurʾān), Abū ʿUbayd said that the motive for mentioning the peculiar reading is to interpret the *mashhur* (acceptable) reading, and to clarify its meanings. For instance, in Āʾishah and Ḥafs's (*shādhdh*) reading at Q2, 238: "... the Middle Prayer is the ʿAsr (afternoon) prayer ..." (adding the last four words to the text); and Ibn Masʿūd's (*shadhdh*) reading at Q5, 38: "... cut off his or her right hands ..." instead of the standard "... cut off his or her hands ..." and Jābir's (*shadhdh*) reading at Q24, 33: "... for indeed Allāh, after such compulsion, is all-forgiving, Most Merciful to them", where he adds the last two words to the text. Abū ʿUbayd said that these expressions and their likes have become a form of interpretation of the Qurʾān. A similar report was narrated on the authority of the Successors, saying that they approved this type of Qurʾān interpretation. How much more so when it was also narrated on the authority of the greatest of the Companions, then it came with the same reading. For it is more and stronger than *tafsīr* (Qurʾān interpretation). For the least of what results from these expression is the knowledge of correct *taʾwīl*. End of Abū ʿUbayd's remark.

I (Suyūṭī) have examined in my book *Asrār al-Tanzīl* (Secrets of the Revelation) the explanation of readings which provide additional meaning to the standard reading.

The fifth caveat

There are differences concerning the use of the *shādhdh* readings: In his *al-Burhān* (The Proof) Imām al-Ḥaramayn al-Juwainī related, on the authority of the apparent meaning of the Shāfiʿī school of Law, that such usage is not permitted; Abū Naṣr al-Qushayrī followed him in this. Ibn al-Ḥājib disagreed with them, saying that the peculiar readings were Qurʾān, but this was never established. The two qadis Abū'l-Ṭayyib and al-Ḥusayn, al-Rawyānī, and al-Rāfiʿī used them, granting them the status of recitations transmitted by *aḥād* Traditions. In his books *Jamʿ al-Jawāmiʿ* (The Collections of the Collections) and *Sharh al-Mukhtaṣar* (Explication of the Summary), Ibn al-Subkī confirmed this view.

The Companions of the Prophet had already based the cutting off of the thief's right hand on Ibn Masʿūd's reading (and) Abū Ḥanīfa supports him in this. They also based the obligation of fasting on serial days for atonement, on Ibn Masʿūd's adding the word "serial" to Q5, 88: (". . . a fast of three days shall be your atonement for your oaths . . .") our friends did not take it as its abrogation is confirmed as will be shown.

The sixth caveat

The *tawjih* (assigned meaning) of the readings are important. The *imāms* dealt with this, and devoted books specifically to this topic, e.g. Abū ʿAlī al-Fārisī's *al-Ḥujja* (The Proof); Makkī's *al-Kashf* (The Uncovering); al-Mahdāwī's *al-Hidāya* (The Guidance); and Ibn Jinn's *al-Muhtasib fī Tawjīh al-Shawādhdh* (The Controller of the Peculiar Readings' [*tawjīh*] Meanings).

Al-Kawāshī said that the value of knowledge of the applied meaning is that it amounts to a guide, or an indication according to what needs proof. But one must be careful of one thing: the probability of one reading so preferred as to almost eliminate another from consideration. This is not desirable, because both of them are *mutawātir*.

In his book *al-Yawāqīt* (The Rubies), Abū ʿUmar al-Zāhid reported on the authority of Thaʿlab, who said that if one case ending on a word in the Qurʾān differs from another, he would not prefer one over the other, but when he moved to colloquial speech then he would choose the more correct.

Abū Jaʿfar al-Naḥḥās said that for the People of the Religion the safe course is that if both recitations are correct, not to say that one or the other is better, because both are from the Prophet (peace and blessings be upon him).

Whoever maintains this sins, and the chief Companions rejected this kind of argument.

Abū Shāma said that the authors made much of the probabilities of the readings *mālik* and *malik* and they go to such extremes that they almost eliminate the validity of the other reading. This is hardly desirable after both have been determined to be *mutawātir*. End of comments on this topic.

Some authorities said that the *tawjīh* of the peculiar readings is even stronger than the *tawjīh* of the *mashhūr* (accepted) recitations.

Conclusion

Al-Nakhaʿī said that they disliked saying "ʿAbd Allāh's recitation", "Salim's recitation"; "Ubayy's recitation"; "Zayd's recitation"; they would rather say: "So-and-so used to recite with this *wajh*" and "someone else would recite with that *wajh*". Al-Nawawī said that the truth is that the former expressions are not disliked.

Chapter twenty-eight

KNOWLEDGE OF (WHERE TO) PAUSE AND (WHERE TO) COMMENCE (IN RECITATION)

Many people have devoted works to this topic: Abū Jaʿfar al-Nahhas, Ibn al-Anbārī, al-Zajjāj, al-Dāni, al-ʿUmānī, al-Sajawandī, among others. This is a noble subject, from which one may come to know the correct pronunciation of a recitation.

Its basis was established by al-Naḥḥās, who said: "Muḥammad Ibn Jaʿfar al-Anbārī informed us, that Hilal Ibn al-Aʿla Ibn Ubayy and ʿAbd Allāh Ibn Jaʿfar informed us, that ʿAbd Allāh Ibn ʿAmr al-Zuraqī informed us, on the authority of Zayd Ibn Abī Anisa, on the authority of al-Qāsim Ibn ʿAwf al-Bakrī, who said that he had heard ʿAbd Allāh Ibn ʿUmar say: 'We have lived for a while in our era, when one of us was granted belief before knowing the Qurʾān, and when a *sūrah* was revealed to Muḥammad (peace and blessings be upon him) we studied what is allowed and what is permitted in it, and where it was necessary to pause in recitation of it in the same way you study the Qurʾān today. Now we see men, one of whom was granted the Qurʾān before belief, who recites what is in its opening to its ending knowing neither what it commands nor what it prohibits, nor where one must pause during reciting it.'"

Al-Nahhas said that this Tradition shows that they used to study where to pause, just as they used to study the Qurʾān itself. Ibn ʿUmar said that the expression "we have lived for a while in our era" indicates that this is the firm consensus of the Prophet's (peace and blessings be upon him) Companions. I (Suyūṭī) say that in his *Sunan*, al-Bayhaqī reported this *athar* (Tradition).

Concerning Q73, 4: "*Wa-ratil l-Qurʾān tartīla* (. . . and recite the Qurʾān in slow, measured rhythmic tones)", on the authority of ʿAlī, who said "*tartīl* means *tajwīd* (rhythmic recitation) of the *ḥarfs* (letters) and knowledge of the places to pause in recitation."

Ibn al-Anbārī said that for complete knowledge of the Qurʾān one must have the knowledge of where to pause and where to begin in its recitation.

Al-Nakzāwī said that knowledge of where to pause in recitation is of great value and noble risk; for one who is not competent in it can in no way be capable of knowing the Qurʾān's meanings, nor can he judge the implications for the *Sharīʿa* from them except by knowing well the *fawāṣil* (places to pause in recitation).

In his *al-Nashr*, Ibn al-Jazarī said that whenever a reciter cannot recite a *sūrah* nor a narrative in one breath, or if it is not possible for him to take a breath between two words which do not require a pause between them, but this would be like taking a breath within one word, then he must choose to pause to take a breath and relax and indicate the desirability of beginning again after this. Yet he must make certain that this does not detract from the correct meaning, nor vitiate comprehension, because herein lies the Qur'ān's *iʿjāz* (rhetorical inimitability), by which the intention is realized; for this reason the Imāms insisted on teaching and knowing it.

In what ʿAlī said there is an indication that this is an obligation. In what Ibn ʿUmar said there is proof that teaching it is the consensus of the Companions of the Prophet (peace and blessings be upon him).

Truly, we now consider teaching it and researching it to be *mutawātir* on the authority of *al-salaf al-ṣāliḥ* (the first true followers of the Prophet (peace and blessings be upon him)), for instance by Abū Jaʿfar al-Yazīd Ibn al-Qaʿqaʿ: one of the exemplaries of the generation of the followers, and his Companion, the *Imām* Nāfiʿ, Abū ʿAmr, Yaʿqūb, ʿAsim, and other *imāms*. What they have to say on this topic is *maʿrūf* (well-known); and their *naṣṣ* (authoritative texts) are *mashhur* (widespread) in their books. Therefore many of the *khalaf* (later scholars) were authorized to grant teaching licences in Qur'ān recitation on the condition that no one could be licensed until after he had mastered the knowledge of pausing and beginning. It is correctly reported that al-Shab'bi said, that when one recites Q55, 26: "And all that is on earth will perish", one does not (pause) before reciting the following verse: "But will abide forever in the Face of your Lord – full of majesty, bounty and honour."

I (Suyūṭī) say that Ibn Abī Ḥātim reported this.

Section: the types of pause

The *imāms* agreed that the various types of pause and beginning have names, although they differed in this. Ibn al-Anbārī said that there are three kinds of pause: (1) *tāmm* (perfect); (2) *ḥasan* (good); and (3) *qabīḥ* (unacceptable).

In the first type, the perfect, it is proper that one stops after a word; and begins directly after it, as what follows it is not semantically dependent on it – e.g. Q2, 5; ". . . it is those who will prosper", and the following verse: ". . . and if you O Muḥammad do not warn them, they will not believe".

In the second type, the good, it is proper that one stops after a word, but one does not immediately begin with the following word – e.g. Q12: "Praise is Allāh's . . .," because it is a *ṣifa* (attribute) to what precedes it.

The unacceptable: the third type is neither perfect nor good – e.g. stopping after the words, "In the Name of . . ." from the verse "In the Name of God," in Q1, 1.

Ibn al-Anbārī said that, to have a perfect pause, one may not pause after the first member of an *iḍāfa* (annexation) construction and its second member, nor after a noun before its adjective, nor after a verb before its subject, nor after an object before its verb, nor after a verb followed by its cognate accusative, nor after the first member of a combination before the second, nor after a noun before its apposition, nor after *inna*, *kana*, *zanna* and their "sisters" and before their subject nouns, nor after a noun subject which begins a sentence before its predicate, nor after a noun and before its exception, nor after a noun and before its syndetic relative clause, be it nominal or literal, nor after a verb and before its verbal noun, nor after a particle and before its dependent word, nor after the protasis of a conditional sentence and before its apodosis.

Someone else said there are four types of pause: (1) *tāmm mukhtār*; (2) *kaf jāʾiz*; (3) *ḥasan mafhūm*; (4) *qabīḥ matrūk*.

1 According to this system, a pause which is *tamm* (perfect) is one in which there is no semantic with what follows it, so it is proper to pause after that word and begin directly after it; this is almost always at the end of a verse, e.g. Q2, 5: ". . . it is those who will prosper." It may also occur within a verse, e.g. at Q27, 34: ". . . when they enter a country, despoil it, and make the noblest of its people the meanest . . ." this pause is perfect, for here ends the story of *Bilqis* [the Queen of Sheba]; then God (He is exalted) said: ". . . Thus do they behave." Likewise, at Q25, 29: "'He did lead me astray from the message of Allāh after it had come to me!'" for here end the words of the evildoer ʿUbayy Ibn Khalaf; then God (He is exalted) said: "Ah! The Evil One is but a traitor to man!" A perfect pause may occur after a verse, e.g. at Q37, 137: "Verily, you pass by their sites, by day (Q37, 138) and by night . . .", because here the second part of the combination is semantically connected to the first part, "by day and by night".

Similar is His saying at Q43, 34–35: ". . . they could recline; and ornaments . . ."; the end of verse 35 is "they could recline"; ". . . and ornaments . . ." is the completion of the combination, because it is added to the first part.

Pausing at the conclusion of each story, and what precedes its beginning; at the end of every *sūrah*, before the vocative particle, the imperative verb, the *lam* of oath, a statement and a prodosis, as long as the apodosis precedes; and before "Allāh is eternally . . .", ". . . he/it was not . . .", "This is . . ." and ". . . were it not for . . .", is *tamm* most of the time, as long as an oath or an introductory statement or something close in meaning to it does not precede.

2 The *kafi* (sufficient) is the type of pause which occurs at Q4, 23: "Prohibited to you for marriage are your mothers . . ." where there is an interruption in expression, but a connection in meaning to the following words "daughters, sister, etc. . . ." Pausing at this point is good, and so is beginning after it. And thus with each verse's beginning followed by *li* – in the sense of "in order to"; *illa* in the sense of "but"; and *inna* ("verily"); an interrogative; *bal* ("rather"); *a-la* ["is it/he not?"]; *sa-* prefixed and *sawfa* preceding the imperfect tense, indicative mood verb to mark it as a threat for the future; *ni'ma* ("how good is!") and *biʾsa* ("how bad is!") followed by its subject in the nominative case; and *kay-la* ("so that no"); as long as none of these is preceded by an introductory phrase or an oath.

3 The *ḥasan* (good) is like the pause that occurs at Q1, 2: "Praise is Allāh's, the Lord of the Worlds." It is good to pause after it, but it is not good to begin after it.

4 The *qabiḥ* (unacceptable) is the type of pause which causes a lack of understanding, as after "Praise . . ." at Q1, 2; even worse is the pause at Q5, 27 – that is, between "A blasphemy indeed are those that say . . ." and "that Allāh is Christ . . ." because by beginning before the second verse fragment the meaning is vitiated; whoever propounds this view and its import is indeed an unbeliever. Likewise at Q2, 25: pausing and then beginning after ". . . thus was he confounded . . ." and at Q4, 11: pausing and then beginning after ". . . one sister has a share of half; for parents . . .".

Even more unacceptable is pausing after a negative before its affirmer as a Q47, 19; "There is no god except Allāh" and at Q17, 105: "We have not sent you except as a bringer of good news and a warner". If it is necessary to pause in order to catch one's breath, it is permissible. Then one returns to a preceding part of the verse to connect it to what follows it. End.

* * *

Al-Sajawandī said that pause has five levels: (1) necessary; (2) absolute; (3) permitted; (4) allowed for a *wajh* (reason); and (5) tolerated for necessity.

1 The necessary pause is one which, were its two sides connected, would change the meaning. For example, at Q2, 8: ". . . they are not believers", pause is necessary here. Were it connected to the following Q2, 9: "Fain would they deceive Allāh . . .", it would be assumed that the second part would be an attributive phrase to the first, for deception is removed from them, and belief free of deception is attributed to them, as one says: "He is not a deceiving believer." The intention of the verse is to affirm deception after rejecting belief. As at Q2, 71: ". . . a heifer not trained to till the soil . . .", the phrase ". . . to till . . ." is an attributive phrase to ". . . trained . . ." which enters the area of negation – that is, it is not trained as a tiller of the soil. The intention in the verse is the confirmation of deceit after belief. Likewise at Q4, 171: ". . . Far exalted is He above having a son . . ." if one connects this to the following part of the verse ". . . To him belongs all the things of the heavens and the earth . . .", one might assume that the second part is an attributive phrase to ". . . a son . . ." and that the negated "son" is included in ". . . to Him belongs what is in the heavens and the earth . . .", but the intention of the verse is the absolute negation of "the son".

2 The absolute pause is one after which it is good to begin, as with a sentence beginning with an inchoative noun as the subject of the phrase.

For example, at Q42, 13: "... Allāh chooses to himself ...".

Or after one verb synonymous with another, as at Q24, 55: "... 'they will worship me alone and not associate aught with me ...'."

And at Q2, 142: "the fools among the people will say ...".

And at Q65, 7: "... After a difficulty, Allāh will soon grant relief."

Before a suppressed verb, as at Q4, 122: "... Allāh's promise is the truth ..." and at Q33, 38: "... It was the practice approved of Allāh ...".

Before a conditional sentence, as at Q6, 38: "... whom Allāh wills, He leaves to wander ...".

After an interrogative, even if it be suppressed, as at Q4, 88: "... Would you guide those ...?" And at Q8, 67: "... You look for the temporal goods of this world ...".

After a negation, as at Q28, 68: "... No choice have they in the matter ...". And at Q33, 13: "... They intend nothing but to run away." These expressions cannot be said as though they were attached to the previous expressions.

3 The permissible pause is one where it is allowable either to pause or to continue, because of the connectedness of two parts. For example, at Q2, 3: "... and sent before your time (and have the assurance of the Hereafter)." Here the second co-ordinating "and" requires connection to what follows, but the precedence of the object, "Hereafter", before its verb, "have the assurance of", makes the pause acceptable – that is, the actual text, above, differs from the underlying text, which reads: "and in the Hereafter they have assurance."

4 The pause which is allowed for a *wajh* is of the type found at Q286: "These are the people who buy the life of this world at the price of the Hereafter; (for their penalty shall not be lightened nor shall they be helped)", because the particle *fa* ("for") requires cause and effect, and this requires connection. But the inceptive verb "lightened" permits a pause allowed for a *wajh*.

5 The pause tolerated for necessity is one in which the second part is not dependent on the first part, yet it is permitted to allow the reciter to catch his breath due to the length of the recitation, so he may pause without returning some words back before beginning again, because the following phrase is fully comprehensible, as at Q2, 22: "... and the heavens your canopy, and sent down rains from the heavens ..." because the second phrase is not dependent on the first for its contextual meaning (the agent of the second phrase is the same as the agent in the first); thus the second is entirely comprehensible.

As for what does not require a pause: e.g. a protasis without its apodosis, a noun subject beginning a sentence without its predicate and so on. Others say that pause in recitation is of eight types: complete, and similar to it; incomplete, and similar to it; good, and similar to it; defective, and similar to it.

Ibn al-Jazarī said that most of what people have said about pause is not rigorous, and not limited. He said that the nearest to what he said about it is that pause can be either voluntary or compulsory, because speech is complete or not; if it is complete, then pause is voluntary; but being complete it is not directly related to what follows it – that is, not from the point of view of pronunciation or meaning, for this is the pause called "complete" on account of its absolute completeness, so one pauses there and begins immediately thereafter. He, Ibn al-Jazarī, gave examples as was given before in the "*Tamm*".

Ibn al-Jazarī also said that a pause may be perfect from the point of view of its interpretation, desinence (case endings), and recitation; but it may not be perfect in another respect, e.g. at Q3, 7: ". . . but no one knows its true meanings except Allāh" is a perfect pause if the phrase which follows it, "and those who are firmly grounded in knowledge . . ." is inceptive; if it is appositive, the pause is not perfect. A similar case is with the "cut-off letters" which introduce certain *sūrahs*: pausing after them is perfect if they are considered to be an inchoative subject followed by a suppressed predicate, or vice versa, as if to say, "*Alīf Lām Mīm* is thus" or "thus is *Alīf Lām Mīm*". Or, if they are considered a direct object of the suppressed imperative *qul*! ("Say!"), a perfect pause follows them; but this is not so if what follows them is considered their predicate.

Likewise at Q2, 125: After "(Remember we made the house) a place of assembly for men and a place of safety", the pause is perfect if we recite the following word *wa-ittakhidhu* ("And take!") with a *i* vowel after the letter *kh*; but if we read it *wa-ittakhadhu* ("and they took") with an *a* vowel after the letter *kh*, then we have a pause which is *kāf*[in] (sufficient). Likewise at Q34, 6: ". . . (to you from your Lord [*min rabbi-ka*] – that is the Truth and it guides) to the path of the Exalted (in Might), worthy of all praise." If one recites it thus, the pause is *hasan* (good); if one reads *man rabbu-ka* (who is your Lord?) for *min rabbi-ka* (from your Lord) it is not so good.

One may prefer the perfect pause, e.g. at Q1, 3–4: "Master of the Day of Judgement. You do we worship, and Your aid we seek." Both verses are followed by a perfect pause, but the first is more perfect than the second because the second shares with the following verse, "show us the straight way", the sense of speech, as opposed to the first. This is what some have called "quasi-perfect".

Within this class are those pauses in which the intended meaning is stressed; thereby their affirmation as accepted pauses is emphasized. Al-Sajawandi called these *lazim* (necessary). Even if it is connected to what follows it, if it is not solely from the semantic aspect, it is called (*al*)-*kafi* (sufficient), for it suffices as a pause or without one, from what follows it; and by omitting what follows it from it, e.g. Q2, 3: ". . . and spend out of what We have provided for them" and Q2, 4: "(And who believe in the Revelation sent to you) and sent before your time . . . (and have the assurance of the Hereafter)" and Q2, 5: "(They are) on true guidance from their Lord." One might prefer sufficiency or perfection in the pause, e.g. at Q2, 10: "In their hearts there is a disease", pausing here is sufficient. At ". . .

and Allāh has increased their disease", pausing here is more sufficient; at ". . . (and grievous is the penalty they incur] because they are false to themselves", pausing here is more sufficient than in either of the two previous pauses.

A pause may be sufficient for the purposes of interpretation, inflection or recitation, and insufficient for another one of these, e.g. Q2, 102: ". . . teaching men magic . . .": a pause here would be sufficient if one interprets the following word *ma* as a negative (yielding: ". . . and not revealed to the two angles . . .); but the pause would be *hasan* (good) if *ma* were to be interpreted as syndetic [yielding: ". . . and which was revealed to the two angles . . ."].

Q2, 4: ". . . and have the assurance of the Hereafter" (see just above); a pause here would be sufficient if what follows it, Q2, 5: ". . . (they) are on true guidance . . .", is considered to be syntactically an inchoative subject and its predicate; the pause would be good if it is considered to be the predicate of Q2, 3: "Who believe in the unseen . . ." or if it is considered to be the predicate of Q2, 4: "And those who believe in the Revelation sent . . .".

Q2, 137: ". . . and we are sincere (in our faith) in him." Pause here is sufficient for those who read the following word, (Q4, 138) in the second person *am taqūlūna* ("or do you say . . ."); if you recite it in the third *am yaqūlūna* ("or do they say"), then pause here is good.

Q2, 284: ". . . Allāh calls you on account for that . . .". Pause here is sufficient for he who recites the following words ". . . He forgives (*fa-yaghfiru*) whom He pleases, and He punishes (*wa-yuʿ adhdhibu*) whom He pleases . . ." in the indicative mood; if one recites these two words in the jussive mood (*fa-yaghfir . . . wa-yuʿ adhdhib*, meaning "then let him forgive" and "and let him punish"), then pausing here is good; if the context be semantic, then the pause is called "good", because it is good and beneficial in itself. Pausing at such points is allowable without starting the recitation without following by reciting what comes immediately after it because of the semantic connection, except if it be the beginning of the following verse because most of the scholars of recitation (*ahl al-ada*) prefer it so: it is based on the words of the Prophet (peace and blessings be upon him), according to a Tradition from Umm Salamah (which we will supply below).

It is possible for a pause to be "good" based on the deep structure; and "sufficient" or "perfect" otherwise, e.g. Q2, 2: ". . . sure guidance, to those who fear Allāh."

Pausing here is good if one considers the following words ("Those who believe in the Unseen . . .)" an attribute; it is sufficient if one considers them to comprise an underlying predicate or an underlying accusative phrase separated from the preceding phrase; it is perfect if it is considered the inchoative subject having as its predicate [Q2, 5:] "These are . . .".

Even if discourse had not been concluded, pause is required. It is called *qabīḥ* (mistaken), and one may not support the pause in such cases except out of necessity, for example, when running out of breath or because of its lack of benefit or corruption of the sense, as at Q1, 7: "The way of those on whom . . .".

Some cases may be worse than others, e.g. Q4, 11: ". . . (the daughter's) share is half. For parents . . .", because it might imply that the parents share the half-portion with the daughter.

Even more mistaken is to pause after Q2, 26: "Allāh disdains not (to use a similitude of things) . . ."; Q107, 4: "so woe to the worshippers who are neglectful of their prayers)"; and Q4, 43: "Approach not prayers (with a mind befogged) . . .".

This is the rule of pause, voluntary and required.

As for beginning recitation, it must be voluntary, because unlike the pause, you may not assign necessity to it, unless independent of the meaning it fulfils the intention of the text. Like pause, it is divided into four sections; they differ analogously as perfect, sufficient, good and mistaken; according to completeness or its absence, or corruption and disruption of its meaning, e.g. the pause after Q2, 8: "Of the people (there are some who say, 'We believe . . .') . . .". Beginning here with ". . . the people . . ." is mistaken; beginning with ". . . 'We believe . . .'" is perfect. Were one to pause after ". . . those who say . . ." one would be better advised to begin with ". . . say . . ." rather than ". . . who . . .".

Thus the pause after Q2, 7: "Allāh has set a seal . . ." is mistaken; and beginning with "Allāh . . ." is even more mistaken; pausing after ". . . set a seal . . ." is sufficient.

Pausing after Q9, 30: ". . . ʿUzayr is a son of God . . ." and/or ". . . Christ is the son of God . . ." is mistaken; beginning with ". . . son of . . ." is even more mistaken; beginning with ". . . ʿUzayr . . ." and/or ". . . Christ . . ." is the worst possible kind of mistake.

Pausing at Q33, 12: ". . . what Allāh (and his envoy) have not promised us . . ." is necessary; beginning with ". . . Allāh . . ." would be mistaken, with ". . . promised us . . ." even more mistaken, and with ". . . what . . ." more mistaken than either of the former two.

Pause may sometimes be good, while beginning reciting mistaken, e.g. Q60, 1: "They have driven out the Messenger and yourselves . . ." after which pausing is good, but beginning with which is mistaken because it corrupts the meaning, as if it were a warning against believing in God.

It is also possible that pause be mistaken, and beginning good, e.g. Q36, 52: ". . . who has raised us up out of our bed of repose? (This is what the Most Gracious had promised) . . .". Pausing after "This . . ." is mistaken because it separates the inchoative subject from its predicate, and it implies that "this" refers to "our bed of repose". Beginning here is either sufficient or perfect because of its inception.

Caveats

1 Some say that pause is not possible on the genitive rather than the first member of a genitive construct (*iḍāfa*), but this is not so. Bin al-Jazarī said that

practical licence is what is intended here; this improves recitation and purifies recital; it does not imply that it is either prohibited nor undesirable. Only if it is implied that the Qurʾān is corrupted or that it opposes the meaning that God intended! Whoever does so is an unbeliever, not merely a sinner!

2 Ibn al-Jazarī also said that not always when linguistic scholars treat it haughtily, nor when reciters try to lord it over others, nor when some empty heads try to interpret it as to what constitutes pause or beginning is it required that pause be supported by this; rather one must keep scrupulously to the exact meaning and the most appropriate pause, e.g. the pause at Q2, 286 ". . . grant us forgiveness. You . . ." and beginning with ". . . (you are) our Protector. Help us . . .", as an entreaty to God.

Likewise at Q4, 62: Pausing after ". . . then they come to you, swearing (by Allāh) . . ., and beginning with ". . . by Allāh . . .".

Also at Q31, 13: Pausing after ". . . O my son! Join not in worship others (with Allāh)" and beginning with ". . . with Allāh, for false worship is . . .".

And also at Q81, 29: Pausing after "You will not will, except as wills (Allāh, for Allāh is the cherisher of the worlds)" and beginning with ". . . Allāh is . . .".

So at Q2, 158: ". . . it is no sin (in them, should they compass it around . . .)" and beginning with ". . . in them . . .".

All this is haughtiness, trickery and corruption of the words from their contexts.

3 Pausing is pardonable when there is length in separating words, the narrative passages and contrasting sentences. Likewise where there is combination of variant readings, or recitation for ascertaining the text and Revelation while it is not pardonable in other dissimilar cases. Pause and beginning may occur at some of the places they name, and were it not for this fact it would not be allowed. This is what al-Sajawandi called "permitted out of necessity", e.g. at Q2, 22: ". . . the heavens your canopy (and sent down rain from the heavens) . . .".

Ibn al-Jazarī said that the best examples of this are found at Q2, 177: ". . . towards the East or West. (But it is righteousness . . .)" and Q2, 61: ". . . (slaying his) messengers (without cause . . .)"; and at Q2, 177: ". . . to be steadfast in prayer, and practise regular charity. (To fulfil the contracts you have made . . .)", and ". . . (and to be firm and patient . . .)", and likewise at all of the separations at Q23, 1: "The Believers must (eventually) win through . . ." to the end of the narrative.

The author of the *Mustawfā* said that the grammarians disliked the deficient pause along with the execution of the perfect pause. If wording be lengthy, and there is no perfect pause in it, it is good to take a deficient one, e.g. at Q72, 1: "Say: 'It has been revealed . . .'" to Q72, 18: ". . . so invoke not anyone with Allāh" if the following word (Q72, 19) is read *innahu*. If it is read *annahu*, then one continues "(That) the devotee of Allāh stands forth to invoke Him; they just make round him a dense crowd."

Al-Sajawandi added that the deficient pause is improved somewhat if it serves to further better explication, e.g. at Q18, 1: ". . . He allowed therein no crookedness, (straight . . .)". Pausing here clarifies the fact that Q18, 2, "straight . . ." is separated from what precedes it, and that ". . . crookedness . . ." is recited in the circumstantial accusative in order for it to precede "straight . . .". Similar is Q4, 23: ". . . sister's daughters; (foster-mothers . . .)" to distinguish by it the prohibition against combining the relative and the causal. Likewise at Q69, 25, "Ah! Would that my record had not been given to me! (Q69, 16). And that I never realized how my account stood!" where the wording is based on pausing between the two verses.

Just as pause is forgiven for the reasons just described, it might not be forgiven nor approved in phrases which are shortened, or if the connection is not semantic, e.g. at Q2, 87: "We gave Moses the Book (and followed him up with up a succession of Messengers) . . ."; "We gave Jesus, the son of Mary, clear (signs) and strengthened him with the Holy Spirit", pause is not forgiven because of the propinquity of the pauses after ". . . messengers . . ." and ". . . Holy . . .".

Thus pairing is preserved by pause by connecting a part where pause is perfect with a synonymous phrase, and by interrupting its connection with what follows it in the text, e.g. Q2, 134: ". . . They shall reap the fruit of what they did . . ." with ". . . and you shall too . . .". Also at Q2, 203: ". . . But if anyone hastens to leave in two days . . ." with ". . . there is no blame on him . . .". Likewise at Q35, 13: "He merges night into day . . ." with ". . . and He merges day into night". Also at Q41, 46: "Whoever works righteousness benefits his own soul . . ." and ". . . whoever works evil, it is against his own soul . . .".

4 Some authorities allow pause on one word, and others on another; between the pauses one must be observant of any present contradiction. For pause in one location may not obviate pause in the other, e.g. at Q2, 2: "(This is the Book;) it is without doubt; (in it is a guidance sure (to those who fear Allāh);" One may not pause after ". . . in it . . ."; whoever permits pausing after ". . . in it . . ." must prohibit it after ". . . without doubt . . .". Likewise at Q2, 282: ". . . (Let a scribe write down faithfully as between the parties) let not the scribe refuse to write; as Allāh has taught him, (so let him write) . . .", if one allows a pause after ". . . to write . . .", then one must prohibit it after ". . . as Allāh taught him . . .".

Likewise at Q3, 7: ". . . (Seeking discord, and searching for its hidden meanings.) but no one knows its true meaning except Allāh. And those who are firmly grounded in knowledge say . . .". If one allows pause after ". . . except Allāh . . ." then one must be observant not to pause after ". . . those firmly grounded in knowledge . . .".

Ibn al-Jazarī said that the first to notice this strict observation in pause was Abūʾl Faḍl al-Rāzī, who transferred the concept from *ʿarud* (prosody).

5 Ibn Mujāhid said that only a grammarian, one learned in the variant readings, expert in Qurʾān commentary, narrative, distinguishing one part from another, and a savant of the language in which the Qurʾān was revealed, may determine that a pause may be perfect.

Others said this also holds for *figh* (jurisprudence). Thus one may not accept the testimony of a slanderer even if he repent, based on pausing after Q24, 4: "(and those who launch a charge against chaste women, and produce not four witnesses, flog them with eighty stripes) and reject their evidence ever after (for such men are wicked transgressors.)"

Al-Nikzawi was one who stated this, saying in his Book of the Pause that it is absolutely necessary for the reciter to know some of the schools of jurisprudence of the famous *imāms*, because this certifies his knowledge of pause and beginning. Because some of them require pausing at certain places in the Qurʾān, and others prohibit it. As for the necessity of knowing grammar and its underling forms it is because those who recite Q22, 78): "it is the cult of your father Ibrāhīm" in the accusative for instigation pause on what precedes it, or connect it syntactically with what precedes it should refrain from pausing.

As for the need to know the variant readings: as stated above, the pause may be perfect as far as the recitation is concerned, but not perfect from other aspects.

As for the need to know about Qurʾān commentary, at Q5, 26: ". . . therefore will the land be out of their reach for forty years . . .", if one pauses before ". . . therefore . . .", it would simply mean that the land was out of their reach this one time; if one pauses before ". . . their . . .", it would imply that it was forbidden to them forever, and that the period of wandering in the desert was forty years. If one consults the Qurʾān commentaries, one realizes, as has been stated above, that a pause may be perfect according to one interpretation and syntax, and not perfect according to another interpretation and syntax.

As for the need to understand meanings, it is necessary because the understanding of a fragment is only possible tethered with a knowledge of its full meaning as at Q10, 65: "Let not their speech grieve you for all power and honour belong to Allāh . . .". The words ". . . for all power and honour . . ." are inceptive, not ". . . their speech [is 'all power and honour']."

Likewise at Q28, 35: ". . . so they shall not be able to touch you: with our signs shall you triumph . . ." with one pausing after "you" and beginning with the following word "the two of you", resulting in the mistaken ". . . so they shall not be able to touch you with our signs . . .". Shaykh ʿIzz al-Dīn said that it is best to pause after "you" because annexation of the third person to "the signs" is preferable to connecting to it what doesn't properly belong. Because the referent of "signs" is Moses' rod and its attributes, because with it Moses defeated the Egyptian magicians, but did not protect them from Pharaoh. Similar is the case of pausing after Q12, 24: "And with passion did she desire him . . ." and beginning with the following words "and he would have desired her . . ." despite the fact that the meaning is given in the following words ". . . but that he saw the evidence of his Lord . . ." he would have desired her. God placed the apodosis of "but that" before it and thus Joseph's lust is abated. Shaykh ʿIzz al-Dīn thus knew that the knowledge of meanings is a great principle of the subject of pause.

6 Ibn Burhān the Grammarian narrated on the authority of Abū Yūsuf the Judge, the companion of Abū Ḥanīfa leaned towards the view that the repetition of the phrase after which one pauses, when the pause is perfect, deficient, good or incorrect is *bidʿa* (reprehensible innovation), and anyone who intends to pause at such locations is invoking reprehensible innovation. He said that the Qurʾān is *muʿjaz* (inimitably miraculous); it is all of piece; its entirety is Qurʾān and its parts are Qurʾān; all of it is perfect and good; each part of it is perfect and good.

7 The Reciters' *imāms* have their own schools on pause and beginning. Nāfiʿ would adapt their distinguishing terminology according to the meaning; Ibn Kathīr and Ḥamza, according to where one takes a breath; but Ibn Kathīr made an exception of Q3, 7: ". . . but no one knows its true meaning except Allāh . . ." because if one continues directly with the following words ". . . and those who are firmly grounded in knowledge . . ." a false message results; and at Q6, 109: ". . . what will make (you Muslims) realize . . ." because if one doesn't pause (before this phrase – that is, a mistake by Suyūṭī – MS), the message received will be "certainly all Signs are in the power of Allāh and what you realize . . ." and at Q16, 103: ". . . it is a man that teaches them . . .". If one refrains from pausing here, the message becomes ". . . it is a man that teaches him the language of him they wickedly point to . . .". One should make a deliberate pause on these. ʿAṣim and al-Kisāʾi would pause according to where the speech ended. Abū ʿAmr would deliberately pause at the beginnings of the verses, saying that was his favourite method. Some of them said that pausing at the end of the verses is sunna (standard practice).

Al-Bayhaqī in his *Shuʿab*, and others have said that it is most excellent to pause at the ends of the verses, unless they be syntactically connected to what follows them, following the guidance and *sunna* (Exemplary Life-Style) of God's Emissary (peace and blessings be upon him).

Abū Dāwūd and others related on the authority of Umm Salamah, that the Prophet (peace and blessings be upon him) would divide his recitation verse by verse, and would recite (Q1, 1): "In the name of Allāh, the Compassionate, the Merciful", then pause, and recite (Q1, 2): "Praise is Allāh's, Lord of the Worlds", then pause, and recite (Q1, 3): "The Compassionate, the Merciful", and then pause, etc.

8 *Waqf*, *qatᶜ* and *sakt* are the most frequent terms which the scholars of old used to apply to "pause". Later scholars distinguished between them as follows.

I *qatᶜ* – this term is applied to stopping recitation at the end, which is similar to stopping reciting. The reciter here is like one who leaves the recitation and moves to a different situation other than reciting, and thus he must take refuge on continuing the recitation of what follows it. This can occur only at the end of the verse, because the end and the verses are in themselves stops. Saᶜīd Ibn Manṣūr said in his *Sunan*: "Abū'l-Aḥwas related to us, on the authority of Abū Sanan, on the authority of Ibn Abī'l-Hudhayl: 'They disliked reciting part of a verse and leaving part.' The *isnād* of this Tradition is sound. ᶜAbdallah Ibn Abī'l-Hudhayl, a great *tabiᶜi* (member of the second Muslim generation) would say that they used to indicate that the *Sahaba* (Companions of the Prophet (peace and blessings be upon him) and thus the first generation of Muslim) also disliked doing that.

II *Waqf* – they applied this term for temporarily interrupting the voice. Generally this is shorter than the pause, usually without taking a breath.

The terms the *imāms* used concerning the practice differed, which indicates that it can be either short or long. According to Ḥamza *sakt* on a phonetic zero is called a *sakt yasira* (simple); according to al-Ashnānī, a *sakt qasira* (short); according to al-Kisāʾi a *sakt mukhtalisa bi-ghayr ishbāᶜ* (slurred, yet unconsummated); according to Ibn Ghalbun it is a *sakta yasīra*; al-Maki said: *waqfa khafīfa* (light); Ibn Shuraykh called it *wuqayfa* (little pause); Ibn Qutayba: without interruption of breath; al-Dani said: *sakta laṭīfa* (gentle) without interruption; al-Jaᶜbarī said: a temporary interruption of breath for a time less than an exhalation – because if it lasts longer it become a *waqf*. There are other expressions as well.

Ibn al-Jazarī said that the truth lies in *al-samaᶜ wal-naql* (hearing (Traditions) and transmission). Only what has been related is possible: the meaning is self-evident. It is perfectly possible to have connection (that is, omission of pause) at the ends of the verses for the purpose of clarity. Some authorities provided Traditions to support this view.

General rules

1 One may omit pausing before every *alladhī* and *alladhīna* (who, which) if what precedes is an attribute; but one must pause if it is a predicate, except for seven instances where I Pause is indicated:

1 Q2, 121: "Those to whom We have sent the Book study it . . ."
2 Q2, 146: "The People of the Book know this as they know . . ."
3 (Likewise at Q6, 20)
4 Q2, 275: "Those who devour usury . . ."
5 Q9, 20: "Those who believe, and suffer exile. . ."
6 Q25, 34: "Those who will be gathered . . ."
7 Q40, 7: "Those who sustain the Throne . . ."

In addition, according to al-Zamakhsharī's Kashshāf:

8 Q114, 5: "(The same) who whispers . . ."

It is permissible for the reciter to pause on the head noun and begin with *alladhi* if it is considered a break, as opposed to considering it an attributive phrase.

Al-Rummānī said that if the attributive phrase is present for specification, then it is not permissible to pause after the head noun preceding it, but if it is present for the purpose of giving praise, then it is permissible, because the agent of the praise is not the agent of the head noun.

* * *

II There are various opinions concerning pausing on the excepted word.

1 Permission to do so is absolute because the meaning is an inchoative subject whose predicate is suppressed in order to indicate it.
2 Prohibition is also absolute, because it depends on what precedes it semantically, because the usage of "except" and its meaning can be synoptically bound to what precedes it; and syntactically, because what precedes it perfectly singles the word in its meaning. If one says "There is no one in the house . . ." one can correct this by adding ". . . except the donkey." If you were to say ". . . except the donkey" separately, you would be in error.

III Separation: This is permissible if it is clarified by a predicate because of the independence and sufficiency of the phrase from what precedes it; it is not permissible if it does not clarify it because of its insufficiency. Ibn al-Ḥājib reported this in his *al-ʾAmālī*.

Pausing on a vocative phrase is allowed, as Ibn al-Ḥājib transmitted from the *muhaqqiqun* (experts): it is independent, and what follows it is a different phrase, even if the first is syntactically connected to it.

One may not pause at any quotations in the Qur'ān, because what follows is narrative. Thus said al-Juwaynī in his Qur'ān Commentary.

One pauses on the word *kal-la* (by no means!, nay!) the thirty-three times it occurs in the Qur'ān: it is agreed that seven are on account of refection, and are thus paused upon, e.g.

1 Q19, 78: ". . . has he taken a contract with (Allāh) Most gracious?" (Q19, 79) "Nay! . . ."
2 Q19, 81–82: ". . . to give them Power and Glory. (Q19, 82:) "Instead . . ."
3 Q26, 14–15: ". . . I fear they may slay me." (Q26, 15:) "Allāh said: 'By no means!' . . ."
4 Q26, 61–62: ". . . we are sure to be overtaken." (Q26, 62:) "(Moses) said, 'By no means!' . . ."
5 Q34, 27: ". . . Show me those whom you have joined as partners: by no means can you . . ."
6 Q74, 15–16: ". . . That I should add (yet more) – by no means! . . ."
7 Q75, 10–11: ". . . 'Where is the refuge?' (Q75, 11:) "By no means! . . ."

Some of the instances of the remainder are really semantic interruptions, so there is no pause on them. In other cases both possibilities exist, according to the following criteria.

Makkī said there are four divisions.

I Where pause is preferable from the semantic point of view and one may begin with what comes after it, as if to say, "Truly . . ." There are eleven instances of this: two in *sūrah* 19, one in *sūrah* 23, and one in *sūrah* 34; two in *sūrah* 70, 15–16: ". . . that I should add (yet more) (Q70, 16:) By no means! . . ." and *sūrah* 70, 52–53: ". . . Scrolls of Revelation spread out! . . . (Q70, 53:) By no means . . .", *sūrah* 83, 13–14: ". . . 'Tales of the Ancients!' (Q83, 14:) By no means! . . .", *sūrah* 89, 16–17: ". . . 'My Lord has humiliated me!' (Q89, 17:) Nay! nay! . . .", *sūrah* 104, 3–4: ". . . his wealth would make him last forever! (Q104, 4:) By no means! . . ."

II Where pause is appropriate, and beginning is not, e.g. Q26, 14–15: ". . . and I fear that they slay me (Q26, 15:) Allāh said, 'By no means! . . .'" and Q26, 61: ". . . 'We are sure to be overtaken' (Q26, 16:) Moses said, 'By no means ! . . .'"

III Where neither pause nor beginning is permitted but is connected to what precedes it and what follows it in the following two instances.
  1 Q78, 4: "Verily! They shall soon some to know!" and
  2 Q102, 4: "Again, you soon shall know!"

IV Where it is permissible to pause and also to begin. These are the eighteen remaining cases.

* * *

The term *balā* (nay! but yes!) occurs in twenty-two locations, and they are of three types.

I What by general consent may be paused upon because of the semantic dependence of what follows it to what precedes it, e.g.:

1 Q6, 30: ". . . They will say, 'Yes, by our Lord! . . .'"

2 Q16, 38: ". . . Allāh will not raise up those who die, nay but it is a promise binding on Him in truth . . ."
3 Q34, 3: ". . . never will come the Hour. Say, 'Nay! But most surely, it will come . . .'"
4 Q39, 58–59: ". . . among the righteous.' (Q39, 59:) Their reply will be, 'Nay, but there came to you . . .'"
5 Q46, 34: ". . . they will be asked, 'Is this not the Truth?' They will say, 'Yea, by our Lord!'"
6 Q64, 7: "The unbelievers think that they will not be raised up for Judgement. Say: 'Yea, by my Lord! . . .'"
7 Q75, 3–4: "Does man think that we cannot assemble his bones? (Q75, 4:) Nay, we are able to . . ."

II Where there is a difference of opinion, refusing to pause is preferable, as in the following five cases.

1 Q2, 260: ". . . Allāh said, 'Do you then believe?' Moses said, 'Yes! But to satisfy my own understanding . . .'"
2 Q39, 71: "'. . . of the meeting of this day of yours?' The answer will be, 'True! But the Decree of Punishment has been proved true . . .'"
3 Q43, 80: ". . . their secrets and their private councils? Indeed We do, and our messengers . . ."
4 Q57, 14: "'. . . were we not with you?' The others will reply, 'True! But . . .'"
5 Q67, 8–9: "'. . . Did no warner come to you?' (Q67, 9) They will say, 'Yes, indeed, a warner did come to us . . .'"

III Where it is preferable to allow pause, and these comprise the remaining ten cases.

* * *

The word *naʿam* (yes) occurs in the Qurʾān four times.

1 At Q7, 44: ". . . Have you also heard your Lord's promises are true? They shall say, 'Yes, but a crier shall proclaim . . .'". It is preferable to pause here because what follows it is not syntactically connected to what precedes it, because it is not said by the inhabitants of the fire.
2 Q26, 41–42: "'. . . if we win?' (Q26, 42:) He said, 'Yea, and more for in that case you shall be raised to posts nearest to my person'"
3 Q37, 17–18: "And also our fathers of old? (Q37, 18:) Say, 'Yea, and you shall then be humiliated . . .'"
4 Q7, 114. He said: "Yea (and more). For you shall be raised to posts nearest to my person"

It is preferable not to pause on these words, because of the syntactic connection between what precedes them and what follows them.

A constraint: In his *al-Nashr*, Ibn al-Jazarī said that wherever pause is permissible, it is permissible to begin reciting after it.

Section

Concerning the quality of the pause at the end of speech

There are various aspects to pause in the speech of the Arabs. What are utilized by the Imāms of recitation are nine: (1) *al-sukūn* (phonetic zero); (2) *al-rawm* (slurring of a final vowel); (3) *al-ishmam* (colouring toward the *u* sound); (4) *al-ibdāl*; (5) *al-naql*; (6) *al-idghām* (assimilation); (7) *al-hadhf* (suppression); (8) *al-ithbāt*; and (9) *al-ilḥāq*.

1 Phonetic zero: this is the basis of pause on words with vowels as a connection, because the function of the pause is stopping and interrupting; and because it is the opposite of beginning, for just as one does not begin with a phonetic zero one does not pause on a vowel. This is the preference of many of the recites.

2 Slurring of a final vowel: some of the reciters consider this a partial pronunciation of a vowel, and some say it is a major weakening of the voice to the point that most of it is not pronounced. Ibn al-Jazarī said that it amounts to the same thing. This is restricted to the final *u* of the imperfect indicative, the final phonetic zero of the imperfect jussive, the final *u* of a noun in the nominative cases, and the final *i* of a noun in the genitive case, as opposed to the final *a* of a noun in the accusative case, because this *a* is weak. If part of it is pronounced, so is its entirety: it is not divisible.

3 Colouring toward the *u* sound: it is an expression denying the indication of an unpronounced vowel. Another opinion has it that one pronounces it with one's lips in the position of pronouncing *u*. Both opinions are the same.

It pertains only to the *u*, whether it is the final vowel of the nominative desinential inflection, or if it is an inherent part of the word as in, e.g. *min hayth*^{u} (from where, because) if it is compulsory. As for the parenthetical phrase and the *mim* marking the plural among those who add a *u* to it, and the feminine ending *-ah*, there is neither slurring of the vowel nor colouring towards the *u* sound.

Ibn al-Jawzī restricted the feminine *-ah* ending to those places where an *h* must be paused upon, contrary to the pause on the written ending *-at*.

Pausing with slurring or colouring was handed down as authoritative by Abū ʿAmr and the Kūfan grammarians; the others related nothing on this topic. The actual reciters followed this practice willingly. Its advantage lies in the clarity of the vowel expressed with the consonant it belongs to in the pause to demonstrate to the listener or observer how this vowel is paused upon.

4 The *ibdāl* (substitution): one pauses with it on an indefinite noun in the accusative case ending in *-an*. One pauses on it by pronouncing *-a* instead of *-an*. Likewise in the word *idhan* (then). In the singular feminine noun ending in *-at* in pause one reads *-ah* instead. In a word ending in a final *hamza* (glottal stop) following a vowel or an *alif*, Ḥamza requires substituting a *madda* (sign of extension) of the type that precedes it. If it be an *alif*, one may suppress it, as in (Q96, 1:) *igra* (for *iqraʾ* "recite!"); (Q15, 49) *nabbi* (for *nabbiʾ* "inform!"); (Q30, 11) *lyabdal* (for *yabdaʾu*, "begins"); (Q4, 176) *in*^{i} *mri* (for *in*^{i} *miriʾ*, "if a man"); (Q.28, 30) *min shati* (for *min shati*, "from the shore of"); (Q81, 29) *an yasha* (for *an yashaʾa*, "if he wills"); (Q2, 22) *mina al-sama* (for *min al-sama*^{i}, "from the heavens"); (Q24, 45) *min ma* (for *min ma*^{in}, "from water").

5 *Al-naql* (transferring): this occurs in words ending with a phonetic zero followed by a *hamza* (glottal stop). According to Ḥamza, one pauses after one moves the final vowel to the penultimate position where it is pronounced and then suppressed whether or not it is a genuine phonetic zero, as in (q16, 5) *difu* (for *difʾ*, "warmth"); (Q3, 91) *mil* (for *mil'*^{u}, "the fullness of"); (Q78, 40) *yanẓuru al-maru* (for *yanẓuru al-mar'*^{u}, "man will see"); (Q15, 44:) *l-kulli bāb*^{in} *mim-hum juzu* (for *li-kull*^{i} *bāb*^{in} *mim-hum juz'*^{un}, "for each of those is a especial class of sinners"); (Q8, 24) *bayna al-mari wa-qalbi-hi* (for *bayna al-mar'*^{i} *wa-qalbi-hi*, "between a man and his heart"); (Q2, 102) *bayna al-mari wa-zawji-hi* (for *bayna al-mar'*^{i} *wa-zawji-hi*, "between man and wife"); (Q27, 25) *yukhriju al-khaba* (for *yukhriju al-khab'*^{a}, "who brings light"). There is no eighth example of this, but if a *yāʾ* or a *wāw* is an inherent part of the root, whether it be after a lengthening as at (Q40, 58) *al-musi* (for *al-musi*, "those who do evil"); (Q39, 69) *wa-ji* (for *wa-jiʾa*, "will be brought forward"); (Q24, 35) *yuḍī* (for *yuḍiʾu*, "luminous"); (Q5, 29) *an tabu'a* "draw on yourself"); (Q28, 76:) *la-tanu* (for *la-tanuʾu*, "would have been a burden"); (Q3, 30) *wa-maʿamilat min su* (for *wa-maʾamilat min suʾ*, "all the evil it has done"); or if the *yāʾ* or the *wāw* has a phonetic zero and is thus "soft" as at (Q passim:) *shay*, "something"; (Q21, 77:) *qawm*^{a} *saw'*^{in} (for *qawm*^{a}, "a people given to evil"); and (Q16, 77) *mithl*^{u} *al-saw* (for *mithl*^{u} *al-saw'*^{i}, "the similitude of evil").

6 *Al-idghām* (assimilation): in a word ending with a glottal stop after an added *yāʾ* or *waw*, Ḥamza holds that one pauses on it with assimilation after substituting for the glottal stop with the sound preceding it as at (Q9, 37) *al-nasi* (for *al-nasi*^{u}, "transposing"); (Q9, 3) *bari* (for *bari*^{un}, "dissolve treaty obligations"); and (Q2, 228) *quru* (for *quru'*^{in}, "monthly periods").

7 *Al-ḥadf* (suppression): those who pronounce affixed *yaʾs* when not in pause suppress them in pause. Affixed *yaʾs* are written one hundred and twenty-one times of which thirty-five appear in the midst of the verses, and the rest at the end of the verse.

According to Nāfiʿ, Abū ʿAmr, Ḥamza, Kisāʾi, and Abū Jaʿfar one must pronounce these *yaʾs* when not in pause, but suppress them when in pause. Ibn Kathīr and Yaʿqūb say they must be pronounced in either case. Ibn Āmir, Asim and Khalaf say they must be suppressed in either case. It is possible that some of them make exceptions for certain cases.

8 *Al-ithbāt* (pouncing): when not in pause this is to be done when an *-i* or *-in* sound is written as shortened to *-i* as in *had*^{i} (for *hadi*, "guide"); *wal*^{i} (for *wal*^{in}, "protector"); *waq*^{i} (for *waq*^{in}, "guarding") and *baq*^{i} (for *baq*^{in}, "remainder").

9 *Al-ilḥāq* (affixation): this is the usage of those who affix a final *haʾ* to particles in pause, e.g. *ʿam-mah* (for *ʿam-ma*, "concerning what?"); *fi-mah* (for *fi-ma*, "in what?"); *b-imah* (for *bi-ma*, "in what?"); *li-mah* (for *li-ma*, "why?"); and *mim-mah* (for *mim-ma*, "from what?"). They also do this on a final geminated *nūn* as in *hunnah* (for *hunna*, "they [female plural]"); and *mithla-hunnah* (for *mithla-hunna*, "like them").

With a *nūn* followed by a short *a*, as in *al-ʿalaminah* (for *al-ʿalamina*, "the worlds"); *al-ladhinah* (for *al-ladhina*, "those who"); and *al-muflihunah* (for *al-muflihuna*, "the successful ones"). With words with inherently geminated consonants, e.g. (Q27, 31) *al-la taʿlu ʿala-yyah* (for *al-la taʿlu ʿala-yya*, "be not arrogant against me"); (Q38, 75) *Khalaq-tu bi-yada-yyah* (for *khalaq-tu bi-yada-yya*, "I created with my hands"); (Q14, 22) *bi-musrikhi-yyah* (for *bi-musrikhi-yya*, "to my cries") and (Q27, 10) *lada-yyah* (for *lada-yya*, "in My presence").

General rule: The consensus is that it is necessary to follow the written script of the ʿUthmānic codex by pausing using substitution, expression, suppression, and connection, but the early authorities handed down differing opinions in certain cases, e.g. ending a word with *-ah* for *-at*, affixing a *haʾ* to what preceded it, pronouncing a *yāʾ* where it is not written, and the *wāw* at (Q17, 11) *wa-yadʿu al-insan*^{u} (for *wa-yadʿu al-insan*^{u}, "a man prays"); (Q54, 6) *wa-yawm*^{a} *yadʿu al-daʿi* (for *yawm*^{a} *yadʿu al-daʿi*, "the day that the caller will call"); (Q96, 18) *sa-nadʿu al-zabaniyata* (for *sa-nadʿu al-zabaniyata*, "we will call on the agents of punishment"); and (Q42, 24) *wa-yamhu Allāh al-batil*^{a} (for *wa-yamhu Allāh al-batil*^{a}, "and Allāh blots out vanity").

Likewise a final short *a* is lengthened at (Q24, 31) *ayyu-hā almuʾminuna* (for *ayyu-hā almuʾminuna*, "O you believers!") and (Q43, 49) *ayyu-hā al-sāḥir*^{u} (for *ayyu-hā al-sāḥir*^{u}, "O you sorcerer!); and (Q55, 31) *ayyuhā al-thaqalani* (for *ayyuhā al-thaqalani*, "O both you worlds!").

The *nūn* in *wa-ka-ayyin* ("will never") wherever it occurs. Abū ʿAmr pauses on it and pronounces it *-iy*, but does not pause at (Q17, 110) *ayya-ma* ("by whatever"), nor at (Q4, 76; 18; 49; 25; 7; 70; 36) *fa-mal*^{i} ("what is wrong with?"); and at (Q38, 82) *way-ka-anna . . . way-ka-anna- hu* ("It is indeed Allāh who enlarges the provision or restricts it, to any of His servants He pleases! Had it not been that Allāh was gracious to us, He could have caused the earth to swallow us up! Ah! Ah! (Those who reject Allāh will assuredly never prosper!)" Nor does he pause at (Q27, 25) *al-la tasjudu* ("that they should not worship").

Some of the reciters follow the written text to the letter.

Chapter twenty-nine

VERBAL ASSIMILATION BUT SEPARATE MEANING

This is an important branch of study which deserves to be presented in a structured manner; it is an important principle of pause, and thus I (Suyūṭī) have placed it after my discussion of pause.

By means of it one can solve many difficulties and uncover many obscurities, e.g. at Q7, 189–190: "It is he who created you from a single person and made you his mate of like nature . . .; (Q7, 190) . . . they ascribe to others a share in the gift they have received: but Allāh is exalted high above the partners they ascribe to Him." The context requires that this story deals with Ādam and Eve (this is made clear by a tradition with a good *isnād* brought forth by Aḥmad and al-Tirmidhī; al-Ḥākim brought it forth accompanied by a sound *isnād* by way of al-Haṣan on the authority of al-Samūra, the latter who heard it from the Prophet; Ibn Abī Ḥātim and others also mentioned the same Tradition with a sound *isnād*, on the authority of Ibn ʿAbbās). But there is a problem at the end of the verse: when polytheism is ascribed to Ādam and Eve because Ādam was a prophet to whom God spoke directly, and prophets are immune to polytheism at all times before and after they receive prophecy. Thus some authorities were wont to ascribe this verse to someone other than Ādam and Eve, to a certain man and his wife who belonged to one of the other nations, but this led to the weakening of the above-mentioned tradition, and condemned it to be false. But I (Suyūṭī), being in doubt) suspended judgement on this till I came to know Ibn Abī Ḥātim's saying: "Aḥmad Ibn ʿUthmān Ibn Ḥākim related to us, on the authority of Aḥmad Ibn al-Mufaḍḍal, on the authority of Asbāṭ, on the authority of al-Suddi, who said (concerning Q7, 190): 'But Allāh is high above the partners they ascribe to Him' that 'this fragment of a verse is a separation from the verse about Ādam and it concerns the gods of the pre-Islamic Arabs'."

ʿAbd al-Razzāq said: "Ibn ʿUyayna reported to us that he heard from Sadaqa Ibn ʿAbd Allāh Ibn Kathīr al-Makkī, who related on the authority of al-Suddi, who said that this is an example of a separated syndesis.

Ibn Abī Ḥātim said: "ʿAlī Ibn al-Ḥusayn reported to us, on the authority of Muḥammad Ibn Abī Ḥammād, on the authority of Mihrān, on the authority of Sufyān, on the authority of al-Suddi, that Abū Mālik said that this verse fragment is separated in order to obey God's command to procreate; 'But Allāh is exalted high above the partners they ascribe to Him' is directed only at Muḥammad's people."

Thus I felt relieved of this problem, and removed from this difficulty: this explanation made clear that the end of Ādam and Eve's story is at Q7, 190:

". . . in the gift they have received . . ." and not at the following words "But Allāh is exalted high . . .". The words that follow this are shifted to the pre-Islamic Arabs and their worship of idols; this is clarified in the change from the dual ending (of *jaʿala* "the two of them ascribe . . .") to that of the plural (of *yushrikuna*, "They (plural) ascribe partners"). Had the verse fragments been connected semantically, the verse would have ended with *yushrikan*ⁱ ("the two of them ascribe . . ."), as at Q7, 189: ". . . they both pray to Allāh their Lord . . . (Q7, 190): . . . He gave both of them a goodly child, they both ascribe to others a share in the gift they have received . . .". This applies also to the words following directly (Q7, 191): "Do they (plural) indeed ascribe to Him as partners things that can create nothing (but are themselves created?)" Excellence of separation and sound digression are two of the features of Qurʾānic style.

Of such excellence of separation is also verse 7, *sūrah* 3: "and no one knows its true interpretation except Allāh. And those who are firm in knowledge say". This verse in case of assimilation the assumption will be that: Those who are firm in knowledge know its true interpretation as well. In the case of separation it is otherwise. It is reported by Ibn Abī Hashim from Abū al-Sha'tha' and Abū Nahik that the two said "you do assimilate this verse but it is separated". Proof of this is that the verse degrades those who follow the unspecific and describe them as of deviated hearts.

So also is verse 101, *sūrah* 4 "and when you travel throughout the land, there is no blame upon you for shortening the prayer (more so) if you fear that those who disbelieve may disrupt (or attack) you . . .": it is obvious that shortening is conditioned on fear and that there is no shortening in absence of fear. A group of persons among them ʿAisha (the Prophet's widow) took that view. But the cause of revelation made clear that this verse is assimilated. Ibn Jābir reported a tradition related to ʿAlī (b. Abī Ṭālib) that he said: "A group of people from Banu al-Najjār asked the Prophet (peace and blessings be upon him) 'O Messenger of Allāh, we travel in the land, how do we pray?' Allāh revealed the verse: 'If you travel throughout the land there is no blame upon you for shortening the prayer.' The revelation stopped at that. One year after that the Prophet (peace and blessings be upon him) went on a campaign. He and his Companions performed the Afternoon Prayer. The disbelievers said: 'Muḥammad and his Companions have given you their backs. Should not you attack them!' One of the disbelievers said: 'They have a similar prayer close to this.' Allāh revealed in between the two prayers (*Zuhr* and *ʿAṣr*): 'If you fear that those who disbelieve may disrupt (or attack) you' to the end of *sūrah* 102, 'Indeed Allāh has prepared for the disbelievers a humiliating punishment.'" Prayer in case of fear was thus revealed. This Tradition shows that the revelation "if you fear" is a condition for what follows it, which is the prayer in case of fear; not the shortening of prayer. Ibn Jarīr said this interpretation is good but for the fact that there is an "if" in the verse.

Ibn al-Faras said that it would be correct in this case to consider the *waw* (and) as redundant.

I (Suyūṭī) say: that will be putting a condition on the condition. Better than this is to consider *idha* (if) redundant according to those who take it as such.

Ibn al-Jawzī in his book called *al-Tafsīr* said: the Arabs may come with a word near another one as if they are together while both give the meaning. In the Qurʾān verse 110, *sūrah* 7 says: ". . . who wants to expel you from land, the eminent among Pharaoh's people said. 'So what do you instruct?' said Pharaoh."

Similar to this are verses 51–52, *sūrah* 12: "It was I who sought to seduce him, and indeed, he is of the truthful" end of al-Aziz's wife speech. "That is so that he, 'Al-ʿAzīz', will know that I did not betray him in his absence," was Yūsuf's reply.

Also, verse 34, *sūrah* 27. "Indeed kings, when they enter a city, ruin it and render the eminent among its people humbled". End of Queen of Sheba's speech. "And thus they do," Allāh's statement.

Like this is also verse 52, *sūrah* 361 "who has raised us from our sleeping place?! End of the disbelievers' speech. "This is what the Most Merciful has promised," said the Angels. Ibn Abū Ḥātim related from Qatada about this verse that he said: "A verse in Allāh's book, in its first part (there is mention) of the people in error, while in its latter part, (there is mention) of the people of right guidance. They said 'O woe to us! Who raised us up from our sleeping place? This is the speech of the people in error. The people of right guidance, when they were raised up from their graves said: "This is what the Most Merciful has promised, and the messengers told the truth."'"

It is reported from Mujāhid about verse 109, *sūrah* 6: And what will make you perceive that even if it (that is, a sign) came, they would not believe. He said what would make you perceive that they would believe if the sign did come to go to the future with the information that "even if it come they will not believe".

Chapter thirty

ON *IMĀLA* (COLOURING OF THE *A* VOWEL TOWARD *E*), THE *A* VOWEL, AND SOUNDS IN BETWEEN

Many of the reciters treated this as a separate topic. Among them is Ibn al-Qāriḥ, who wrote a book on it entitled *Qurrat al-ʿAyn fī al-Fatḥ wal-Imāla bayna al-Lafẓayn* (Satisfaction concerning the vowel *a* and the *imāla* between words).

Al-Dānī said that the *imāla* and the vowel *a* were both acceptable pronunciations, which are frequent on the tongues of the most elegant Arabic speakers in whose language the Qurʾān was revealed. The *a* vowel is the favoured pronunciation of the people of the Hijaz, and the *imāla* is favoured by the common people of the tribes of Tamim, Asad and Qays of the Nejd. Al-Dani said that the principle is stated in one of the traditions of Hudhayfa, in which the Prophet (peace and blessings be upon him) says: "Recite the Qurʾān in the tribal dialects and pronunciations of the Bedouin Arabs; but beware of the pronunciations of the people of Sin and of the People of the Book." al-Dānī added that the *imāla* was doubtless one of the "seven *aḥruf*" and thus one of the "tribal dialects and pronunciations of the Bedouin Arabs".

Abū Bakr Ibn Abī Shayba reported, on the authority of Wakīʿ, on the authority of Aʿmash, on the authority of Ibrāhīm, who said that they used to consider an *alif* and a *yāʾ* as equals in recitation – that is, the *alif* and the *yāʾ* are equivalent to the *tafkhīm* ("emphatic", or velarized, recitation) and the *imāla*.

In the History of the Reciters it is reported, by way of Abū ʿAṣim al-Ḍarīr al-Kūfī, on the authority of Muḥammad Ibn ʿAbd Allāh, on the authority of ʿAsim, on the authority of Zirr Ibn Hubaysh, who said that someone recited in the presence of ʿAbd Allāh Ibn Masʿūd (Q20, 1): *Ta Ha* without an *i* vowel. The latter corrected him by reciting *Ti Hi* with an *i* vowel. The man repeated *Ta Ha* without an *i* vowel, and ʿAbd Allāh corrected him by reciting *Ti Hi* with an *i* vowel. The man repeated again *Ṭā Hā* without an *i* vowel, and ʿAbd Allāh corrected him again by reciting *Ti Hi* with an *i* vowel, and added that the Emissary of God (peace and blessings be upon him) had taught him to recite it this way. Ibn al-Jazarī said that this Tradition is strange, it comes to us uniquely in this form, and the authoritative tradents in its *isnād* are all trustworthy except Muḥammad Ibn ʿUbayd Allāh, also known as al-ʿAzramī, who is considered weak in *Ḥadīth* transmission; he was a good person, but his books perished, so he relied on his memory, and he was criticized for that.

I (Suyūṭī) say that Ibn Mardawahi reported this Tradition in his Commentary, adding to its end that Gabriel revealed it in this way.

It is reported in the Beauty of the Reciters, on the authority of Ṣafwān Ibn ʿAssal, that he heard the Emissary of God (peace and blessings be upon him) recite (Q19, 12): "O Yahya! . . ." as *ya yahye* rather than *ya yahya*. Ṣafwān asked him, "O Emissary of God! You have pronounced this with *imāla* and this is not the dialect of Quraysh." The Prophet (peace and blessings be upon him) answered: "It is the dialect of my uncles of the Banu Saʿd."

Ibn Ashta reported, on the authority of Ibn Abī Ḥātim, who said that the Kufans argued for *imāla* because they found in their codex *yaʾs* instead of *alifs*, so they followed the written text and recited with *imāla* to approximate the sound of the *yaʾs*.

I *Imāla* may be an *a* vowel coloured towards *e*, and often an *alif* coloured towards a *yaʾ*. The latter is the essential. It is called *al-idjaʿ* (adding an *a* sound to a consonant); *al-bath* (the name given to a *dad* to distinguish it from a *zaʾ* when both are pronounced alike, in the Arabic dialects and in Persian and Turkish); and *al-kasr* (adding a short *i* vowel); these latter three are infrequent, as they occur between words. It is also called *al-taqlīl* (possession of a quality to a degree between the two extremes, Greek: *metrion ti*), *al-talṭīf* (attenuation), and *bayna-bayna* (intermediate pronunciation). These are of two types, *shadida* (strong) and *mutawaṣṣiṭa* (medium), both of which are permitted in recitation. In the intense type complete metathesis is avoided as well as velarization and the medium type between the middle *a* vowel and the strong *imāla*.

Al-Dānī said that our teachers are of differing opinions as to which pronunciation is more proper and appropriate, but he prefers the medium *imāla* which is *bayna-bayna*, because the goal of the *imāla* is achieved by it, and it is the indication that the underlying principle of the *imāla* is the *alif* coloured towards the *yaʾ*, yet preventing it from becoming totally a *yāʾ* anywhere, or resembling an accompanying *i* vowel, or a *yaʾ*.

II Pronouncing the *a* vowel is accomplished by the reciter opening his mouth in pronouncing a word. Some authorities equate it with *tafkhīm* ("emphatic", or velarized, pronunciation), which can be strong or medium. The strong type is the person's final opening of his mouth on that word; it is not permitted in the Qurʾān, and it is extinct in the language of the pre-Islamic Arabs.

The medium is what falls between the strong pronunciation of *a* and the medium *imāla*. Al-Dānī said that this is what the partisans of the *a* among the reciters use.

There are differences of opinion as to whether the *imāla* is a branch of the *a* or whether it is an independent principle in itself.

The first view is that the *imāla* may not occur except for a specific reason, and if this reason be absent, it must be pronounced *a*. If the reason be present, either the *imāla* or the *a* is permissible. There is not a single word where the *imāla* is pronounced but that there is among the Arabs someone who would pronounce it with *a*. Thus the persistence of *a* indicates that if there is the *a* is the principle and the *imāla* as a franch of it.

The speech about the *imāla* revolves around five aspects: (1) its causes; (2) its types; (3) its advantages; (4) who it is that pronounces it with *imāla*; and (5) what is pronounced with *imāla*.

1 Its causes: the reciters mentioned ten. Ibn al-Jazarī said they concern two matters, the first is the *i* vowel, and the second is the *yaʾ*. Either of them may precede or follow a point of *imāla* in a word, or it may be suppressed at that point.

An *i* vowel or a *yāʾ* may not be present at such at such a point in a word, and suppression also may be absent, but it may be present in some surface manifestations of that word.

An *alif* or an *a* vowel may be pronounced with *imāla* due to another *alif* or *a* vowel which is pronounced with *imāla*; this is called "*imāla* caused by *imāla*". An *alif* may also be pronounced to emphasize another *alif* which is pronounced with *imāla*.

Ibn al-Jazarī said that one may also pronounce with *imāla* because of the frequency of its use, to separate a noun from a particle, and thus the number of reasons come to twelve.

Concerning the *imāla* which occurs because of a preceding *i* vowel, it is conditioned on that it is separated by one letter between it and an *alif*, as in the words *kitāb* and *ḥisāb*. This separation is possible only by pronouncing the *alif*.

As for the *a* which is pronounced with *imāla*, there is no separation between it and the *i* vowel, or between two letters the first of which has a phonetic zero, as in the word *insān* (meaning a person); or, if there are two *a* vowels, the second of which accompanies a *haʾ*, because of its softness.

Concerning the preceding *yaʾ*, it is either connected to the *alif* as in the words *hayah* and *al-ayama*, or it is separated by two letters, one of which is *haʾ*, e.g. *yadu-ha*.

As for the *i* vowel that follows, the same is true whether it is necessary, as in *ʿabid*, or accidental as in *min al-nas* and *fi al-nar*. As for following *yaʾ*, it is as in *muabayiʾ*. As for the suppressed *i* vowel it is as in *khafa*, where the underlying root is *khawifa*.

As for the suppressed *yaʾ*, as in *yakhshā*, *al-hudā*, *atā* and *tharā*, the *yaʾ* is methathesized into an *alif*, and the consonant preceding it is followed by an *a* vowel.

As for the accidental *i* vowel in some forms of words such as *taba*, *jaʾa*, *shʾa* and *zada*, it is because in the imperfect tense, nominative mood, the first letter of the root will be pronounced with *i* vowel.

As for the accidental *yaʾ*, as in *tala* and *ghaza*, the *alifs* represent an underlying *was*, and thus they are pronounced with *imāla* only in such internal passive forms as *tuliya* and *ghuziya*.

As for the *imāla* caused by an *imāla*, this is similar to al-Kisāī's pronouncing of the *alif* following the *nūn* at Q2, 156, *inna li-llah*, because of the pronunciation of the *alif* with *imāla* in *li-llah*. But he did not pronounce the following words, *wa-inna ilay-hi* with *imāla* because of the lack of the word *li-llah* after it. *Al-Kisaʿi* followed this practice with *al-duha*, *al-qura*, *duha-ha* and *tala-ha*.

As for the *imāla* because of similarity, this occurs on the feminine *alif* of *al-husna* and on the *alifs* of Mūsā and Isa because of their resemblance to the *alif* in *al-hudā*.

As for the *imāla* due to frequency of usage, it is like the *imāla* on *al-nās* in the three cases, according to what the author of al-Mubhij reported.

As for the *imāla* used to separate a noun from a particle, this occurs in the "separated letters" which begin some *sūrahs*; Sībawayhi said that the *imāla* on *bāʾ* and *tāʾ* are on letters of the alphabet, not on actual words which are pronounced, e.g. *mā* and *lā*, and other particles.

* * *

There are four reasons for the *imāla*, and they all correspond to the two already mentioned, affinity and assigning a watchword.

As for affinity, it is monolithic; it occurs both with what is pronounced near it, and for an *imāla* pronounced elsewhere. The reciters intended that the action of the tongue and the vicinity of the letter's point articulation with *imāla* be the reason for the *imāla*, and that it should be for one reason and have one form.

As for the assigning a watchword, there are three parts: inherent assignation, assignation on account of the accidental form of a word because of its syntactic function, and assignation because of similarity to something assigned inherently.

* * *

Its advantage lies in the simplicity of its pronunciation because the tongue is elevated in pronouncing the *a* vowel, and lowered when pronouncing with *imāla*. Lowering the tongue is easier than elevating it, for this one pronounces with *imāla* when one should, and one pronounces the *a* vowel when one considers it to be stronger or an inherent part of the root.

* * *

Of the ten principal reciters, all used *imāla* except Ibn Kathīr, who did not use it even once in the entire Qurʾān.

* * *

As to where and to what extent one employs *imāla*, there are the books on variant readings and books on the *imāla*.

We mention here what of necessity must be noted: Ḥamza, al-Kisaʿi and Khalaf used *imāla* on every *alif* formed by metathesis from *yāʾ*, wherever it appears in the Qurʾān, whether in a noun or in a verb, e.g. *al-hudā*, *al-hawā*, *al-fatā*, *al-ʾmā*, *al-zinā*, *atā*, *abā*, *sāʿā*, *yakhshā*, *yarḍā*, *ijtabā*, *ishtarā*, *mathwā*, *maʾwā*, *adnā* and *azkā*.

And in addition, very feminine *alif* on words with the morphological patterns *fuʿlā*, *fiʿlā* and *faʿlā*, e.g., *ṭūbā*, *bushrā*, *quṣwā*, *qurbā*, *unthā*, *dunyā*, *iḥdā*, *dhikrā*, *siyamā*, *dīzā*, *mawtā*, *marḍā*, *salwā* and *taqwā*. Some authorities added to these Mūsā, ʿIsā and Yaḥyā.

And all words on the morphological patterns *fuʿalā* and *faʿalā*, e.g. *sukārā*, *kusālā*, *usārā*, *yatāmā*, *naṣārā* and *ayāmā*.

Every word in the codices which is written with a final *yaʾ*, e.g. *balā*, *matā*, *yā asafā*, *yā waylatā* and *yā hasratā* and the interrogative *annā*. Excepted from these are *ḥattā*, *ilā*, *ʿalā*, *ladā* and *mā zakā*, never read with *imāla*.

Likewise they would read words whose roots ended with *wāw* with *imāla*, whether the preceding vowel was either *i* or *u*, e.g., *al-ribā* and *al-ḍuḥā* (however they were written) and also *al-quwa* and *al-ʿula*.

They also pronounced with *imāla* the ends of verses *ayas* in *sūrahs* that followed a pattern and these are: *Ṭā Hā* (20), *Al-Najm* (53), *Saʾala* (= *al-Maʿārij*, 70), *al-Qiyāma* (75), *al-Nāziʿāt* (79), *ʿAbasa* (80), *al-Aʿla* (87), *al-Shams* (91), *al-Layl* (92), *al-Ḍuḥā* (93), and *al-'Alaq* (96). Abū ʿAmr and Warsh agreed on these.

Abū ʿAmr would pronounce with *imāla* every word containing a *raʾ* followed by an *alif*, e.g. *dhikrā*, *bushrā*, *asrā*, *arā-hu*, *ishtarā*, *yarā*, *qurā*, *al-naṣārā*, *asārā* and *sukārā*. He did likewise on the *alifs* in words on the morphological pattern *fuʾla* as they occurred.

Abū ʿAmr and al-Kisaʿi would pronounce with *imāla* every *alif* followed by a final *raʾ* and then the *i* vowel of the genitive case, e.g. *al-dārī*, *al-nārī*, *al-qahhāri*, *al-ghaffāri*, *al-nahāri*, *al-diyāri*, *al-kuffāri*, *al-abkāri*, *bi-qinṭāri*, *abṣāri-him*, *awbāri-ha*, *ashʿāri-ha ḥimāri-ka*, whether or not the *alif* was an integral part of the root.

Ḥamza would pronounce with *imāla* ten verbs with a medial *alif* in their various past tenses from: *zāda*, *shāʾa*, *jāʾa*, *khāba*, *rāna*, *khāfa*, *zāgha*, *ṭāba*, *ḍāqa* and *ḥāqa* wherever and however they occurred.

Al-Kisāʿi would pronounce with *imāla* the feminine *haʾ* and what precedes it with an absolute pause after letters, whose mnemonic is *fa-ja'that Zaynab li-dhawd shams* (Zaynab urged on Sham's female camels). The *faʾ* as in *khalīfa* and *raʾfa*; the *jīm* as in *walīja* and *lujja*; the *thāʾ* as in *thalātha* and *khabītha*; the *taʾ* as in *bughta* and *mayta*; the *zāy* as in *bārīza* and *a'azza*; the *yāʾ* as in *khashya* and *shayba*; the *nūn* as in *sunna* and *janna*; the *baʾ* as in *habba* and *tawba*; the *iam* as in *layla* and *lujja*; the *dhal* as in *lidhdha* and *mawqudha*; the *wāw* as in *quswa* and *al-marwa*; the *dāl* as in *balda* and *ʿidda*; the *shin* as in *fāḥisha* and *ʿisha*; the *mīm* as in *raḥma* and *niʿma*; and the *sin* as in *al-khamisa* and *khamsa*.

Al-Kisāʾī would pronounce with a clear *a* vowel after the ten "elevated" consonants: *jim*, *ʿayn*, *qaf*, *zaʾ*, *khaʾ*, *sad*, *taʾ*, *dad*, *ghayn* and *tʾ*, He would pronounce four other letters, *alif*, *kaf*, *haʾ* and *raʾ*, when preceded by *yāʾ* with a phonetic zero, or before a connected *i* vowel, or before an *i* vowel separated by a phonetic zero, he would pronounce with *imāla*; otherwise, he would pronounce them with a clear *a* vowel.

There remain letters on which there is disagreement and division, but there is no need to list them. Expect to find them in specialist books.

As for the "separate letters" which introduce certain *sūrahs*, Ḥamza, al-Kisaʿi, Khalaf, Abū ʿAmr, Ibn Āmir and Abū Bakr pronounced "*Alīf Lām Rāʾ*" which precede five *sūrahs* with *imāla*; Warsh pronounced them with an intermediate pronunciation.

Abū ʿAmr, al-Kisāʾī and Abū Bakr pronounced the *haʾ* at the beginning of the *sūrahs Maryam* (19) and *Ṭa Ha* (20) with *imāla*; Ḥamza and Khalaf did so on the letters, but not on the former.

Those who pronounced "*Alīf Lām Rāʾ*" with *imāla* also pronounced the *yāʾ* at the beginning of *sūrah Maryam* with *imāla*; except Abū ʿAmr, who became well known for this.

The first three, as well as Abū Bakr, pronounced the introductory letters of *sūrah* 36 with *imāla*: *Yā sīn*.

These four pronounced the *taʾ* at the beginning of *sūrah* 20 with *imāla*; they did so also with "*Ṭāʾ Sīn Mīm*", "*Ṭā Sīn*" and the seven instances (*sūrahs* 40–46) of "*Ḥāʾ Mīm*"; Ibn Dhukwan agreed with them concerning the latter.

Conclusion

Because of the Tradition which says, "The Qurʾān was revealed in *tafkhim* ('emphatic', or velarized pronunciation)", some authorities disliked employing *imāla*. This was replied to (as follows).

1 Thus it was revealed, but later *imāla* was permitted.
2 This means that it is recited to men, and one does not lower the voice in reciting it as in women's speech.
3 This means that it was revealed with extreme severity against the polytheists, as the author of Jamal al-Qurrāʾ said: "This is far from the interpretation of the Tradition, because it was also revealed with mercy and gentleness."
4 This means that it was revealed with awe and veneration – that is, they called it awesome and venerated. By this they emphasized the Qurʾān's awe and veneration.
5 The meaning of *tafkhīm* of the pronunciation of the middle of words with a *u* vowel or an *i* vowel in various places instead of pronouncing a phonetic zero because it embellishes and fulfils the pronunciation.

Al-Dānī said that such was the interpretation according to Ibn ʿAbbās. Then he said: "Ibn Khāqān informed us, on the authority of Aḥmad Ibn Muḥammad, on the authority of ʿAlī Ibn ʿAbd al-ʿAzīz, on the authority of al-Qāsim, who said that he heard al-Kisaʾī say that he heard Salmān say, on the authority of al-Zuhrī, who said, on the authority of Ibn ʿAbbās, who said: 'The Qurʾān was revealed with *tathqīl* (increment) and *tafkhīm*, as God says Jumuʿa [for jumʿa] and the like with this increment.' Then we received al-Hakim's Tradition, on the authority of Zayd Ibn Thābit, who heard from the Prophet (peace and blessings be upon him): 'The Qurʾān was revealed with *tafkhim*.'"

Muḥammad Ibn Muqātil, one of the reciters, said: "I heard ʿAmmar recite Q77, 6: 'Whether of justification or of warning . . ." (. . . *ʿudhran aw nudhran as ʿudhuran aw nudhuran*); and Q18, 96: '. . . the two steep mountainsides . . .' (. . . *al-ṣadfayni as al-ṣadafayni*)" – that is, with an added vowel in the middle of the word.

This is supported by Abū ʿUbayda, who said that the people of the Hijaz pronounce everything with *tafkhīm*, except for one word, "ten" *ʿashra* (for *ʿashara*), in which they pronounce the second consonant with a phonetic zero; the people of the Najd eschew *tafkhīm* in their speech, except for the same word, which they pronounce "*ʿashira*", with an *i* vowel after the second consonant.

Al-Dānī said that this latter interpretation of the Tradition is preferable.

Chapter thirty-one

ASSIMILATION AND CONSERVING; SUPPRESSION AND METATHESIS

A large number of the reciters have dedicated books to this topic.

I *Idghām* (assimilation) is pronouncing two consonants as the second consonant, doubled. This may be the major or the minor type.

a The major type: when the first of the two consonants is followed by a vowel, whether the two consonants are identical, similar or proximate. It is called major due to its frequency of occurrence, because a vowel more frequent than a phonetic zero. Another opinion is that it is called major because of its effect of nullifying the vowel before assimilating its consonant. A third opinion; on account of the difficulty in performing it. The fourth opinion: because it includes the identical, similar, and proximate consonants.

Of the ten Reciters, the one most famous in this matter is Abū ʿAmr Ibn al-ʿAlāʾ. Others concerned themselves with this topic, e.g. Ḥasan al-Basri, al-Aʿmash, Ibn Muhaysin and others.

Its cause is the desirability of facilitation in recitation.

Many of the authors of books concerning variant readings do not concern themselves with this topic at all, e.g. Abū ʿUbayd in his book (*al-Imām*), Ibn Mujāhid in his *al-Musabbaʿa*, al-Makkī in his *Tabṣira*, al-Ṭalamnakkī in his *al-Rawḍa*, Ibn Sufyān in his *al-Hādī*, Ibn Shurayh in his *al-Kāfī*, al-Mahdāwī in his *al-Hidāya*, and others.

The author of *Taqrīb al-Nashr* (Ibn al-Jazarī) said that by "paired sounds" we mean those sounds with the same points of articulation and the same executions. By "similar sounds" we mean those with the same points of articulation but different execution. By "proximate sounds" we mean those sounds with a proximate point of articulation or proximate means of execution.

As for the "paired sounds" which undergo assimilation, they total seventeen: the *baʾ*, *taʾ*, *thaʾ*, *haʾ*, *raʾ*, *sin*, *ayn*, *ghayn*, *faʾ*, *qaf*, *kaf*, *lam*, *mim*, *nun*, *waw*, *laʾ* and *yaʾ*, e.g. Q4, 105: reading for *al-kitaba bil-ḥaqqi*, *al-kitabbil-ḥaqqi*; Q5, 106: for *al-mawti taḥbisūna-ha*, *al-mawttaḥbisūna-ha*; Q2, 191: *haythu thaqiftumū-hum*, *hayththaqiftumū-hum*; Q2, 235: *al-nikāḥi ḥattā*, *al-nikāḥḥatta*; Q2, 185: for *shahru ramaḍāna*, *sharramaḍāna*; Q22, 2: *al-nāsu sukārā*, *al-nāssukārā*; for Q2, 225: for *yashfaʿu ʿinda-hu*, *yashfaʿ ʿinda-hu*; Q3, 85: *yabtaghī ghayra al-islāmi*, *yabtaghghyri al-islāmi*; Q2, 213: *fa-khtulifa fī-hi*, *fa-khtuliffi-hi*; Q7, 143: *afāqa qāla*, *afāqqāla*; Q12, 29: *inna-ki kunti*, *inna-kkunt*; Q27, 37: *lā qibala la-hum*, *lā-qiballa-hum*; Q1,

3–4: *al-raḥīm māliki, al-raḥimmāliki*; Q2, 3: *wa-naḥnu nuṣabbihu, wa-naḥnnusabbihu*; Q16, 63: *fa-huwa waliyyu-hum, fa-huwwaliyyu-hum*; Q2, 2: *fi-hi hudan, fi-hhudan*; and Q2, 254: *yaʾtiy yawmun, yaʾtiyyawmun.*

This is conditioned on that the two sounds are not separated in the written text, e.g. Q29, 50: *ana nadhirun*, because the two words are separated by an *alif* in the text; they must also appear as *sandhi* phenomena – that is, across words; if the sequence occurs within one word, assimilation will not occur, unless they are identical consonants, e.g. Q2, 200: *manāsika-kum* pronounced *manasikkum*; Q74, 42: and *mā salaka-kum*, as *mā salakku*. This does not occur, however, if the first letter is a *taʾ* referring to the first or second person singular, e.g. Q78, 40: *kuntu turaban*; and Q10, 42: *a-fa-anta tusmiʿu*. It also will not occur if the first consonant is geminated, e.g. Q54, 48: *massa saqara*; and Q15, 39: *rabbi bi-ma*. Neither will it occur if the first consonant is nunated, e.g. *ghafurun rahim* or *samiʿun ʿalīm.*

There are sixteen letters which comprise the "similar sounds" and "proximate sounds", and their mnemonic is *ruḍ sa-nashuddu ḥujjata-ka bi-dhullin fa-nam* ("live abstemiously, and we will strengthen your plea with subservience, so sleep (well)"). This assimilation is conditioned on that the first consonant is not geminated, e.g. Q2, 200: *ashaddu dhikran*; nor nunated, e.g. Q39, 6: *fi ẓulumāt thalathin*; nor has the pronominal *taʾ*, as at Q17, 61: *khalaq-ta ṭīnan.*

The *bāʾ* is assimilated into the *mīm* only in the case of *yuʿadhdhibu man yashaʾu* ("He Punishes whom He wills").

The *tāʾ* is assimilated into ten letters: (1) the *thaʾ*, e.g. Q2, 92: *bil-bayyināt thumma*, pronounced as *bil-bayyināththumma*; (2) the *jīm*, as at Q14, 23: *al-ṣāliḥāti jannatin, al-ṣālihajjannatin*; (3) the *dhal*, Q11, 114: *al-sayyiʾati dhalika, al-sayyiʾadhdhālika*; (4) the *zay*, Q39, 73: *al-jannati zumaran, al-jannazzumaran*; (5) the *sin*, Q4, 57: *al-ṣāliḥāt sa-nudhkilu-hum, al-ṣāliḥāssa-nudhkhilu-kum*; but not at Q2, 247: *walam yuʾta saʾatan*, because the weak *a* vowel is apocopated; (6) the *shīn*, Q24, 4: *bi-arbaʾati shuhadāʾ, bi-arbaʾbi-rbaʾashuhadāʾ*; (7) the *sād*, Q78, 38: *wal-malāʾikatu ṣaffa, wal-malaʾikaṣṣaffa*; (8) the *ḍād*, Q100, 1: *wal-ʿādiyāt ḍadḥan, wal-ʿādiyaḍḍabhan*; (9) the *taʾ*, Q11, 114: *wa-aqim al-ṣalāta ṭarafayi al-nahāri, wa-aqim al-ṣalāṭṭarafayi al-nahari*; and (10) the *zaʾ*, Q4, 97: *al-malaikatu zalimi, al-malaikazzlimi.*

The *thaʾ* is assimilated into five letters: (1) the *taʾ*, Q15, 65: *haythu tuʾmaruna, hayttuʾmaruna*; (2) the *dhal*, Q3, 14: *wal-harthi dhālika, wal hardhahālika*; (3) the *sīn*, Q27, 16: *wa-waritha sulaymānu, wa-warissulaymānu*; (4) the *shīn*, Q2, 35: *haythu shiʾtuma, hayshshiʾ tuma*; (5) the *dad*, Q51, 24: *ḥadīthuḍayfi, ḍayfi, hadiḍḍayfi*. The *jim* is assimilated into two letters: the *shin*, Q48, 29: *akhraja shaṭʾa-hu*, pronounced as *akhrashshaṭʾa-hu*, and *tāʾ*; Q70, 3: *dhī al-maʿāriji taruju, dhi al-maritta'ruju*. The *haʾ* is assimilated into the *ayn* only at Q3, 185: *zuḥziḥa ani al-nāri, zuḥzi ani al-nār*. The *dāl* is assimilated into ten letters: (1) the *tāʾ*, Q2, 187: *al-masajidi tika, almasajatika*; (2) the *thaʾ*, Q4, 134: *yurīdu thawāba, yurīththaw āba*; (3) the *jīm*, Q2, 251: *dāwūdu jālūta, dāwūjjālūta*; (4) the *dhāl*, Q5, 97: *wal-qalāʾida dhālika*, *wal-qalā'idhdhālika*; (5) the *zay*, Q24, 35: *yakādu zaytu-ha*, *yakāzzaytu-ha*; (6) the *sīn*, Q14, 49–50: *al-aṣfādi sarābīlu-hum*, *al-aṣfāssarābīlu-um*; (7) the *shīn*, Q12, 26: *wa-shadida shāhidun*, *wa-shahishshāhidun*; (8) the *ṣad*, Q12, 72: *nafqidu ṣuwāʿ*, *nafqissuwāʿ*; (9) the *ḍād*, Q1, 21: *min baʿdi ḍarrā'a*, *min baʿḍḍarrā'*; and (10) the *ẓā'*, Q40, 31: *yurīdu ẓulman*, *yurī dẓulam*.

A letter followed by a short *a* vowel, and which follows a letter with a phonetic zero is not assimilated unless it is *ta'*, because of the strength of the similarity with the follwing sound.

The *dhāl* is assimilated into the sīn, Q18, 61: *fa-ttakhadha sabīla-hu*, *fa-ttakkkhassabīla-hu*.

The *ṣād* is assimilated into the *dhas*, Q72, 3: *mā ittakhadha ṣaḥibatan*, *mā ittakhaṣṣāḥibatan*.

The *rā'* is assimilated into the *lām*, Q11, 78: *hunna atharu la-kum*, *hunna athalla-kum*; Q2, 285: *al-maṣīru layukallifu*, *al-maṣīlla yukallifu*; Q3, 190: *wal-nahāri la-ayatin*, *wa-nahalla-aytin*. If the *rā'* is followed by a short *a* vowel, and follows a letter followed by a phonetic zero, it does not assimilate, Q27, 8: *wa-ḥamīra li-tarkab ū-hā*.

The *sīn* is assimilated into the *zay*, Q81, 7: *wa-idhā al-nufūsu zuwwijat*, *wa-idhā al-nufsuzzuwwijat*; and into the *shin*, Q19, 4: *al-ra'su shayban*, *al-raʿshshayban*.

And the *shīn* is assimilated into the *sīn*, only at Q17, 42: *dhī al-ʿarshi sabīlan*, *dhī al-ʿarssabīlan*.

The *ḍāḍ* into the *sīn* only at Q24, 62: *li-baʿdi sha'ni-him*, *li-baʿshsha'ni-him*.

The *qāf* is assimilated into the *kāf* when the former is followed by a vowel, e.g. Q5, 64: *yunfique kayfa yashā'u*, *yunfikkayfa yashā'u*; likewise, if both letters are followed by a mim at morpheme boundaries within a word, e.g. Q2, 21: *khalaqa-kum*, *khalakhum*.

The *kāf* is assimilated into the *qāf* when the former has a vowel following it, e.g. Q2, 30: *wa-nuqaddisu la-ka qāla*, *wa-nuqaddisu la-qqāla*; but not if it is followed by a phonetic zero, Q62, 11: *wa-tarakūq-ka qā'iman*.

The *lām* followed by a vowel is assimilated into the *rā'*, e.g. Q11, 81: *rusulu rabbi-ka*, *rusurrabbi-ka*; or when the letter preceding it is followed by a phonetic zero, and it itself is followed by a short *u* vowel, Q81, 19: *la-qawolu rasūlin*, *la-qaworrasūlin*; or a short *i* vowel, Q27, 125: *ilā sabīli rabbi-ka*, *ilā sabīrrabbi-ka*; but not if it is preceded by a short *a* vowel, Q63, 10: *fa-yaqūlu rabbi*, except for the last syllable of the word *qala* wherever it occurs, e.g. Q3, 38: *qāla rabbi*, *qarrabbi*, Q5, 23: *qāla rajulani*, *qārrajulani*, etc.

The *mīm*, when preceded by a consonant with a vowel, will drop its short vowel at a word boundary before a *ba'*, but if the preceding consonant is pronounced with a vowel after it, the vowel following the *mim* will be softened by nasalization, e.g. Q6, 53: *bi-aʿlama bil-shākirīna*, Q2, 113: *yaḥkumu bayna-hum* and Q4, 156: *maryama buhtānan*. This one method of softening is mentioned in the *Tarjama*. Ibn al-Jazarī mentioned in his *Anwāʿ al-idghām* that some of the ancient authorities accepted this as true; but the author of the *al-Nahr* (Ibn al-Jazarī) said that this is wrong. But if the letter preceding it is followed by a phonetic zero, then it is pronounced, e.g. at Q2, 132: *Ibrāhīm banī-hi*.

The *nūn*, when preceded by a letter followed by a vowel, is assimilated if the *rā'* or the *lām* following it, Q7, 168: *ta'adhdhana rabbu-ka*, *ta'adhdharrabbu-ka*; Q2, 55: *lan nu'mina la-ka*, *lan nu'milla-ka*; but if the preceding letter is followed by a phonetic zero, it is pronounced, Q27, 50: *yakhāfūona rabba-kum*; Q2, 266: *an takūna la-hu*; except for the *nūn* in the word *naḥunu*, which is assimilated, Q2, 138: *wa-naḥun la-hum*, *wa-naḥlla-hum*; Q11, 53: *wa-ma naḥnu la-ka*, *wa-ma naḥlla-ka*. This is because of the frequency of its occurrence and the repetition of the *nūn* in it, and the necessity of providing it with an anaptyctic (helping) vowel, and its phonetic weight.

Two caveats

1 Abū ʿAmr, Ḥamza and Ya'qūb agree about certain assimilated letters. This was made into a general rule by Ibn al-Jazarī in his books *al-Nashr* and *al-Taqrīb*.

2 The Ten Reciters are agreed that there is assimilation of the *mim* and the *nūn* in the fourth word at Q12, 11: *ma la-ka la ta'mannā ʿalā yūsufa*, but they differed on its exact execution. Abū Jaʿfar recited it with complete assimilation, and the others added a sign for slurring and *ishmām* (*umlaut*).

Rule

Ibn al-Jazarī said that every identical or proximate letter Abū ʿAmr would assimilate at the boundaries of the *sūrahs* would amount to one thousand, three hundred and four, e.g. to connect the ending of *sūrah* 96 with the following *sūrah*. But if one separates them with the *basmalla*, and then recites *sūrah* 97 followed by the *basmalla*, then the total is one thousand, three hundred and five because of connecting the ending of *sūrah* 13 with the beginning of the following *sūrah*, and that one with one following it. If one separates the *sūrahs* with silence by not reciting the *basmalla*, the total is one thousand, three hundred and three.

b The "minor" assimilation: this occurs when the first letter is followed by a phonetic zero; it may be obligatory, prohibited or allowed. When one follows the practices of the reciters as written in the books of their differences, one may conclude that it is permissible because the reciters differed in two ways: (1) the assimilation of a letter into various letters in numerous words; these are limited to *idh*, *qad*, the feminine suffix *-t*, *hal* and *bal*. They differed on whether *idh* should be assimilated or not into six letters: the *ta'*, Q2, 166: *idh tabarra'a*; the *jīm*, Q48, 26: *idh jaʿala*; the *dāl*, Q18, 39: *idh dakhal-ta*; the *zāy*, Q33, 10: *idh zāghati*; the *sīn*, Q24, 12: *idh samiʿtunu-hu*; the *ṣād*, Q46, 29: *wa-idh ṣaraf-na*.

They differed on whether *qad* should be assimilated into eight letters: the *jīm*, Q2, 92: *wa-la-qad jaʾa-kum*; the *dhal*, Q7, 179: *wa-la-qad dharʾ-nā*; the *zāy*, Q67, 5: *wa-la-qad zayyan-na*; the *sīn*, Q5, 102: *qad saʾala-hum*; the *shīn*, Q12, 3: *qad shaghafa-hā*; the *ṣād*, Q17, 41: *wa-la-qad ṣarraf-na*; the *ḍād*, Q4, 167: *la-qad ḍallū*; and the *ẓaʾ*, Q2, 231: *fa-qad ẓalam*.

They differed on whether the feminine suffix *-t* should be assimilated or not with six letters: the *thaʾ*, at Q11, 95: *baʿidat thamūdu*; the *jim*, Q4, 56: *naḍijat julūd-hum*; the *zay*, Q17, 97: *khabat zidna-hum*; the *sīn*, Q2, 261: *anbatat sabʿa sanābila*; the *ṣād huddimat ṣawāmiʿu*, Q22, 40; and the *ẓaʾ*, Q21, 11: kānat ẓālimatan.

They differed on whether the *lam* or *hal* or *bal* should be assimilated or not into eight letters. *Bal* was associated with five: the *zāy*, Q13, 33: *bal zuyyin;* the *sin*, Q12, 18: *bal sawwalat*; the *ḍād*, Q46, 28: *bal ḍallu*; the *taʾ*, Q4, 155: *bal tabaʾa*; and the *ẓaʾ*, Q48, 12: *bal ẓanan-tum*.

Hal was associated with the *thāʾ*, Q83, 36: *hal thuwwiba*; and both the particles *hal* and *bal* share in cases of the *taʾ* and the *nūn*, e.g. Q5, 59: *hal tanqimūna*; Q21, 40: *bal taʾtī-him*; Q26, 203: *hal naḥnu*; and Q2, 170: *bal nattabiʾu*.

Assimilation of letters with proximate points of articulation

They disagreed on seventeen of these: (a) the *bāʾ* into the *fāʾ*, Q4, 74: *aw yaghlib fa-sawfa*; Q13, 5: *fa-in taʿjab fa-ʿajabʿ*, Q17, 63: *idhhab fa-man*; *fa-ahab fa-inna*; and Q49, 11: *wa-man lam yatub fa-ulāʾika*; (b) Q2, 284: *wa-yuʿadhdhibu man yashaʾ*; (c) Q11, 42: *irkab maʾa-nā* (d) Q34, 9: *nakhsif bi-him*; (e) *raʾ* followed by a phonetic zero into the *lam*, Q3, 31: *yaghfir la-kum*; and Q52, 48: *wa-ṣbir li-ḥukmi rabbi-ka*; (f) the *lam* followed by a phonetic zero into the *dhāl*, Q2, 231: *wa-man yafʿal dhālika* (and wherever else it occurs); (g) *thāʾ* into *dhāl*, Q7, 176: *yalhath dhālika*; (h) *the dāl* into the *thāʾ*, Q3, 145: *wa-man yurīd thawāba* (and wherever else it occurs); (i) *dhāl* into the *tāʾ*, Q2, 51: *ittakhadh-tum* (no matter the resulting pronunciation); (j) *dhāl* into *tāʾ*, Q20, 96: *fa-nabadhtu-ha*; (k) same as at Q44, 27 and Q42, 20: *udhtu*; (1) the *thʾ*, as at Q17, 52: *labith-tum*, and at Q2, 259: *labith-tu*, however they occur; the *thaʾ* at Q7, 43 and Q43, 72: *ūrithtumū- hāʾ*; (m) *dāl* into *dhal*, Q19, 1–2: *kāf hāʾ yāʾ ʿayn ṣād dhikru*; (n) *nūn* into *wāw*, Q36, 1: *yā sīn wal-qurʾān*; (o) *nūn* into *was* Q68, 1: *nūn wal-alam*; and (p) *nun* into *mim*, Q26, 1 and Q28, 1: *ṭā sīn mīm*.

Rule

The rule to be derived is that for any two adjacent letters which are identical or similar, and the first is followed by a phonetic zero, the first must be assimilated into the second, in speech as well as in recitation.

The identical; e.g. Q2, 60: *iḍrib bi-ʿaṣā-ka*; Q2, 16: *rabiḥat tijarātu-hum*; Q5, 61: *wa-qad dakhalū*; Q27, 28: *idhhab bi-kitābi*; Q4, 63: *wa-qul la-hum*; Q27, 89: *wa-hum mani*; Q2, 48: and *nafsin*; Q4, 78: *yudrik-kum*; and Q27, 76: *yuwajjih-hu*.

The similar: e.g. Q3, 72: *qalat ṭā'ifatun*; Q29, 38: *wa-qad tabayyana*; Q43, 39: *idh ẓalam-tum*; Q83, 14: *bal rāna*; and Q17, 24: *hal ra'ay-tum* and *wa-qul rabbī*.

The first of the two similar letters must not be followed by a long vowel for assimilation to occur: Q6, 96: *qālū wa-hum*; Q114, 5: *alladhī yuwaswisu*; nor may the first letter be a guttural as at Q43, 89: *fa-ṣfaḥ ʿan-hum*.

Note

The rule is that people disliked assimilation in the Qur'ān. Ḥamza said that he disliked it in prayer, and he provided us with three principles.

Addition

To the two former sections another is added, about which some differed, e.g. the *nūn* followed by a phonetic zero and nunation. For these two we have four rules: *iẓhār* (expression); *idghām* (assimilation); *iqlāb* (metathesis); and *ikhfā'* (lightening).

1 *Iẓhār*: all of the reciters employed this with the six guttural letters: the *hamza*, *hā'*, *thā'*, *ʿayn*, *hā'*, *ghayn* and *khā'*, e.g. at Q6, 26: *wa-yan'awna*; Q2, 62: *man āmana*; Q9, 109: *fa-nhāra*; Q13, 33: *min hadin*; Q9, 109: *jurufin hārin*; Q1, 7: *anʿamta*; Q10, 61: *min ʿamalin*; Q2, 7: *ʿadhabun ʿaẓīmun*; Q108, 2: *wa-nḥar*; Q41, 42: *ḥakīmin ḥamīd*; Q17, 51: *fa-sa-yughiḍūna*; Q7, 43: *min ghillin*; Q7, 59: *ilahin ghayru-hu*; Q5, 3: *wal-munkhaniqatu*; Q2, 197: *min khayrin*; and Q43, 58: *qawmun khaṣimuna*. Some of them, however, would soften recitation with the *kha'* and *ʿayn*.

2 *Idghām*: the reciters used this with six letters; two without resonance, the *lām* and the *rā'*, e.g. at Q2, 24: *fa-in lam tafʿalu*, read as *fa-illam tafʿalu*; Q2, 2: *hudan lil-muttaqīna*, as *hudallil-muttaqīn*; Q2, 5: *min rabbi-him*, *mirrabbi-him*; and Q2, 25: *thamaratin rizqan*, *thamaratirrizqan*. Four letters were recited with resonance: the *nūn*, *mīm*, *yā'*, and *wāsw*, e.g. at Q2, 48: *ʿan nafsin*; Q2, 58: *ḥittatun naghfir*; Q23, 55: *min mālin*, *mimmālin*; Q2, 62: *mathalan mā*, *mathalammā*; Q13, 11: *min wālin*; Q2, 19: *wa-raʿdun wa-barqun*; Q2, 8: *man yaqūlu*; and Q2, 19: *wa-barqun yajʿalūna*.

3 *Iqlāb*: this was used with only the *ba'*, e.g. at Q2, 33: *anbi'-tum*, pronounced as *ambi-tum*; Q2, 253: *mim ba'di-him*, *mim ba'di-him*; and Q2, 18: *ṣummon buknun ṣummunbukmun*. The *nūn* and the nunation metathesize to *mim* exclusively, and are pronounced with resonance.

4 *Ikhfā'*: this is used with the remaining fifteen letters, the *ta'*, *thā'*, *jīm*, *dāl*, *dhā*, *zāy*, *sīn*, *shīn*, *ṣād*, *ḍāḍ*, *ṭā'*, *ẓā'*, *fā'*, *qaf*, and *kāf*, e.g. at Q2, 23: *kun-tum*, read

as *kut-tum*; Q11, 112: *wa-man tāba, wa-mattāba*; Q2, 25: *jannātin tajrī, jannātittajrī*; Q2, 178: *bil-unthā*; Q2, 25: *min thamaratin, mith thamaratin*; Q73, 5: *qawlan thaqīlan, qawlaththaqīlan*; Q10, 22: *anjayta-nā, ajjayta-nā*; Q28, 71: *in jaʿala, ij jaʿala*; Q17, 49: *khalqan jadīdan, khalqajjadīdan*; Q2, 22: *andād, addādan*; Q19, 91: *andaʿaw, ad daʿaw*; Q78, 34: *wa-kaʾsan dihāqan, wa-kaʾsaddihaqan*; Q2, 6: *a-andharta-hum, a-adhdharta-hum*; Q18, 31: *min dhahabin, midhdhahabin*; Q17, 2–3: *wakīlan dhuriyyata, wakīladhdhuryyata*; Q41, 2: *tanzīlun min, tanzīlummin*; Q14, 44: *min zawālin, mizzzawālin*; Q18, 40: *ṣaʿīdan zalaqan, ṣaʿīdazzalaqan*; Q4, 28: *al-insānu, al-issānu*; Q12, 51: *min sūʾin, missūʾin*; Q39, 29: *wa-rajulan salaman, wa-rajulassalaman*; Q80, 22: *anshara-hu, ashshara-hu*; Q2, 70: *in shāʾ, ishshāʾ*; Q35, 30: *ghafūrn shakūrun, ghafūrushshakūrun*; Q9, 100: *wal-anṣāri, wal-aṣṣāri*; Q5, 2: *an ṣaddū-kum, aṣ ṣaddū-kum*; Q77, 33: *jimālatun ṣufrun, jimālatuṣṣufrun*; Q11, 82: *manḍūḍin, maḍḍūdin*; Q5, 105: *man dalla, maddalla*; Q25, 39: *wa-kullan ḍarab-n, wa-kullaḍḍarab-nā*; Q3, 14: *al-muqanṭarati, al-muqaṭṭarati*; Q6, 2: *min ṭīnin, mit ṭīnin*; Q4, 43: *ṣaʿīdan ṭayyiban, ṣaʿīdaṭṭayyiban*; Q2, 210: *yanẓurūna, yaẓẓurūna*; Q34, 22: *min ẓahīrin, miẓẓahīrin*; Q4, 57: *ẓillan ẓalīlan, ẓillaẓẓalīan*; Q26, 63: *fa-nfalaqa, fa-ffalaqa*; Q2, 90: *min faḍli-hi, miffaidi-hi*; Q4, 14: *khālidan fī-hā, khālidaffī-hā*; Q12, 62: *inqalabu, iqqalabu*; Q14, 26: *min qarārin, miqqārarin*; Q34, 50: *samīʿūn qarībun, samīʿuqqaribun*; Q3, 104: *al-munkari, al-mukkari*; Q3, 81: *min kitābin, mikkitābin*; and Q27, 29: *kitābun karīmun, kitābukkarīmun.*

Ikhfāʾ is a position between expression and assimilation, and always requires resonance.

Chapter thirty-two

REGARDING *MADD* (LENGTHENING) AND *QAṢR* (SHORTENING)

A number of reciters authored works on this subject.

The basis for *madd* (lengthening) is what has been narrated by Saʿīd ibn Manṣūr in his *Sunan*: "Shihāb ibn Khirāsh informed us, saying: Masʿūd ibn Yazīd al-Kindī informed me, saying:

"Ibn Masʿūd was teaching a man to recite, when the man read (*Innamā al-ṣadaqātu li-l-fuqarā wa-l-masākīn*) (Q9, 60) without the *alif madd*[1] ending (on the word fuqarāʾ). So Ibn Masʿūd said, 'The Messenger of Allāh did not teach me to recite it thus.' The man said, 'How did he teach you to recite it, O Abū ʿAbd-al-Raḥmān?' So he said, 'He taught me to recite it (*Innamā al-ṣadaqātu li-l-fuqarāʾi wa-l-masākīn*)', and he pronounced (and lengthened) the *alif madd*."

This narration is a powerful evidence for lengthening, and is authoritative in this regard, its transmitters being trustworthy. It is also narrated by al-Ṭabarani in his al-Kabīr.

Madd (lengthening) is equivalent to extending a long vowel over its natural length – this being the minimum length required in the pronunciation of a long vowel.

Qaṣr (shortening) is omitting this extension, and leaving the natural long vowel as it is.

The long vowels are the *alif*, whenever it appears; the vowelless *wāw*, when immediately preceded by a letter bearing a short u vowel; and the vowelless *yāʾ*, when preceded by a letter bearing a short i vowel.

Lengthening may occur either for:

(I) a phonetic reason.
(II) a semantic reason.

I The phonetic reason is linked to the appearance of either:

(1) a hamza
(2) a vowelless letter.

1 The hamza may appear after a long vowel or before it, examples of the latter being: (*ʾādam*) (Q2, 31); (*raʾā*) (Q53, 11); (*ʾīmān*) (Q2, 93); (*khāṭi'īn*) (Q12, 97); (*ʾūtū*) (Q2, 101); and (*al-mawʾūda*) (Q81, 8).

As for the former,[2] if the *hamza* and the long vowel are both in the same word it is known as the *muttaṣil* (connected) form of the *madd*. For example: (*ulāʾik*)

(Q2, 5); (*shāʾa Allāh*) (Q2, 20); (*al-sūʾā*) (Q30, 10); (*min sūʾ*) (Q3, 30); and (*yaḍīʾ*) (Q24, 35).

And if the long vowel is at the end of one word, and the *hamza* at the beginning of the next it is known as the *munfaṣil* (disjoined) form of the *madd*. For example: (*bi-mā ʾanzal*) (Q2, 90); (*yā ʾayyuha*) (Q2, 21); (*qalū ʾāmanna*) (Q2, 14); (*amruhū ʾilā Allāh*) (Q2, 275); (*fī ʾanfusikum*) (Q2, 235); and (*bihī ʾillā al-fāsiqīn*) (Q2, 26).

The reason for extending when there is a *hamza* is that long vowels are subtle and the *hamza* is difficult to pronounce; so the subtle letter is extended in order to ease the pronunciation of the difficult one.

2 The vowelless letter (that follows a long vowel) can be either obligatory, meaning it does not change under any circumstance, such as with: (*al-ḍāllīn*) (Q1, 7); (*dābba*) (Q2, 164); (*alif lām mīm*) (Q2, 1); (*a tuḥājjūnnī*) (Q6, 80); or casual, meaning that it is apparent only due to the reciter pausing or some other reason – as with (*al-ʿibād*) (Q2, 207); (*al-ḥisāb*) (Q2, 202); (*nastaʿīn*) (Q1, 5); (*al-raḥīm*) (Q1, 1); and (*yūqinūn*) (Q2, 4) in the case of a pause; and (*fīh-hudan*) (Q2, 2); (*qāl-lahum*) (Q2, 243); (*yaqūr-rabbana*) (Q2, 201) when read with assimilation, as shown.

The reason for extending when there is a vowelless letter is in order to allow the amalgamation of two following vowelless letters. Thus it is as if it takes the place of a short vowel.

* * *

The Reciters are in agreement about extending the long vowel when followed by a *hamza* in the same word (the *muṭṭaṣil*), and the long vowel followed by an obligatory vowelless letter, although they are at variance as regards their lengths. However, they differ concerning whether to shorten the other two types: the long vowel followed by a *hamza* in a separate word (the *munfaṣil*), and the long vowel followed by a casual vowelless letter.

As for the *muttaṣil*, the majority view is that it is extended by one full measure, but no more.

Others hold the view that it can be graded in the same way as the *munfaṣil*: so it is extended most in the recitations of Ḥamza and Warsh, slightly less in that of ʿĀṣim, less again in those of Ibn ʿĀmir, al-Kisāʾī and Khalaf, and less still in the recitations of Ibn ʿAmr and the rest.

Yet others hold the view that it has only two degrees of extension: longer, as per above,[3] and middling for the rest.

As for the extension due to a vowelless letter – also known as the *madd al-ʿadl* (extension of equality), due to it being equal to one measure – the majority view is that it also is extended by one full measure, and no more, although some hold that it has various grades.

As for the *munfaṣil* – which is also known as the *madd al-faṣl* (extension of division), since it divides between two words; as the *madd al-basṭ* (extension of extending), due to it extending between two words; as the *madd al-iʿtibār* (extension of consideration), due to two words being considered as one word; as the *madd ḥarf bi-ḥarf* (extension of a letter with a letter) – that is, the extension of one word with another; and as the *al-madd al-jāʾiz* (permissible extension) due to the difference about whether to extend it or not – statements about the measure of its extension differ so much that it is not possible to enumerate them all. However, in brief, it has seven grades.

1 Shortening. Meaning removing the unessential extension and leaving the long vowel in its natural state without any lengthening. This is restricted to the *munfaṣil* in the recitations of Abū Jaʿfar and Ibn Kathīr, and also Abū ʿAmr according to the majority view.

2 Slightly longer than shortening. This is measured as being the length of two *alifs*, or one and a half according to some. This is found in the recitation of Abū ʿAmr in both the *muttaṣil* and *munfaṣil* forms of the *madd*, according to the author of *al-Taysīr*.[4]

3 Slightly longer than the last. This is a middle length extension according to the majority view, and is measured as being three *alifs* in length, although it is also said to be two and a half, and also two by those holding that the previous grade is measured as one and a half. This is found in the recitation of Ibn ʿĀmir and al-Kisāʾī in both (the *muttaṣil* and *munfaṣil*), according to the author of *al-Taysīr*.

4 Slightly longer than the last. This is measured as four *alifs* in length, although it is also said to be three and a half, and it is also said to be three as per the preceding dispute. This is found in the recitation of ʿĀṣim in both forms, according to the author of *al-Taysīr*.

5 Slightly longer than the last. This is measured as five alifs in length, and as four and a half, and as four as per the dispute. This is found in the recitations of Ḥamza and Warsh in [the *munfaṣil*], according to the same.

6 Longer than that. This is measured by al-Hudhalī as being five *alifs* in length, on the assumption that the fifth grade is four. He states that this is found in the recitation of Ḥamza.

7 Excessive. This is measured as being six, and al-Hudhalī states that it is found in the recitation of Warsh.

However, Ibn al-Jazarī states: "This debate about measuring the grades in terms of *alifs* does not lead to any precision; rather it is merely verbal, since if the lowest degree – which is shortening – is added to by the smallest amount it becomes the second degree, and so forth until the last."

* * *

As for the long vowel followed by a casual vowelless letter, in all of the recitations each of the three forms is allowed: lengthening (both fully and to a medium extent) and shortening; this being a matter of choice.

II The semantic reason (for lengthening) lies in the wish to be emphatic in negating. This is a powerful reason, to which the Arabs paid great attention, even though it is regarded as weaker than the phonetic one by the scholars of recitation. An example of it is the *madd al-taʿẓīm* (extension of glorification), such as is found in *lā ilāha illā hū*, *lā ilāha illā Allāh* and *lā ilāha illā ant*.

This form of lengthening, used with this purpose, is attributed to those who shorten the *munfaṣil* form of the *madd*, and it is known as the *madd al-mubālagha* (extension of exaggeration). Ibn Mihrān in *Kitāb al-Maddāt*, states: "It is called the extension of exaggeration since it is used for exaggerating the divinity that is solely for Allāh, Most High." He then says: "This is widely used by the Arabs, who lengthen when supplicating and when seeking God's help, and also when exaggerating in negating something. They even lengthen things, with this purpose, for which there is no basis." Ibn al-Jazarī states: "The use of lengthening in exaggeration has been narrated from Ḥamza for negating with the particle *lā*, such as in (*lā rayba fīh*) (Q2, 2); (*lā shiyata fīhā*) (Q2, 71); (*lā maradda lah*) (Q13, 11); and (*lā jaram*) (Q11, 22). Its length in this case is middling, not being full due to the reason behind it being weak." This was stated by Ibn al-Qaṣṣāʿ.

The two reasons, the phonetic and the semantic, may coincide, such as in (*lā ʾilāha illā*) (Q2, 255); (*lā ʾikrāha fī al-dīn*) (Q2, 256); and (*lā ʾithma ʿalayh*) (Q2, 182), in which case the long vowel is extended one full measure as usual when lengthening due to a *hamza*; and the (shorter) extension due to the semantic reason is cancelled, thus acting upon the stronger and leaving the weaker.

Rule

If the reason for the lengthening changes, it is permissible to lengthen, out of consideration of the original form, or shorten, with regard to the pronunciation. This is regardless of whether the reason for the extension is the appearance of a *hamza* or a vowelless letter, and regardless of whether the *hamza* (should this be the reason) is pronounced as a sound halfway between a *hamza* and a *yāʾ* (*bayna bayn*), is altered, or is omitted completely. Furthermore, lengthening is preferable when a trace of the hamza remains following a change, such as in (*hāʾulāʾi in kuntum*) (Q2, 31) in the recitations of Qālūn and al-Bizzī; and shortening is preferable when no trace remains, such as with the same verse in the recitation of Abū ʿAmr.

Rule

There is consensus that when two reasons (for lengthening) combine, one strong and the other weak, the strong is acted upon and the weak is cancelled. This brings about certain subsidiary issues, among which is that just seen, regarding the coinciding of the phonetic and semantic reasons. Another appears in cases such as (*jāʾū ʾabāhum*) (Q12, 16) and (*raʾā ʾaydiyahum*) (Q11, 70) in the recitation of Warsh, when shortening and extending to a medial length are not allowed, but only extending fully. This is out of acting upon the stronger of the two reasons, which is extending the long vowel due to the following *hamza*. However, if a pause is made on *jāʾū* or *raʾā*, all of the three forms are allowed, due to the long vowel being preceded by a *hamza*, and as the other reason, the following *hamza*, has gone.

Point of benefit

Abū Bakr Aḥmad ibn al-Ḥusayn ibn Mihrān al-Naysabūrī states: The extensions found in the Qurʾān are of ten types.

1 *Madd al-ḥajz* (extension of separation), such as in (*ʾā ʾandhartahum*) (Q2, 6); (*ʾā ʾanta qulta li-l-nās*) (Q5, 116); (*ʾā ʾidhā mitnā*) (Q23, 82); and (*ʾā ʾulqiya al-dhikr ʿalayhi*) (Q54, 25). It is called this because it occurs between two *hamzas* as a partition between them, since the Arabs found it too difficult to combine them. By consensus it is one complete *alif* in length, by which separation is obtained.

2 *Madd al-ʿadl* (extension of equality), found in every doubled letter preceded by a long vowel or a diphthong, such as in (*al-ḍāllīn*) (Q1, 7). It is called this because it is equivalent to a short vowel – that is, it takes its place in separating between two vowelless letters.

3 *Madd al-tamkīn* (extension of enablement), such as in (*ulāʾik*) (Q2, 5); (*al-malāʾika*) (Q2, 31); and (*shaʿāʾir*) (Q2, 158). This is one of the extensions which is followed by a *hamza*, the accurate pronunciation of which it is used to enable.

4 *Madd al-basṭ* (extension of expansion) – and it is also called the *madd al-faṣl* (extension of division) – such as in (*bi-mā ʾanzal*) (Q2, 91), since it expands between two words, and joins between two adjacent words.

5 *Madd al-rawm* (extension of slurring), such as in (*hā antum*) (Q3, 66), because they slur the *hamza* of the word *ʾantum*, not pronouncing it precisely, nor leaving it altogether; rather they soften it, and allude to it. This is following the rule of those who do not pronounce the hamza of *hā ʾantum*. Its length is one and a half *alifs*.

6 *Madd al-farq* (extension of differentiation), such as in (*ʾāʾlān*) (Q10, 51), since it differentiates between the interrogative and the declarative statement. Its length is one complete alif by consensus. However, if there is a doubled letter following the long *alif*, a second *alif* is added, so as to enable the *hamza* to be pronounced correctly, such as in (*ʾā-dh-dhākirīn Allāh*) (sic).

7 *Madd al-binya* (extension of structure), such as in (*māʾ*) (Q2, 22); (*duʿāʾ*) (Q2, 171); (*nidāʾ*) (Q2, 171); and (*zakariyyāʾ*) (Q19, 7), since the noun is composed with an *alif madd* ending, so as to distinguish it from those words ending in an *alif maqṣūra*.[5]

8 *Madd al-mubālagha* (extension of exaggeration), such as in (*lā ʾilāha illā Allāh*) (Q47, 19).

9 *Madd al-badal min al-hamza* (extension of substitution for a *hamza*), such as in (*ādam*) (Q2, 35); (*ākhir*) (Q2, 8); and (*āman*) (Q2, 177). Its length is a complete *alif* by consensus.

10 *Madd al-aṣl* (extension of the verbal root), found in verbs with an *alif madd* ending, such as in (*jāʾ*) (Q110, 1) and (*shāʾ*) (Q2, 70). The difference between this and *madd al-binya* above is that those nouns are built with an *alif madd* ending, so as to distinguish them from those words ending in an *alif maqṣūra*, whereas these are long vowels which are part of the original root letters of verbs, and which were formulated for certain considerations.

Chapter thirty-three

REGARDING LIGHTENING THE *HAMZA*

There are a number of works dedicated to this topic.

Know, that since the *hamza* is the heaviest of letters to pronounce, and comes from the furthest inside the mouth, the Arabs devised various means of lightening its pronunciation. The tribe of Quraysh and the rest of the people of the Hijaz went further (than all other Arabs) in lightening the *hamza*. Thus, most instances of lightening it are found in the recitations which they have narrated, such as that of Ibn Kathīr narrated via Ibn Fulayḥ, that of Nāfiᶜ narrated via Warsh, and that of Abū ᶜAmr, because his recitation is taken from the people of the Hijaz.

Ibn ᶜAdiyy narrates via Mūsā ibn ᶜUbayda, from Nāfiᶜ, from Ibn ᶜUmar, saying:

The Messenger of Allāh (peace and blessings be upon him) did not pronounce the *hamza*, nor did Abū Bakr, ᶜUmar, or any of the (early) caliphs. Rather, saying the *hamza* is nothing but a reprehensible innovation, begun by those that followed them.

Abū Shāma states: "This *ḥadīth* cannot be used as an evidence, since Mūsā ibn ᶜUbayda al-Rabadhī is considered weak by the scholars of *Ḥadīth*."

I myself add that this is also the case with the *ḥadīth* narrated by al-Ḥākim in his Mustadrak, given on the authority of Ḥamrān ibn Aᶜyan, from Abū al-Aswad al-Duᵓalī, from Abū Dharr, saying:

A bedouin came to the Messenger of Allāh (peace and blessings be upon him), and said: "O Nabī' Allāh (Prophet of Allāh)." He replied: "I am not the Nabīᵓ Allāh, but I am the Nabiyy Allāh."

Al-Dhahabī states: "This is a rejected *ḥadīth*, as Ḥamrān is a *rāfiḍī*,[1] and is thus untrustworthy."

The rules regarding the *hamza* are many and cannot be enumerated in less than a complete volume, but what we will mention here is that it can be pronounced properly in four ways.

1 Transferral of its short vowel to a preceding vowelless letter. The *hamza* is thereby dropped, for example (*Qada-flaḥa al-muᵓminūn*) (Q23, 1) with the *dāl* taking the short *a* vowel. This is found in the recitation of Nāfiᶜ transmitted via Warsh. It occurs when the vowelless letter is sound and at the end of a word, and the *hamza* is at the beginning of the next. The students of Yaᶜqūb, who transmitted from Warsh, excluded from this rule (*kitābiyah. Innī ẓanant*) (Q69, 19), where they made the *hāᵓ* vowelless and pronounced the *hamza*. As for the

rest of the reciters, they pronounced the hamza and left the preceding letter vowelless, throughout the Qurʾān.

2 Substitution, such that a vowelless *hamza* is turned into a long vowel corresponding to the short vowel on the preceding letter – that is, it is turned into an *alif* after a short *a* vowel, such as with (*wa āmur ahlak*) (Q20, 132) (originally *wa ʾmur ahlak*, but now pronounced *wāmur ahlak*), into a *wāw* after a short *u* vowel, such as with (*yūminūn*) (Q2, 3) (originally *yuʾminūn*), and into a *yāʾ* after a short *i* vowel, such as with (*jīt*) (Q2, 71) (originally *jiʾt*). This occurs in the recitation of Abū ʿAmr. It also makes no difference whether the *hamza* is the first, second, or third of the word's root letters.

(This rule is followed) as long as: (a) the *hamza* is not vowelless – either by being in the jussive case, e.g. (*nansaʾhā*)[2] (Q2, 106), or by being indeclinable, e.g. (*arjiʾhu*) (Q7, 111); (b) leaving out the *hamza* does not make the word more difficult to pronounce, such as with (*tuʾwī ilayk*) (Q33, 51); (c) no ambiguity is caused, as is the case with the word (*riʾyā*) (Q19, 74).

If the *hamza* carries a short vowel, however, there is agreement that it is pronounced fully, e.g. (*yuʾaddih*) (Q3, 75).

3 Easing it, by pronouncing it between a *hamza* and the short vowel it is carrying. Thus, if there are two successive *hamzas* both carrying a short a vowel, Ibn Kathīr and Nāfiʿ,[3] Abū ʿAmr and Hishām ease the second *hamza* – although Warsh (one of the narrators of the recitation of Nāfiʿ) turns it into an *alif*; Ibn Kathīr does not insert an *alif* before it; and Qālūn (the other narrator of the recitation of Nāfiʿ), Hishām and Abū ʿAmr do insert an alif before it – while the rest of the seven Reciters [ʿĀṣim, Ḥamza and al-Kisāʾī] pronounce it fully.

If the two *hamzas* carry two different vowels, the first being a short *a* vowel, and the second a short *i* vowel, Ibn Kathīr, Nāfiʿ and Abū ʿAmr ease the second – with Qālūn and Abū ʿAmr inserting an alif before it – and the rest pronounce it as a proper *hamza*.

If the first carries a short *a* vowel and the second a short *u* vowel, this occurring only in (*Qul ʾaʾunabbiʾukum*) (Q3, 15), (*ʾAʾunzila ʾalayhi al-dhikr*) (Q38, 8), and (*ʾAʾulqiy*) (Q54, 25), the same three (Ibn Kathīr, Nāfiʿ, and Abū ʿAmr) ease the second *hamza* – with Qālūn inserting an *alif* before it – and the rest pronounce it as a proper *hamza*.

Al-Dānī states: "The Companions alluded to the use of easing here by writing the second *hamza* on top of a *wāw*."

4 Dropping the *hamza* without transferring its short vowel (see 1 above). This is found in the recitation of Abū ʿAmr when two successive *hamzas* carry the same short vowel but are in two separate words.

If both *hamzas* carry a short *i* vowel, such as with (*hāʾulāʾi ʾin kuntum*) (Q2, 31), Warsh and Qunbul make the second into a vowelless *yāʾ*, Qālūn and al-Bazzī make the first a *yāʾ* carrying a short *i* vowel, Abū ʿAmr drops it, and the rest pronounce both the *hamzas*.

If they both carry a short *a* vowel, such as with (*jāʾa ʾajaluhum*) (Q7, 34), Warsh and Qunbul make the second a long vowel, the other three (Qālūn, al-Bizzī and Abū ʿAmr) drop the first, while the rest pronounce both the *hamzas*.

If they both carry a short *u* vowel, the only occurrence of this being (*awliyāʾu ʾulāʾik*) (Q46, 32), Abū ʿAmr drops the first, Qālūn and al-Bizzī make it into a *wāw* carrying a short *u* vowel, the other two (Warsh and Qanbal) make the second *hamza* into a vowelless *wāw*, and the rest pronounce both the *hamzas*.

They also differed about which of the *hamzas* is the one dropped: is it the first or the second? That it is the first is the opinion of Abū ʿAmr, and that it is the second is the opinion of the grammarian al-Khalīl. The benefit of this dispute becomes apparent when lengthening (*madd*) occurs; since if it is the first *hamza* which is dropped, it is the *munfaṣil* form of the *madd* which occurs, and if it is the second *hamza*, it is the *muttaṣil* form of the *madd*.

Chapter thirty-four

REGARDING THE MANNER OF RECEIVING THE QURʾĀN

Know that memorizing the Qurʾān is a collective duty upon the Muslim community, as has been declared by al-Jurjānī in *al-Shāfī*, *al-ʿIbādī* and others. Al-Juwaynī states:

The meaning of this is that it should not cease to be known by a number of people large enough to be considered as *mutawātir*, so that it can never be altered or corrupted. If this is undertaken by enough people to reach this number, the obligation is removed from the rest, but if not, all are sinful.

Teaching it is also a collective duty, and is one of the best actions in bringing one near to God. Thus one sound *ḥadīth* states:

The best of you is the one who learns the Qurʾān and then teaches it.

The methods of receiving knowledge, according to the scholars of Ḥadīth, are listening to a teacher reading a text and reading to him, listening while another person reads to a teacher, being handed a text by a teacher, being given permission to teach, written correspondence between a teacher and a pupil, a teacher bequeathing a text to a pupil, receiving information from a teacher, and finding a text (belonging to a teacher). Only the first two of these are valid (in the case of the Qurʾān), as will become clear from what is mentioned below.

Reading to a teacher is the mode that has been used throughout the ages. As regards listening to a teacher read, it is probably allowable here, since it was through hearing the Prophet (peace and blessings be upon him) that the Companions (God be pleased with them) received the Qurʾān. However, none of the scholars of recitation considered merely hearing from the teacher to be enough, the reason being obvious, since what is intended is the manner of performing the recitation, and not everyone who hears the pronunciation of the teacher is able to recite in the same manner as him. This is not the case with *Ḥadīth*, in which the goal is understanding the meaning, and the pronunciation of the *Ḥadīth* does not follow the required manner used in reciting the Qurʾān. As for the Companions, their purity of language and sound nature ensured their ability to recite correctly, just as they had heard it from the Prophet (peace and blessings be upon him), because it was revealed in their language.

Evidence for the practice of learning to recite from a teacher is found in the fact that the Prophet (peace and blessings be upon him) reviewed the Qurʾān by reading it to the Angel Gabriel each year in the month of Ramaḍān.

It is reported that the Shaykh Shams al-Dīn ibn al-Jazarī, when he came to Cairo and vast numbers came to learn from him, did not have sufficient time to listen to everyone. Thus he would recite a verse of the Qurʾān himself, and then everyone would repeat it to him with one voice. Hence he did not suffice with merely reciting it himself.

A student is allowed to recite before a teacher even if someone else is also reciting to him at the same time, as long as the teacher is still able to follow the recitation of each. The Shaykh ʿAlam al-Dīn al-Sakhāwī used to listen to two or three students, each reciting different parts of the Qurʾān, and he would correct each of them as necessary. The same is true if the teacher is occupied with something else, such as copying or reading a text.

It is also not necessary for the student to recite from memory; reading from a copy of the Qurʾān is sufficient.

Section

Recitation can be done in three ways.

1 *Taḥqīq*. This means giving each letter its due, by lengthening the different types of madd, pronouncing the *hamza*, giving the vowels their proper length, paying due attention to letters which should be articulated fully or doubled, and clarifying all letters and separating them one from another, by pausing, by reciting slowly and deliberately, and with attention being paid to only stopping where the meaning allows, and without shortening or decreasing in any way, or removing any vowel, or improperly assimilating any vowelled letter.

This method of recitation is used for exercising the tongue and perfecting the recitation of the words. It is preferable that those still learning should recite in this manner. However, care should be taken not to go to excess by turning short vowels into long ones, repeating the *rāʾs*, vowelizing vowelless letters, or reverberating the *nūns* by exaggerated nasalization. Thus, Ḥamza said to one individual he heard going to excess in this manner: "Do you not know that what exceeds white (with regards skin) is leprosy, what exceeds wavy (with regards hair) is frizzy, and what exceeds recitation is not recitation." Similarly, it is not allowable to increase the length of separation between the letters of words, such as the one who pauses briefly on the *tāʾ* of *nastaʿīn* (Q1, 5), claiming that he is reciting with *tartīl*.[1]

This was the manner of recitation of Ḥamza and Warsh. Regarding it, al-Dānī narrates a *ḥadīth* in his *Kitāb al-Tajwīd* with a chain of narration going back to Ubayy ibn Kaʿb, which states that the latter recited to the Messenger of God (peace and blessings be upon him) in the style of *taḥqīq*. Al-Dānī states, however, that this *ḥadīth* is strange but with a sound chain of narration.

2 *Ḥadr*. This is to recite swiftly and flowingly, and by making it lighter by shortening certain long vowels, removing certain short vowels, contracting, changing, performing the major form of assimilation (*al-idghām al-kabīr*), lightening the *hamza*, and by other means authenticated by narration. This is while showing consideration to desinential inflection, correct pronunciation, and

firmly establishing the letters, and without cutting short long vowels, contracting the majority of short vowels, losing the sound of the *ghunna* (nasalization), or being negligent to such an extent that the recitation is incorrect and cannot be described as recitation.

This was the manner of recitation of Ibn Kathīr and Abū Jaʿfar, and of those who shortened the *munfaṣil* form of the *madd*, such as Abū ʿAmr and Yaʿqūb.

3 *Tadwīr*. This is midway between *taḥqīq* and *ḥadr*. It is narrated from the majority of scholars, those who lengthened the *munfaṣil* form of the *madd* yet not to its full extent. It was the manner of recitation of the rest of the Reciters, and is that chosen by most who perform this art.

Point of note

In the type that follows this (the thirty-fifth type), the desirability of reciting with *tartīl* will be discussed. The difference between the latter and *taḥqīq* – as given by some – is that *taḥqīq* is done for the purpose of exercising the tongue, teaching and practising, while *tartīl* is done for reflection, contemplation and gaining further understanding. Thus, all *taḥqīq* is *tartīl*, but not all *tartīl* is *taḥqīq*.

Section

It is important to recite the Qurʾān in the prescribed manner of *tajwīd*, and a great number of scholars have authored works on this subject, among them al-Dānī and others. Al-Dānī himself narrates that Ibn Masʿūd stated: "Recite the Qurʾān with *tajwīd*."

The scholars of recitation have said:

Tajwīd is the adornment of recitation. It consists of giving the letters their due and their proper order, and pronouncing each letter from its point of articulation and its source, and pronouncing it gently, in its perfect form, without excess, exaggeration or affectation.

This was alluded to by the Prophet (peace and blessings be upon him) when he said: "Whoever wishes to recite the Qurʾān purely, as it was revealed, then let him recite it in the manner of Ibn Umm ʿAbd" – that is, Ibn Masʿūd, who (may God be pleased with him) was endowed with great skill in the correct recitation of the Qurʾān.

There is no doubt that just as the Muslims are expected to worship God by seeking to understand the meaning of the Qurʾān and follow its injunctions, they are also expected to worship Him by pronouncing it correctly and articulating the letters in the manner imparted by the authorities of this art, and which has been narrated from the noble Prophet. In fact, scholars consider recitation without following the rules of *tajwīd* to be erroneous. They have divided error in recitation into two forms: manifest and hidden. Error in recitation is a defect that impinges on the words causing a violation. However, the manifest form causes an obvious violation, known to both the scholars of recitation and others besides – this being an error in *iʿrāb*; while the hidden form causes a violation only known to the scholars of recitation and those reciters who have taken this art from the mouths of the scholars, and have mastered it based on the pronunciation of the experts in this field.

Ibn al-Jazarī states:

I know of no means of achieving perfection in *tajwīd* like unto exercising the tongue and repeating the pronunciation taken from the mouth of an expert. Its basis is knowledge of the manner of stopping, of inclining the short *a* vowel towards a short *i* vowel, and of assimilation, and knowledge of the rules of the *hamza*, of softening (*tarqīq*) and enlarging (*tafkhīm*) letters, and of the points of articulation of the letters.

The first four of these have already been discussed. As for softening the letters, all the *mustafil* (low)[2] letters are rendered delicately, and it is not allowed to enlarge them. The only exceptions are the *lām* in the name 'Allāh' when it follows a short *a* vowel or a short *u* vowel, as is agreed by all, or when it follows any of the *muṭbaq* (covered) letters,[3] according to one opinion; and also the *rāʾ* when it bears a short *u* vowel or a short *a* vowel, or, in certain circumstances, when it is vowelless. And as for the *mustaʿlī* (elevated) letters, these are all enlarged in all circumstances.

With regard to the points of articulation of the letters, the correct opinion in the view of the reciters and the early grammarians, such as al-Khalīl, is that they are seventeen in number.

A large number of these two groups have, however, stated that they number sixteen, eliminating thereby the point of articulation of the letters coming from the chest (*jawf*), these being the long vowels and the diphthongs. They then gave the point of articulation of the *ā* as being the bottom of the throat, and that of the *ū* and *ī* as being from the point of articulation of the vowelled letters.

Some also numbered them as fourteen, eliminating the points of articulation of the *nūn*, the *lām*, and the *rāʾ*, and instead giving them a single shared point.

Ibn al-Ḥājib states: "This is all an approximation, and were it not so then each letter would have its own separate point of articulation."

The Reciters state that the best way of determining the point of articulation of a letter is to pronounce a short a vowel followed by the particular letter given either vowelless or doubled, the latter being clearer, with the characteristics of the letter being noticed. The points of articulation are:

1 The chest for the *ā*, *ū* and *ī*.

2 The bottom of the throat for the *hamza* and *hāʾ*.

3 The middle of the throat for the *ʿayn* and *ḥāʾ*.

4 The closest part of the throat to the mouth for the *ghayn* and the *khāʾ*.

5 The bottom part of the tongue, just above the throat, and the adjacent part of the palate, for the *qāf*.

6 A little higher on the tongue above the bottom of the point of articulation of the *qāf*, and the adjacent part of the palate, for the *kāf*.

7 Between the middle of the tongue and the middle of the palate for the *jīm*, *shīn*, and *yāʾ*.

8 For the *ḍād*, from the first part of the side of the tongue, and the adjacent molar teeth on the left (and it is also said 'the right') side.

9 For the *lām*, from the side of the tongue at its upper end until the tip of the tongue, and the adjacent part of the hard palate.

10 For the *nūn*, from the tip of the tongue, yet slightly lower (on the palate) than for the *lām*.

11 For the *rāʾ*, from the point of articulation of the *nūn*, although closer to the top of the tongue.

12 For the *ṭāʾ*, *dāl* and *tāʾ*, from the tip of the tongue and the bases of the upper incisors up towards the palate.

13 The sibilants, the *ṣād*, *sīn* and *zāy*, from between the tip of the tongue and a little above the lower incisors.

14 For the *ẓaʾ*, *thāʾ* and *dhāl*, from between the tip of the tongue and the edges of the upper incisors.

15 For the *fāʾ*, from the inside of the lower lip and the edges of the upper incisors.

16 For the *bāʾ*, *mīm* and the *wāw* which is not a long vowel, from between the two lips.

17 The nose, for the *ghunna* (nasalization) which comes with assimilation, the *nūn*, and the vowelless *mīm*.

(Ibn al-Jazarī) states in al-Nashr:

The *hamza* and the *hāʾ* share in their point of articulation, and in both being open and low letters; although the *hamza* is set apart by it being a voiced (*majhūr*) and an occlusive (*shadīd*) letter.

The *ʿayn* and the *ḥāʾ* similarly share their point of articulation; yet the *ḥāʾ* is distinguished by being an unvoiced (*mahmūs*) and a fully constrictive letter.[4]

The *ghayn* and the *khāʾ* share their point of articulation, and are both constrictive, elevated, and open. The *ghayn* is set apart by being voiced.

The *jīm*, *shīn* and *yāʾ* share their point of articulation, and are open and low. However, the *jīm* stands apart by being occlusive, and it shares with the *yāʾ* being voiced. The *shīn* stands apart by being unvoiced (*mahmūs*) and by being pronounced with the spreading of air in the mouth, and it shares with the *yāʾ* being constrictive.

The *ḍād* and the *ẓāʾ* share being voiced, constrictive, elevated and covered. Nevertheless, they differ in points of articulation, and the *ḍād* stands alone as being recited by stretching the sound from one side of the tongue to the other.

The *ṭāʾ*, *dāl* and *tāʾ* share their point of articulation, and are occlusive. The *ṭāʾ* is set apart by being covered and low, and both it and the *dāl* are voiced. The *taʾ* is distinguished by being unvoiced, and both it and the *dāl* are open and low.

The *ẓāʾ*, *dhāl* and *thāʾ* share their point of articulation and are constrictive. The *ẓāʾ* stands apart by being elevated and covered, and both it and the *dhāl* are voiced. The *thāʾ* is distinguished by being unvoiced, and both it and the *dhāl* are open and low.

The *ṣād*, *zāy* and *sīn* share their point of articulation, and both are constrictive and sibilants. The *ṣād* is set apart by being covered and elevated, and both it and the *sīn* are unvoiced. The *zāy* is distinguished by being voiced, and both it and the sīn are open and low.

If the Reciter masters the pronunciation of each letter by itself, giving it its due, then he should apply himself to doing so when combining it with other letters. This is because combining the letters produces characteristics that are not present when the letters are pronounced in isolation, depending upon whether it adjoins a letter with a similar (*majānis*) or approximate (*maqārib*) point of articulation, or one which is strong or weak, or one which is enlarged or soft. In this case the strong letter attracts the weak, and the enlarged overpowers the soft, and it becomes difficult for the tongue to pronounce it as it should be; except as the result of intense practice. Thus, whoever masters correct pronunciation when the letters are combined, has achieved the essence of *tajwīd.*

From the poem about *tajwīd* of Shaykh ʿAlam al-Dīn, from whose own handwriting I have quoted, comes the following,

Do not consider *tajwīd* excessive extension (of long vowels)
Or the extending of what should not be extended by a weak reciter,
Or that you double a *hamza* after an extension
Or that you stammer with the letters like a drunkard
Or that you pronounce a *hamza* as if vomiting
So that the listener would flee from nausea
For each letter is a fine balance so do not exceed
or diminish in the balance
So if you pronounce a hamza, do so gently
Without panting, and without hesitating

And extend long vowels when stopping
Or when there is a hamza; this is good, O brother of perfection!

Point of benefit

(Al-Sakhāwī) states in *Jamāl al-Qurrā*ʾ:

People have (reprehensibly) innovated with regard to reciting the Qurʾān by using singing voices. It is said that the first verse of the Qurʾān to have been sung are the words of God, Most High:

Ammā al-safīnatu fa kānat li-masākīna yaʿmalūna fī al-baḥr (Q18, 79).

This was copied from their singing of the poet's words:

Ammā al-qaṭātu fa innī sawfa anʿatuhā
Naʿtan yuwāfiqu ʿindī baʿda mā fīhā.

It is about these people that the Prophet (peace and blessings be upon him) said:

"Misguided are their hearts and the hearts of those who are pleased by their manner."

Among the things that they innovated is something which they call *tarʿīd* (thundering), which is when they make their voices tremble, like the one who trembles from cold or pain.

Another is what they call *tarqīṣ* (making dance), which is when they slur a vowelless letter, and then hurriedly give a short vowel as if it is running or hurrying.

There is another called *taṭrīb* (chanting), which is when they chant and sing the Qurʾān, and extend in the wrong places and for longer than should be done.

There is another called *taḥzīn* (making sad), which is when they recite in a very sad manner, almost weeping with humility and submissiveness.

Another is one invented by those who unite and read with a single voice, so that for the words of God, Most High *a fa lā taʿqilūn* (Q2, 44) they say *a fa la taʿqilūn*, leaving out the *ā*, and also *Qālu āmannā* (instead of *Qālū āmannā* (Q2, 14), leaving out the *ū*. They also extend what should not be extended in order to maintain the style they have chosen; although, this should be called perversion.

Section

Regarding the manner of performing the various recitations separately and in combination

The path followed by the early Muslims was that they would complete an entire reading of the Qurʾān with just one style of recitation. They did not combine it with another style except during the fifth century, when combining different styles in a single reading appeared, and became well established. However, they only allowed those to combine the recitations who had first studied and had mastered them separately, and had made a complete recitation of the Qurʾān in the style of each [of the acknowledged] reciters by itself. In fact, if a recitation was narrated (differently) by two transmitters, they would read a complete recitation of the Qurʾān in the style of each transmitter, before combining them, and so on.

A group of scholars were more lenient in this regard, and so they would allow one to make just one complete recitation of the Qurʾān for each of the seven reciters except Nāfiʿ and Ḥamza, for whom they would require one complete recitation for Qālūn, one for Warsh, one for Khalaf, and one for Khallād.[5] They would only let someone combine after having completed this. Admittedly, if they saw that someone had recited (the different styles) separately and in combination at the hands of a respected teacher, and had been authorized (to teach) and become qualified, and he wanted to combine the recitations in a single rendering of the Qurʾān, they would not expect him to recite them all separately first. This is because they knew that he had reached a high level of knowledge and proficiency.

They have two methods for combining:

1 *Jamʿ bi-l-ḥarf* (combining by word), whereby the Reciter begins his recitation, and if he passes by a word for which there is a variant reading he repeats it in isolation, showing its different possible readings. He stops on the word if permitted, or else links it (with what follows) using the last style (with which he was reciting) until he reaches a stopping place. If the point of variance is related to two words, such as with the madd *munfaṣil*, he stops on the second, and takes in the difference, and then moves on to what follows.

This is the methodology of the Egyptian reciters, and reciting in this manner is more reliable and easier to master. However, it detracts from the splendour and beauty of the recitation.

2 *Jamʿ bi-l-waqf* (combining by stopping place), whereby the Reciter begins using one recitation until he comes to a stopping place. Then he goes back using the recitation that follows it up to the same point. Then he goes back again, and continues doing so, until he completes them all.

This is the methodology of the Syrian reciters. It is more easily visualized, clearer, takes longer, and is more clearly eminent.

Some reciters used to combine by verse, in the same manner.

Abū al-Ḥasan al-Qabaḥātī states in his poem and its commentary:

For the one combining the recitations there are seven conditions, which can be condensed into five:

1 Choosing a good stopping place.

2 Choosing a good starting place.

3 Good rendition.

4 No mixing of recitations. So that if he reads in the style of one recitation, he does not move on to the next until he completes the first (up to the stopping place). If he contravenes this rule, the teacher should not ignore it, but instead should signal to him with his hand. If he does not understand, he should say: "You did not connect (to what follows)." If he still does not comprehend, the teacher should wait until he remembers. If he is unable to do so, then he should remind him.

5 Observing the correct order with regard to the recitations; beginning with that which the scholars have put first in their books. Thus one should begin with the recitation of Nāfiʿ before that of Ibn Kathīr, and with Qālūn's (transmission of the recitation of Nāfiʿ) before that of Warsh.

Ibn al-Jazarī states:

The correct opinion is that this is not a requirement, but rather is a preference. Indeed, those teachers who we have met only consider one to be skilled if one continually gives precedence to one reciter in particular. Some of them, however, would observe symmetry when combining recitations. Thus they would begin by shortening (the appropriate long vowels – the *munfaṣil*), then by reciting with the next grade of extension, and so on until the longest grade of extension. They would begin with the longest grade of extension, and then with the next shortest, and so on until they were reciting by shortening. This technique would, however, only be followed with a skilled teacher, of great ability to recollect. Otherwise, one standard order would be followed.

He also stated:

The one combining should look at the differences in the recitations, in terms of principles and details. For that which can be superimposed, one should suffice with just one version. That which cannot requires careful attention: if one is able to adjoin it to the one, two, or more words preceding it, without causing confusion or complexity, one should do so; if one is unable, one should go back to the place where one began, so that all the versions can be comprehended without any omission, complexity, or repetition – the first of which is prohibited, the second disliked, and the third deficient.

As for recitation by piecing together and mixing one recitation with another, this will be expounded in the subsequent type.

With regard to the recitations (*qirāʾāt*), transmissions (*riwāyāt*), paths (*turuq*) and versions (*awjuh*), it is not allowed for a reciter to omit or disturb any of them, for it is a shortcoming in perfecting the transmission. This is with the exception of the versions (*awjuh*), for these are a matter of choice; whichever version one employs is sufficient for that transmission (*riwāya*).

As for the amount which one should read when learning, the early Muslims would not exceed ten verses, no matter who they were. As for those who followed them, then it would depend on the individual's ability.

About this Ibn al-Jazarī states:

It has become customary when learning recitations separately to take 1/120th of the Qurʾān at a time, and when learning in combination to take 1/240th of the Qurʾān.

Al-Sakhāwī states that others have not given a limit to the amount (which should be studied at one time), and that it is a matter of choice.

I have summarized this type, and have organized what is a miscellany of sayings made by the scholars of recitation. This is an important type, which the reciter needs, just as the scholar of *ḥadīth* requires its like for the science of *ḥadīth*.

A point of benefit

Ibn Khayr claims that there is scholarly consensus that it is not allowed for anyone to relate a *ḥadīth* from the Prophet (peace and blessings be upon him) unless he has a chain of narration for it, even if it is with scholarly authorization (*ijāza*). Would the same rule then apply to the Qurʾān, such that no one would be allowed to quote a verse or read it if he had not previously read it before a teacher? I find no narration to this effect. However, there is a reason (why this might be required) in that the degree of caution required in reading the Qurʾān is greater than that in reading the *ḥadīth*. There is also a basis for why this is not necessary, in that the reason for this being a requirement as regards *ḥadīth* is only for fear that additional material might be added to the *ḥadīth*, or that statements which the Prophet (peace and blessings be upon him) did not make might be claimed as being his; yet the Qurʾān is preserved, well learned, widely circulated, and has been made easy. This is what is clear.

A second point of benefit

Being given authorization from a teacher is not a requirement for teaching people to read. So whoever knows oneself to be qualified, is permitted to do so, even if no one has given them authorization. This was the practice of the earliest Muslims and the pious from amongst the subsequent early generations.

The same is true of every discipline, and for both teaching and giving opinions, contrary to what is imagined by the ignorant, who believe it to be a condition. Rather, people only adopted the system of authorization because a person's competence is not usually known by those novices and such like who wish to study with them. This is due to the insufficient rank of these novices in this regard. And as seeking someone qualified before studying with them is a condition, the authorization is like a proof from the teacher to the one authorized, of the latter's competence.

A third point of benefit

There is scholarly consensus that the practice of many of the leading reciters, as regards only giving authorization in return for money, is not allowed. In fact, if the teacher knows of someone's competence, it is obligatory that they give them authorization to teach. And, likewise, if they know of that person's lack of competence it is forbidden for them to do so. An authorization is not something which can be repaid with money, so no-one may take money in return for it, nor a fee for it.

Among the *fatwas* of al-Ṣadr Mawhūb al-Jazarī, who is a companion of ours, is that he was asked whether a teacher who asks his student for something in return for an authorization should be taken to the ruler by the student and compelled to give the authorization. He replied: "(No, because) one should not be compelled to give an authorization, and one may not take a fee for it."

He was also asked about a man whom a teacher has authorized to teach recitation; if it becomes clear that the man is irreligious, and the teacher fears that he will be negligent, should he revoke his authorization?

He replied: "The authorization is not nullified by his being irreligious."

As for taking a fee for teaching, this is allowed, since in *Ṣaḥīḥ al-Bukhārī* (it is reported that the Prophet (peace and blessings be upon him) said): 'The most worthy thing for which you can take a fee is the Book of God.' However, it has been said that if it becomes encumbent upon him to teach, it is not allowed. This is the opinion of al-Ḥalīmī. And it also said that it is not allowed under any circumstance. This was the opinion of Abū Ḥanīfa, due to the ḥadīth reported by Abū Dāwūd, from ʿUbāda ibn al-Ṣāmit, that he taught a man from the Ahl al-Ṣuffa the Qurʾān, who then gave him a bow. So the Prophet (peace and blessings be upon him) said to him: 'If you are happy to have a collar of fire put around your neck on account of accepting this, then accept it.'

Those who permit it reply that doubt has been cast on the chain of this narration. And also that, since he undertook the teaching voluntarily, he did not deserve anything for it; then he was given something by way of recompense, so it was not permissible to take it. This is in contrast to one who forms an agreement prior to teaching.

In the *Bustān* of Abū al-Layth, (he states):

Teaching is of three types:

1 For the sake of God alone, and for this recompense is not sought.

2 For a fee.

3 Without stipulation, when if one is given something as a gift it can be accepted.

The first of these is rewarded by God, and this is the practice of the prophets. The second is a point of disagreement, but the more weighty opinion is that it is allowed. And there is scholarly consensus that the third is allowed, because the

Prophet (peace and blessings be upon him) used to teach mankind, and yet he also used to accept gifts.

A fourth point of benefit

Ibn Baṣḥān, if he repeated to a student some part of the Qurʾān that the latter had missed, and they did not know it, he would write it down, and then, when they had completed the whole Qurʾān and sought authorization from him, he would ask them about those places. If they knew them, he would give them authorization, and if not he would leave him to make another complete recitation.

Another point of benefit

The one who wants to perfect the recitations and the correct reciting of the letters should memorize a complete book by which he can recollect the differences of recitation and distinguish between what is an obligatory and an acceptable difference.

Another point of benefit

Ibn al-Ṣalāḥ states in one of his *fatwas*: Reciting the Qurʾān is a blessing which God has bestowed on mankind; it is narrated that the angels were not given this, and as a result they are eager to hear it from man.

Chapter thirty-five

REGARDING THE ETIQUETTES OF RECITING IT AND ITS RECITERS

A number of scholars have authored works on this subject. Among them is al-Nawawī in his *al-Tibyān*, in which he mentions – as well as in *Sharḥ al-Muhadhdhab* and in *al-Adhkār* – a number of etiquettes. I will summarize these here, will increase them in number many times over, and will classify them into separate issues for the sake of ease.

Issue

It is recommended that one should read and recite the Qurʾān much. The Almighty has said, in praise of the one who is in the habit of doing this: *Yatlūna āyāti Allāhi ānāʾi al-layl* (Who recite God's revelations during the night)[1] (Q3, 113).

It is related in the two books of *Ṣaḥīḥ* (of al-Bukhārī and Muslim), in a *ḥadīth* narrated by Ibn ʿUmar, (that the Prophet (peace and blessings be upon him) said): "Envy is forbidden except in two matters: a man to whom God has given the Qurʾān and he concerns himself with it by day and by night . . ."

Al-Tirmidhī relates, from a *ḥadīth* narrated by Ibn Masʿūd, (that the Prophet (peace and blessings be upon him) said): "Whoever recites a single letter from the Book of God, has earned thereby a good deed. And a good deed is rewarded tenfold."

He also relates, from a *ḥadīth* narrated by Abū Saʿīd (al-Khudrī), (that the Prophet (peace and blessings be upon him) said): "The Lord, glorified be He, says: Whoever is so preoccupied with the Qurʾān and with remembering Me that they cease asking Me, I will give them the best of that which is given to those who ask. The superiority of the Speech of God over the rest of speech is like the superiority of God over His creatures."

Muslim relates, from a *ḥadīth* narrated by Abū Umāmah, (that the Prophet (peace and blessings be upon him) said): "Recite the Qurʾān, for it will come on the Day of Resurrection as an intercessor for those who engage themselves with it."

Al-Bayhaqī relates, from a *ḥadīth* narrated by ʿĀʾisha, (that the Prophet (peace and blessings be upon him) said): "The house in which the Qurʾān is recited appears to the inhabitants of the heavens as the stars appear to the inhabitants of the earth."

He also relates, from a *ḥadīth* narrated by Anas, (that the Prophet (peace and blessings be upon him) said): "Illuminate your houses with prayer and the recitation of the Qurʾān."

He further relates, from a ḥadīth narrated by al-Nuʿmān ibn Bashīr, (that the Prophet (peace and blessings be upon him) said): "The best form of worship undertaken by my community is the recitation of the Qurʾān."

And again, from a *ḥadīth* narrated by Samūra ibn Jundab, (that the Prophet (peace and blessings be upon him) said): "Every host is pleased that people come to his banquet, and the banquet of God is the Qurʾān so do not desert it."

He also relates, in both *marfūʿ* and mawqūf form,[2] a *ḥadīth* narrated by ʿUbayda al-Makkī, (that the Prophet (peace and blessings be upon him) said): "O people of the Qurʾān! Do not hide the Qurʾān under your pillow, but recite it as it should be recited, by day and by night, and propagate it, and contemplate what it contains, so that you might prosper."

The early Muslims had certain habits as regards the quantity they would recite. The most that is narrated concerning the amount recited is that some would complete the Qurʾān eight times in a day and a night; four times by day, and four times by night. Second to this is that some would complete it four times in a day and a night; then three times, then twice, and then once.

However, ʿĀʾisha criticized all of this. Ibn Abī Dāwūd relates that Muslim ibn Mikhrāq declared: "I said to ʿĀʾisha: 'There are men who read the Qurʾān twice or three times in one night.' To which she replied: 'They read without reading. I used to stand in prayer with the Prophet (peace and blessings be upon him) the entire night, and he would recite al-Baqara, āl ʿImrān, and al-Nisāʿ.[3] And whenever he passed by a verse containing glad tidings, he would supplicate and ask (for that good); and whenever he passed by a verse evoking fear, he would supplicate and seek refuge with God.' "

Then there are those who completed the Qurʾān in two nights; and then those who completed it in three, which is good.

A number of people disliked it that the Qurʾān should be completed in any shorter time than that (that is, three nights), because of the *ḥadīth* related by Abū Dāwūd and al-Tirmidhī (who declares it a sound *ḥadīth*), narrated by Abdullāh ibn ʿUmar back to the Prophet (peace and blessings be upon him), who said: "The one who completes the Qurʾān in less than three (nights) does not understand (it)."

Ibn Abī Dāwūd and Saʿīd ibn Manṣūr relate from Ibn Masʿūd, who said: "Do not read the Qurʾān in less than three (nights)."

Abū ʿUbayd relates from Muʿādh ibn Jabal that the latter used to dislike the Qurʾān being recited in less than three (nights).

Aḥmad and Abū ʿUbayd relate from Saʿīd ibn al-Mundhir – who narrated only this one *ḥadīth* from the Prophet (peace and blessings be upon him) – who declared: "I said: 'O Messenger of God! Can I recite the Qurʾān in three (nights)?' He said: 'Yes, if you are able.' "

Then there are those who complete it in four, then in five, then in six, and then in seven (nights), which is the middle and best of courses to follow, and was the habit of the majority of the Companions and other early Muslims.

Al-Bukhārī and Muslim[4] relate from ʿAbdullāh ibn ʿAmr, who said: "The Messenger of God (peace and blessings be upon him) said to me: 'Complete reading the Qurʾān in a month.' I said: 'I have strength (to do more than that).' He said: 'Read it in ten (nights).' I said: 'I have strength (to do more than that).' He said: 'Read it in seven [nights], and do not do more than that.'"

Abū ʿUbayda and others relate via Wāsi ʿIbn Ḥibbān, from Qays ibn Abī Ṣaʿṣaʿa – who narrated only this one *ḥadīth* from the Prophet (peace and blessings be upon him) that he said: "(I asked): 'O Messenger of God, in how many (nights) should I complete the Qurʾān?' He said: 'In fifteen.' I said: 'I find myself to be stronger than that.' He said: 'Read it in a week.'"

Then there are those who complete it in eight (nights), then in ten, then in a month and then in two months.

Ibn Abī Dāwūd relates from Makḥūl, who said: "The strong Companions of the Messenger of God (peace and blessings be upon him) used to recite the Qurʾān in seven (nights); and some of them would do so in a month, and some in two months, and some would take longer than that."

Abū al-Layth states in al-Bustān: "One reading the Qurʾān should complete it at least twice each year, if they are not able to do so more than that."

Al-Ḥasan ibn Ziyād relates that Abū Ḥanīfa said: "Whoever recites the Qurʾān twice each year has done his duty, because the Prophet (peace and blessings be upon him) recited it to Gabriel twice in the year in which he passed away."

Others have said that it is disliked that one should take more than forty days to complete the Qurʾān without an excuse. This was stipulated by (Imām) Aḥmad, based on the fact that ʿAbdullāh ibn ʿUmar asked the Prophet (peace and blessings be upon him): "In how many (days) should we complete the Qurʾān?" He said: "In forty days." This *ḥadīth* is related by Abū Dāwūd.

Al-Nawawī states in *al-Adhkār*: "The preferred opinion is that this differs for each person. Thus, if subtleties and points of learning become apparent to someone through meticulous contemplation, that person should limit themselves to that amount which results in their perfect understanding of what they are reading. Likewise, whoever is busy with spreading knowledge or judging between disputants, or any other important matters of religion or public welfare, they should limit themselves to an amount whereby no harm, nor loss of perfection, is caused to that which he is observing. And if they are not from amongst those mentioned above, they should do as much as possible, without doing so much that they become bored, and without racing so much as to be babbling in their recitation."

Issue

Forgetting the Qurʾān is a major sin, as has been stated by al-Nawawī in *al-Rawḍa* and elsewhere, due to the *ḥadīth* related by Abū Dāwūd and others (in which the Prophet (peace and blessings be upon him) said): "The sins of my community were shown to me, and I did not see a sin greater than that of a man forgetting a chapter or a verse of the Qurʾān which he had been given."

He also related the *ḥadīth* (in which the Prophet (peace and blessings be upon him) said): "Whoever learns the Qurʾān and then forgets it, will meet God with missing limbs on the Day of Resurrection."

Al-Bukhārī and Muslim relate (the *ḥadīth*): "Keep reading the Qurʾān; by the one in whose hand is Muḥammad's soul, it is quicker to slip away than camels from their hobbles."

Issue

It is preferable to have *wuḍūʾ* when reciting the Qurʾān, since it is the best means of remembering God, and (the Prophet) (peace and blessings be upon him) disliked making remembrance of God except while in a state of purity, as has been established in the *ḥadīth* literature.

Imām al-Ḥaramayn stated: "It is not disliked for the one in a state of minor ritual impurity to recite the Qurʾān, since it is narrated authentically that the Prophet (peace and blessings be upon him) used to recite while in a state of minor ritual impurity. (Al-Nawawī) states in *Sharḥ al-Muhadhdhab*: "If one is reciting and is about to break wind, one should cease reciting until it has passed."

As for the one in a state of major ritual impurity and the menstruating woman, it is forbidden for them to recite, although it is allowed for them to look at a copy of the Qurʾān, and to read it in one's mind.

With regards to the one with an impure mouth, it is disliked for him to recite; and some hold that it is forbidden, just as it is forbidden to touch a copy of the Qurʾān with an impure hand.

Issue

It is recommended to recite in a clean place, and the best place is the mosque. Some scholars disliked that the Qurʾān be recited in the washroom and in the street. Al-Nawawī states: "Our school of law holds that it is not disliked in these two." He also states: "Al-Shaʿbī believed it to be disliked in unclean places and in the mill while it is turning." He adds: "This is in accordance with our school of law."

Issue

It is preferable that one should sit facing the *qibla*, displaying humility, in a state of calm and sobriety, and with bowed head.

Issue

It is commendable to use a toothstick, in order to honour the Qurʾān and purify (one's mouth). Ibn Mājah relates a *ḥadīth* with two chains of narration, one of which stops at ʿAlī, and another with a good chain from al-Bazzār that goes all the way back to the Prophet, (in which the Prophet (peace and blessings be upon him) states): "Your mouths are paths for the Qurʾān, so make them pleasant with the toothstick."

I would add here that if one stops one's recitation and then returns to it shortly thereafter, the desirability of saying the formula for seeking refuge indicates that one should also reapply the toothstick.

Issue

It is commendable to pronounce the formula for seeking refuge before reciting. God, Most High, states: *Fa idhā qaraʾta al-Qurʾāna fa istaaʿidh bi Allāhi min al-shayṭāni al-rajīm* (When you recite the Qurʾān, seek God's protection from the outcast Satan) (Q16, 98). Meaning if you wish to recite it.

Some scholars gave the opinion that one should seek refuge after reciting, taking the literal meaning of the verse [which is in the past tense];[5] and some that it is an obligation, due to the use of the imperative.

Al-Nawawī states: "So if one passes by a group of people, one should greet them and then continue reciting. And if one repeats the formula for seeking refuge, then that is good." He adds: "Its preferred form is: *Aʿūdhū bi-llāhi min al-shayt āni al-rajīm* (I seek refuge with God from the cursed Satan). And a group of the early Muslims used to add (after the name of God): *al-Samīʿi al-ʿAlīm* (the All Hearing, the All Knowing)."

And from Ḥamzah (the following variations to Aʿūdhū are related): *Astaʿīdhu* (I seek refuge), *Nastaʿīdhu* (We seek refuge), *Istaʿadhtu* (I have sought refuge), these being considered preferable in form by the author of al-Hidāya, from the Ḥanafī school, due to their conformity with the wording of the Qurʾān.

From Ḥumayd ibn Qays (is related the formula): *Aʿūdhu bi-llāhi al-Qādir min al-shayṭāni al-ghādir* (I seek refuge with God, the All Powerful, from the treacherous Satan). From Abū al-Simāl (is related the formula): *Aʿūdhu bi-llāhi al-Qawiyy min al-shayṭāni al-ghawiyy* (I seek refuge with God, the Strong, from the misguided Satan).

Some (have related the formula): *Aʿūdhu bi-llāhi al-ʿAẓīm min al-shayṭāni al-rajīm* (I seek refuge with God, the Great, from the cursed Satan).

Others (have related the formula): *Aʿūdhu bi-llāhi min al-shayṭāni al-rajīm, inna Allāha huwa al-Samīʿu al-ʿAlīm* (I seek refuge with God from the cursed Satan. Truly God is the All Hearing the All Knowing).

There are also other formulas. Al-Ḥulwānī states in his *Jāmiʿ*: "There is no particular constraint to the formula for seeking refuge; whoever wishes can extend it, and whoever wishes can shorten it."

Ibn al-Jazarī states in *al-Nashr*: "The preferred opinion of the scholars of recitation is that it should be read aloud. It is also said that it should be said quietly in all circumstances, and again [that it should be said quietly when reciting] anything other than *sūrah al-Fātiḥa*."[6] He adds: "They made their preference of saying it aloud universal. However, Abū Shāma placed a very important restriction upon it: that (the Reciter) be in the presence of someone who can hear him." He continues: "This is because reciting the formula of seeking refuge aloud is a sign (that one is going) to recite, just as saying aloud the talbiya and the takbīrs of Eid[7] (are signs). One of the benefits of doing so is that the one listening can pay attention to the recitation right from the start, without missing anything. Yet if the formula of seeking refuge was said quietly, the one listening would only know after having missed some of the recitation. This is the difference between reciting for the prayer and not."

He also states: "Later scholars have differed about what is meant by saying it quietly. Most hold the opinion that what is intended is whispering it, and that one must pronounce it and recite it such that one can hear it oneself. Another opinion is that it means to conceal it, remembering it in one's heart without pronouncing it."

He adds: "If one's recitation is interrupted by turning away from it or by saying something else – even if it be merely replying to a greeting – one should repeat the formula of seeking refuge; but if one says something related to the recitation, one does not need to do so." He continues: "Is it a collective or an individual duty; such that if a group of people recite together, is it sufficient for just one of them to pronounce the formula – as is the case with pronouncing the *basmala*[8] over food – or not? I can find no specific text about this, yet the second would appear to be the correct opinion, since what is intended is the safeguarding of the reciter, and his taking refuge with God from the evil of Satan; thus, one person's saying of the formula would not be sufficient for another."

Issue

One should take care to recite the basmala at the beginning of every *sūrah*, except *sūrah* Barā'a,[9] since most scholars are of the opinion that it is an actual verse.

Thus if one abandons it, in the view of the majority of scholars, they will have left out a part of the entire Qurʾān.

And if one starts reciting at some point within the *sūrah*, it is also preferred for them to read the *basmala*. This was stipulated by al-Shāfiʿī, as has been reported by al-ʿIbādī. The Reciters state that this is imperative when reciting verses such as: *Ilayhi yuraddu ʿilmu al-sāʿah* (Knowledge of the hour belongs solely to Him) (Q41, 47), and *Wa huwa alladhī anshaʾa jannāt* (It is He who produces gardens) (Q6, 141) as it is distasteful to recite it after the formula for seeking refuge, due to the possible delusion that the pronoun refers back to Satan (rather than to God).

Ibn al-Jazarī states: "As for beginning with verses in the middle of *sūrah Barāʿa*, there are few who object (to reciting the *basmala* when beginning with them), while Abū al-Ḥasan al-Sakhāwī stresses that it should be recited, although al-Jaʿbarī opposes him in this."

Issue

Recitation of the Qurʾān does not require an intention as do other forms of remembrance of God, unless one makes a vow to read it outside the prayer. In this case, the intention of doing it in fulfilment of the vow, or as an obligation, is required. This is so even if, in one's vow, one has specified the time that one will fulfil it. If one leaves the intention, the recitation is not valid. This was stipulated by al-Qamwalī in al-Jawāhir.

Issue

It is commendable to recite the Qurʾān with *tartīl* (in a measured way). God, Most High, states: *Wa rattil al-Qurʾāna tartīlā* (Recite the Qurʾān slowly and distinctly) (Q73, 4).

Abū Dāwūd and others relate from Umm Salamah that she described the recitation of the Prophet (peace and blessings be upon him) as: "Having distinct pronunciation; letter by letter."

Al-Bukhārī relates from Anas that he was asked about the recitation of the Messenger of God (peace and blessings be upon him), and he said: "It was protracted." Then he recited *Bismi Allāhi al-Raḥmānī al-Raḥīm* (Q1, 1), and he lengthened the long vowels in *Allāh*, and in *al-Raḥmān* and in *al-Raḥīm*.

In the two books of *Ṣaḥīḥ* (of al-Bukhārī and Muslim, it is related) from Ibn Masʿūd that a man said to him: "I recite all the mufaṣṣal *sūrahs*[10] in a single *rakʿa*." He replied: "Reciting hurriedly, as you do with poetry. There are indeed people who recite the Qurʾān, but it does not get further than their collarbones. However, if it reaches the heart, and settles therein, then it benefits."

Regarding those who have memorized the Qurʾān, al-Ājurrī relates from Ibn Masʿūd, that the latter said: "Do not throw it away as one would throw away inferior dates, and do not recite hurriedly as you do with poetry. Pause at its wonders, and move hearts with it, and do not let your concern be the end of the *sūrah*."

He also related in a *ḥadīth* narrated from Ibn ʿUmar (that the Prophet (peace and blessings be upon him) said): "It will be said to the one who recited the Qurʾān: 'Read, and ascend in degrees. And recite with *tartīl* as you did in the world. For your rank is (indicated) by the last verse that you recited.' "

(Al-Nawawī) states in *Sharḥ al-Muhadhdhab*: "The scholars are in agreement about the abhorrence of reciting excessively fast."

(The scholars) also state that reciting one thirtieth portion of the Qurʾān with *tartīl* is preferable to reciting twice that amount in the same length of time without *tartīl*.

They further mention that the preference of reciting with *tartīl* is because it enables contemplation, shows greater respect and reverence, and has a deeper effect on the heart. As a result, it is preferable for the non-Arab, who does not understand its meaning.

(Ibn al-Jazarī states) in *al-Nashr*: "It is a point of dispute as to whether it is better to recite with *tartīl* and only a little, or recite quickly and hence a lot. Regarding this, one scholar has spoken well in saying: 'The rewards gained for reciting with *tartīl* are greater in degree, and the rewards gained for reciting a lot are greater in number, since each letter recited is counted as ten good deeds.' "

Al-Zarkashī states in *al-Burhān*: "Perfection of *tartīl* is to pronounce the words in a grand manner and to make the letters distinct, and not to merge one letter with another. And it is also said that this is its lowest level, and that perfection of it is to recite according to the circumstance: so that if one recites a passage containing a threat, one does so in a threatening manner, and if one recites a passage glorifying God, one does so in a glorifying manner.

Issue

It is commendable to recite with contemplation and comprehension, as this is the ultimate aim and the most important requirement (when reading the Qurʾān), and it is in this way that hearts are opened and obtain enlightenment. God, Most High, states: *Kitābun anzalnāhu ilayka mubārakun li yaddabbarū āyātih* (This is a blessed Scripture which We sent down to you (Muḥammad), for people to think about its messages) (Q38, 29).

He also states: *A fa lā yatadabbarūna al-Qurʾān* (Will they not think about this Qurʾān) (Q4, 82). The way of doing this is to occupy one's mind with contemplating the meaning of that which one is pronouncing, so that one knows the meaning of every verse, and ponders the commands and prohibitions, and one believes in accepting these. So, if one recites something in which one has previously fallen short, one apologizes and seeks forgiveness; and if one recites a verse relating to mercy, one rejoices and requests it; or a verse relating to punishment, one is fearful and seeks refuge from it; or relating to God being unlike His creation, one declares Him so, and exalts Him; or relating to calling upon God, one beseeches and asks Him.

Muslim relates from Ḥudhayfa, who said: "I prayed with the Prophet (peace and blessings be upon him) one night, and he began reciting *sūrah al-Baqara* (Chapter 2), then *sūrah al-Nisāʿ* (Chapter 4), which he completed, and then *sūrah āl ʿImrān*, which he also completed, reciting at a slow pace. If he passed by a verse glorifying God, he would glorify Him, and if he passed by one in which God is besought, he would beseech Him, and if he passed by one in which God is sought refuge with, he would seek refuge with Him."

Abū Dāwūd, al-Nisāʾī, and others relate from ʿAwf ibn Mālik, who said: "I stood in prayer with the Prophet (peace and blessings be upon him) one night, and he recited *sūrah al-Baqara*; whenever he passed by a verse mentioning mercy he stopped and asked for it, and whenever he passed by a verse mentioning punishment he stopped and sought refuge from it."

Abū Dāwūd and al-Tirmidhī both relate the following *ḥadīth*: "Whoever recites *Wa al-tīni wa al-zaytūn* (Chapter 95) until its end, then let them say: '*Balā, wa ana ʿalā dhālika min al-shāhidīn*' ('Yes indeed! And I am one of those who testify to that').[11] And whoever recites *Lā uqsimu bi-yawmi al-qiyāma* (Chapter 75) until its end: '*A laysa Dhālika bi-qādirin ʿalā an yuḥyiya al-mawtā*' ('Is That not able to bring the dead to life?'), then let them say: 'Balā' ('Yes indeed!'). And whoever recites *Wa al-Mursalāt* (Chapter 77), until they reach: '*Fa bi-ayyi ḥadīthin baʿdahu yuʾminūn*' ('Then in which speech thereafter will they believe?'), then let them say: '*Āmannā bi-Allāh*' ('We believe in God')."

Aḥmad and Abū Dāwūd relate from Ibn ʿAbbās, that the Prophet (peace and blessings be upon him), whenever he recited: "*Sabbiḥi isma Rabbika al-Aʿlā*" ("Glorify the name of your Lord, the Most High") (Q87, 1), would say: *Subḥāna Rabbiya al-Aʿlā* ("Glory be to my Lord, the Most High").

Al-Tirmidhī and al-Ḥākim relate from Jābir, who said: "The Messenger of God (peace and blessings be upon him) came out to his Companions, and recited to them *sūrah al-Raḥmān* (Chapter 55) from beginning to end. They remained quiet, and so he told them: 'I recited it to the Jinn and they were better in response than you. Whenever I came to God's saying: "*Fa bi-ayyi ālāʾi Rabbikumā tukadhdhibān*" ("Then which of the favours of your Lord do you deny?"), they replied: "*Wa lā bi-shayʾin min niʿamika Rabbanā nukadhdhib, fa laka al-ḥamd.*" ("None of Your favours, O Lord, do we deny, and to You is all praise").'"

Ibn Marduwayh, al-Daylamī, Ibn Abī al-Dunyā in al-Duʿā, and others relate, with a very weak chain of narration, from Jābir, that the Prophet (peace and blessings be upon him) recited: *Wa idhā saʾalaka ʿibādī ʿannī fa innī qarībun . . .* ([Prophet], if My servants ask you about Me, I am near) (Q2, 186) until the end of the verse, and then said: "O God, You have ordered us to supplicate, and You have taken it upon Yourself to respond (to our supplication). I am at Your service, O God, I am at Your service. I am at Your service, You have no partner, I am at Your service. Praise and blessings belong to You, as does sovereignty. You have no partner. I bear witness that You are Unique, One, Eternal; You beget not, neither were You begotten; and there is nothing like unto You. And I bear witness that Your promise is true, and that the meeting with You is true, and that Paradise is true, and that hellfire is true, and that the Hour is coming, without doubt, and that You will raise up those who are in the graves."

Abū Dāwūd and others relate from Wāʾil ibn Ḥujr, (who said): "I heard the Prophet (peace and blessings be upon him) recite: *Wa lā al-ḍāllīn* (Q1, 7)", and he said: '*Āmīn*' ('Amen'), lengthening it with his voice."

Al-Ṭabarānī relates the same *ḥadīth*, with the wording: "He said: '*Āmīn*' three times." And al-Bayhaqī relates it with the wording: "He said: '*Rabbi ighfir lī. Āmīn*' ('O Lord, forgive me, Amen')."

Abū ʿUbayd relates, from Abū Maysara, that Gabriel taught the Messenger of God (peace and blessings be upon him) to say "Āmīn" at the end of *sūrah al-Baqara*.

He also relates, from Muʿādh ibn Jabal, that when he would complete *sūrah al-Baqara*, he would say: "*Āmīn*."

Al-Nawawī states: "It is good manners, when one recites a verse such as: *Wa qālati al-yahūdu ʿuzayrun ibnu Allāh* (The Jews said, 'Ezra is the son of God') (Q9, 30), or: *Wa qālati al-yahūdu yaddu Allāhi maghlūla* (The Jews have said, 'God is tight-fisted') (Q5, 64), to lower one's voice. This is what al-Nakhaʿī used to do."

Issue

There is no harm in repeating a verse one or more times. Al-Nisāʾi and others relate, from Abū Dharr, that the Prophet (peace and blessings be upon him) stood in prayer, reciting a verse, repeating it until morning came; this being the verse beginning: *In tuʿadhdhibhum fa innahum ʿibāduk* . . . (If You punish them, they are Your servants) (Q5, 118).

Issue

It is preferable to cry when reciting the Qurʾān, and for one who is unable to cry, then to attempt to do so. Sadness and humility are also desirable. God, Most High, says: *Wa yakhirrūna li al-adhqāni yabkūn* (They fall down on their faces, weeping) (Q17, 109).

In the two *Ṣaḥīḥ* books (of al-Bukhārī and Muslim), in the *ḥadīth* regarding Ibn Masʿūd's reciting to the Prophet (peace and blessings be upon him), it is mentioned: ". . . and his eyes were shedding tears".

Al-Bayhaqī relates in *al-Shuʿab* from Saʿd ibn Mālik that the Prophet (peace and blessings be upon him) said: "This Qurʾān came down with sadness and sorrow. So if you recite it, then cry, and if you cannot cry then try to cry."

He also relates from ʿAbd al-Mālik ibn ʿUmayr, that he was told that the Prophet (peace and blessings be upon him) said: "I am going to recite to you a *sūrah*, and whoever cries will have gained Paradise. So if you cannot cry, then try to cry."

In the Musnad of Abū Yaʿlā, is mentioned the *ḥadīth*: "Recite the Qurʾān with sadness, as it came down with sadness."

Al-Ṭabarānī mentions the *ḥadīth*: "The best Reciter is the one who feels sad when they recite the Qurʾān."

Al-Nawawī states in *Sharḥ al-Muhadhdhab*: "The way to make oneself cry is to ponder the warnings and grave threats which one is reading, and also the covenants, and then to think about one's shortcomings regarding them. If one does not feel grief and cry because of this, then one should cry at the lack of one's grief, since this is a disaster."

Issue

It is commendable to beautify one's voice when reciting, based on the *ḥadīth* related by Ibn Ḥibbān and others: "Embellish the Qurʾān with your voices." And al-Dārimī gives it with the wording: "Beautify the Qurʾān with your voices, because the beautiful voice increases the Qurʾān in beauty."

Al-Bazzār and others relate the *ḥadīth*: "Loveliness of voice is the adornment of the Qurʾān."

Regarding this there are numerous sound *ḥadīth*. Hence if one does not have a beautiful voice, one should beautify it as much as possible, yet without distorting (his recitation).

As for reciting with melodies, al-Shāfiʿī stated in *al-Mukhtaṣar* that it was unobjectionable, or – as narrated by al-Rabīʿ al-Jīzī – that it was disliked.

Al-Rāfiʿī states: "The majority of scholars do not differ about this. Rather what is disliked is going to excess in extending the long vowels, and in lengthening the short vowels until they become long vowels, or in assimilating letters in the wrong place. If it does not reach to this extent, then it is not disliked."

Al-Rāfiʿī states in his additional comments on *al-Rawḍa*: "The correct position is that exaggerating in the way mentioned is forbidden, for which the reciter is in great error and the listener is sinful due to having deviated from the proper course." He also states: "This is what al-Shāfiʿī meant by it being disliked."

In this regard, I would add the *ḥadīth*: "Recite the Qur'ān according to the melodies and voices of the Arabs, and beware of the melodies of the people of the two Books and the people of sin. There will come people who will chant the Qurʾān with a quavering voice as if singing, or in the style of monks. It will not pass their throats. Their hearts are infected, as are the hearts of those who admire them." This *ḥadīth* was related by al-Ṭabarānī and al-Bayhaqī.

Al-Nawawī states: "It is preferable to request recitation from one with a beautiful voice and to listen attentively to it, due to the sound *ḥadīth* (in this regard). There is also no harm in group recitation; nor in group reciting in rotation, meaning that part of the group recite one portion, and then another part recite another."

Issue

It is preferable to recite in a grand manner, in accordance with the *ḥadīth* related by al-Ḥākim: "The Qurʾān descended with grandeur." Al-Ḥalīmī states: "The meaning of this is that one recites it in a man's voice, not making the voice submissive, like the speech of women." He adds: "Imāla,[12] which is preferred by some of the scholars of recitation, is not included in the stated dislike. It is possible that the Qurʾān was revealed with grandeur, and yet nevertheless it was made permissible to perform imāla when appropriate."

Issue

There are *ḥadīths* related, stipulating the preferability of raising one's voice when reciting, and other *ḥadīths* that specify that one should remain quiet, and lower one's voice. Among the first, there is the *ḥadīth* related in the works of Bukhārī and Muslim: "Allāh does not listen to anything as He does to a prophet with a beautiful voice chanting the Qurʾān aloud."

Of the second type there is the *ḥadīth*, related by Abū Dāwūd, al-Tirmidhī, and *al-Nasāʾī*: "The one who recites the Qurʾān aloud is like the one who gives charity openly, and the one who recites the Qurʾān secretly is like the one who gives charity secretly."

Al-Nawawī states: "One can harmonize between these two types of *ḥadīth* by the fact that reciting secretly is preferable when one fears hypocrisy, or if one would disturb people praying or sleeping; and reciting aloud is preferable otherwise, since it requires more effort and its benefits the listeners as well. Furthermore, it stirs the reciter's heart, increases one's intention to reflect, directs one's hearing towards what is being recited, repels sleep, and is enlivening."

Evidence for this understanding can be found in the sound *ḥadīth* related by Abū Dāwūd from Abū Saʿīd, that: "The Messenger of God (peace and blessings be upon him) secluded himself in the mosque, and heard them reciting aloud, so he drew back his curtain and said: 'You are all communing with your Lord, so do not disturb one another, and do not raise your voices above one another when reciting.' "

Some have said: "It is preferable to read partly aloud and partly in secret, since the one reciting secretly may become bored, and thus find relief in reciting aloud; and the one reciting aloud may become weary, and thus find relief in reciting secretly."

Issue

Reading from a written copy of the Qurʾān is preferable to reciting from one's memory, because looking at the Qurʾān is a required form of worship. Al-Nawawī states: "This is what has been stated by those from our school and by the early

Muslims, and I find no dispute regarding this." He adds: "If it is stated that this differs according to the individual – so that reading from a copy is preferable for the one whose level of humility and contemplation is equal whether reading from a copy or reciting from memory, and reciting from memory is preferable for the one for whom this causes greater humility and contemplation – then this is a good opinion."

I would add that evidence for the desirability of reading from a copy of the Qurʾān can be found in the *ḥadīth* related by al-Ṭabarānī, and by al-Bayhaqī in his *al-Shuʿab*, coming from Aws al-Thaqafī that the Prophet (peace and blessings be upon him) said: "A man's recitation when not looking at a copy of the Qurʾān is worth a thousand ranks of reward, and his recitation from a copy is doubled, at two thousand ranks of reward."

Abū ʿUbayd relates with a weak chain of narration: "The superiority of reciting the Qurʾān by sight over the one who recites it from memory is like the superiority of the obligatory form of worship over the supererogatory."

Al-Bayhaqī relates from Ibn Masʿūd that the Prophet (peace and blessings be upon him) said: "Whoever is happy to love God and his Messenger, let him read from a written copy of the Qurʾān." Al-Bayhaqī states: "This *ḥadīth* is rejected."

He also relates, with a good chain of narration ending at the Companion, "Keep looking at the text of the Qurʾān."

Al-Zarkashī, in *al-Burhān*, reports what al-Nawawī discusses as one opinion, and reports along with it a further opinion, that reciting from memory is better no matter what; Ibn ʿAbd al-Salām chose this opinion, because it causes a level of contemplation not obtained from reading from the written text.

Issue

(Al-Nawawī) states in al-Tibyān: "If the reciter falters and does not know what follows and so asks someone else, then he should be guided by what has been reported from Ibn Masʿūd, al-Nakhaʿī, and Bashīr ibn Abū Masʿūd, who stated: 'If one of you asks their brother about a verse, then recite what comes before it and then fall silent. And do not say: "How is such and such", as this will confuse him.'"

Ibn al-Mujāhid states: "If a reciter has doubt about a letter, is it a *tāʾ* or a *yāʾ*, then they should recite it as a *yāʾ*, because the Qurʾān follows the masculine gender. And if one doubts as to whether a letter carries a *hamza* or not, one should recite it without the *hamza*. And if one doubts as to whether a letter is joined or cut, one should recite it joined. And if one doubts as to whether a letter should be lengthened or shortened, one should recite it shortened. And if one doubts as to whether a letter carries a short *a* vowel, or a short *i* vowel, one should recite it as a short *a* vowel, since the first is not ungrammatical in one place, and the second is sometimes ungrammatical.

ʿAbd al-Razzāq relates that Ibn Masʿūd stated: "If you dispute about whether a letter is *ayāʾ* or *atāʾ*, make it *ayāʾ*. Make the Qur'ān masculine." From this

Thaʿlab understood that whatever can take the masculine or feminine form, giving it the masculine form is better. This is refuted by the fact that it is not permissible to make masculine that which is a "non-real" feminine (that is, one which is only grammatically, but not literally, feminine),[13] due to the prevalence of this in the Qur'ān in the feminine form, such as: *al-nāru waʿadahā Allāh* (Q22, 72); *Iltaffati al-sāqu bi al-sāq* (Q75, 29); *Qālat lahum rusuluhum* (Q14, 11). And if it is prohibited to do so with the "non-real" feminine, then it is even more so the case with the "real" feminine. Scholars have stated that it is not correct that that which can be treated as both masculine and feminine, comes mainly in the masculine; thus, for example, Allāh, Most High, states *Wa al-nakhla bāsiqā* (Q50, 10) and *Aʿjāzu nakhlin khāwiya* (Q69, 7), making it feminine even though the masculine is admissible, as in *Aʿjāzu nakhlin munqaʿir* (Q54, 20); and *Min al-shajari al-akhḍar* (Q36, 80).

Scholars state: "What is intended by the word 'Dhakkirū'[14] is not admonishing and calling people, as in the words of the Most High: *Fa dhakkir bi al-Qur'ān* (Q50, 45) but just with the preposition *bi* being omitted; what is intended is 'Make people remember the Qur'ān' – that is, induce them to memorize it so that they do not forget it."

I would add that the beginning of the above narration negates this understanding.

Al-Wāḥidī states: "It is as Thaʿlab has stated, and what is intended thereby is that if the wording allows both the masculine and feminine form, and adopting the masculine form does not require one to go against the text of the Qurʾān, then do so, e.g. *Wa lā yuqbalu minhā shafāʿa* (Q2, 48)." He adds: "Evidence for this opinion can be seen from the fact that the students of ʿAbdullāh from among the reciters of *al-Kūfa*, such as Ḥamza and al-Kisāʾī, followed this rule, and thus read anything of this type in the masculine form, for example the verse: *Yawma tashhadu ʿalayhim alsinatuhum* (Q24, 24); and this is not a true feminine."

Issue

It is disliked to interrupt one's recitation in order to speak to someone. Al-Ḥalīmī states: "This is because no one else's speech should be preferred to the Speech of Allāh."

Al-Bayhaqī strengthens this with the *ḥadīth* related by al-Bukhārī and Muslim: "When Ibn ʿUmar used to recite the Qur'ān, he would not speak until he had finished."

It is also disliked to laugh, play with anything, or look at that which distracts one's attention.

Issue

It is not allowed to recite the Qurʾān in a foreign language under any circumstance; whether one is proficient in Arabic or not; during prayer or out of it. Although, it is reported from Abū Ḥanīfa that it is allowed in any cirmcumstance, and from Abū Yūsuf and Muḥammad (the two companions of Abū Ḥanīfa) that it is allowed for the one who is not proficient in Arabic. However, in the commentary on al-Bazdawī it is stated that Abū Ḥanīfa withdrew this opinion. The reason for the prohibition is that this removes its intended inimitability.

It is related from al-Qaffāl, of the Shāfiʿī madhhab: "Reciting in Persian is unthinkable." It was said to him: "In that case no one can elucidate the Qur'ān." He replied: "Not so, because in this case it is allowed to give some of what God intends and be incapable of giving some. However, if one wants to recite in Persian, it is not possible to give all that is intended by God, Most High, because translation is changing one wording for another which can substitute it; this is not possible, while it is possible with exegesis."

Issue

It is not allowed to recite with a non-canonical (*shādhdh*) recitation of the Qurʾān. Ibn ʿAbd al-Barr reports that there is consensus about this, however Mawhūb al-Jazarī mentions that it is allowed outside the prayer, by analogy with narrating *ḥadīth* by their meaning.

Issue

It is preferable to recite the Qur'ān sequentially. (Al-Nawawī) states in *Sharḥ al-Muhadhdhab*: "This is because there is wisdom behind its order, so one should not leave it except where stated by the law, such as reciting *sūrah al-Sajda* (Chapter 32) and *sūrah al-Insān* (Chapter 76) in the morning prayer on Friday. If one breaks up the *sūrahs* or recites them contrary to their order it is allowable, although one has left that which is preferable." He adds: "As for reciting *sūrahs* from back to front, it is agreed that this is prohibited, because it removes some of its inimitability and the wisdom behind its order."

I would add that there is a narration regarding this point, wherein al-Ṭabarānī relates, with a good (*jayyid*) chain of narration, from Ibn Masʿūd that he was asked about a man who recites the verses of the Qur'ān in reverse order, and he said: "Such a man has a twisted heart."

* * *

I would add that there is a narration regarding this point, wherein al-Ṭabarānī relates, with a good (*jayyid*) chain of narration, from Ibn Masʿud that he was asked about a man who recites the verses of the Qurʾān in reverse order, and he said: "Such a man has a twisted heart."

* * *

As for mixing one *sūrah* with another, al-Ḥalīmī considers abandoning this practice is erring in propriety. When Abū ʿUbayd, on the authority of Saʿid ibn al-Musayyat, narrated that the Emissary of God (peace and blessings be upon him) passed by Bilāl when the latter was reciting from one *sūrah* and then from another *sūrah*, he said: "O Bilāl, I passed by you when you were reciting first this *sūrah* and then another one." (Bilāl) answered: "I combine the good with the good." (The Prophet) then said: "Read each *sūrah* in its entirety or to its end." This tradition is related to the Prophet (peace and blessings be upon him), (*mursal*), yet *ṣaḥīḥ* (sound), according to Abū Dawud on the indirect and sole authority of Abū Hurayra.

Abū ʿUbayd related it with a different chain of transmitters, viz. from ʿUmar, the client of Ghafra: The Prophet (peace and blessings be upon him) said to Bilāl: "Whenever you start a *sūrah*, finish it."

(Abū ʿUbayd also) said: "Muʿadh related to us on the authority of Ibn ʿAwn: 'I asked Ibn Sīrīn about a man who recites two verses, and then leaves them and begins reciting somewhere else. He answered: "Beware lest any one of you sin, because it is a grave sin he does unawares."'"

It was related on the authority of Ibn Masʿud, who said: "Whenever you begin (reciting) a *sūrah*, and you want to change your recitation to a different *sūrah*, you recite: 'Say: "He is Allāh, the One,'" (Q112, 1), and when you do so, continue reciting to the end of that *sūrah*."

It was related on the authority of Ibn Abī al-Hudhayl who said: "They used to dislike reciting a verse and leave out parts of it."

Abū ʿUbayd said: "The situation with us is that our reciters dislike reciting verses from different places, as the Emissary of God (peace and blessings be upon him) enjoined Bilāl, and which Ibn Sīrīn also disapproved of.

"Concerning the narration of ʿAbd Allāh according to my understanding is that one begins one *sūrah*, intending to complete it, but then turns to recite from another one that appears to him. And whoever begins reciting with the intent of passing from verse to verse, and abandons the proper order of the verses of the Qurʾān – it is only out of ignorance he does this, because, had God wanted, He would have revealed them in that order."

The Qadi Abū Bakr reported the consensus that reciting one verse from one *sūrah* and then a verse from another *sūrah* was not allowable.

Al-Bayhaqī said: "The best argument against this practice is to say that the arrangement of the Book of Allāh is taken from the Prophet (peace and blessings be upon him); he took it from Gabriel. The right thing for a reciter is to recite it in its proper revealed order." As Ibn Sīrīn said: "God's arrangement is better than yours."

Question

Al-Ḥalīmī said: "The rule is to recite every letter fixed by a reciter properly to achieve reciting the entirety of the Qurʾān."

Ibn al-Ṣalāh and al-Nawawī said: "Whenever a reciter follows a particular recitation of a leading reciter, he must continue in that recitation as long as the words are connected. When the connection is broken, then he can begin a different recitation. However it is better that he remains in the first recitation in this session."

In addition to the two authorities above, others demanded absolute prohibition of changing from one recitation to another.

Ibn al-Jazarī said: "It is correct to say that if one recitation is based on another, then this is prohibited with a *haram* prohibition, as if reciting 'Ādam received the names from his Lord' (Q2, 37), with both words 'Ādam' and 'words' (*kalimat*) pronounced in the nominative case (with final vowel *-u*) or in the accusative case (with final vowels *-a* and the second with *-i*), and taking the nominative case of 'Ādam' from (Reciters) other than Ibn Kathir, and the nominative case of 'words' from (Ibn Kathir's) reading. And such is unallowable in the Arabic language and in practice."

If it is not like that then one distinguishes between the place of the narration and others. And if it were by way of narration (*riwaya*), it would also be prohibited, because it is mendacious adulteration; but if is by way of recitation (*tilawa*), it is permissible.

Question

When listening to the recitation of the Qur'ān the rule is to desist from gabbing or conversing at the time of the recitation. Allāh said:

God said: "When the Qur'ān is recited, listen to it and be silent, so that you may receive mercy" (Q7, 204).

Question

It is a rule to prostrate at the recitation of the Prostration Verses. These are fourteen found in *sūrahs The Heights*, *The Thunder*, *The Bees*, *The Night Journey* and *Maryam*; there are two prostrations each in the *sūrahs* of *The Pilgrimage*, *The Discernment* (*al-Furqan*), *The Ants*, *Alīf Lam Mim Tanzil*, *Fussilat*, *The Star*, *Idha al-Sama Inshaqqat*, and *Iqra BiSmi Rabbika*. As for *Surat Sad*, prostration is recommended, but not binding – that is, it is not a major matter. Some (authorities) added (to these) the final verses of *Surat al-Hijr*; Ibn al-Faras narrated this to us in his *Aḥkām*.

Question

Al-Nawawī said: "The most excellent time chosen for prayer is the night, and it is best to do so in the latter half of the night. The time between the Maghrib prayer and the ʿIsha prayer is commended for recitation; the best part of the day for recitation is the morning. Recitation at other times is not unseemly in regard to time, concerning what Ibn Abī Dawud narrated on the authority of Muʿadh ibn Rafaʿa, on the authority of the elders who disliked recitation after the al-ʿAsr prayer, alleging that this is the practice of *Yahud* (the Jews), is unacceptable, and is baseless."

Among the best of days (for recitation) is the Day of ʿArafah, then Friday, then Monday, and then Thursday; also during the last ten days of Ramaḍān, and the first day of Dhu al-Hijja. Of the months it is Ramaḍān.

Preferred for the beginning of recitation is Friday night, and for concluding is Thursday. Ibn Abī Dawud narrated this on the authority of ʿUthman ibn ʿAffan who used to practise this.

The most preferable time for concluding is the beginning of the day or the beginning of the night, as al-Dārami narrated on the authority of Saʿd ibn Abī Waqqaṣ with a sound chain of transmission: "When the conclusion of the Qurʾān recitation corresponds to the first part of the night, the angels pray along until morning; and if it corresponds to the beginning of the day, then the angels pray along until the evening."

(Al-Ghazālī) said in his *Ihyaʾ* that when the conclusion is at the beginning of the day it is done with the two *rakʿas* (prostrations) of the al-Fajr prayer, and if it is at the beginning of the night, it is done customarily with the two *rakʿas* of the al-Maghrib prayer.

On the authority of Ibn al-Mubārak: in the winter it is preferable to conclude recitation at the beginning of the night; in summer, at the beginning of the day.

Question

Ibn Abī Dawud, on the authority of the consensus of the second generation of Muslims, says that it is a tradition to fast on the day of conclusion. Al-Ṭabarānī related, on the authority of Anas, that one's family and friends should be present. Whenever he would conclude the Qurʾān recitation he would gather his family together and prayed.

Ibn Abī Dawud narrated, on the authority of al-Hakam ibn ʿUtayba, who said: "Mujāhid and Ibn Abī Amama (other edition: Lubaba) who both said: 'We have invited you to come because we are about to complete the recitation of the Qurʾān, as prayer is answerable at that time.'" He also narrated, on the authority of Mujāhid, who said: "They used to gather together for prayer at the conclusion of reciting the Qurʾān for at that time mercy descends."

Question

Saying *takbīr* (veneration of God) "Allāh is great" is desirable from the *sūrah al-Duha* (the Dawn) to the end of the Qurʾān – such is the recitation of the Meccans.

In his Shuʿab, al-Bayhaqī related, as did Ibn Khuzayma by way of Ibn Abī Bazza, who said: "I heard ʿIkrama ibn Sulayman say: 'I recited to Ismaʿil ibn ʿAbdulla the Meccan, and when I reached *sūrah al-Duha*, he said: "Say the *takbīr* 'God is great' whenever you conclude because I recited before ʿAbdullah ibn Kathir who commanded me to do so, saying: 'I recited to Mujāhid, and he commanded me to do so.' " ' "

Mujāhid related that he recited before Ibn ʿAbbās, who ordered him to do likewise.

Ibn ʿAbbās related that he recited before Ubayy ibn Kaʿb, who also commanded him to do likewise. We also report it without a chain of transmitters.

Al-Bayhaqī reported the same in a different way from Ibn Bazza as *marfuʿ*.

In his *Mustadrak*, al-Hakim related (this Tradition) in the same way as *marfuʿ* regarding it as *ṣaḥīḥ* (sound). Al-Bāzzi narrated it in many ways.

Musa ibn Harun related: "Al-Bāzzi told me: 'Muḥammad ibn Idris al-Shāfiʿī told me: "If you refrain from reciting the *takbīr* 'God is great' you have lost one of your Prophet's *sunnas* (practices)." ' "

Al-Hāfiẓ ʿImad al-Dīn ibn Kathir said: "The *ḥadīth* (Traditions) is thus confirmed as *ṣaḥīḥ* (sound)."

Abū al-ʿAlaʾ al-Hamdani narrated, on the authority of al-Bāzzi that the basis for this is that at an interruption in the Revelation to the Prophet (peace and blessings be upon him) the polytheists said: "Muḥammad's Lord had forsaken him." The Prophet (peace and blessings be upon him) recited the *takbīr* "God is great" when the *sūrah al-Duha* was revealed. Ibn Kathir said: "This narrative was related with a chain of transmission which was not examined either for soundness or weakness."

Al-Ḥalīmī said: "The point in reciting the *takbīr* 'God is great' during recitation is similar to reciting it during the Ramaḍān fast: after completion of a portion of fasting one recites it, and after completing of the recitation of the said *sūrahs* one does so also."

He added: "Its characterization is that one pauses at the completion of each *sūrah*, and recites the formula 'God is great.' "

One of our fellow commentators, Sulaym al-Rāzī said likewise: "One recites the *takbīr* 'God is great' once between every two *sūrahs*, without connecting the *takbīr* to the end of the *sūrah*; one separates between *sūrahs* with a silent pause." He added: "Those among the Reciters who do not pronounce the *takbīr* 'God is great' claim that this practice is harmful because it is an otiose addition to the text of the Qurʾān, and in time this practice makes one imagine that it is an inherent part of the Qurʾānic text.

"In the Nashr, the Reciters are in disagreement concerning its beginning, viz. does one begin (with the recitation of the *takbīr* 'God is great') at the beginning of *sūrah al-Duha*, or at its end? As for completing it, does one do so at the beginning of *sūrah al-Nas*, or at its end? Does one connect or interrupt at its beginning or at its end? The difference of opinion is based on the following principle: does it belong to beginning of the *sūrah* or to its end?"

Regarding its words some say "Allāhu Akbar" (God is great), while others say there is no god except Allāh, and God is great!", be it during prayer or outside of it. Al-Sakhawi and Abū Shama made this explicit.

Question

After completion (of recitation), prayer is a tradition. Al-Ṭabarānī and others narrate a (*ḥadīth*) Tradition on the authority of al-ʿIrbād ibn Saria (which has a chain of transmission that is *marfuʿ* (disconnected): "For him who has completed the recitation of the entire Qurʾān, prayer is *mustajaba* (answerable)."

(One finds in) the *Shuʿab* the following *marfuʿ* Tradition: "Whoever recites the entire Qurʾān and praises his Lord, and prays for the Prophet (peace and blessings be upon him), and begs forgiveness for his sins from his Lord, goodness, he certainly has prayed at the right place."

When one has concluded a complete recitation, it is commendable to begin a new recitation according to the Tradition recorded by al-Tirmidhī and others, viz: "Completing the recitation of the Qurʾān is the most favourable act to God when it is done in the mannar of *al-hal al-murtahil* (arriving-departing), as by one who begins the recitation of the Qurʾān and completes the whole recitation only to begin a new complete recitation."

Al-Dārami recited the following Tradition with a good (*hasan*) chain of transmission: "On the authority of Ibn ʿAbbās, on the authority of Ubayy ibn Kaʿb, who said: 'Whenever the Prophet (peace and blessings be upon him) recited "I take refuge in the Lord of Mankind . . ." (Q114, 1–6), he would begin reciting the *hamd* (the *bismalla* formula – that is, the first *sūrah* of the Qurʾān – and then continue with the second *sūrah*, *al-Baqara* (The Cow), up to the verse "They are the successful ones" (Q2, 5), then he would pray the prayer of conclusion, and then he would stand up.' "

Question

On the authority of Imām Aḥmad the repetition of the 112th *sūrah*, *al-Ikhlas* (Sincerity) at the conclusion of the recitation, is forbidden, yet people would do so. Some of them said, "The point in this is that (this *sūrah*) is equivalent in worth to one-third of the Qurʾān. Repeating it three times is equal to reciting the whole of the Qurʾān."

If it is said: "Were this the case, one would have to recite (*sūrah* 112) four times to reach two conclusions," We say that what is meant is to be certain of a complete recitation, be it the one recited or the one for which one is to receive recompense for repeating.

In my opinion, the result would be to make up for some error in the recitation. And as al-Ḥalīmī considered repetition at closure as equal to repetition at the end of Ramaḍān, so one should compare the completion of *sūrah al-Ikhlāṣ* with following Ramaḍān with six days of fasting in Shawwāl.

It is reprehensible to use the recitation of the Qurʾān to earn a living. Al-Ajarī narrated a Tradition from ʿUmrān ibn al-Ḥusayn with a *marfūʿ* chain of transmission: "Whoever recited the Qurʾān – should only ask God for help, for a group of people reciting the Qurʾān will ask others for help by reciting the Qurʾān.

In his Comprehensive History, al-Bukhārī related the following Tradition with a sound chain of transmission: "Whoever recited the Qurʾān in the presence of an evil doer, he is cursed tenfold for each letter (*harf*)."

Question

It is wrong to say "I forgot (*nasītu*) such and such a verse, but one must rather say: 'I was made to forget (*unsītu-ha*).'" This prohibition is found in both the *Ṣaḥīḥ* collections (of al-Bukhārī and Muslim).

Question

The three *imāms* claim that the reward (from reciting) goes to the deceased; our practice is the opposite (Q53, 39): "And that a man will have only what he has striven for."

Section on quotation and the like

Quotation (*iqtibās*) is the inclusion in either poetry or prose text of the Qurʾān as not part of it, not by saying "God (He is forever exalted) said . . ." or the like; for if one says so it is no longer quotation.

The Mālikis are well-known for their opposition to this practice, and their firm prohibition of it. As for the followers of our school (*madhhab*), our early teachers did not thwart this practice, not did their followers, despite the prevalence of quotation in their eras and the usage of poetry early on and lately.

A group of later scholars did thwart this practice. Shaykh ʿIzz al-Dīn ʿAbd al-Salam was asked about it, and he permitted it. What the Prophet (peace and blessings be upon him) said in prayer and elsewhere supports this view (Q6, 79): "I have turned my face (to Him who created the heavens and the earth, as a man of pure faith . . .)" and (Q6, 96): ("O God! (*allāhumma*): 'You who split the sky in the morning, and make the night a rest, and the sun and the moon as a reckoning' remove debt from me and enrich me from poverty."

Regarding the speech of Abū Bakr (Q26, 227): ". . . Those who do wrong will surely know by what overturning they will be overturned."

And again in the last Tradition transmitted by Ibn ʿUmar: "Verily, in your Emissary you have a good example."

All this indicates that it is permissible (to use quotations) in sermons, encomia, and in prayer. This is only in prose. There is no indication that this is so with poetry, with the distinction made by the Malikite Judge Abū Bakr that including poetry is reprehensible, but it is permitted in prose.

The Judge ʿIyāḍ used (to quote prose) in contexts of prayers of asking for healing.

In his Summary of the Garden (*al-Rawda*) the Yamānī al-Sharaf Ismāʿīl ibn al-Muqriʾ said in the Explanation of (of Ibn Hajja) Eloquence that it is appropriate to (insert prose) in prayers (for healing) and in praise for (the Prophet) (peace and blessings be upon him) and his family and his Companions, even if it is inserted within poetry. Otherwise it is rejected.

According to Ibn Ḥajja's Explanation of Eloquence, quotation has three divisions, viz. acceptable (*maqbūl*), permitted (*mubāḥ*) and rejected (*mardūd*). The first division encompasses speeches, sermons and contracts. The second, in speech, letters and stories. The third has two parts: the first is what God related to Himself, and we seek refuge in God from whatever person who relates this to himself, as was reported concerning one of Marwan's sons who signed a document concerning criticism of his actions: "To Us is their return; then upon Us will rest their reckoning" (Q88, 25–26).

The last type is including a verse intending mockery; we take refuge in God from this, e.g. *arkhā* [in another ed. *awḥā*] "He leaned over sideways to his lovers (How impossible!) what are promised (Q23, 36) while his buttocks muttered from behind him (For work like this people should compete) (Q37, 36).

In my opinion this division is sound, and I endorse it.

The Shaykh Tāj al-Dīn ibn al-Subkī in his *Ṭabaqāt* mentioned that in the *Tarjama* (biography) of the Imām Abū Manṣūr ʿAbd al-Qāhir ibn al-Ṭāhir al-Tamīmī al-Baghdādī, one of the great and glorious Shāfiʿite (scholars), that an example of his poetry is: "You who transgressed and then were hostile and then committed a crime; and then stopped and then reverted and confessed; Take the good news of Allāh's speech from His verses (Q8, 38): '. . . if they cease (their unbelief) forgiveness will be granted to them for what is past.'"

He added that the use of this example by such as *al-Ustādh* (Master) Abū Manṣūr to the quotation in his poetry, for he is of great standing (*jalīl al-qadr*), has merit; yet people prohibited it, even if some of their studies of this concluded that it should be permitted.

It is said that this is done only by those poets who wander aimlessly in every valley (see Q26, 224–225), and seize upon any expression available without consideration. This *Ustādh* Abū Manṣūr is one of the *imāms* of the religion, and the *Ustādh* Abū al-Qāsim ibn ʿAsākir practised this, relating two lines of poetry from the former.

In my opinion these two lines of poetry do not constitute quotation because he clearly distinguished God's speech, as we have explained previously.

Concerning the saying of his brother, al-Shaykh Bahaʾ al-Dīn, he reported in his Bride of the Joys (*ʿArūs al-Afrāḥ*) that one must abstain from and abjure this practice entirely, and that the speech of God and His Emissary must be completely free from this.

From my viewpoint, I have witnessed a number of prominent *imāms* employ this practice, one of whom is Abū al-Qāsim al-Rafiʿ, who read in his Dictations (*Amālī*) and that other great *imāms* quoted it from him.

Kingdom is God's to which all faces turn; the great are humbled by Him.
Singular in dominion and power; those who strive to have such are sure to fail.
Leave them and their claim for dominion on the day of their delusion.
For tomorrow they will know who is the liar.

In his *Shuʿab al-Īmān* (Pillars of Belief), al-Bayhaqī on the authority of his Shaykk, Abū ʿAbd-al-Raḥmān al-Sulami said: "Aḥmad ibn Muḥammad ibn Yazīd recited to us some of his poetry.

"Ask God for his grace and be pious, for piety is the best of what might be obtained;

"And he who fears God, He will make for him, and provide him from sources he never could expect (Q65, 3)."

There are two things related to quotation: (1) the recitation of the Qurʾān as speech. In his Tibyān, al-Nawawī said: "Ibn Abī Dāwūd mentioned that controversy hovers over this question, and he related on the authority of al-Nakhaʿi that he was loath to reciting the Qurʾān for a mundane matter.

It is narrated that ʿUmar ibn al-Khaṭṭāb recited during the sunset (*maghrib*) prayer in Mecca (Q95, 1–2): "By the figs and olives, By Mount Sinai." Then, he raised his voice and recited (Q95, 3): "By this secure territory." It was narrated on the authority of al-Ḥukaym [another ed: Hakim] ibn Saʿid: "One of the Kharijifes (*min al-muḥakkama*) approached ʿAlī while the latter was at the morning prayer, and said (Q39, 65): 'If you associate others with God, your work will surely fail . . .' Upon which ʿAlī answered with (Q30, 60): 'So have patience. Allāh's promise is true. (Do) not let those who have no certainty make you unsteady.'"

Another (authority claimed) that it is prohibited to coin parables during the recitation of the Qurʾān. Our companion, ʿImad al-Bayhaqī, al-Baghawiʾ's disciple, clarified this and Ibn al-Ṣalāh reported it in his *The Advantages of Travel* (*Fawaʾid al-riḥla*).

Secondly: inserting expressions from the Qurʾān into poetry and the like is doubtless permissible. We have related on the authority of al-Sharif Taqiy al-Dīn al-Ḥusayni that when he composed the following verses:

Metaphor is its truth, so pass over it, do not inhabit it but belittle it, little it will be.
What good is a decorated house, if you see that after an earthquake, it's not there.

he was afraid that he might commit a great sin by using these Qurʾānic phrases in poetry, so he approached Shaykh al-Islām Taqiy al-Dīn ibn al-Daqīq al-ʿId to ask him about this, and the latter approved of it and said to him say: "What good is a decorated balm [another ed. has *kahf* (cave)]," so the former answered: "O Sir, you have helped me and given me permission (*aftayta-ni*)."

Conclusion

In his *Burhān*, al-Zarkashī said: "One must not transgress Qurʾānic examples."

Thus he disapproved al-Ḥarīrī, saying: "Put me in a house narrower than a coffin (Noah's Ark), and weaker than the spider's web" (reference to Q29: The Spider).

What meaning is more eloquent than Allāh's meaning which He emphasized in six aspects, when He said (Q29, 41): "Verily, the frailest of houses is the house of the spider." Allāh employed "verily" (*inna*) (for emphasis); and used the superlative elative derived from the word "frail" (*al-wahn*); and added to that the plural (noun "houses" (*buyūt*)); and made (this plural definite "the houses" (*al-buyut*) with the definite article; and He emphasized the predicate by preceding it with the (emphatic particle) *la-*.

The proof of the pudding is found at Q2, 26: "Allāh is not ashamed to coin a simile of a gnat or even greater (in size or in minuteness) [see Zamakhsharī ad loc.]." But the Prophet (peace and blessings be upon him) has indeed coined a simile of something smaller than a gnat, when he said: "If Allāh weighed this lower world, it would be smaller than a gnat's wing to Him."

Some people say that the verse "or even greater (in size or in minuteness"), is in relation to its coarseness (*al-khissa*). (Others said that it meant "or even lesser") and so the ambiguity was unsolved.

Endnotes

Chapter fifteen

1 Abū al-Ḥasan Muslim Ibn al-Ḥajjāj Ibn Muslim al-Qurayshi, author of one of the two most authoritative collections called "the two *Ṣaḥīḥs*". Died 261/845. (From Zb I 32, note 3.)
2 He is mentioned as one of the Companions who had memorized the Qur'ān in Zb I 243 top. (MBS)
3 Q2.
4 Compare the "Lord's Prayer" in Matthew 6 9–13 and, in a shorter version, Luke 11 2–4. (For God's throne in the Bible, see Isaiah 66 1 and I Kings 22 19.)
5 The Imām Abū Bakr Aḥmad Ibn al-Ḥusayn Ibn ʿAlī Ibn Abd Allāh al-Bayhaqī, author of a Sunan, Dalaʾil al-Nubuwwa, etc. Died 458/1066. From *Ṭabaqāt al-Shāfiʿīa III* 3–5. (From ZbI 190, note 2.)
6 The Imām Abū Abd Allāh Muḥammad Ibn ʿAbd Allāh, known as (al-Ḥakam sic) al-Ḥākim, author al-Mustadrak aʾla al-Ṣaḥīḥayn. Died 405/1013. From Zb I 190, note 1.
7 Q9, 112.
8 Q23, 1–11 (Ibrāhīm has "Sūrat al-Muʾmin [*40 sic], here, instead of the correct Sūrat al-Mu'minin).
9 Q33.35.
10 Q70, 23–33.
11 Abū ʿAbd Allāh Muḥammad Ibn Ismaʿīl Ibn Ibrāhīm al-Bukhārī, the Imām, learned in *ḥadīth* and author of al-Jamiʾ al-Ṣaḥīḥ. Died 510/1115–16. (See Ibn Khallikan I 146 for biography.) (From Zb I 33, note 1.)
12 Q33, 45.
13 Q6, 1.
14 Q17, 111.
15 Q11, 123 to end.
16 Q6, 151.
17 Ibid.
18 See Q12, 24.
19 Q82, 10–12.
20 Q10, 61.
21 Q13, 33.
22 Q17, 32.
23 Q12, 24.

Chapter sixteen

1 Q2, 185.
2 Q97, 1.
3 The *lawḥ al-maḥfūẓ* in the highest heaven.
4 Baʾthatu-hu.
5 Q25, 33.
6 Q17, 106.
7 According to the context, *dhikr* may also mean: "admonition" or "warning". See Sh. EI 273, col. 2 end.

8 *Bayt al-iʿzza.*
9 Manuscript T has here: "Then the Qurʾān was revealed in instalments". See Introduction, p. 11 top.
10 Q2, 185 (not in Ib).
11 Q97, 1 (not in Ib).
12 Rasalan.
13 Manuscript T has: "It was brought down in its entirety on the Night of Power in Ramaḍān, then it was brought down in instalments, piece following piece, slowly and with deliberation."
14 See note 41 for Chapter sixteen.
15 The Imām Abū al-Ḥasan ʿAlī Ibn Ḥabīb al-Shāfiʿī author of *Kitāb Adab al-Dunyā wa-l-Dīn*, *Al-Ḥāwī* and a *Tafsīr*. Died 450. (From *Shadharāt al-Dhahab III* 285–286). [From Zb I 187, note 2.]
16 Q2, 283 (4) (not in Ib).
17 Manuscript T has: ". . . His sending of Muḥammad (peace and blessings be upon him) . . ."
18 Q2, 185 (not in Ib).
19 Q97, 1.
20 Q96, 1 (not in Ib).
21 *Buʿitha.*
22 Q25, 32.
23 Ibid.
24 Ibid.
25 Ibid.
26 Q25, 33.
27 Q25, 7.
28 Q17, 94.
29 Q12, 109.
30 Q13, 38.
31 Q7, 144.
32 Q7, 145.
33 Q7, 150. (N.B. Ib has Q7.105 (sic) here.)
34 Q7, 154.
35 Q7, 171.
36 See note 125 for Chapter seventeen.
37 Q24, 11–19 (not in Ib).
38 Q9, 28.
39 Q56, 75.
40 More formal Arabic would have "the other (*al-ʾākharu*)" instead of Suyūṭī's "second (*al-thānī*)".
41 The Imām Fakhr al-Dīn Muḥammad Ibn ʿUmar al-Razī, author of the voluminous *tafsīr Mafatih al-Ghayb*. Died 606/1208–1209. (From Ibn Khallikān I 474.) (From Zb I 13, note 5.)
42 Q26, 193 (not in Ib).
43 Q26, 194.
44 Q97, 1.
45 (Ib. has "qālū (sic) "they say".)
46 Q34, 23.
47 Q80, 15–16.
48 Here *ʾakhar* is used, correctly. See note 31 for Chapter sixteen.
49 (Previous to this page in Ib.)
50 Q17, 1.
51 Here begins Q93, 6–8.
52 Sic. Ib. has *aʾjid*, "I found", for the Qurʾān's *yajid*, "He found".

53 Likewise, Ib has ʾ*away-tu* (first person) for the Qurʾān's ʾ*awā* (third person).
54 Ib has *wa-dāllan fa-haday-tu* for the Qurʾān's *wa-wajada-ka dāllan fa-hadā.*
55 Ib has wa–āʾilan fa–ʿaghnā–tu for the Qurʾān's *wa–wajada–ka–aʾilan fa–aʾghnā.*
56 Here begins a paraphrase of Q94, 1–2.
57 Here it ends. Ib has *wa-sharaH-tu la-ka Sadra-ka wa-Haṭṭaṭ-tu* ʿ*an-ka wizra-ka* for the Qurʾān's ʾ*a-lam nashraḥ la-ka Ṣadra-ka wa-waḍa*ʿ*-nā* ʿ*an-ka wizra-ka.*
58 Manuscript T adds here: "until the Day of Resurrection".
59 Ib has a misprint here: *ka-hay*ʾ*at-ṭin* (sic).
60 Q77, 6.
61 Q18, 96.
62 Q7, 54.
63 Ibn Ḥajar mentions him in his *Lisān al-Mīzān*, 272. He said: "Concerning the rest, He brought them with miracles." Al-Azdi said this *ḥadīth* is based on a false *isnād* (*matruuk*).
64 The expression *shāfin kāfin* is an example of ʾ*itbā*ʿ – "imitative pleonasm". Compare: "helter-skelter", " namby-pamby", etc.
65 The corresponding section of Zb is entitled "(Concerning the seven qiraʾat {variant readings})" (I 213 to end). Is this (the same) editor's addition? (MBS)
66 Q5, 60. See al-Qurtubi's *tafsīr* VI 235.
67 Q17, 23. Same X 243.
68 Q2, 282. (The "Debt Verse", see above.) See same III 405.
69 Q34, 19. See same XIV 291.
70 Q2, 259. See same III 295.
71 Zb I 214 end vocalizes *nunshiru-haa.*
72 Q56, 29. See same XVII 208.
73 Q50, 19. See same XVII 12.
74 Q92, 3. See same XX 80.
75 Q101, 5.
76 Q4, 37.
77 Q2, 37.
78 Q10, 30.
79 Q1, 6.
80 Q15, 65.
81 These last two Arabic words are mistakes: *fa* should be substituted for *wa*. See Zb I 215 end.
82 Q9, 111.
83 Q40, 35.
84 *Shāfin kāfin.* See note 54 for Chapter 16.
85 Q2, 20.
86 According to Zb I 220, note 9, the occurrence of *marruu fii-haa* is a mistake.
87 At first, the Qurʾān was only memorized. The earliest written fragments contain neither *nuqat* (diacritical points) nor *tashkil* (vowel signs). (MBS)
88 Q44, 43–44.
89 See Ibn Fāris al-Ṣaḥāba, 28. (From Zb I 283, note 2.)
90 Compare Zb I 283 end.
91 Addition from Zb I 283 top.
92 Same.
93 Q14, 4.
94 See Zb I 284, note 5.
95 Ib has "he [sic] related it".
96 Worship, etc. See Zb I 224 end. (MBS)
97 The author listed only these, although he mentioned above that there were forty views.
98 He is Abū Ḥātim Muḥammad Ibn Ḥabban al-Bustī, thus al-Qurtubī's *tafsīr* I 42.

99 Ib has a mistaken *tanwin* here, perhaps meant for the previous "dialect".
100 Ib misspells this word, omitting the *yāʾ*.
101 See note 55 for Chapter sixteen.
102 Tradition holds that ʿUthmān, the third Caliph, had the texts of the Qurʾān then extant (from the time of Abū Bakr, or before) destroyed; under ʿUthmān's direction, the Prophet's secretary Zayd Ibn Thābit produced the standard text, known as the "ʿUthmanic codex." (MBS)
103 See notes 56 and 74 of Chapter sixteen.
104 In ms T.
105 See note 86 in Chapter 16.

Chapter seventeen

1 This paragraph is Suyūṭī's addition to what generally follows Zb I 273 and the following pages.
2 Ib clarifies the first vowel as *u*: (4) Uzayzi.
3 Ms T has "Saydhala" with a *sīn* instead of a *shīn*. Ibn Khallikān clarified this by saying: "(His name) is spelled with an *a*, a *shin* and a *dhaal*. This is his nickname (*laqab*), and, despite my research efforts, I don't know what it means." (Ibn Khallikān also) clarified that the name "ʿAzīzi" should be spelled with an *ayn* with *a* (sic! sic) and two *zaaʾs* (sic). He is Ibn Abd Allāh, one of the Shāfiʿite jurisprudents, author of the book *al-Burhān fī Mushkilāt al-Qurʾān* (*Clarification of the Difficult (Passages) in the Qurʾān*). He died in the year 494 AH. See Ibn Khallikān I 318, Shadharat al-Dhahabī III 401, and Kashf al-Ẓunūn 241.
4 See note 3 above.
5 Q44, 1–2.
6 Q36, 77.
7 Q9, 6.
8 Q4, 174.
9 Q10, 57.
10 Q25, 1.
11 Q17, 82.
12 Q10, 57.
13 See note 2 from Chapter 16.
14 Q21, 50.
15 Q36, 77.
16 Q54, 5.
17 Q10, 1 Ib has Q10, 2 (sic); Zb I 274 note 5 has Q10, 1–2 (sic).
18 Q5, 48.
19 Q3, 103.
20 Q6, 153.
21 Q18, 2. Ib has Q18, 3 (sic); Zb I 274 note 10 has Q18, 1–2 (sic).
22 Q86, 13.
23 Q78, 1–2.
24 Q39, 23. Zb I 274 note 13 has Q39, 2 (sic).
25 Q26, 192.
26 Q42, 52.
27 Q21, 45.
28 Q12, 2.
29 Q7, 203.
30 Q3, 138.
31 Q2, 45.
32 Q3, 62.

33 Q17, 9.
34 Q72, 21.
35 Q69, 48.
36 Q2, 256.
37 Q39, 33.
38 Q6, 115.
39 Q65, 5.
40 Q3, 193.
41 Q2, 97.
42 Q85, 21.
43 Q21, 105.
44 Q41, 3–4.
45 Q41, 41.
46 Q14, 52.
47 Q12, 3.
48 Q80, 13–14. This gives us a total of forty-six names for the Qurʾān, despite the mention of fifty-five above. (MBS)
49 The original Arabic meaning of the root *KTB* is "to bind or sew together". Fischer W. *Grundriss der arabischen Philologie*. Wiesbaden 1982. 144 mid.
50 Compare Zb I 276 end.
51 Ib mistakenly has *lugharatan* (sic) here. See also Schub, M. "Panchronic Actions in Arabic" *JSS Journal of Semitic Studies* (Manchester) 27/1. 1982. 59 note 12.
52 Compare Zb I 279 mid.
53 Zb I 277 top suggests that it is derived from the root *KRY*, "to collect together". The original meaning of the root *QR* in Arabic is "to collect together". See Fischer, same place.
54 Ib has "two phonetic zeros preceding it", which makes no sense. See Zb I 278 end.
55 Ib has a misprint *ruhjaan* (sic!) here.
56 See note 38 in Chapter seventeen.
57 Zb I 277 end explains that what is "displayed" is (menstrual) blood (*qarʾ*). Without this, Suyūṭī's paragraph doesn't make much sense.
58 Compare Zb I 279 top.
59 Zb same.
60 This dubious linguistic "explanation" is absent in Zb same.
61 Compare ZB I 280 top: "It is called 'the Discriminator (*al-furqaan*)' because it discriminates between Truth and falsehood, the Muslim and the unbeliever, and the (true) believer and the hypocrite. Thus was ʿUmar Ibn al-Khatab nicknamed 'al-Faruq'."
62 Compare Zb I 280 end.
63 Q43, 44.
64 Compare Zb I 279 mid.
65 Compare Zb I 280 mid.
66 See note 2 for Chapter seventeen.
67 Compare Zb I 280 mid.
68 This paragraph is absent from Zb.
69 Same as previous note.
70 Zb I 280 top adds that *al-mathaani* is applied as a name to only one *sūrah*, the *Fātiḥa*. [*1]
71 Q87, 18.
72 See note 8 for Chapter seventeen. This paragraph is absent in Zb.
73 See note 10 for Chapter seventeen. This paragraph is absent in Zb.
74 See note 26 for Chapter seventeen. Compare Zb I 280 end, 281.
75 See note 29 for Chapter seventeen.
76 Zb I 279 end.

77 See note 15 for Chapter seventeen. Compare Zb I 279 mid.
78 Abū Ṭāhir Aḥmad Ibn Muḥammad Ibn Aḥmad al-Silāfi, d. 572 AH. From Ibn Khallikān I 31 (From Zb I 282, note 1).
79 Q14, 52.
80 In his *al-Murshid al-Wajīz* (The Abridged Guide). See Zb I 281 end.
81 Q20, 131.
82 The Judge Shihāb al-Dīn Ibrāhīm Ibn ʿAbd Allāh Ibn Abī al-Dam al-Ḥimawi, d. 632 AH (From Zb 281, note 3).
83 Compare Zb I 281 end 282.
84 Muḥammad Ibn ʿAbdullah Ibn Ashta, a scholar of Arabic and (variant) readings, who wrote a book on rare readings. He died in 306 AH (from *Ṭabaqāt al-Qurra'* (The Generations of the Readers) p. 1842).
85 These last two paragraphs do not appear in Zb I 282.
86 Muḥammad Ibn Ayyūb Ibn Yaḥyā Ibn al-Durays al-Bajalī, a tradant (transmitter of *ḥadīths*) who wrote the book *Fī Faḍāʾil al-Qurʾān* (*Concerning the Excellencies of the Qurʾān*).
87 Q2, 53.
88 Ib has "Al-Qutabi" (sic). See Zb I 263 end.
89 (Suyūṭī) took this from (al-Zarkashī's) Burhān I 64, and II 264. (Ib) This corresponds to Zb I 264 top. (MBS)
90 Dīwan 13.
91 Q38, 21.
92 He is Ibrāhīm Ibn ʿUmrān Ibrahīm Abū Isḥāq al-Jaʿbarī, one of the Shāfiʿite jurisprudents. He wrote about one hundred books, most of which deal with the (variant) readings. Among them are *Sharḥ al-Shāṭibiyya*, *Ḥadiqat al-Ẓahr fī ʿAdad Āy al-Suwar*, *Jāmilat Arbāb al-Maqasid fī Rasm al-Maṣḥaf* and others. He died in 732 AH. (This is from) al-Durar al-Kamina I 50.
93 *Surat al-Kawthar* [*108]. See Zb I 264 end.
94 *Suyūṭī: bi-tawqīfin mina al-nabi . . .*, which is a mistaken usage of an agent in the passive voice. (MBS)
95 Q15, 95.
96 Q13, 39.
97 Q43, 4.
98 Q3, 7.
99 Ib mistakenly has *mufzigh* (sic) here for mufziʿ.
100 Same as above note.
101 Ib has two otiose words here: *li-ʿumm al-qurʾaan*. Sic.
102 See note 77 from Chapter sixteen (*ʾitbāʿ*).
103 Compare Zb I 280 top: ". . . because one may not divide it up . . .".
104 Algar translation page 193 top.
105 Tabari continues with a *ḥadīth* on the authority Jarīr Ibn ʿAbdullah al-Ansāri: ". . . he shall have what he has asked for." See Cooper 81 end.
106 Q1, 6.
107 Q1, 4.
108 Ibid.
109 Q9, 117.
110 See Lane 155, col. 3 end and 156.
111 Q78, 1.
112 Q78, 14.
113 Q111, 5.
114 Ib has *lam*, but reports that the Burhān has *lan*.
115 Zb I 270 mid, and following.
116 Ib I–II 160 top vocalizes *khuluq*; in Zb I 270 mid, he vocalizes *khalq*.

117 Ib I–II 160 top mistakenly has *sbq* (sic!). Zb I 270 mid has the correct *ʾasbaq*.
118 See Lane 2532 end, 2533.
119 Q6, 142–144.
120 The Burhān has "in this *sūrah*" instead of "his *sūrah*".
121 Added here in Zb I 271 mid.
122 Same.
123 Q37, 101–107.
124 Abū ʿAlī al-Ishbīlī ʿUmar Ibn Muḥammad Ibn ʿUmar al-Azdi, known as al-Shalawbiin, who wrote a commentary on Sībawayhi's *Kitab and al-Musannafat fī al-Nahw*. Died 645/1246–47. (See *Bughāt al-Wuʿāt* 364.) (From Zb II 239, note 4.)
125 *al-mufaṣṣal.*
126 *Sūrahs* beginning with the "mysterious letters" *Ḥā Mīm*.
127 According to the *qamūs* (dictionary): the *qawāriʿ* are the Qurʾānic verses, which protect whoever reads them from devils, men and *jinn* as if to say: they repulse the satans (Ib).
128 Q17, 111.

Chapter thirty-two

1 A word ending composed of an *alif* followed by a *hamza*.
2 Where the *hamza* appears after a long vowel.
3 That is, in the recitations of Ḥamza and Warsh.
4 *Al-Taysīr*, Abū ʿAmr al-Dānī.
5 An ending found on certain words, written as ى but pronounced as *ā*, although which (unlike the preceding words) is not followed by a *hamza*.

Chapter thirty-three

1 Lit. a 'rejectionist'; i.e. a shiʿi who rejects the caliphates of Abū Bakr, ʿUmar and ʿUthmān.
2 This and the following Qurʾānic quotation are given according to the recitation of Abū ʿAmr.
3 Lit. "The two from the two noble sanctuaries".

Chapter thirty-four

1 Recitation of the Qurʾān done at a very slow pace, in which great care is given to the correct pronunciation of each letter and to all the rules of recitation. *See*: M.I.H.I. Surty, *A Course in the Science of Reciting the Qurʾān*. Leicester: The Islamic Foundation, 1988, p. 197.
2 The Arabic letters can be separated into *mustaʿlī* letters – the elevated letters (*khāʾ*, *ṣād*, *ḍād*, *ṭā'*, *ẓā'*, *ghayn*, *qāf*), where the tongue is elevated to the hard palate for pronunciation – and *mustafil* letters – the low, depressed letters (the remaining twenty-two letters), where the tongue is lowered to the lowest part of the mouth for pronunciation. *See*: Surty, *Reciting the Qurʾān*, p. 65.
3 Another division of the Arabic letters is into *muṭbaq*, these being the *ṣād*, *ḍād*, *ṭāʾ* and *ẓāʾ* – *Iṭbāq*, meaning 'to cover, put a lid on', is used to describe the position of the tongue in the production of these letters, when it is effectively covered by the hard palate – and *munfatiḥ* 'open, uncovered', the other twenty-four letters, the production of which required the opening of the palate. *See*: *ibid*; *EI*, III:596b, X:83a.
4 As opposed to the *ʿayn*, which was one of those letters classed by the Arabs as being between the occlusive and the constrictive. *See*: *EI*, III, 596b.

5 The point being that each of the seven Reciters had their recitations narrated by two transmitters, yet this group of scholars would accept just a single recitation for all of the reciters except Nāfiʿ and Ḥamza, for whom they would require a recitation for each of the two transmitters. Qālūn and Warsh are the two transmitters of the recitation of Nāfiʿ, and Khalaf and Khallād the two transmitters of the recitation of Ḥamza.

Chapter thirty-five

1 The English translations for this and subsequent verses of the Qurʾān have been taken wholly or with slight adaptations from: *The Qurʾān; A new translation by M. A. S. Abdel Ḥaleem.* Oxford, 2005.

2 A *marfuʿ ḥadīth* is one whose chain of narration goes all the way back to the Prophet (peace and blessings be upon him), as opposed to a *mawquf ḥadīth*, which is one that stops at the Companion.

3 The second, third, and fourth *sūrahs* of the Qurʾān, respectively.

4 Lit. 'The two Shaykhs'.

5 The verse in the previous paragraph is actually given in the past tense in Arabic; literally: "When you have recited the Qurʾān . . .".

6 The opening chapter of the Qurʾān.

7 Specific formulas repeated at the times of pilgrimage and Eid festivals respectively.

8 The formula *Bismi Allāh*.

9 The ninth chapter of the Qurʾān, more commonly known as Sura al-Tawba.

10 Those starting from Chapter 36 until the end of the Qurʾān, according to one view.

11 This is in response to the last verse of Chapter 95, which asks: "Is God not the most decisive of judges?"

12 Inclining the *a* vowel towards an *i* vowel.

13 Arabic distinguishes between two types of feminine noun, one which is actually physically feminine in gender (real feminine); and the other which is only grammatically feminine, and which would generally be considered as being neuter in English. Hence in the following examples, *Nār* (fire), *sāq* (leg) and *rusul* (messengers) are all referred to by the feminine pronoun.

14 Translated in the previous paragraph as "Make masculine", as opposed to its alternative meaning given here.

INDEX

ʿAbd Allah Ibn ʿUmar 171, 201, 278
ʿAbd Khayr 138, 161
ʿAbd al-Mālik ibn ʿUmayr 272
ʿAbd-al-Raḥmān b. Ghanam 28
ʿAbd-al-Raḥmān b. Kaʿb b. Mālik 79
ʿAbdullah b. Abī Bakr b. Ḥazm 35
ʿAbdullah b. ʿAmr 51
ʿAbdullah b. Masʿūd 21–2
ʿAbdullah b. Salām 10, 15–16, 19
ʿAbdullah b. al-Zubayr 61–2
ʿAbdullah Ibn Abī'l-Hudhayl 213
ʿAbdullah Ibn ʿAmir Ibn al-ʿAs 88
ʿAbdullah Ibn ʿAmr 265
ʿAbdullah Ibn Kathīr 281
ʿAbdullāh Ibn ʿUmar 265
Abī Dharr 84–5
Abī Qullaba 95
Abī Umama 88
ablution 26–7, 34, 78–9
Abode of Glory 100
Abrāhām 63, 67, 88, 102
  Book of 94
  Station of 71
"abrogating" and "abrogated" verses 110, 115
Abū ʿAbbās Ibn ʿAmmar 193
Abū ʿAbd Allah al-Mawṣilī 160
Abū al-ʿAla al-Hamadani 110
Abū ʿAlī al-Ahwāzī 108, 110
Abū al-Āliyah 47, 98
Abū ʿAmr 158, 194, 217, 219, 229, 236, 243–4, 248–9
Abu ʿAwāna 102
Abū Ayyāsh al-Zarqī 26
Abū Bakr 28, 43, 55, 59–60, 67, 78, 115, 121–2, 137–43, 171, 188, 191, 230, 245, 278, 283–4
Abū Bakr al-Baqillānī 143, 146–7
Abū Bakr b. al-Ḥārith b. Abyad 45
Abū Bakr Ibn al-Anbārī 148
Abū Bakr Ibn al-ʿArabī 193
Abū Bakra 105, 107
Abū al-Dardāʾ 145, 170–1
Abū Dharr 272
Abū al-Ḍuḥā 47
Abū al-Faḍl al-Rāzī 106
Abū Ḥanīfa 198, 261, 265, 277
Abū al-Ḥasan al-Qabaḥātī 258–9
Abū al-Ḥasan al-Rūmanī 121
Abū al-Ḥasan b. al-Haṣṣār 5
Abū Ḥātim al-Sijistānī 108
Abū Ḥayyān al-Badrī 12, 15, 193
Abū Ḥirzah 29
Abū Hurayrah 10–11, 26–8, 35, 68, 107, 125, 186, 278
Abū Iyās 167
Abū Jaʿfar Ibn Zubayr 148–9
Abū Jaʿfar al-Naḥḥās 3, 149, 198
Abū Khuzaima al-Anṣārī 138
Abū al-Layth 261, 265
Abū Mālik 48, 221
Abū Manṣūr 284
Abū Maryam al-Ghassāni 32
Abū Maysara 272
Abū al-Miqsam 185
Abū Mūsā 41, 172
Abū Naṣr al-Qushayrī 197
Abū al-Qāsim al-Ḥasan 1
Abū al-Qāsim Ibn ʿAsākir 284
Abū al-Qāsim al-Rafīʿ 285
Abū Rāfi 17
Abū al-Rajāʾ al-Utārīdī 41
Abū Rawq 155
Abū Saʿīd b. al-Muallā 32
Abū Saʿīd al-Khudrī 12, 26, 28, 98
Abū Salamah b. ʿAbd-al-Raḥmān 42
Abū Shāma 92–4, 100, 109–10, 140, 181, 184–5, 189, 193, 198, 247, 268
Abū al-Simāl 267
Abū Sufyān 34
Abū Sulaymān al-Dimishqī 9
Abū Turāb 156
Abū ʿUbayd 7, 22, 27, 42, 87, 108, 155, 172, 192, 197, 275, 278
Abū ʿUbayda 120, 125, 231
Abū Umāmah 84–5, 263
Abū ʿUmar al-Zāhid 198
Abū Yaʿlā 37, 104, 166, 273
Abū Yūsuf 212
Abū Zayd 172–3

Ādam 279
aḥād recitations 181, 186
Aḥmad ibn Muḥammad ibn Yazīd 282, 285
ahruf 104–5
Āʾishah 21, 26–7, 32–4, 36–7, 41, 43–4, 51, 57, 72, 78, 97, 104, 186, 263–4
al-Ājiri 160
ʿAlam al-Dīn, Shaykh 256–7
ʿAlī b. Abī Ṭalha 5, 8
ʿAlī b. Abī Ṭālib 7, 13, 85, 138, 142, 155, 201–2, 222, 285
ʿAlī b. al-Ḥusayn 45
ʿAlī Ibn Muḥammad 165
ʿAmar Ibn ʿAbd al-Mālik 103
Āmir b. Rabīʿah 65
ʿAmmāra Ibn Ghaziyya 141
ʿAmr b. Madī Karab 56
Anas b. Mālik 8–9, 13, 31, 37, 52, 71, 83–4, 131, 169–70, 190, 264, 269, 280
al-Anbārī 187
Arabic dialects 108–9, 225–6
articulation, points of 254–6
Asʾad b. Zarārah 79
al-Asfahānī 98–9
al-Ashʿarī 119
al-Ashnānī 213
Āṣim b. ʿUmar b. Qatāda 35
Asla b. Shurayk 26
Asmāʾ bt. Yāzīd 10, 26
assimilation of verse 222, 233–8
see also idgham
ʿAtāʾ Ibn al-Ṣaib 81, 103
ʿAuf b. Mālik al-Ashjaʿī 19
ʿAwf ibn Mālik 271
Aws al-Thaqafī 275
Ayfaʾ al-Kalāʾī 84
al-ʿAzrami 225

al-Baghawī 115, 147, 195
Baqi Ibn Mukhlad 124
al-Barāʾ 11, 31, 49–50
basmala recitation 268
al-Bayhaqī 4, 26, 43–4, 77, 87, 98, 100, 110, 123, 137, 149–50, 156, 160, 172, 182, 212, 275, 278
al-Bazzār 189, 191
al-Bazzāz 77
al-Bāzzi 281, 244
Bilāl al-Ḥabashī 18
Bishr Ibn Mūsa 138
al-Bizzī 249
al-Bukhārī 7, 26–7, 33, 37, 62, 68–9, 97, 125, 137, 141, 145, 149, 151, 169–70, 186, 283
Burayda 89, 189

chains of transmission, authenticity of 63–6
Companions of the Prophet 104
crying when reciting 272–3

al-Ḍahhāk 9, 28, 49, 83–4
al-Dāni 158–9, 182, 186, 213, 225–6, 231, 248, 252
al-Dārami 166, 282
al-Dāraquṭnī 124–5, 161
al-Dārimī 273
al-Daylamī 159
al-Dhababī 83, 247
dying without heirs 35

Elite of Hawāzin 108
eloquence 284

al-Farrāʾ 119, 151
Farwah b. Nusayk al-Muradī 18
fasting 280
Fātiḥa, the 126–7
fatwas 261–2
al-Fayḍ 160
feminine forms in the Qurʾān 275–6
fighting, verses concerned with 47
al-Firyāni 88
Friday prayer 79

Gabriel 41–2, 44, 68–9, 73, 76, 83–4, 91–5, 98–103, 105, 109, 115, 144–8, 155–6, 189–90, 225, 251, 265, 272, 278
al-Ghāfiqī 156
al-Ghazālī 280
group recitation 273

ḥadīths 97–102, 107–10, 123, 260
ḥadr style 252–3
Al-Ḥāfiẓ 281

Hafṣ b. Maysarah 64
al-Ḥākim 10, 29, 47, 62, 83, 87–8, 93, 137, 141, 151, 160, 186, 221, 274
al-Ḥalīmī 261, 274, 278, 281–2
Ḥamza 212–13, 218, 229, 238, 242–5, 252, 267
hamzas, use of 244, 275
lightening of 247–9
al-Ḥaramayn 52, 57, 197, 266
al-Ḥarīrī 286
al-Harith al-Hasibi 140, 143
harfs 107–11, 114–15, 182–4
al-Haṣan 44, 124, 155, 161, 187
'height' 179
Hibatullah 39
Hishām Ibn Hakim 109
Holy Spirit, the 102, 210
Hudhaifa al-Thaqafī 149–50
al-Hudhalī 23, 39, 157, 166
Hudhayfa 26, 36, 141, 225, 271
al-Ḥukaym 285
al-Ḥulwānī 268
Ḥumayd Ibn Qays 267
Ḥusayn b. Abī l-Ḥasan 4
Ḥusayn b. Alī 45
Ḥusayn b. al-Faḍl 7

ibdāl 218
Ibn ʿAbbās 3–5, 8–12, 16–19, 26–9, 32, 43–4, 47, 49, 51–3, 56–9, 63–70, 81, 85, 87–9, 92, 94–7, 104–5, 108, 128, 130–1, 144, 151, 155–6, 186, 189–90, 231, 271, 281
Ibn ʿAbd al-Barr 27, 107, 109
Ibn ʿAbd al-Birr 78
Ibn ʿAbd al-Salām 275
Ibn Abī Dawud 138–9, 142–6, 152, 171, 173, 280, 285
Ibn Abī Ḥasan 172
Ibn Abī Ḥātim 155, 158, 202
Ibn Abī al-Hudhayl 278
Ibn Abī Mulaykah 29
Ibn Abī Shayba 149
Ibn ʿĀmir 182
Ibn al-Anbārī 103, 201–2
Ibn al-ʿArabī 1, 39, 61, 159
Ibn ʿAsākir 131
Ibn Ashitta 139–40, 142, 148, 155
Ibn Ashta 34, 115, 122, 150, 152, 171
Ibn ʿAskar 103
Ibn ʿAṭiyya 7, 108, 110, 149
Ibn Baṣḥān 262
Ibn Bazza 281
Ibn Buraydah 12, 122
Ibn Daqīq al-ʿĪd 55
Ibn Dhukwān 230
Ibn Durays 83–4, 124, 138, 156, 159
Ibn al-Faras 9–11, 15, 21, 79, 222
Ibn Fāris 147
Ibn Furāk 95
Ibn Ghalbūn 213
Ibn al-Ghars 127–9
Ibn Ḥabbān 111, 114
Ibn Ḥabīb 28–9, 31, 33, 83
Ibn Ḥajar 14, 31–2, 43, 45, 50, 64, 67, 69, 93–4, 130–1, 138–42, 146, 149, 171–3, 191–2
Ibn al-Ḥājib 193, 197–8, 214, 254
Ibn Ḥajja 284
Ibn al-Haṣṣār 13, 18, 22, 25, 28, 52, 68, 75, 78, 147, 149
Ibn Ḥayyan 134, 194
Ibn Ḥazm 191
Ibn Jarīr 52, 171, 124–5, 222
Ibn al-Jawzī 123, 167, 217, 223
Ibn al-Jazarī 19, 106–7, 115, 178, 181–7, 193, 201, 206–13, 217, 225, 227, 235–6, 243–4, 251–5, 259–60, 268–70, 279
Ibn Jubayr al-Makki 194
Ibn Jurayj 26, 49, 156
Ibn Kathīr 12, 51, 68, 75, 92, 119, 171, 177, 182, 212, 228, 243, 248, 279, 281
Ibn al-Kawāshī 196
Ibn al-Khattāb 156
Ibn Khayr 260
Ibn Mājah 267
Ibn Mandaḥ 179
Ibn Mardawahi 225
Ibn Marwān 156
Ibn Masʿūd 2, 10, 16, 23, 33, 39, 47, 66, 68, 77–8, 81, 100, 107–9, 121–3, 131, 135, 147, 152, 155, 167, 189, 191–2, 197–8, 225, 241, 253, 269, 272–8
Ibn Maysara 89
Ibn Mihrān 244
Ibn Muʿīn 152, 160
Ibn al-Mubārak 280
Ibn Mujāhid 193–4, 211, 275
Ibn al-Naqīb 1–2, 44, 83, 111
Ibn ʿUmar 284
Ibn al-Qāriḥ 225

Ibn al-Qaṣṣāʿ 244
Ibn Qutayba 108, 192, 213
Ibn Rahawayh 84
Ibn al-Ṣabbāgh 192
Ibn Saʿd 4, 173
Ibn Saʿdān 104
Ibn al-Ṣalāh 81, 262, 285
Ibn Shanbūdh 163
Ibn Shihāb 49, 92
Ibn Shuraykh 213
Ibn Sīrīn 115, 124, 139, 172, 278
Ibn al-Subkī 198, 284
Ibn Taymiyah 55, 59, 62
Ibn Thābit 131
Ibn al-Ṭīn 27
Ibn ʿUmar 27–32, 47, 63–4, 71–2, 81, 123, 128, 201–2, 247, 263, 270, 276
Ibn ʿUṣfūr 134
Ibn Wahb 141, 146
Ibn Yazīd al-Nakhaʾi 191
Ibn al-Zubayr 9, 187
Ibrāhīm 25, 225
idgham 233, 238
see also assimilation
ikhfaʾ 238–9
Ikrama 123, 138–9
Ikrimah 44, 72
ʿImad al-Bayhaqī 285
Imād al-Dīn b. Kathir 2
al-Imām, Fakhr al-Dīn 22
imāla 225–31
Imrān b. Ḥusayn 28, 33
Inspiration 101–4
iʾnzāl, interpretations of 99–100
iqlāb 238
al-ʿIrbād ibn Saria 282
al-Isbahānī 21
al-Islām Abū al-Faḍl b. Ḥajar 55
al-Islām Taqiy al-Dīn ibn al-Daqīq al-ʿId 286
Ismah b. Mālik al-Khutamī 32
Ismaʿīl b. Rāfiʿ 83–4
Ismaʿīl ibn ʿAbdulla 281
isnāds 177–9, 186
Isrāfīl 103
ʿIyād 284
iẓhar 238
ʿIzz al-Dīn, Shaykh 211–12, 283

al-Jaʿbarī 9, 22, 55, 123, 133, 184, 213, 269
Jābir b. ʿAbdillah 42
Jābir b. Zayd 9, 16, 45
al-Jadd b. Qays 35
Jaʿfar b. Abī Ṭālib 24
al-Jāḥiẓ 117
Jamʿ bi-l-ḥarf and *Jamʿ bi-l-waqf* 258
Jarīr Ibn ʿAbd al-Ḥamīd 152
Jesus, son of Mary 210
Joseph 89, 212
Jubayr 21
Jundab 15–16, 64
jurisprudence 211
al-Juwaynī 100–1, 214, 251

Kaʿb al-Qurazī 32, 88, 172
al-Kalbī 14
al-Kawāshī xxxiii, 195–6, 198
Khālid Ibn Maʿdan 127
al-Khalīl 249, 254
al-Khaṭṭābī 102
al-Khaṭīb 67
al-Khaṭībī 137, 141
al-Khattābi 151
al-Khudrī 263
Khuzayma Ibn Thābit 140, 142
al-Kirmānī xxxii, xxxiii, 43, 45, 121, 130, 148, 169
al-Kisāʾī 213, 228–30, 243

al-Liḥyāwī 120

madd 241–6
Makḥūl 265
al-Makkī, ʿUbayda 22–3, 146, 184, 194, 215, 264
Mālik 146–8, 155
Maʿqal b. Yasar 83–4
Marwān b. Ḥakam 29, 56–7
masculine forms in the Qurʾān 275–6
Masrūq 19
al-Māwardī xxxiii, 92, 93, 110, 125, 131, 151
Mawhūb al-Jazarī 277
al-Mawṣilī 160, 163, 165
Maymūn b. Mihrān 22
al-Māzirī 169
al-Mazzi 12
Mecca, revelations in 1–24, 64–5
Medina, revelations in 1–24, 65

melodies accompanying recitation 273
menopausal women 56
menstruation 196, 266
Michael 105, 107
al-Miqdād 128
Miswar b. Makhramah 29
Moses 87, 94–7, 102, 122, 133, 210, 212
Muʾadh Ibn Anas 135
Muʿadh Ibn Jabal 264, 271
Muāwiyah b. Abī Sufyān 51
Muḥammad b. Barakāt al-Saʿdī 33
Muḥammad b. Kaʿb al-Quraẓī 26, 58
Muḥammad b. Shurahabīl 72
Muḥammad Ibn Idris al-Shāfiʿī 281
Muḥammad Ibn Kaʿb al-Quraẓī 89
Muḥammad Ibn Muqatil 231
Muḥammad Ibn Naṣr al-Marzawi 156
Muḥammad Ibn Sīrīn 138, 142, 171
Mujāhid 7–9, 43, 47, 65, 71, 81, 280
Muqātil 4, 15
mursal tradition 63
al-Mursī 114, 124, 126–7
Mūsā Ibn ʿUqba 141
Musʿab b. ʿUmayr 72
al-Musayyib 67
Muslim Ibn Mikhrāq 87, 127, 137, 145, 264
mutawātir recitation 181, 187–96, 202, 251
'Mutual Agreement' 177–8
al-Muẓẓaffarī 121

Nāfiʿ 212, 247
al-Naḥḥās xxxii, 8, 201
al-Nakhaʿī 285
al-Nakzawī 98, 151, 201
al-Nasafī 9, 30, 45
Al-Nasaʾī 92, 105
al-Nawawī 13, 67, 191, 199, 263–7, 270–80
Night of the Ascension 102
Night of Power 6, 91–2, 94, 100
al-Nikzāwī 211
al-Nisābūrī, ʿAlī Ibn Sahl 100
al-Nisāʾī 145, 171
Noah 132–3
al-Nuʿmān ibn Bashīr 264

"paired sounds" 233–4
pauses in recitation 202–17
  levels of 204–5
Persian language, recitation in 277
phonetic zero 217
poetry, Qurʾānic verses used as 285–6
polytheism 221, 281
Preserved Tablet 99–100
prostration and the Prostration Verses 279–80
"proximate sounds" 233–4

al-Qāḍī Abū Bakr 2, 51, 170
al-Qāḍī Jalāl al-Dīn 28, 31 33, 37, 181
Qālūn 244, 248–9
Qamwalī 269
al-Qarrāb 195
Qāsim Ibn Thābit 106
qaṣr 241
qatʿ 213
Qatāda 5, 8, 14, 16, 19–20, 27, 77, 122, 128, 158, 169, 223
Qays ibn Abī Ṣaʿṣaʿa 265
qiblah, turning towards 31, 56–7, 64–5
Qunbul 248–9
quotations from the Qurʾān, use of 283–5
Qurʾān, the
  collection and arrangement of 137–53
  division into *sūrahs* 157–8
  first parts to be revealed 41–8
  general and *specific* verses in 59–61
  last parts to be revealed 49–53
  manner of reception 251–62
  manner of revelation 91–115
  memorizers and narrators of 169–75
  naming of 117–21
  number of letters in 167
  number of verses in 159–61
  number of words in 166–7
  pronunciation of name of 119–20
  reading of 274–5
  singing of 157
  time taken in recitation 264–5
  verses associated with sayings of the Companions 71–3
  verses revealed several times 75–6
al-Qurṭubī 111, 170
al-Qushayrī 155
Qutayba 105–6
al-Qutaybi 122
Quṭrub 120

Rabīʿ 150

al-Rāfiʿī 37–8, 273
al-Rāghib 120, 151
Ramaḍān 95, 280, 283
al-Rāwi 151
al-Rāzī 60, 92, 99, 157, 191, 211, 281
recitation
best times for 280
commencement of and pauses in 201–20
completion of 282
error in 253–4
etiquettes of 263–86
in foreign languages 276–7
forgetting verses in the course of 283
interruption of 276
learning in combination 260
manner of performance 252–3, 257–60
sequential 277
starting and stopping places 258–9
revelation
accompanied by angels and unaccompanied 83–5
attributable to several verses 69
in daytime and at night 31–4
on earth and in heaven 39
in instalments 94–8
in Mecca and in Medina 1–24
to Muḥammad the Prophet and to several prophets 87–9
multiple occasions of 67–8
related to a particular occasion 55–60
in summer and winter 35–6
verses anticipating or anticipated by an ordinance 77–9
when in bed or sleeping 37–8
while The Prophet was in residence or travelling 25–30
al-Rummānī 214

Saʿd b. Muʿādh 72
Saʿd Ibn Abī Waqqaṣ 186
Saʿd Ibn Mālik 272
Saʿd Ibn ʿUbayd 172
al-Ṣadr Mawhūb al-Jazarī 261
Saʿīd b. Abī Waqqāṣ 27
Saʿīd b. Jubayr 8, 30, 48–9, 72, 84
Saʿīd b. al-Musayyab 49–50
Saʿīd b. Musayyib 72
Saʿīd Ibn Jubayr 189
Saʿīd Ibn Manṣūr 88, 186, 213
Saʿīd Ibn al-Mundhir 264
Ṣafwān b. Ummayah 25
Ṣafwan Ibn ʿAssal 226
Sahl b. Saʿd 66
Saʿīd Ibn Khālid 149
al-Sajawandi 204, 206, 209–10
al-Sakhāwī 21, 29, 33, 76, 94, 129, 133, 135, 139, 151, 167, 252, 257, 260, 269
al-Samargandi 196
Samūra Ibn Jundab 264
secret recitation 274
al-Shabī 16, 202
shadhdh recitations 181
al-Shāfiʿī 57, 187, 268–9, 273
al-Shalawbin 134
al-Sharaf Ismāʿīl ibn al-Muqriʾ 284
al-Sharīf Taqiy al-Dīn al-Ḥusayni 285–6
al-Shaṭibī 186
Shaydhala 117
Sībawayhi 228
"similar sounds" 233–4
Solomon 89
al-Subkī 60
al-Suddī 25, 52, 88, 221
Sufyān al-Thawrī 104
Sufyān Ibn ʿUyayna 126
sūrahs 22–3, 37–8, 157–8
naming and vocalization of 122–35
revealed in successive segments and as a whole 81

al-Ṭabarānī 87, 155–6, 163, 167, 191, 273
tadwīr style 253
al-Ṭaḥawī 108
taḥqīq 252
tajwīd 253–6
takbīr 281–2
tartīl 269–70
al-Ṭayyibī 99, 148
Thābit Ibn al-Ḥajjaj 97
al-Thaʿlabī 126
Thaubān 27
al-Tirmidhī 28, 167, 186
toothsticks, use of 267
Torah, the 88–9, 94–7, 122, 129–30

ʿUbadā ibn al-Ṣāmit 261
ʿUbayd Ibn ʿUmayr 128

ʿUbayda al-Salmani 115
Ubayy b. Kaʿb 3, 12–13, 28, 50, 81, 107, 281–2
Ubayy b. ʿUmayr 42
ʿUdayy Ibn Thābit 102
ʿUmar b. al-Khaṭṭāb 25, 33, 35, 49, 67, 77, 98, 107, 109, 115, 137–41, 145–6, 187, 278, 285
Umm ʿAmr 26
Umm Maktūm 70
Umm Salamah 51–2, 69, 188, 207, 212, 269
Umm Waraqa bint ʿAbd Allah Ibn al-Ḥārith 173
ʿUmran ibn al-Ḥusayn 283
ʿUrwah 57
ʿUthmān 9, 51, 56, 115, 141–5, 155, 194
ʿUthman b. Abī al-Ās 16
ʿUthman Ibn Waqqaṣ 280
ʿUthmānic codes 219
ʿUthmanic codices 115

veiling 71

al-Wāḥidī 35, 55, 61, 63, 158, 276
Waʾil Ibn Ḥujr 272
Waʾila Ibn al-Asqaʿ 135
Walīd b. Muslim 2
al-Wāqidī 45
Waraqah 43–4
Warsh 230, 242–3, 245, 247, 249
wine, drinking of 47–8, 56

Yaḥyā b. Salam 2
Yūnis 134

al-Zaʿfarani 166
Ẓāhirī School 56
al-Zajjāj 120
zakāt 78–9
al-Zamakhsharī 58, 157–9, 214
Zarara Ibn Awfa 131
al-Zarkashī 62, 75, 132, 148, 157, 192–3, 279, 286
Zayd b. Arqam 29, 33
Zayd Ibn Thābit 69–70, 115, 137–42, 182, 231
al-Zuhrī 25, 29, 42